Rituals of National Loyalty

Rituals of National Loyalty

An Anthropology of the State and
the Village Scout Movement in Thailand

Katherine A. Bowie

COLUMBIA UNIVERSITY PRESS   NEW YORK

Columbia University Press

New York   Chichester, West Sussex

Copyright © 1997 Columbia University Press

All rights reserved

Library of Congress Cataloging-in-Publication Data

Bowie, Katherine Ann, 1950–

Rituals of national loyalty : an anthropology of the state and the village scout

movement in Thailand / Katherine A. Bowie.

p.   cm.

Includes bibliographical references and index.

ISBN 0-231-10390-5 (cloth : alk. paper). — ISBN 0-231-10391-3 (pbk. : alk.

paper)

1. Thailand—Politics and government. 2. Communism—Thailand.

3. Insurgency—Thailand. I. Title.

DS586.B69   1997

306.2'09593'08047—dc20   96–38184

Casebound editions of Columbia University Press books are printed

on permanent and durable acid-free paper.

Printed in the United States of America

c 10 9 8 7 6 5 4 3 2 1

p 10 9 8 7 6 5 4 3 2 1

❧

To my children,
Matthew and James,
*whose births during the course of writing
this book taught me the power
behind the symbolism of family.*

Contents

Acknowledgments

I had never intended to write this book. I wrote it because of memories that would not fade and because various friends and colleagues encouraged me to record my observations for the historical record. The writing proceeded in two major stages. Immediately after I observed a Village Scout initiation ritual in the 1970s I wrote up my thoughts in a lengthy paper for a class I took with Frank Reynolds. I would like to thank Ajarn Frank and, subsequently, Charles Keyes and Stanley Tambiah, who also read this early draft, for urging me to publish my observations. The second stage began six years ago, spurred primarily by Al McCoy, whose enthusiasm for my village data and whose willingness to interview Filipino military colonels forced me to confront my lack of courage.

Many other friends and colleagues have played a role in helping me write this book. From the the heyday of the Village Scout movement I recall warmly many impassioned discussions with Marjorie Muecke, Walter Irvine, Narong Mahakhom, Surasinghsamruam Shimbhanao, and Chayan Vaddhanaphuti. I regret that Surasinghsamruam did not live to see this book finished. For reflections on the scouts and the period of the

1970s in Thailand I would particularly like to thank Sumali Conlon, Samart Srijumnong, Wutisak Lapcharoensap, Thongchai Winichakul, Phibul Manaskriangsak, Winyu Anganarak, Wasit Dejakhun, Narong Mahakhom, Praphan Muunprakan, Samraan Bunmaamanii, Uthaj Bunchyyn, and Mae Liang Inthong Suriyasak. Police Lieutenant General Somkhuan Harikul has been exceptionally helpful. His graciousness touched and overwhelmed me as he endured two lengthy interviews with me, the first complicated by my hungry six-week-old infant and the second, a year later, by a very sick one-year-old. His assistance in subsequent telephone calls and in providing access to photographs and statistics is greatly appreciated.

Framing the information I gathered on the Village Scout movement was also a long process. I wish to recognize the many stimulating discussions I have had over the years with John Conlon, whose gentle questioning helped shape the overall structure of this book. For comparative discussions about the nature of ritual I would particularly like to thank Jack Kugelmass and Maria Lepowsky. Students of my seminar, "Peasant Politics," and Thongchai Winichakul's seminar, "Politics and Culture in Recent Thai History," both held in the spring semester 1994, provided helpful reflections on an earlier draft of this manuscript. Similarly, I appreciate the comments of Al McCoy, Biff Keyes, Rita Kipp, Jan Opdyke, Carol Compton, Arjun Guneratne, Kate Bjork, Lee Wengraf, Eric Zolov, Susan Hangen, Louis Immendorf, Kevin McIntyre, and Walter and Trudi Bowie on various chapter drafts. Julie Rath, Aree White, Christopher Bowie, Gay Seidman, Ruth Dunnell, Ade Sutopo, David Streckfuss, Doug Bloch, John Davis, Nalinee Tantuvanit, Thitaya Phaobtung, Robert E. Jones, John Smail, and Rosanne Rutten, Jarin Boonmathya, Joanne Moller, and Daniel Arghiros also provided appreciated assistance.

John Michel and Ron Harris helped see this book through its various stages at Columbia University Press. Megan Sinnott rendered bibliographical help, Sarah Short provided photographic assistance, Mary Pixley helped with graphs, Sandra Austin typed the many tables in the appendix, and Janpanit Surasin and Kannikar Elbow reviewed the transliterations. The editorial comments of my husband, Hugh Wilson, improved my argument and my prose; without his help both would have remained more rough-hewn. Fresh in my mind at this moment is my gratitude to Polly Kummel, whose meticulous copyediting is teaching me even more about the craft of writing.

I would also like to recognize the assistance of the National Research Council of Thailand for its support of my research in Thailand. The Luce Foundation and the Center of Southeast Asian Studies at the University of Wisconsin at Madison provided support and much needed time in which to complete this manuscript. Finally, I would also like to express my appreciation to the many scout instructors and villagers, both scout and nonscout, who shared their thoughts on this fascinating movement and complicated historical period; for their sakes I have left them anonymous.

NAMES, TRANSLITERATION, AND TRANSLATION

Unlike the custom of many Western societies, Thais are most frequently referred to by their first names. In fact, last names came into use in Thailand only in the twentieth century. Consequently, I use both first and last names the first time an individual is mentioned in the text, and I subsequently refer to Thais by their first name. Similarly, the Thai language bibliography is listed alphabetically by first names in accordance with Thai convention. Thai authors whose works appear in English appear under their last names, in accordance with English-language convention.

With the exception of proper names and place names, I am following a variant of the Haas system of transcription without the tone marks. Proper names are transliterated, whenever possible, according to the individual's preferences. For place names I am using common spellings as they appear on maps. Unless otherwise noted, all translations of texts and conversations are mine.

A Note on the Photographs

Determining appropriate illustrations for this book proved to be a larger undertaking than I had anticipated. Cameras were scarce among villagers twenty years ago. Older villagers possess few pictures of themselves beyond the posed photographs taken in preparation for their funerals. Because I was a guest at the Village Scout initiation I observed, I did not feel comfortable taking photographs and had been advised by uncertain scout instructors not to do so. Although it was relatively easy to obtain photographs of individual scouts posing before a scenic spot, it proved difficult to obtain photographs depicting key moments of the initiation or key village events. Consequently, although the quality of the photographs is not always good, I have included villagers' pictures of the initiation and other events because of their rarity.

I wish to express my appreciation to various villagers and Village Scouts for giving me permission to use these photographs. Their willingness to authorize use of these pictures should in no way be construed as their agreement with the analysis presented in this book. I am sure that several would disagree heartily with aspects of my interpretation.

I also know that the photographs of the events of October 6, 1976, are painful for virtually all Thais to see. Many would prefer that this moment in history remain buried in the past. Even among Village Scouts many did not agree with the direct politicization of the movement in this manner. As Lieutenant General Somkhuan Harikul told reporters at the time and reiterated in his more recent interviews with me, although he and others sought to benefit the public through the Village Scouts, some sought to use the movement to further private ends. The Village Scout movement was multifaceted, and I seek in my illustrations to reflect its political complexity.

According to various journalists and newspaper editors with whom I have talked or corresponded, photographs of events that occurred on October 6 were on a proscribed list, and police confiscated film of the event from many newspaper offices. Although many more photographs survived, I did not wish to place any Thai photographers in a politically sensitive position and so have included only photographs that are available through international film archives. In this regard I particularly wish to thank Neil Ulevich for his time in recounting what he saw and for his assistance in retrieving his Pulitzer prize–winning photographs, some of which are reprinted here.

Photographs

FIGURES AND TABLES

Figures

Tables

Rituals of National Loyalty

A Village Scout, flanked by police and Border Patrol officers, escorts a captured and wounded student through the campus gates in the aftermath of the main assault at Thammasat University on October 6, 1976.

(Photo by Neil Ulevich; used by permission of AP/WideWorld Photos.)

Introduction: Toward an Anthropology of the Right

❖

Clenched fists raised against the night sky.

Cries of hundreds of villagers shouting, "We will fight! We will fight! We will fight!"

The smell of gunpowder and the sight of thatched roofs burning yellow and red against the smoky blackness.

A crisp white Styrofoam replica of a Buddhist temple lying flat in the settling dust.

Thai government officials acting the roles of Lord Robert Baden-Powell confronting Zulu warriors.

Thick ropes cordoning off throughways for stretcher after stretcher to pass, bearing villagers sobbing uncontrollably.

These images are indelibly etched in my memory, despite the passage of twenty years. They were moments in a five-day initiation ritual for the largest right-wing mass organization in Thai history, innocently called the Village Scouts or, translated more accurately, the "Village Tiger Cubs." Since its founding in 1971 about five million people have been initiated into its ranks, approximately one-fifth of Thailand's adult population.

State sponsored, the Village Scouts were intended to counter the "communist threat." War was raging in the countries bordering Thailand—Vietnam, Cambodia, and Laos. The Thai government was embroiled in the war in Indochina; Thai troops were fighting in Vietnam, and the United States was flying bombing runs from airbases in Thailand. Simultaneously, the Thai government found itself facing a growing communist guerrilla campaign within its borders. The Village Scout movement, directly linked to the Border Patrol Police and the all-powerful Ministry of Interior, had a twofold purpose. Viewed broadly, the movement sought to inoculate the Thai body politic against communism by injecting its citizenry with a dose of nationalism. Viewed more immediately, the movement served to intimidate anyone critical of the government into silence and to inform on those who refused to be intimidated. Upon initiation Village Scouts throughout the country were encouraged to become "eyes and ears" (*pen huu pen taa*) for the government and "to inform local officials about any strangers entering their village" (McNabb 1978:142). As one Village Scout song, "News," explains,

> What is he doing?
> Where is he doing it?
> When is he doing it?
> Whom is he doing it with?
> Who is he?
> And how is he doing it?
> Just tell us!
> (McNabb 1978:142)

Most Village Scout activities appeared to be innocuous. Members spent their time visiting the evening campfire sessions of scout troops undergoing initiation, receiving troop flags, or celebrating the annual anniversaries of their initiations. Scouts also swept the streets in their neighborhoods or cleaned up canalways, parks, and other public areas. They participated in local temple festivals and made donations to scouts or others whose homes had burned down or who had experienced similar disasters. Yet other activities were highly politicized. The scouts visited government soldiers wounded in combat with communist guerrillas. Apparently innocent street-cleaning projects often were timed to coincide with progressive rallies organized by workers, peasants, or students.

By far the most terrifying moment of the Village Scout movement was scouts' frenzied participation in the bloody and gruesome attack at Thammasat University on October 6, 1976. Village Scouts enthusiastically assisted in the beating and killing of scores of university students; some students were shot, others garroted, and yet others doused with gasoline and set ablaze. The day ended with the dissolution of Parliament and the return of military rule.

For me, as for many Thais, October 6 is emblazoned in memory. I was working as a research assistant for a faculty member at Thammasat University and had friends among both faculty and students. I recall listening in horror to the radio descriptions of what was happening. I looked with disbelief at the horrible photographs of the atrocities in an early edition newspaper distributed before the military seized control of the media. I never planned to write a book on the Village Scouts; although my overall interest is on the effects of development on village life, my dissertation focused on nineteenth-century Thailand.

I first traveled to Thailand in 1974 as a graduate student in anthropology. I arrived just months after a massive popular uprising had ousted a long-entrenched military regime on October 14, 1973. The newly inaugurated civilian interregnum proved increasingly tumultuous. Reformers and reactionaries clashed with growing frequency. The old guard fought back with a political arsenal that ranged from intimidation to assassination. With the war in Indochina raging at the borders the defenders of the status quo conflated reformers and communists in order to defame both. Students and others who traveled to rural areas with every intention of helping villagers became embroiled in the political battle between the illusive "communist terrorist" and the very real Village Scouts. During my first two years in Thailand I sometimes worked as a freelance journalist; in the course of researching articles for a local Thai newspaper I too was threatened by Village Scouts.

Thus, for those of us who had occasion to observe aspects of Village Scout activities, investigating the movement meant facing the stark realities that underlie the "cultural elaboration of fear" (Taussig 1987:8). The state groomed the Village Scouts as partisans at a time when politics had become deadly serious. As increasing numbers of villagers and townspeople were initiated into the movement, Village Scouts seemed to be everywhere, their telltale maroon kerchiefs serving as a constant reminder of the visible and invisible agencies of the state. Despite its omnipresence, as anthropologist Marjorie Muecke noted at the time, "it is difficult for persons who are not members of the organization to attain access to information on the Village Scouts" (1980:*n*408). The movement was surrounded with an aura of the illicit. With few exceptions outsiders were forbidden to attend Village Scout initiations (see Muecke 1980:*n*408). Even those allowed to join were made to feel that they were part of a selected minority. Furthermore the Village Scout movement was closely affiliated with the king of Thailand; any commentary on the movement therefore risked allegations of lèse majesté, a treasonous crime against the monarchy.

Because of a fortuitous convergence of events I became one of the only foreigners to observe the full five-day initiation rite. By August 1976 I had decided to move to the northern province of Chiang Mai. The particular initiation I witnessed took place in mid-1977. At the time I was living with a village family that had been approached by Village Scout organizers to house new initiates. A rather awkward situation arose because non-scouts were not supposed to see the initiation. After some consultation and discussion the organizers decided that because I was American and had been a Girl Scout (an entirely different organization in fact), I would be permitted to observe the initiation.

Nonetheless throughout the course of the initiation I was often led to feel that I was seeing something I was not supposed to see. I was repeatedly told that outsiders were not allowed to attend the initiations. The only exceptions were the village peddlers who were allowed to hawk refreshments at the evening campfire sessions on the nights that senior scout troops visited. Although other villagers stopped and watched from a distance on their way to market or to their fields, the initiation site was cordoned off. Consequently, I was made to feel like a voyeur of a private moment when the Thai state sought to penetrate deep into the hearts and minds of its subjects.

Perhaps what frightened me about the initiation was less what I saw with my eyes than my recollections of history and my visions of future nightmares. While the instructors at the initiation revealed their activities with pride, film clips of Nazi Germany flashed through my mind, a macabre déjà vu of fascism. By this time my life had been threatened and the October 1976 bloodbath at Thammasat University had already occurred. Thus I could not separate the ethereal realm of ritual from its earthly consequences of intimidation and violence.

Throughout the civilian period I had friends on both sides of the political divide. However, as the right grew bolder, my friends interested in social reform suffered increased harassment. Some were arrested, and someone I knew and respected was murdered. Thais have a saying, "To kill a chicken for the monkeys to see" (*khaa kaj haj ling duu*). The gratuitous violence of October 6 and what had happened to some of my friends taught me, among the monkeys, that the stakes were indeed high.

Faced with that "space of death" (Taussig 1990:3) that looms before a curious academic on the precipice of personal danger—fear of jeopardizing friends, worry about visa renewals, not to mention the unspeakable—I froze. The images of the initiation froze too, crisp and still, awaiting that time when I would confront them again. Despite all the years that have passed, I have been unable to dispel the macabre images. I have felt torn between my fascination and horror at what I saw and my fear of repercussions, not only for my friends but also for myself. As James Scott has written of his fieldwork experience, "It was not long before I noticed how I measured my own words before those who had power over me in some significant way" (1990:ix).

Twenty years have passed. The Village Scout movement was at its zenith during the mid-1970s, and no analysis of the course of Thai national politics during this period is complete without reference to it. Yet with the notable exceptions of articles by Muecke (1980) and Kawiirat Khunnaphat (1986), no scholarly study has focused on this quasi-fascist, quasi-farcical right-wing movement. Because I am among a few social scientists who have observed a full initiation session in a village context, I have long felt an obligation—at once moral and intellectual—to make my observations public. Although the coup in 1991 and the bloody military suppression of the popular prodemocracy uprising in May 1992 are dramatic proof that politics remains a deadly serious business in Thailand, I hope sufficient time has passed that the material in this book is no longer politically sensitive for villagers, scout instructors, or others involved.

This book, then, is part of a delayed effort to confront the position of the anthropologist doing fieldwork under conditions of intense political conflict. As Carolyn Nordstrom and JoAnn Martin point out, "The widespread sociopolitical violence in the world, especially in the Third World, has altered the terrain of ethnographic research, raising new questions and requiring different types of ethnographic presentations" (1992:3). Although we may debate whether the degree of violence has changed in the modern world, certainly more anthropologists feel compelled to engage the subject. This shift of emphasis results in part because the theoretical issues of growing concern to anthropologists center less on the reconstruction of "traditional" societies and more on understanding the dynamism of a "post-traditional" world. Our concerns are nurtured by our prolonged periods of residence in other societies during which we often develop friendships with people whose lives are embroiled in political struggles. As we become better informed about the ongoing events in a country, it is difficult—and at times even irresponsible—to avoid forming opinions.

However, studying politics poses major methodological challenges. The inherently partisan nature of political strife and the disciplinary exhortations to remain neutral place anthropologists, among other scholars, in a difficult situation. Obtaining equal access to all participants of a political debate is often not possible. When I observed the Village Scout initiations, I was generally associating with members of the rural elite. Only later did I learn how reluctant members of the landless poor were to confide in me, lest I create problems for them with their landlords or moneylenders. Dilemmas of partisanship—whether voluntary or involuntary—have made many anthropologists reluctant to focus on politics directly. However, the injunction to be objective would require of us that we confront all aspects of society as truthfully as possible. Avoiding the subject of the state and the techniques of power because of personal fears or fears of bias only skews the record and undermines our ability to engage the full complexity of modernity.

Further complicating the study of politics is the disjuncture between the inherent dynamism of politics and the inescapable constraints of academic training. As graduate students we must pass various stages of preparation for fieldwork, culminating in faculty approval of our fieldwork proposal. When I was taking courses and preparing for fieldwork, I had no idea that the Village Scout movement existed—it was still in its infancy—let alone the significance it was to achieve during my stay in Thailand. Nor could I know I would observe its initiation rite. Thus this book is a post facto response to unanticipated events rather than the careful result of a preconceived plan.

The anthropological method has traditionally been more qualitative than quantitative, relying on participant observation and in-depth interviewing. In part because of this methodological preference most anthropologists base their fieldwork on the study of a single village or other similarly well-circumscribed social group. Because anthropologists traditionally have been reluctant to generalize beyond the confines of the community they observe firsthand, they have preferred to leave the study of the state and nation to political scientists. Conversely, political scientists, although adept at the study of national events, have rarely included village-based politics in their accounts. Grappling with the problem of understanding the motivations of literally millions of people is daunting, especially in a Third World country where few opinion polls exist and politics is a dangerous and taboo subject about which villagers are often reticent, even cagey.

Thus, even when I had confronted my personal hesitance in writing this book, I found I faced other difficulties. The Village Scout movement was designed to draw in ordinary people living in thousands of villages and towns across a country. To fully understand such a movement requires some access to the thoughts and motivations of both planners and participants. Interviewing members of the elite and reading urban-based newspapers is helpful but not enough. By combining village-based ethnography with more traditional elite-based sources, I have tried to provide one way to cope with the methodological problems in understanding the interplay of agrarian and national politics. Accordingly, this book draws upon four primary sources: printed materials, such as newspaper accounts and secondary sources; memories from my two years of residence in Bangkok (1974–1976); field notes compiled during five years of fieldwork in northern Thailand, drawing primarily from the period of 1976 to 1979; and interviews conducted with key individuals involved in the Village Scout movement during briefer stays in Thailand in 1991 and 1992. By embracing both historical and sociological approaches, this book seeks to erase the traditional disciplinary boundaries of political science and anthropology. Bridging macro- and microlevels of historical analysis, it analyzes the dynamics of a national political movement by integrating village ethnography with the national and international context.

At its most basic level this book addresses the evolving theoretical discussions about the use of ritual in nation-state formation. The Village Scout movement was a state-sponsored, right-wing mass movement. The primary criterion for membership was participation in a five-day initiation rite. There is a growing literature on the various processes by which states develop and exercise their control over their citizenry.[1] Despite the belief of many scholars that such visible manifestations of state power as rituals are less relevant for an understanding of the modern state than its use of invisible techniques (e.g., Foucault 1979), increasing attention is being paid to the role of ritual as one cultural mechanism important in state formation. The Village Scout movement was an attempt by the Thai state, whose legitimacy was contested, to use ritual to sway a citizenry whose loyalties were in doubt. Brandishing the mantra of "Nation, Religion, and King" the Village Scout initiation ritual sought to inspire nationalist sentiment in order to ward off apparent external threats of communism and real internal challenges to government authority.[2]

However, as I studied the literature on state rituals, I was frustrated by its narrow focus on the rituals themselves and its neglect of their social contexts and consequences. Writing this book two decades after the heyday of the Village Scout movement provides the advantage of historical perspective. Although the initiation rite underwent little fundamental change, its historical context changed dramatically. The first initiation was held in 1971, for reluctant and unwilling villagers living in the remote mountainous villages of northeastern Thailand. Within a few years the movement became urban-based, and demand for initiation exceeded the spaces available. In 1976 alone about two million Thais became Village Scouts. After the coup of October 1976 the new government called a temporary halt to new initiations. When initiations resumed in May 1977, the movement returned to its incarnation as a rural-based counterinsurgency force. Although the organization continues to initiate new members every year, the Village Scout movement has faded into a mere continuing presence since about 1981. Now about two hundred initiations are held each year. Thus the level of popular interest in the movement has fluctuated dramatically over time. The Village Scout movement was nurtured in magic, peaked in mayhem, and eventually subsided as the national political struggle metamorphosed.

Understanding this changing trajectory involves understanding the movement's sociohistorical context. Given the intensity of the class conflict in which Thai society was embroiled throughout the birth and growth of the Village Scouts, a class analysis becomes an inevitable component in understanding the rise and decline of the Village Scout movement. Consequently, this book argues for the importance of incorporating a class-based analysis in any scholarly examination of political and, particularly, state rituals. As I suggest in chapter 1, a class-based analysis encourages a recognition of the following four aspects of state ritual: *agency*, or who and whose interests lie behind the state ritual; *efficacy*, or the ritual's effect on its intended audience; *cross-class symbolism*, or the role of symbols in masking class conflict; and *dynamism*, or the never-ending historical process of change in state rituals as the inevitable result of the ongoing tension between the classes.

Too many anthropological analyses of state rituals have assumed that the state and the people have common interests based upon a shared culture. Maurice Bloch, one of the few Marxist anthropologists to have written on ritual, even goes so far as to ridicule the idea that rituals could be "created as a plot by cynical rulers who deliberately invent subtle and totally convincing mystifying devices for the domination of others" (1986:6). Bloch concludes that "the theory of ideology as a plot on the part of power-holders is ridiculous" (1986:177). Yet the Village Scout movement is a clear-cut case of a state's deliberately inventing a ritual to use as a weapon in its struggle for survival.[3]

However, once we acknowledge that ritual can be used as a device for domination, the relationship of the state to the balance of forces between the classes demands investigation. Like many scholars I view the state as closely aligned with the dominant economic class. However, as a student of Theda Skocpol, I was influenced by her thought-provoking work in political and historical sociology. Consequently, I have come to share her position and that of other "structural Marxists," which argues for "the relative autonomy of the state" (see discussions in Block 1977; Carnoy 1984; Evans, Rueschemeyer, and Skocpol 1985; Hamilton 1982; Miliband 1969; Poulantzas 1973; Skocpol 1979). As Skocpol explains, this position developed in critical reaction to "a widespread vulgarization—the notion that states were nothing but instruments manipulated consciously and directly by leaders and interest groups representing the dominant class" (1979:27). She continues, "State rulers may have to be free of control by specific dominant-class groups and personnel if they are to be able to implement policies that serve the fundamental interest of an entire dominant class" (1979:27). Although the Thai state and the Thai ruling class often work in tandem, there are times—coups being the most obvious example—when the two are in temporary conflict. As this book shows, shifting relations between the Thai state and the dominant class motivated the rise and demise of the Village Scout movement.

Neither the Thai state nor the Thai ruling class is monolithic, except at the crudest level of analysis. Consequently, following Nicos Poulantzas who wrote of class fractions (1973; see also Williams 1981:74–81), I refer to both state factions and class fractions throughout this book as a way of recognizing the divisions and debates both within the state and within each of the broader social classes. Given both the myriad ways in which *class* can be defined (e.g., recent discussions in Blumberg 1980, Wright 1985, and Wright et al. 1989), and the lack of detailed systematic research on the more subtle social or economic divisions of Thai society, I have not attempted a systematic catalogue of classes and class fractions. Rather, I am working within the most rudimentary division of Thai society—the elite, the middle class, and the poor majority, which includes most of the peasantry. Among the peasantry I describe additional class fractions based primarily on socioeconomic status: the wealthy, the subsistence level, and the landless and land-poor villagers. Within the middle class, largely urban, I note the development of a major split between "progressives" sympathetic to democratic reforms under a civilian government and "conservatives" sympathetic to military rule and the status quo. The elite is characterized by a complex series of overlapping interests and even contradictory identities that can be subdivided into such categories as royalists versus commoners, parliamentarians versus militarists, businessmen versus bureaucrats, or Chinese-Thai versus "ethnic" Thai. Further divisions can be made within these categories according to such criteria as occupation, gender, school attended, and even class in school. Although no complete social mapping of the elite has been undertaken, coups and countercoups intimate the divisions within the power elite.[4]

Because the Village Scout movement can only be understood in the context of struggles within the state and between the state and competing social classes, this book is also a case study of an experiment in the establishment of hegemony by a state under siege. Although the meaning of the term *hegemony* is still debated (see discussions in Scott 1985:314–18; Comaroff and Comaroff 1991:19–27; Williams 1976), most interpretations focus on the ways the elite mask their control over the forces of production in a veil of legitimacy. As Scott explains, "The ruling class dominates not only the means of physical production but the means of symbolic production as well," seeking "to disseminate those values that reinforce its position" (1985:315). Stuart Hall expands upon the political significance of this attempted "monopoly of the means of mental production," noting that ruling conceptions of the world seek to become "the horizon of the taken-for-granted . . . setting the limit to what will appear as rational, reasonable, credible, indeed sayable or thinkable" (1988:44). The Village Scout movement was an attempt by the Thai elite to define, through the medium of ritual, the boundaries of discourse tolerated under the rubric of nationalism. Going beyond these boundaries and criticizing government policies was portrayed as a betrayal of the nation.

However, discussions of hegemony raise the question of false consciousness among the subaltern. This book is also a study of Thai villagers' interpretations of the Village Scout movement. I would suggest that because of differences in class position, cultural hegemony is always only partial. As Paul Willis explains, "Social agents are not passive bearers of ideology, but active appropriators who reproduce existing structures only through struggle, contestation, and a partial penetration of those structures" (1977:175). James Scott has even suggested that "a hegemonic ideology must, by definition, represent an idealization, which therefore inevitably creates the contradictions that permit it to be criticized *in its own terms*" (1985:317; emphasis his). Faced with a growing communist guerrilla movement and intensifying demands for social reform, the Thai elite experimented with the Village Scouts. However, the movement's effects varied, even backfiring in unanticipated ways. Thus this book argues for the importance of a temporal perspective in understanding the dialectic between elite struggles to achieve ideological hegemony and subaltern unmaskings of false pretenses.

Because of its emphasis on both state hegemony and peasant political consciousness my analysis of the Village Scout movement is divided in two parts. Part One focuses on the state and Part II focuses on peasant reactions. The division also corresponds to a major chronological juncture in the history of the rise and fall of the Village Scout movement. The events of October 6, 1976, provide the watershed date. Part One, which begins with chapter 2, is divided into three chapters, covering the early history of the movement.

Chapter 2 begins with a discussion of the movement's founding by Major General Somkhuan Harikul, a high-ranking officer in Thailand's premier counterinsurgency agency, the Border Patrol Police (BPP). Although the idea for the movement was conceived by Somkhuan Harikul, he in turn was embedded within broader social forces. Consequently, this chapter not only explores the biography of Somkhuan Harikul but also considers the development of the Communist Party of Thailand and locates the Border Patrol Police within the spectrum of government agencies charged with fighting the growth of communism.

Chapter 3 examines major political and economic forces behind the rapid growth of the scout movement during the civilian period, focusing on the changing interaction of the monarchy and the middle classes. The Village Scout movement came under royal patronage in 1972. I argue that the significance of royal patronage was less the result of the institution of monarchy per se and more the consequence of the king's alignment in Thai society. When the Village Scout movement was beginning, the king was extremely popular, particularly because of his critical stance toward the entrenched dictatorship. However, as Thai society polarized in the mid-1970s, the middle classes split, with one wing supporting liberal reform and the other supporting the status quo. Encouraged by the king's move to the right, the conservative wing became active in the Village Scout movement. Thus I suggest that understanding the rise of the Village Scouts involves understanding the symbolic appeal of the monarchy amid the intensifying polarization of the period. The monarchy served simultaneously as a symbol of progressive reform and of conservative reaction.

In the wake of the coup of October 6, 1976, the new government imposed a moratorium on Village Scout initiations from December 11, 1976, to May 15, 1977. Chapter 4 focuses on this period. I describe five major fissures within the ruling elite that contributed to the government's decision to call a moratorium. I then consider the reasons for the movement's resumption, noting the growth of the Communist Party of Thailand and the crisis in the reputation of the monarchy in the months after October 6.

In Part Two the focus shifts from the national level to local villages. The theoretical emphasis also shifts from issues of agency and the state to an examination of the efficacy of the Village Scout movement among the peasantry. Chronologically, this part of the book concentrates on the second phase of the movement, after the moratorium ends and initiations resume. This transition from the national to the village level corresponds not only to thematic and chronological divisions but also, fortuitously, to when I moved from the capital city of Bangkok to a village in northern Thailand. The style of the book changes with my move. Whereas Part One relies more heavily on newspaper accounts and other written sources, Part Two draws more on my personal experiences, both as a journalist and as an anthropologist. These latter chapters are based primarily on field notes I recorded at the time. Thus my analysis of the efficacy of the Village Scout movement among the peasantry is primarily ethnographic. The village analysis is based upon my prolonged residence in Chiang Mai Province, one of the most prosperous provinces of northern Thailand. Part Two is also divided into three chapters, beginning with chapter 5.

Chapter 5 begins with a panoramic overview of political conditions and a description of scout activity in the Chiang Mai Valley region of northern Thailand in the aftermath of the October 6 coup. I focus on San Patong District, located about twenty-five kilometers southwest of the provincial capital of Chiang Mai. I then turn to a more finely grained presentation of local discussions of the scout movement, taking the village I call Samsen Village as my primary case study. My narrative begins when village leaders are informed that their village is to be the site of a scout initiation session. Chapter 6 presents a detailed account of a Village Scout initiation. Chapter 7 analyzes the immediate effects of the session, discussing some of the initiation's themes and village response. In this chapter I show how the responses of villagers vary with their class position within the village.

The concluding chapter places the movement in its contemporary historical context. The chapter centers on the important administrative changes initiated by General Kriangsak Chomanan that served to declaw the Village Tiger Cubs, as the Village Scout movement is more literally translated. Kriangsak's government came to power in a coup in October 1977. The chapter closes with a brief consideration of some of the broader comparative implications of the Village Scout movement. The themes of symbolism and dynamism are developed throughout the book because they link the interactions of the state and peasantry.

In trying to understand the origin and development of the Village Scout movement this book balances the interrelationship of agency and structure. As Paul Ricoeur explains, one kind of history focuses on the role of individuals, whereas another seeks to find structure and system; the challenge is to "tackle an event-filled history and a structural history at the same time," to acknowledge both "the great personages who make their appearance and the slowly progressing forces" (1965:39; see also Plekhanov 1940). By exploring the dynamic relationship of individuals and the broader social forces, this book is a case study of a particular political experiment, a "study of individual creativity in relation to cultural constitution over time" (Fox 1991:110). As Richard Fox explains,

> Experiments, however they progress, are not, then, anonymous; they are authored by individual dreams, authorized by group struggle, and deauthorized by the opposition they meet—until the next time. This progression in turn authorizes a culture history that is at once structural and singular.
>
> (1991:108)

The Village Scout movement was the brainchild of a single individual, Somkhuan Harikul, and benefited tremendously from the support of members of the royal family. However, as I show in this book, the movement flourished only to the extent that it received the support of the state and certain class fractions. Even the popularity of the monarchy was a response to the individual actions of the king, who had aligned himself with the sentiments of the national majority against a corrupt military minority; he jeopardized his position when he later became identified with a controversial minority faction.

In its inclusion of the views of ordinary people this book is also intended to be a contribution to understanding "false consciousness" and right-wing political movements. The literature on fascism excepted, few scholarly studies have explored the popular bases of conservatism (a 1988 essay by Stuart Hall on Thatcherism is a lonely herald of the possibilities). Even within the huge literature on fascism far less attention has been paid to the rural bases of fascist support than the urban (Cardoza 1982, P. Schneider 1986, and Tilton 1975 are notable exceptions).

With further examination of other conservative movements it may become possible to generalize about structural differences between left- and right-wing movements. This book begins to suggest that right-wing movements may have a character fundamentally different from that of left-wing movements. Although definitions vary, by *left-wing* I mean social movements seeking to change the overall structure of society on behalf of the majority, and by *right-wing* I mean efforts to maintain a status quo benefiting the interests of an elite minority.

Whereas genuine left-wing movements generally seek to appeal to the interests of subaltern classes or form united fronts based primarily upon reason and shared material interests and only secondarily upon emotion, a right-wing movement appears more likely to make a cross-class appeal based primarily upon emotion and only secondarily upon reason and material interests. To the extent that a left-wing movement makes use of symbols it is to express shared interests and aspirations. Right-wing movements use symbols to blur and mask the conflicting interests inherent in a cross-class alliance. As Daniel Guerin explains in his analysis of fascism, "Fascism would rather arouse faith than address itself to the intelligence":

> A party supported by the subsidies of the propertied classes, with the secret aim of defending the privileges of property owners, is not interested in appealing to the intelligence of its recruits; or rather, it considers it prudent not to appeal to their understanding until they have been thoroughly bewitched.
>
> (1973:63)[5]

As will become clear, the Village Scout movement evoked the powerful emotional bonds of family. Indeed the family motif is commonplace in conservative rhetoric around the world, including in the United States. The choice of this motif by conservative movements is not accidental but results from the political contradiction inherent in justifying a hierarchical society to those lower down on the socioeconomic ladder.

Finally, in its effort to include the international context within which the Village Scout movement developed, this book contributes to the new and growing anthropological literature on "transnationalism" and the international constitution of any society's "culture." Whereas the earlier literature on culture was essentialist, contemporary approaches are beginning to emphasize the "complex, transnational cultural flows" that link societies (Appadurai 1991:209). As Arjun Appadurai explains, a perspective of the anthropological terrain as broader "ethnoscapes" opens up explorations into "the ways in which local historical trajectories flow into complicated transnational structures" (1991:209).

Although the origins of scouting in Thailand are complex and an indigenous analogue for an adult form of scouting exists (see Vella 1978; Bowie 1993), official accounts of the inspiration of the Village Scout movement cite the Boy Scout organization founded by Lord Baden-Powell in England.[6] A closer analysis of Baden-Powell's Boy Scout organization reveals in turn its complex international origins. As Michael Rosenthal explains in his fascinating account of the origin of the British Boy Scouts,

> Baden-Powell never claimed that the principles behind his scheme for training youth were uniquely his. On the contrary, he always emphasized that his system drew on many sources, including his own scouting practices with the South African Constabulary. While the extent of his scholarly investigations is no doubt mildly exaggerated, Baden-Powell indicated that between 1906 and the time he started to compose the text of *Scouting for Boys* he had read Epictetus; Livy; Pestalozzi, the Swiss educator; Jahn on physical culture; as well as the *Broadstone of Honour* by Kenelm Digby; had looked into the technique for educating boys to be found among the Spartans, the Zulus and other African tribes, as well as the ancient British and Irish; had studied the Bushido of the Japanese and the educational methods of John Pounds, the Portsmouth shoemaker who founded the "ragged schools" for destitute boys; and consulted the practices of contemporaries, such as William Smith, Ernest Thompson Seton, and Dan Beard, among others.
>
> (1986:64)

The Village Scout movement was also strongly influenced by British and American counterinsurgency strategies. Furthermore, during the Village Scout movement's rapid expansion the Thai government was undergoing political and economic crises that can only be understood in the context of the Vietnam War and the international oil crisis.

My efforts to confront the moral challenge of exploring a permutation of state power in a period of intense political conflict forced me to encounter a series of intellectual challenges. Underlying all the broader subjects broached by this book and its discussion of the Village Scout ritual is the issue of class. How a nation is formed, how the villages and towns are integrated into the urban-based state, and how the nation is in turn integrated into the dynamics of international affairs are all ultimately discussions involving the differential economic and political power of various interest groups or class fractions. Although the Thai state sponsored and supported the Village Scouts, the interests that gave rise to the movement were fundamentally class based. The movement's growth and decline can ultimately be understood only by understanding the vicissitudes of the struggle between classes and class fractions as they worked themselves out in Thailand at the village, national, and even global levels. As Stanley Tambiah and Valerio Valeri can attest from my days at the University of Chicago as a graduate student taking their seminars on ritual, I never imagined that I would devote much attention to something as epiphenomenal as the study of ritual. Thus, ironically and unexpectedly, my forays beyond the traditional boundaries of the anthropological domain forced me to reembrace one of its core subjects, ritual, and led me to formulate the argument I present in this book, an argument for a class-based analysis of state ritual.

Standing in front of a mural depicting two lynched activists, Thailand's famous band Kamachon performs at a prodemocracy rally at the National Student Center of Thailand on October 4, 1976. After the October 6 coup several band members joined the underground movement.

(Photo by Neil Ulevich; used by permission of AP/WideWorld Photos.)

1

Magic and Mayhem: Of Ritual and Class

✤

In Thailand the 1970s were a strange amalgam of magic and mayhem. Rumors of magical potions that shrank penises abounded. Allegedly part of a Vietnamese communist conspiracy to render Thai men impotent and thus unable, literally, to reproduce the Thai nation, mysterious penis-shrinking additives were said to have been mixed in food sold in Vietnamese-owned restaurants. In northeastern Thailand, where many Vietnamese refugees had settled, the rumors abetted attacks on shops and other businesses owned by Vietnamese.

During these surreal days rumors of blood-sucking vampires also proliferated. The vampires were said to nab unsuspecting village children, sucking their bodies dry to provide transfusions for wounded communist guerrillas. The government, and particularly the military, controlled virtually all radio broadcasts in Thailand. Radio stations broadcasting into rural areas described the vampires as wearing indigo-dyed shirts, flip-flops, shoulder bags, and, significantly, eyeglasses—the characteristic attire of progressive university students seeking to demonstrate their solidarity with the village poor. Consequently, well-intentioned students who traveled to rural areas came under attack by terrified villagers. During this strange period a newly created religious institute sponsored seances during which mediums communicated with the spirit of Karl Marx, who was now eagerly proclaiming his nineteenth-century mistakes to all who would listen. High-ranking monks blessed thousands of sacred amulets and holy *phaa yan* cloths that military officers distributed to their soldiers to protect them from guerrilla forces.[1] But these appeals to magic and superstition were not spontaneous; they were carefully orchestrated stories planted by men trained in psychological warfare.

A civil war was under way. Demands for more democratic government were growing. Peasants, workers, and activists were pressing for long-awaited reforms. The Communist Party of Thailand was expanding. The Thai state was responding by deploying every force at its disposal, both real and fantastic, to buttress its position.

Among its seemingly surreal responses to the growing popular demands for reform was the inauguration of the nationwide Village Scout movement. At first glance it was an unlikely candidate to succeed in the serious business of combating communist insurgency. The main criterion for membership was participation in a rite of initiation that involved five days and four nights of entertainment interspersed with a few didactic lessons.[2] Participants performed skits, sang lighthearted songs specially written for the movement (such as "Holiday in America" and "Smile! Smile!"), and danced such moves as the bump, then popular in the United States, and the duck-waddle dance (*ram pet*), a dance unique to the Village Scouts that mimicked a duck's waddle. And yet the Village Scout movement succeeded in becoming the largest right-wing popular organization ever fabricated in Thai history.

The movement spun its magic by drawing on the aura of the Thai monarchy. Intoning the nationalistic rhetoric of loyalty to Nation, Religion, and King, the counterinsurgency spin doctors deployed the mystique of royalty. A rumor circulated that King Naresuan, a famous sixteenth-century monarch who had been victorious against the Burmese, had appeared in a dream to the queen of Thailand, telling her that "Thailand would fall unless the people were united, and that the Village Scouts was the means to unite them" (Muecke 1980:n413).[3] Combining royal majesty with village beliefs in sacred amulets, the Village Scout designers developed a magical folklore centering on the scout kerchiefs. Worn by all Village Scouts, these maroon kerchiefs were the most obvious feature distinguishing them from the population at large. The kerchiefs, given to each initiate at the close of the five-day initiation rite, were a special gift from the king of Thailand. They were portrayed as having mystical powers. During the course of the initiation scout instructors told of fires in which householders lost their homes and all their possessions except the sacred scout kerchief; amazingly, the residents retrieved their scarves completely intact from the burning ashes.

These tales, once deployed, fused with existing lore about sacred amulets that protected their wearers from misfortune. The stories developed a life of their own. Scouts also told various anecdotes about villagers who lost their kerchiefs and met with sundry calamities. For example, I heard frequent variations of a story about a man who had left his kerchief on the dashboard of his car. While he was driving, the royal scarf slipped to the floor near his feet. Because the foot is the most vulgar part of the body, he immediately went berserk. His car came to a stop and he ran about the road, hysterical, until some passing villagers found his scout scarf on the car floor. As soon as they picked up his scarf, he recovered his sanity. In some versions the victim ran about naked; in other versions the kerchief fell to the floor in the house. So engulfing and so plausible was this realm of ritual magic that the Thai state had created that a participant committed suicide, apparently because he had lost his kerchief, on the first night I attended a Village Scout event.

In the course of this five-day ritual initiates were transformed into sobbing masses of humanity, overwhelmed by their new-found love of the Thai nation and their intensified love of the monarchy. This love of nation rendered initiates capable of hysterical hatred, never made clearer than in the murderous participation of Village Scouts in the atrocities against university students on October 6, 1976. Nurtured in magic, the movement peaked in mayhem.

Mayhem and October 6

The full potential of the Village Scout movement became apparent only gradually. Intellectuals paid little attention during its initial years in the early 1970s. They dismissed the movement as a harmless, even naive, attempt at counterinsurgency. However, the organization was taken more seriously as it grew. By the mid-1970s scholars such as Frank Reynolds note its "strong ritualistic and revivalistic overtones" (1977:279), and many were beginning to characterize the movement as fascist. As David Morell and Chai-anan Samudavanija write, "With their uniforms and massive ral-

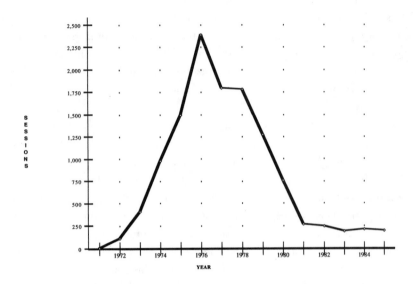

Figure 1.1. Number of Village Scout Initiations by Year, 1971–1985
Based on figures from VS history (1987).

lies, and by the extensive reliance on emotional ideology, the Village Scouts by 1976 clearly had many attributes of a fascist organization" (1981:244).[4]

The first year of the movement saw only eight initiation rituals, all held in the impoverished northeastern region. The number gradually increased, although the average number of initiates per session remained low. However, a sharp increase both in the number of initiations and in the average number of initiates attending each session began in 1975. The year 1976 marked the most dramatic surge: 2,387 initiation sessions were held, with an average of 795 scouts initiated at each session. In this one year alone almost two million Thais, nearly 10 percent of the country's adult population, became members (see figures 1.1 and 1.2).[5] Overall about five million Thais in a population estimated at fifty million have been initiated as Village Scouts, or about one adult Thai in every five.

Both men and women were involved. Unlike ostensibly parallel organizations, such as the Boys Scouts, which are gender specific, the Village Scout organization sought a gender balance. Recruitment of women often entailed overcoming villagers' reluctance to allow wives and daughters to participate. Nonetheless national guidelines recommended that the positions of president and vice president of each scout chapter be gender bal-

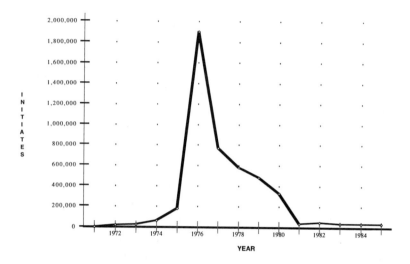

Figure 1.2. Number of Village Scout Initiates by Year, 1971–1985
(Based on figures from VS history (1987).

anced, that is, one male and one female, and scout organizers even returned to villages in which few women had registered in order to encourage their participation.[6] Because of such special efforts almost as many women joined the movement as men.[7] The inclusion of women gave the initiation rite a festive and flirtatious character, greatly enhancing its appeal. The participation of women also served to depoliticize the organization, giving it a friendly and familial aura that an all-male movement would not have had.

The peak years of the Village Scout movement coincided with the period of civilian government in Thailand. After a massive popular uprising in October 1973 the military was temporarily ousted from direct control of the government. As the pressures for progressive reform gained momentum, the conservative response began to form. The Village Scout movement was a major channel of conservative reaction. Mimicking the recruiting strategy of the Communist Party of Thailand, which relied on the continuing expansion of tiers of three-person cells, organizers encouraged new Village Scout initiates to recruit new members, each of whom would become the nucleus of a new three-person cell.[8] By 1975 and 1976 the maroon kerchiefs of the Village Scouts seemed omnipresent. The movement was mushrooming.

The vast majority of Village Scout activities seemed innocuous, oriented toward internal activities such as attending each other's initiations and public service projects such as street cleaning. Over time scout activities became more politicized. Increasingly, Village Scouts intimidated university students, journalists, and other urban intellectuals visiting villagers. Activists informing villagers of their rights under existing laws, particularly those regarding minimum wages or tenancy, received threats from local Village Scout groups. On a growing number of occasions progressive rallies met with countergatherings of Village Scouts. Such mobilizations of scouts were consciously and often explicitly intended to intimidate and counterbalance the left.

And then October 6, 1976, arrived. On that day the horrible potential that had lain dormant in the Village Scouts became manifest. Even now, for a generation of Thai, time is marked by whether events happened before or after this gruesome day. The momentum leading up to the bloodbath at Thammasat University, one of Thailand's most prestigious universities, had been building during the preceding three turbulent years of civilian rule. By August 1976 everyone could see that events were rapidly coming to a head.

The immediate sequence leading up to October 6 began with the returns of exiled field marshals Praphat Charusathien and Thanom Kittikachorn in August and September 1976, respectively. The two men were part of the military triumvirate expelled from the country after the massive popular uprising of October 14, 1973. Praphat's return provoked student demonstrations, forcing him back into exile. Thanom's return was more sophisticated; he had himself ordained as a Buddhist novice in Singapore and completed his ordination into the monkhood at Wat Bovornives in Bangkok. Because Wat Bovornives is the royal temple most directly linked with the royal family—the king was ordained there—and because the king made a personal visit to Thanom at the temple, public opposition to Thanom's return became a politically delicate matter. All the while rumors of an imminent restoration of military rule were mounting; both student and labor leaders feared that any demonstrations they organized might serve as a pretext for the impending coup. Protest was muted. The leaders of the main student organization, the National Student Council of Thailand (NSCT), distributed posters and leaflets asking the government to expel Thanom.

As if to bait student leaders, two students were garroted while putting up anti-Thanom posters on September 24. With virtually unprecedented efficiency and candor the police department announced that low-ranking police officers were involved in this atrocity (see, for example, "Srisuk Admits" 1976). On the weekend of October 2–3, relatives of the "Martyrs of October 14," those who had been killed in the popular uprising that had led to the expulsion of the military in 1973, held a protest rally at Thammasat. That Sunday, October 3, students boycotted their scheduled exams in solidarity. The following day, October 4, students at Thammasat University held a rally on the university campus. One skit was a reenactment of the garroting. The next morning two extreme right-wing papers reported that the university students had hung the crown prince in effigy. Conservative newspapers and radio stations vilified the students, describing the NSCT as riddled with communists and accusing the students of lèse majesté. Students continued to gather at Thammasat; all classes were suspended. By evening about ten thousand people, students and members of the public, had gathered at Thammasat to listen to speeches and music (Shawcross 1976:60).

Yarn Kroh, the radio station of the army's armored division, began to escalate its attacks. Lieutenant Colonel Uthan Sanitwong na Ayuthaya, a close relative of the queen, was the station's director. The station had long been denouncing students and other activists as "the scum of the earth" and "a burden to the land." As the *Bangkok Post* reported on October 6, "Some of the speakers were so strong in their speeches that at times they were shouting 'Kill them . . . kill them' (meaning the activist groups)" ("Probe Ordered" 1976).

Throughout the night of October 5 the radio station began to orchestrate the mobilization of right-wing forces—most important, Nawaphon, the Red Gaurs, and the Village Scouts. Nawaphon was a clandestine organization founded by a group of senior military officers in the intelligence and countersubversion branches of the government; its membership consisted primarily of the conservative elite, "ultra-conservatives such as provincial governors, large landowners, district and village heads" (Mallet 1978:84).[9] The Red Gaurs (*Krathing Daeng*) were more visible because they were openly associated with such acts of violence as throwing bombs into gatherings of students, labor unions, and other progressive organizations. Formed by groups within the Internal Security Operations Command (ISOC) and other army intelligence agencies, the Red Gaurs were basically a group of vigilantes composed of "ex-mercenaries, school drop-outs, unemployed youths and some vocational students" (Mallet 1978:84). However, neither Nawaphon nor the Red Gaurs were as numerous as the Village Scouts. For any right-wing demonstration to appear to have popular broad-based support, mobilizing the Village Scouts was essential. Throughout the night the official head of the Village Scouts, Major General Charoenrit Chamrasromrun of the Border Patrol Police, called upon Village Scouts to gather in Bangkok at the site of the statue of King Rama V, located in front of the National Assembly (Marks 1977:60).

In addition to calling for the protection of the Nation, Religion, and King, the military radio broadcast claims that students were planning to attack Wat Bovornives, where Field Marshal Thanom was staying. The Village Scouts were told to prepare to defend the temple. The explicit nature of the radio broadcasts makes apparent just how thoroughly the mayhem of October 6 was orchestrated. The following is an excerpt from a transcript made by the BBC, which was monitoring the station at 1 A.M. on October 6, while Nawaphon was being mobilized: "Now is the time for Thai patriots to rise up and fight. . . . Nawapol men throughout the country are urgently requested to contact Nawapol coordinators in their provinces. In the Bangkok area they should report at once to Operations Centres" (Shawcross 1976:60).

At 1:45 A.M. the military radio castigated the police for failing to act in support of Nawaphon (Shawcross 1976:60). However, by 2:40 A.M. Border Patrol Police and municipal police units had surrounded the university. The military radio announced, "The police are now doing their duty. . . . The public should stay away from the university" (Shawcross 1976:61; see also Marks 1977:60). The police locked the gates of the university, keeping the students and other supporters trapped inside. Outside the university was a growing mob of Red Gaurs, Nawaphon, and Village Scouts, the last easily recognizable in their maroon kerchiefs. Observers estimated that four thousand rightist supporters—primarily scouts—were milling about outside the university in the early hours of the morning in response to the army radio station's broadcasts (Morell and Samudavanija 1981:275).

The shooting began at about 5:45 A.M. and lasted more than an hour (Marks 1977:61). According to one foreign journalist who was there, the firepower was more intense than anything he had ever seen or heard in all his years in Vietnam. The brutal attack at Thammasat University is graphically summarized by David Morell and Chai-anan Samudavanija:

> As dawn broke over the city . . . hundreds of armed policemen and several heavily armed Border Patrol Police units had joined the Village Scouts, Red Gaurs, and other vigilantes. As the mob tried to

force its way through the locked gates of the campus, shooting broke out. Armed with M-16s, M-79 grenade launchers, carbines, and even recoilless rifles, the BPP and other armed individuals cut loose with a withering volume of fire. (1981:275)

At 7 A.M. there was a lull in the shooting as the police and the mob stormed onto the campus. William Shawcross describes what transpired:

> The students were set upon by the police and the crowds, including thousands of right-wing students. Some were dragged out of the buildings, and forced to strip off their shirts and crawl under police guard onto the football field. The stands around the ground were filled with vigilantes and right-wing young people cheering wildly. Other students attacked by the mob were strung up and beaten to death with chairs, axes, and guns. Wounded young men and women were dragged off stretchers and pummelled to death.
>
> (1976:61)

Dr. Puey Ungphakorn, then the rector of Thammasat University, provides one of the most detailed hour-by-hour accounts of the events of October 6. The following excerpt from his account provides some insight into the level of gratuitous violence:

> **09:00** A.M Period of heavy fighting as police attack individual buildings and student bases. Two police killed. Many students wounded and killed. While police use heavy weaponry, Red Gaurs, Village Scouts and right-wing groups, having seized ten to fifteen wounded or escaping students including two girls, beat, mutilate, hang and burn them, occasionally with police watching. One girl stripped and shot repeatedly. Large numbers of students try to escape but are arrested.
>
> **09:06** A.M. The Red Gaurs began to pour kerosene on and to burn four people, one of whom was still alive.
>
> **09:20** A.M. Four students, their hands on their heads symbolizing surrender, came out through the front gate and were brutally beaten and shot by the Red Gaurs. One was hung. A girl, who had been shot to death, was sexually abused by plainclothes policemen; they used a stick on her vagina. At a nearby site, a man was severely beaten and burned. Another person was hung while he was still alive.
>
> (1977:8)

Morell and Samudavanija provide a terse summary: "The carnage was almost unbelievable. Some students were burned alive or lynched from nearby trees; others were simply shot at point-blank range, some on the university grounds, others as they attempted to flee the campus on foot or swim to safety (Thammasat University is located on the bank of the Chao Phya River)" (1981: 275).

As the shooting subsided, government forces entered the university and began to arrest the students. They ordered everyone, male and female alike, to strip to the waist and lie on the ground. Police, scouts, and other right wingers seized the opportunity to strip the gold necklaces with Buddha images that many Thai wear, taking them ostensibly because communists are not Buddhists. The exact number of dead and wounded is not clear. The official figure acknowledged by the government was 46 dead, 145 students wounded, and 3,059 arrested (Marks 1977:61; see also Zimmerman 1978:58). However, officials of the Chinese Benevolent Foundation, which transported and cremated many of the dead, said that they had handled more than a hundred corpses that day (Ungphakorn 1977:9). That evening at 6 P.M. the National Administrative Reform Council (NARC), a navy–army–air force coalition, declared it had taken control of the government.

To this day the full story of who was behind the mobilization of October 6 has not become public. Nonetheless it is clear that, as Marks writes, "the operations at Thammasat had been carried out by police and right wing groups, particularly the Village Scouts with their royal insignia prominently displayed" (1977:61).[10] Responding to the military radio station's all-night broadcasts of patriotic music and emotional speeches, Village Scouts massed outside Thammasat University during the early morning hours of October 6, and thousands of other Village Scouts poured into Bangkok throughout the rest of the day. By 9:30 A.M. a crowd of thirty thousand had gathered at the statue of Rama V (Ungphakorn 1977:9). Village Scouts had begun demonstrating there the day before, demanding the resignation of leading members of the civilian government. Scouts also gathered at three other points in the city: Wang Saranrom Park, located near Thammasat University; the race grounds (Sanam Maa); and the zoo (Khaw Din Wannaa), the last two located near Chitrlada Palace. The Border Patrol Police provided trucks for transportation, and Village Scouts came from as far away as Ayuthaya, about ninety kilometers from Bangkok. The numbers of Village Scouts increased steadily throughout the day. Not until the evening of October

Thai Border Patrol Police, Metropolitan Police, and other paramilitary groups, including Red Gaurs and Village Scouts, surround Thammasat University on October 6. *(Photo used by permission of UPI/Bettmann.)*

6, after NARC had seized power, did the Village Scouts disperse. By that time 200,000 Village Scouts were estimated to have arrived in the capital city.[11]

Village Scouts in Bangkok were also involved in at least one further incident on October 6. In the hours after the attack at the university leaflets began circulating in Bangkok accusing Dr. Puey Ungphakorn, rector of Thammasat University, of seeking to destroy the monarchy. Friends advised Dr. Puey to leave the country, at least temporarily. At the airport he learned that his flight had been delayed. When the formation of the National Administrative Reform Council was announced, an immigration official came up to Dr. Puey. As Dr. Puey explains, "He told me the radio had denounced me and had warned the airline not to carry me. I was told that the Village Scouts were rushing out to the airport to get me" (Shawcross 1976:61). Dr. Puey was then arrested by a police officer who said that three of Dr. Puey's students had denounced him as a communist. The officer told Dr. Puey that he would have to walk out through the mob of more than one hundred Village Scouts gathered at the airport (Morell and Samudavanija 1981:245). Fortunately, Dr. Puey was able to contact

In this now famous photograph a policeman takes aim at people inside the university.
(Photo used by permission of UPI/Bettmann.)

members of the privy council, and he was allowed to leave the country (see Shawcross 1976:61).

With the return of military rule on the evening of October 6 the immediate mission of the Village Scouts and other right-wing forces had been accomplished. The rumormongering broadcast over state radio stations had apparently succeeded in its bewitchment. The everyday world had been converted into a phantasmagorical nightmare in which university students were transformed into blood-sucking vampires and Vietnamese infiltrators. The right became the self-righteous heralds of a new order. In the days that followed the coup student dorms, newspaper offices, and political party headquarters were ransacked. Sulak Sivaraksa estimated that 100,000 books were burned at his bookshop and warehouse alone (1985:371). Thousands of students, teachers, labor organizers, and journalists who had not already fled were arrested on suspicion of being "dangers to society" (*phai sangkhom*). In the tense calm that followed, the daily news reports consisted largely of announcements of scout training sessions, scout gatherings, scout contributions to temples, and scout visits to wounded soldiers in hospitals. The right had triumphed.

In the days after the coup I witnessed a police truck bearing six police-

A rightist beats a dead student.
(Photo by Neil Ulevich; used by permission of AP/WorldWide Photos.)

men armed with semiautomatic weapons pull in to a gas station. The police arrested a gas station attendant. After they drove off, I joined one of the hushed huddles of onlookers to ask why he had been arrested. It seemed the attendant had said something negative about the Village Scouts to a taxi driver who was filling his tank. The taxi driver apparently

Students, stripped to the waist, lie under guard on the university soccer field before being taken to jail. According to official figures, 3,059 students were arrested. *(Photo by Neil Ulevich; used by permission of AP / WorldWide Photos.)*

was a Village Scout; he drove to the nearby police station to report the incident. The charge was lèse majesté.

Ironically, the Village Scout movement began to fade almost as quickly as it had risen to prominence. During its peak years from 1975 to 1979 more than a thousand new initiation rites were held each year. Yet by 1981 the pace of initiations had slowed to an average of two hundred rites per year. That number has held more or less steady since. The movement continues to hold new initiations, but the Village Scouts rarely make headlines. Thus within a few short years after the bloodbath at Thammasat University the Village Scout movement shrank into virtual oblivion. What happened? Why would a movement grow so rapidly, become capable of participating in such an atrocity, and then almost vanish?[12]

At its inception the Village Scout organization appeared an unlikely prospect for such astounding growth. The initiation rite was conceived by Major General Somkhuan Harikul of the Border Patrol Police, a quiet unassuming man without the obvious, flashy charisma of figures inspiring the rapid-fire growth of similar movements elsewhere. The movement itself was sponsored by the Thai state, a notoriously bureaucratic institution and long mistrusted by the Thai people. To compound this unlikely enterprise further, the key framework of the nationalistic rite was imported from the Boy Scouts and adapted for use with adult villagers and townspeople. Accordingly, the Village Scout initiation did not resonate in any obvious way with indigenous practices. And yet during the mid-1970s this movement exploded, creating a demand for new initiation rites that the Thai state could not satisfy.

The explanation of the movement's rise and fall lies in the relationship between the ritual and the broader social context. Although the initiation rite was emotionally powerful, the actual form and content of the Village Scout initiation rite changed little over the course of the two decades. Some variation occurred in the explicitly political content of ad-libbed speeches and skits, and the lavishness of stage props and costuming showed some diversity, but the basic format of the five days remained remarkably constant. Nonetheless the movement as a whole underwent dramatic transformations. Because the ritual changed relatively little, the Village Scout phenomenon becomes a window through which to observe the kaleidoscopic patterns of what I am calling class fractions and state factions.[13] Viewed narrowly the rise and fall of the Village Scout movement provides insight into a fascinating and volatile chapter of Thai history. Seen more broadly this movement illustrates the importance of incorporating a greater sensitivity to class in scholarly efforts to explain the functioning of state ritual in stratified societies.

A Class-Based Analysis of Ritual

Over the centuries rulers and their advisers have developed an appreciation for the political utility of state rituals. The founder of the Han dynasty (206 B.C.–221 A.D.) is said to have balked when advised that the time had come to consult books on Confucian ethics and ritual. "All I possess I have won on horseback," he exclaimed. "Why should I now bother with those musty old texts?" "Your Majesty may have won it on horseback," retorted his chief counselor, "but can you rule it on horseback?" (C. Bell 1992: 193). But if rulers have long understood the political dimensions of ritual, scholarly appreciation of the use of state rituals has been more recent.[14] Although the literature on the use of ritual by the state is growing, much of the discussion has focused on premodern states. Some scholars have gone so far as to associate the visible state rituals primarily with the premodern state and emphasize the invisible techniques of rule in the modern state (e.g., Foucault 1979).

States governing societies with significant economic and political inequalities face problems of legitimacy. Such states face a choice, whether to rule by consensus or force. As Machiavelli writes, "The first way is natural to men, and the second to beasts. . . . So a prince must understand how to make a nice use of the beast and the man" (1961 [1517]:99). In general states prefer to govern by consensus rather than overt coercion. Among symbolic forms of domination (Bourdieu 1977a, 1977b) ritual remains a vital political technique. As E. P. Thompson observes, "A great part of politics and law is always theater: once a social system has become 'set,' it does not need to be endorsed daily by exhibitions of power (although occasional punctuations of force will be made to define the limits of the system's tolerance); what matters more is a continuing theatrical style" (1974:389). The Village Scout movement is a fascinating demonstration of a contemporary application of ritual by the modern state.

Given that social stratification is an inherent characteristic of state societies, it is remarkable that, even within the scholarly literature on ritual, the relationship of state ritual to social class has received so little attention.[15] In 1975 Steven Lukes noted the failure of the prevailing scholarship to consider the place of ritual in a "class-structured, conflictual, and pluralistic model of society" (301). Little has changed in the twenty years since. As Maurice Bloch points out, "Few Marxist writers have discussed ritual" (1986:6), and non-Marxist anthropologists have generally shunned the subject of class (see Ortner 1984; R. Smith 1984; Leach 1984). Many scholars appear to regard the subject of class as inherently crude and vulgar. As R. H. Tawney wryly remarks, "The word 'class' is fraught with unpleasing associations, so that to linger upon it is apt to be interpreted as the symptom of a perverted mind and a jaundiced spirit" (1931:65). Paul Blumberg calls class "America's forbidden thought" (1980:53).[16] Paul Fussell notes that "although most Americans sense that they live within an extremely complicated system of social classes," it remains a "touchy subject" for Americans: "You can outrage people today simply by mentioning social class, very much the way, sipping tea among the aspidistras a century ago, you could silence a party by adverting too openly to sex" (1983:15).

Nonetheless social stratification is an important characteristic of state societies, and a complete understanding of state rituals requires explicating the complex manner in which state rituals function in class-differentiated societies. In fact Maurice Bloch goes so far as to suggest that because rituals are highly limited codes of information and can be easily manipulated by the holders of power to falsify the sense of reality of the exploited classes, their usage is greatest in those societies that are the most politically differentiated (1977; Zuesse 1987:419). Christel Lane makes a similar observation about the political possibilities of ritual, noting that in societies "where a marked discrepancy between the ideological definition of social relations and their actual state has not yet led to *open* conflict," ritual "is a tool of political elites in their effort to perpetuate the political *status quo*" (1981:16). She continues:

> Rulers can resort to three basic strategies to induce the ruled to accept their definitions of social reality. They can change social conditions to bring them closer to their ideological definition, they can change the consciousness of the ruled to bring perceptions of social reality into line with their ideological definition or they can influence the ruled, by various means, to accept the discrepancy between the ideological definition and the reality of social relations. In other words, rulers can initiate social revolution, or cultural revolution, or they can maintain social control through coercion or remuneration.
>
> (1981:27).

The creation of the Village Scouts was an attempt by the Thai state at "cultural management," an effort to both mold the consciousness of the more compliant citizens and to intimidate the more intractable elements into inaction, thereby changing the balance of forces in favor of the state (Marriott 1963:29; Lane 1981:2). Thus the Village Scout movement provides a particularly dramatic example of the interplay of different class positions and hence a clear example for analyzing the social tectonics of Thai society. However, analyzing the Village Scout movement in its entirety requires an expansion of existing theories of political ritual to incorporate a class-based analysis. A class-based analysis allows more careful attention to key aspects of state ritual: the question of agency, the issue of efficacy, the ambiguity inherent in symbolic multivocality, and the dynamism of historical context.

Returning Agency to Hegemony

A major problem in discussions of state ritual in complex societies has been the failure of scholars to confront the underlying assumptions about how a society is held together and the extent to which the state is assumed to be ruling through "fundamentally consensually based legitimate authority, or fundamentally coercive domination" (Skocpol 1979:25). The vision of too many anthropologists has been blurred by the disciplinary preoccupation with describing "culture"; as a consequence both social stratification and the power of the state have been portrayed as the uncontested reflections of the popular will.[17]

The work of Clifford Geertz, one of the most prominent and influential anthropologists to write on state rituals, is a classic example. To a remarkable degree Geertz portrays the state as an epiphenomenon of the popular will, as if social hierarchy were the voluntary creation of subaltern culture. Thus he writes of nineteenth-century Bali:

> Rather than flowing down from a pinnacle of authority or spreading out from a generative center, power seems instead to be pulled up toward such a pinnacle or to be drawn in toward such a center. The right to command was not delegated from king to lord, lord to lordling, and lordling to subject; rather, it was surrendered from subject to lordling, lordling to lord, and lord to king. Power was not allocated from the top, it was cumulated from the bottom.
>
> (1980:62–63).

So extreme is his position that his analysis of Balinese state ritual portrays state ceremonials not as an instrument in buttressing the political power of the state but as a royal response to the cosmological imperatives of a shared agentless and homogeneous culture. He writes,

> The expressive nature of the Balinese states was apparent through the whole of its known history, for it was always pointed not toward tyranny, whose systematic concentration of power it was incompetent to effect, and not even very methodically toward government, which it pursued indifferently and hesitantly, but rather toward spectacle, toward ceremony, toward the public dramatization of the ruling obsessions of Balinese culture. . . . Court ceremonialism was the driving force of court politics; and mass ritual was not a device to shore up the state, but rather the state, even in its final gasp, was a device for the enactment of mass ritual. Power served pomp, not pomp power.
>
> (1980:13)

A similar view is put forward by Stanley Tambiah (1976). Drawing upon

Geertz's notion of a "theatre-state," Tambiah writes of a galactic polity "integrated through collective cosmic rituals," which serve as "embodiments of the collective aspirations and fantasies of heavenly grandeur" (1976:487).

To a certain extent the presumption that state rituals express the common cultural values of the people as a whole follows from the Durkheimian tradition of seeing ritual and its symbolism as playing a role in recreating and strengthening social solidarity.[18] As Durkheim writes of public ceremonials, "There can be no society which does not feel the need of upholding and reaffirming at regular intervals the collective sentiments and the collective ideas which make its unity and its personality" (1915:475).

Sharing this perspective, Monica Wilson suggests that ritual is a "key to culture" that reveals the "values of the group" (1954:241; see also Goody 1977:32; Munn 1973:605; V. Turner 1969:6). Lloyd Warner interprets various American holidays, such as Thanksgiving, Christmas, Memorial Day, and the Fourth of July, as "rituals of a sacred symbol system which functions periodically to unify the whole community" (1962:8). Such rituals "draw all people together to emphasize their similarities and common heritage" (Warner 1962:7; see also Bellah 1967). Similarly, Shils and Young describe the British coronation as "a series of ritual affirmations of the moral values necessary to a well-governed and good society" and "as a great act of national communion" (1953:67, 80).

Thus in the prevailing paradigm state rituals have generally been interpreted as occurring within the context of a consensual society in which the people see their rulers as legitimate and the rituals as expressing shared cultural values. This view of state rituals is being challenged as discussions of hegemony and resistance receive greater play (e.g., Comaroff and Comaroff 1993; Apter 1992). A close reading of Geertz reveals contradictions in his argument. In his famous article "Centers, Kings, and Charisma," he concedes in passing the illegitimacy of most states:

> No matter how democratically the members of the elite are chosen (usually not very) or how deeply divided among themselves they may be (usually much more than outsiders imagine), they justify their existence and order their actions in terms of a collection of stories, ceremonies, insignia, formalities, and appurtenances that they have either inherited or, in more revolutionary situations, invented.
>
> (1977:152)

The possibility that state ceremonials play an active part in the creation of state power—in effect, a cynical effort to manipulate the cultural beliefs of the masses—lies behind Geertz's concession that the "elaborate mystique of court ceremonial" is supposed to conceal "that majesty is made, not born" (1977:153). Thus in his description of Queen Elizabeth I's progresses he writes of her attempt to appear as the incarnation of moral ideals such as "Chastity, Wisdom, Peace, Perfect Beauty and Pure Religion," noting that "Elizabeth not only accepted its transformation of her into a moral idea, she actively cooperated in it" (1977:156).

Once the idea that state rituals might be part of the technique of governance is admitted into consideration, ascertaining agency becomes an important part of the analysis of ritual. Lloyd Warner provides a rare study sensitive to issues of both class and ritual. In his analysis of the tercentenary celebration of the founding of Yankee City (his pseudonym for a city in New England), he noted that the decisions regarding the choices of themes to be included (and excluded), on the specific guidelines for their enactment, and on other preparations, lay with the elites of the community (Warner 1961:89–159). Furthermore, elite involvement in the design of the rituals served elite interests. Thus Lukes argues that political rituals should be analyzed as part of what can be called the "mobilization of bias," that these rituals "operate systematically and consistently to the benefit of certain persons and groups at the expense of others" (1975:305). Consequently, Lukes proposes the following checklist of questions that he believes should be raised in any study of ritual:

> Who (i.e., which social groups) have prescribed their performance and specified the rules which govern them? Who (which social groups) specify the objects of thought and feeling they symbolize—specifically, certain forms of social relationship and activity—as of special significance? Who exactly holds them to be specially significant, and significant in what ways? In the interests of which social groups does the acceptance of these ways of seeing operate?
>
> (1975:302)

Although a class perspective on state ritual makes the need to consider agency clear, determining agency may not be straightforward.[19] The conceptualization and authorization of state rituals necessarily involves more than one individual. Furthermore the state is not a monolithic entity but often rife with bureaucratic factionalism. In addition the various factions of the state respond to and support a range of class fractions in society at large. The state is only "relatively autonomous" and must be understood in relation to the broader society (see the introduction for a discussion of the "relative autonomy" of the state). In the case of the Village Scout movement two individuals played key roles: the founder, Major General Somkhuan Harikul of the Border Patrol Police, and the king. However, the success of each of these men also was dependent upon the support and cooperation of various competing class fractions and state factions. Thus, as this book shows, class fractions and state factions constitute a form of "collective agency" that must be understood, along with the actions of specific individuals, in the analysis of state rituals.

False Consciousness and the Issue of Efficacy

A second important aspect of state ritual ignored in the consensual model is efficacy, by which I mean the effect of the ritual on its participants or audience. For some scholars mere participation in a ritual performance signifies that "the performer accepts, and indicates to himself and to others that he accepts, whatever is encoded in the canons of the liturgical order in which he is participating" (Rappaport 1979). The ritual is assumed to reflect the shared cultural ideology of rulers and people. However, once the possibility that rulers are manipulating ritual for their own interests enters into consideration, it is necessary to confront the possibility that the interests of the rulers and the people are not the same. Basing their analysis upon Marx, Nicholas Abercrombie and Bryan Turner suggest that "since social classes have different economic circumstances, they also have different interests, so that ideas grasp, represent and promote separate interests. In short, each class forms its own system of beliefs, the character of which is determined by the particular interests of the class" (1978:150–51). The contrast with the consensualist paradigm is made clear when they argue that subordinate classes "rarely, or never, shared the ideology of the dominant class" (1978:150).

Thus, if the rulers' interests are different from those of the people, and if ritual is a means by which the rulers are trying to advance their case to the people, the question that naturally follows is, how effective is their appeal? Although scholars suggest the possibility that ritual is a form of manipulation of public opinion, few fully address its effect. Accounts by Geertz and others assert awe or astonishment as the popular reaction to the pomp of royal processions. Consider, for example, Geertz's account of the royal procession made by Hayam Wuruk in Java during the fourteenth century:

There were about four hundred ox-drawn, solid-wheel carts; there were, more for effect than anything else, elephants, horses, donkeys, and even camels (imported from India); there were swarms of people on foot, some carrying burdens, some displaying regalia, some no doubt dancing and singing—the whole lurching along like some archaic traffic jam a mile or two an hour over the narrow and rutted roads lined with crowds of astonished peasants.

(1977:159)

The imagined reception by the spectators of all these accounts of royal processions is favorable, although why the peasantry would be astonished, if in fact peasants and rulers shared a common cultural ideology, is unclear. Nor does Geertz consider whether this awe or astonishment reinforced or undermined the legitimacy of royal rule: villagers may have resented the grandiose display and obvious wealth of the king. Like other consensualists, Geertz makes no effort to document the thoughts of any spectators, leaving open the question of the ritual's actual reception.

James Scott provides an excellent discussion of the problem of determining what lies behind what he calls the "official transcript" of relations between the dominant and the subordinate. As he writes, the official transcript almost invariably "provides convincing evidence of willing, even enthusiastic complicity. In ordinary circumstances subordinates have a vested interest in avoiding any *explicit* display of insubordination" (1990:86). The official transcript presents difficulties for historical research, not only because these are generally "records of elite activities kept by elites in ways that reflect their class and status" but also because of "the more profound difficulty presented by earnest efforts of subordinate groups to conceal their activities and opinions, which might expose them to harm" (1990:87). As innumerable revolts prove, peasants have risen up and monarchies toppled despite the performance of grandiose state rituals.

Thus the effect of ritual on its intended audience must be established and cannot simply be assumed. The methodological issues involved in determining effect are daunting. As Christel Lane, one of the few scholars of ritual to confront the issue, writes, "This is a very difficult problem which is usually neglected in the analysis of ritual" (1981:239). Moore and Myerhoff present a good summary of the issue:

A field worker is confronted with difficult technical problems if he/she wants to ascertain the specific effects on all the individuals present at a collective ceremony. Numbers are an obstacle. Further, much information may be inaccessible for many reasons: psychological, cultural and technical. In the absence of an ideal universe of complete, precise information the field worker must rely on what people tell him/her, piecing data together, drawing on empathy and intuition.

(1977:13)[20]

Nonetheless, however difficult the problem of determining efficacy is, the scholarly failure to do so is as much a consequence of the prevailing classless academic paradigm of ritual as the failure of an honest attempt to surmount the methodological challenges. By presuming that rituals are expressing some essential cultural truth, rituals have been simply assumed to be efficacious. The inclusion of class in the analysis of ritual forces the scholar to grapple with the effect of the ritual on its viewers and participants.

As with agency, the problems of determining efficacy in a complex society are immense. In part the problem of deciding whether a ritual is effective requires knowing what the intentions of its planners actually were. Furthermore, given the variety of state factions and class fractions involved in supporting a certain version of a state ritual, there may be a range of intersecting and diverging purposes. In cases like the Village Scout movement, where politically sensitive issues of psychological warfare and counterinsurgency are involved, the intentions of planners of state rituals may be tacit or even denied. Nonetheless, although actual aims may be hard to ascertain and assess, the ritual's effect on its intended audience needs to be considered. To fail to address the issue of efficacy in the performance of state ritual is to assume the success of state efforts in establishing hegemony and to attribute, unchallenged, a monolithic false consciousness to the subordinate classes.

Including Class in the Multivocality of Symbolism

A class perspective of rituals also expands our understanding of what has long been recognized as a key component of rituals, the use of symbols. As Victor Turner summarizes, "The symbol is the smallest unit of the ritual" (1967:19), the ritual itself being the "performance of a complex sequence of symbolic acts" (1988:75). As Nancy Munn explains, symbols condense meaning, thereby creating "the communicative economy and generalizing power of ritual" (1973:592; see also A. Cohen 1979; Firth 1973; Dolgin, Kemnitzer, and Schneider, eds. 1977). Munn suggests that "ritual should be viewed as a societal control system, a generalized medium of social interaction, linking the individual to a community of significant others through the symbolic mobilization of shared life meanings" (1973:605; see also work by V. Turner 1957, 1967, 1969; Tambiah 1979). However, far more work remains to be done in understanding the role that symbols play in the rituals of class-stratified societies.

Much early work on symbols, even while recognizing the spectrum of referents that a given symbol may evoke (e.g., V. Turner 1957, 1967), viewed these multiple referents as essentially accessible to all participants in ritual.[21] However, as Lukes points out, symbolic mobilization may be strategic and in the interests of one subgroup or another in society. Lukes describes the role of ritual in foregrounding certain interpretations of society, noting that ritual "helps to define as authoritative certain ways of seeing society," adding that "at the same time, therefore, it deflects their attention from other forms, since every way of seeing is also a way of not seeing" (Lukes 1975:301; see also Moore and Myerhoff 1977:5). More recently, Valerio Valeri has made a similar argument, noting that "ritual produces social order by producing conceptual order" and explaining that "the creation of conceptual order is also, constitutively, the suppression of aspects of reality" (1985: xi). He elaborates upon the potential of this cognitive aspect of ritual in the context of hierarchy:

> From this point of view the ordering virtue of ritual is not due simply to enlightening, but also to blinding. . . . Most give sense and efficacy to the subject's actions by stressing that they are part of a harmonious hierarchical whole. But this also implies suppressing in the subject's experience all that points to the conflictual character of social relations and to the exploitative nature of the nobility's rule.
>
> (1985:xii)

In a class-stratified society the symbols deployed in the interest of the elite may include intimidating references to the raw power of the state; these references may range from indirect allusions to graphic depictions. Thus Michel Foucault analyzes public executions in pre-nineteenth-century France as examples of state rituals of intimidation:

> Although the redress of the private injury occasioned by the offence must be proportionate, although the sentence must be equitable,

the punishment is carried out in such a way as to give a spectacle not of measure, but of imbalance and excess; in this liturgy of punishment, there must be an emphatic affirmation of power and its intrinsic superiority. And this superiority is not simply that of right, but that of the physical strength of the sovereign beating down upon the body of his adversary and mastering it. . . . The ceremony of punishment, then, is an exercise of 'terror.'

(1979:48–49)[22]

However, state rituals may also make a more subtle appeal to persuasion, attempting to win over the hearts and minds of the subaltern classes.

The complex properties of symbols provide a range of intriguing possibilities for the mediation of the disparities across classes. As Kertzer comments, multivocality—the different meanings that a symbol may have such that it may be understood by different people in different ways—is "especially important in the use of ritual to build political solidarity in the absence of consensus" (1988:11). Moore and Myerhoff note that rituals may express deep contradictions in the social or cultural system or "just the opposite, it may be designed to mask these, to deny and disguise them and gloss the difficulties they present" (1977:16).

Glossing over inequality presents a complicated challenge to the creators of state rituals because complex societies are often "not *Gemeinschaften* [communities] or even systems of accepted rank" (Hobsbawm 1983:9). Not all state rituals are effective.[23] To the extent that state rituals succeed in their appeal, the issue of the existence of false consciousness is raised. As Bourdieu argues, "Symbolic systems owe their particular force to the fact that the power relations which they express are only manifest in the *misrecognizable* form of relations of meaning (displacement)" (1977a:117; emphasis added). He suggests that ideologies "serve sectional interests which they tend to present as universal interests common to the group as a whole" and thereby contribute to the "bogus integration of society as a whole and therefore to the demobilization (i.e., false consciousness) of the dominated classes" (1977:114). Marx and Engels also refer to the power of ideology to make "men and their circumstances appear upside down, as in a *camera obscura*" (1970:247).

Our understanding of how state rituals may draw upon symbols is only in its initial phases. Some symbols may be on such a level of generality that they are indeed shared by all members of the society; thus the differences between the classes are temporarily disregarded in an appeal to collective solidarity. Rituals may also attempt to draw upon the views and values of the subaltern classes, putting them forward as if they were part of the beliefs of the elite.[24] Rituals may create a new set of appeals that become attractive to the subaltern. In considering these respective approaches Marx and Engels's argument that the ideas of "the ruling class are in every epoch the ruling ideas" (1970:64) must be counterbalanced with Gramsci's view that, at least to some extent, the subaltern classes participate in forming the values by which the elite govern (1971:52).

Regardless of the source of the symbols upon which state rituals draw, the important point is that, in contradistinction to theories of symbols that emphasize the rich layers of meaning available to any and all of its participants, a class-based theory of symbolic interpretation must consider seriously the likelihood that the same symbols may in fact be interpreted quite differently by various participants. The Village Scout movement evoked the powerful emotional bonds of monarchy and family. Because the nation was portrayed as a large family with the king as the royal father, the family motif was primary. However, the family imagery had different meanings for the elite espousing it and the peasantry embracing it. For the elite the authoritarian structure of the family provided a perfect paradigm to justify the continuation of the status quo from which they benefited. For the poor the familial ideology represented a yet-to-be-actualized ideal of a caring government protecting and nurturing its dependents. The social tectonics shifted again once growing numbers of the poor despaired of the establishment of such a loving government.

Dynamism: Toward a Trajectory of Rituals

How long can a misrecognition of respective class interests last? A ritual based upon illusion is, after all, quite insecure. As Christel Lane points out, rituals can succeed only if they "in some way answer the needs of those who enact them" (1981:34). Considering ritual from the perspective of class struggle favors a more dynamic perspective in which state ritual is assumed to be a manifestation of the ongoing dialectic between rulers and ruled. Ritual, rather than merely an expression of long-standing social truths, then is seen as a weapon in a struggle, a language of manipulation. Traditional definitions have emphasized the elements of ritual that are unchanging and repetitious, as "almost all action that is standardized in some way or other" (Goody 1977:27; see also Kertzer 1988:9; Lukes 1975:290; Mead 1973; Zuesse 1987:405).[25] This earlier static view has been challenged by performative approaches to ritual. As

Victor Turner writes, "The great genres, ritual, carnival, drama, spectacle, possess in common a temporal structure which interdigitates constant with variable features, and allows a place for spontaneous invention and improvisation in the course of any given performance. The prejudice that ritual is always 'rigid,' 'stereotyped,' 'obsessive' is a peculiarly Western European one" (1988:26; see also Tambiah 1979).

However, whereas the performative approach focused more on improvised changes made in successive individual performances, a new generation of scholars is seeking to place ritual in a broader historical context. Christel Lane's study of changes in Soviet socialist rituals over the course of the twentieth century (1981), Maurice Bloch's analysis of the circumcision rite in Madagascar over the course of two centuries (1986), and Emiko Ohnuki-Tierney's exploration of the changing symbolism of monkey performances over virtually a millennium of Japanese history (1987) have been pioneering studies. Perhaps the single work that has had the greatest effect in pointing to the dynamism of ritual has been *The Invention of Tradition* (Hobsbawm 1983). As Hobsbawm explains in the introduction to his book, " 'Traditions' which appear or claim to be old are often quite recent in origin and sometimes invented" (1983:1). Don Handelman develops this point in his work, noting that "all public events began sometime and somewhere, regardless of whether their existence is attributed to 'tradition' or to invention" (1990:17). Kertzer suggests that it is precisely "because people create and alter rituals that they are such powerful tools of political action" (1988:12).

In fact it can be argued that many scholars who have focused on the repetitiveness of ritual have allowed themselves to fall victim to the deliberate illusion of stasis. Hobsbawm argues that this illusion is an important strategy in state rituals, noting that invented traditions use repetition to imply continuity with the past (1983:1). Similarly, Moore and Myerhoff comment,

> Ritual must be orderly because it frequently interrupts or manages or accompanies various forms of disorder, ranging from the ordinary rough and tumble confusion of everyday life, through the disorder of choice, and the multiplicity of inconsistencies in ideologies and in social arrangements. . . . Ceremonies are paradoxical in this way. Being the most obviously contrived forms of social contact, they epitomize the made-up quality of culture and almost invite notice as such. Yet their very form and purpose is to discourage

untrammeled inquiry into such questions. Ceremonies convey most of their messages as postulates.

(1977:17–18)[26]

A broader historical perspective of ritual change sheds light on the dynamic manner in which rituals are integrated into society. As Goody observes, "The function of 'ritual' can be better elucidated under changing rather than static conditions" (1977:34). A class-based analysis of ritual requires locating ritual in its historical context. The tension caused by the differing material interests of the various social classes becomes a central component of the analysis. Ritual serves as an important avenue of negotiation used by age-old partners in the tango between the classes. A class-based analysis of state ritual presumes a consciously manipulative aspect of ritual design. State ritual becomes a deliberate political overture, with public reception an uncertain outcome. Depending on the context and the sense of public reaction, the ritual can then be modified or discontinued. Thus the arena of social change provides "a kind of laboratory, where we can observe at first hand how a new ritual develops and establishes itself" (Beattie 1966:71).

The Village Scout movement is an example of a newly created state ritual. Both its creation and its perpetuation over time raise questions about the conditions within Thai society to which the Thai state was responding through this ritual medium. Not only was the Village Scout movement created de novo, it in turn underwent significant transformations during the two decades that followed its inception. However, these changes were primarily in the relationship of the movement to the broader society rather than in the ritual itself. The Village Scout movement began with a specific individual working within a particular agency of the Thai state, the Border Patrol Police (BPP). However, the BPP and other counterinsurgency agencies of the Thai government have sponsored numerous counterinsurgency programs, the vast majority of which have left no mark. The movement's rise cannot be explained without an understanding of the support of the middle and upper classes. Similarly, explaining the movement's decline involves understanding a new historical context and a new balance of power between the classes. The rise and fall of the Village Scout movement was part of a dynamic historical context in which ritual and the shifting alignments of class fractions and state factions were in constant tension and undergoing constant change. As this book shows, the Village Scout movement can best be understood through an exploration

State procession of King Rama VII to the northern city of Chiang Mai in 1926.
(Photo used by permission of Phayab University Archives Photograph Collection.)

of the fourfold issues of agency, efficacy, symbolic ambiguity, and historical dynamism.

Awe to Persuasion

Although this book focuses on the two decades of the Village Scout movement's rise and fall, placing a state ritual in its historical context involves more than understanding a single ritual. As political rituals rise and fall, they become part of a longer historical trajectory of the use of ritual by states. A broader historical perspective illuminates the negotiation between the classes, the overture by the state, and the response by the people. The Thai state has had a long tradition of buttressing its claims to legitimacy through ritual (see Chaloemtiarana 1979; Desai 1980; Gerini 1895; Wales 1931; B. Smith 1978; F. Reynolds 1978; Riggs 1966; Wells 1939). Although a full comparative history of Thai political rituals remains to be written, even a cursory overview reveals significant changes from the nineteenth to the twentieth century. Locating the Village Scout movement in the broader historical context of Thai state rituals sheds further light on the novelty of the movement and the extent of the crisis that confronted the Thai state in the 1970s.

Until 1932 Thailand was ruled by absolute monarchs. In royal rituals in general the primary role of the people has been to serve as spectators rather than as participants. In fact many royal rituals took place within the court or within the capital city. Ordinary villagers probably would have seen a royal spectacle only when a trip to the capital city coincided with an important holiday or when royal processions passed through their villages. The animated account left by the nineteenth-century missionary Clifton Dodd suggests that state ritual was intended to awe and impress its viewers:

> The Chow Fa of Kengtung, the Kun chief, rides a very richly caparisoned elephant. His state robes are entirely of cloth of gold, and his pagoda-like coronet or tiara is also covered with gold. There is one big procession during the year, when the Chow Fa goes out to take his annual bath in the hot sulphur springs, about an hour's ride across the plain to the southeast. He remains there five days. On his return he rides his small elephant with no more sign of rank than the large white satin umbrella carried over him. When he arrives at a rest house outside the city gate, just below our mission compound, he stops to change into his state robes. His large elephant gorgeously arrayed is waiting for him, also a large concourse of people. It is always on big bazaar days that this procession takes place, and the market is thronged. As soon as the procession appears everything stops and there is almost absolute silence as the Chow Fa passes slowly through the market until he disappears into the grounds of his palace. It is most impressive.
>
> (1923:201).

Until the middle of the nineteenth century a considerable portion of Thai court rituals involved Hindu-Brahmanical elements, thereby in effect accentuating the difference between the court religious authority and the Buddhist population. Beginning particularly during the reign of King Rama IV (1851–1868), increasing efforts were made to tap into the Buddhist beliefs held by the majority of the country's population. The court added Buddhist modifications to nearly every state ceremony. As Tambiah summarizes, "The verdict is that the Mongkut era saw an expanded and elaborated ceremonialism surrounding kingship, his contribution being to make Buddhist additions to existing rituals and to introduce new festivals" (1976:227). Riggs suggests that "it was part of Mongkut's policy not only to reduce the emphasis placed on the royal coronation and cremation ceremonies, as expressions primarily of the old cult of the divine king, but also to give greater attention to the role of the king as leading patron of Buddhist ceremonials and activities" (1966:100).[27] Through this involvement in Buddhist rites the king "does not separate himself from the people, but projects his role into the midst of those activities which are most sacred to them" (Riggs 1966:1010). H. G. Quaritch Wales makes a similar comment, noting that "the King was wise enough to found nearly all the component parts of the new ceremony on rites drawn from the stock of Siamese religion and culture—the material that lay ready to hand and was most easily understood by the people" (1931:214).

Nonetheless the state ceremonials that drew upon Buddhist symbolism also relied heavily on spectacle. The annual royal *kathin* ceremony, an occasion on which the king gives robes to the monks, involved the typical grand procession:

> The Royal *Kathina* processions by land and by water are almost the only occasions, other than the Coronation, on which the people can see their monarch pass by in the pomp and circumstance of Old Siam. While the State Processions on these occasions are not so magnificent as those which take place at the Coronation, yet I think they are of greater sociological value, for they take place, not once in a life-time, but every year, and the volume of the crowds that line the route can leave no doubt as to the great hold which royal pageantry still exercises over the minds of the people. Indeed, it is above all the frequency and regularity of these occasions which given them such great value. (Wales 1931:201)[28]

The reign of King Rama VI, also called King Vajiravudh (1910–1925), saw a further general transformation in the use of court ritual. In addition to his lavish coronation and other more traditional forms of spectacle-based ritual, Rama VI developed political institutions that were intended to reach out to the hearts and minds of at least a portion of the population. Faced with a hostile military and a highly factionalized government bureaucracy, Rama VI sought to develop nationalist sentiments by using a strategy related to that of the Village Scouts. However, unlike the Village Scouts, which sought to reach ordinary villagers, Rama VI focused on officials in the state bureaucracy. To further this end in 1911, a year after ascending to the throne, he founded an indigenous form of quasi-scout

organization called the "Wild Tiger Corps" (*sya paa*).[29] The Wild Tiger
Corps started with an enrollment of 200 or 300 volunteers from among
the civilian officials of Bangkok, but by 1924 it numbered more than
10,000 and included "practically every officer of the civil government of
the country" (Graham 1924:242). The corps had an initiation ritual and
spent considerable time in military marches, drills, exercises, sports, war
games, and camping outings (Vella 1978). To reach the youth Rama VI
also founded the Thai form of Boy Scouting (*luuk sya*, which translates literally as 'tiger cubs'; for more on this period see Graham 1924; S. Greene
1971; C. Reynolds, ed. 1991; Vella 1978). However, as Vella notes, the
king's "primary audience was the educated element in the population—
the elite, the leaders"; Vella observes that it was "unlikely that the population at large, the vast mass of Siam's farmers, was deeply influenced by the
King's nationalistic messages" (1978:260–61).

The mantra Nation, Religion, and King, which came to be so closely
identified with the Village Scout movement and bandied about as if it were
a natural and ancient component of Thai identity, in fact dates from Rama
VI's reign. The phrase was popularized by King Rama VI in order to incul-
cate "devotion to Fatherland, Nation, and our Holy Religion" (Vella
1978:33; Girling 1981:139; see F. Reynolds for a discussion of the emergence of "nation" in 1977:267–82; 1978:134–46; see also C. Reynolds,
ed. 1991). During his reign Rama VI did much to promote a militarist
interpretation of nationalism. Using theater, he reenacted stories from the
lives of ancient Thai heroes, at once emphasizing their military virtues and
using them to glorify Thai culture (F. Reynolds 1977:275).[30] He fostered
a Thai identity by juxtaposing it against the Chinese, whom he described
as the "Jews of the Orient." He also encouraged an interpretation of
Buddhism in which he sought "to combat the more pacifist tendencies in
the Buddhist tradition" by affirming "the right to take military action
either in self-defense or in the cause of justice" (F. Reynolds 1977:
274–75). King Rama VI's three-part mantra was given concrete shape in
the new national flag he introduced, its red, white, and blue stripes representing the Nation, Religion, and King, respectively (F. Reynolds
1978:136). The mantra Nation, Religion, and King has been revived by
the leaders of one military coup after another, most notably during the
military coup of 1947, Sarit's coup of 1957, and again during the mid-
1970s (Girling 1981:139). Thus the reign of Rama VI marked a period of
interesting experimentations in efforts to shape public political consciousness, at least among a sector of urban middle-class officialdom.

The overthrow of the absolute monarchy and the establishment of a constitutional monarchy in 1932 curtailed court power and ceremony. Indeed the lavish expenditures of King Rama VI had done much to undermine the legitimacy of the throne, particularly because his extravagance occurred at a time of budget cutbacks at other levels of government, including layoffs of many low-ranking officials. Not until Field Marshal Sarit seized power in 1957, after World War II, did court ritual receive significant government support. The newly resurrected court rituals included the first plowing ceremony, the drinking of the water of allegiance, and the seasonal changing of the clothes of the Emerald Buddha (see Tambiah 1976:229; see also Chaloemtiarana 1979). In 1962 the royal kathin ceremonial was particularly grand, staged with royal barges traveling in procession by river (Tambiah 1976:229). As Tambiah notes, the emergence of these rituals must be understood in the context of "the emergence of military dictatorship and an era of collaboration with the United States against communism" (1976:229); see chapter 3 for a more detailed discussion of this period). The context of Thai society had changed dramatically from the nineteenth century. However, with the exception of the Wild Tiger movement, the basic approach of the court ritual had not altered; it remained one of impressing its spectators.[31]

The Village Scout movement marks a dramatic departure. Just how striking a change in state policy the Village Scouts represents can be seen from the following description, provided by George Tanham, an expert in Thai counterinsurgency, of the general preference of the Thai elite to maintain a depoliticized peasantry:

> The ruling elite over the years, in trying to restrict political power to itself, has maintained an apolitical population, and has attempted to provide enough services and security to keep the people content. Inciting the masses to political action, trying to organize them in large groups, and developing a greater popular awareness have not been part of Thai politics. Rather the leaders have tried to keep the people away from political matters and have them concentrate on their own mundane affairs.
>
> (1974:37).

Although state processions can be seen as an effort to bring the state to the local villages, they rely on external spectacle and appeal only secondarily to the moral values of the people.[32] The Village Scout movement sought not merely to impress people but to reach the hearts and minds of all citizens. If the movement could not win villagers over, it could strengthen the state by at least intimidating its opposition. In this latter aspect the Village Scout movement functioned like Foucault's "panopticism" in which "inspection functions ceaselessly. The gaze is alert everywhere" (1979:195–228). The movement relied on establishing an internalized obedience enforced by surveillance as the basis for social discipline rather than external ceremonies of intimidation and spectacle. Instead of mass spectacle the Village Scout movement was simultaneously a manipulation of hearts and minds of individual citizens and the establishment of eyes and ears for the government. Consequently, virtually every village in the country had a panoptican cell, always watching.

The Village Scout initiation rite had virtually no direct connection with any significant preexisting Thai rituals. It cobbled together sleep deprivation from psychological warfare theories with skits, songs, and knot tying from the international Boy Scout movement. The Village Scout movement appears to have been a quixotic bricolage of political desperation, an unlikely strategy for success.[33] When the Village Scout initiation ritual was developed, Thailand was a rapidly polarizing society. From the perspective of the elite the stakes were high and the existing strategies failing. The rapid growth of the Communist Party in Thailand forced the Thai elite to overcome their concerns about a potentially explosive mix of right-wing ideology and popular mobilization; they were ready to risk a new experiment.

PART ONE

Agency and the State

Somkhuan Harikul gives an award to a villager at the first Village Scout initiation in Loei Province in 1971.

(Photo used by permission of Somkhuan Harikul, director of Village Scout Operations Center.)

2

Genesis in Conflict

The man officially credited with founding the Village Scout movement is a soft-spoken self-effacing officer of the Border Patrol Police (BPP), Major General Somkhuan Harikul. He developed the idea of creating an initiation rite to counter communism after he attended a Wood Badge leadership camp, the elite training camp of the Boy Scouts. However, as Somkhuan Harikul explains the movement's origin, the impetus for the Village Scout movement was a devastating battle between government forces and communist guerrillas in December 1968. This encounter, the most serious engagement that had occurred until then, dramatized the growing military strength of the communist opposition and made it clear that government strategies were failing. More effective approaches had to be found; pressure on the state to take risks and experiment with innovations was mounting.

Although conceived by one man, the genesis of the Village Scouts can be understood only in the context of the maelstrom of escalating class conflict, of rapidly metamorphosing relations between the state and those who opposed it. This chapter considers the relationship between the founder and the broader social context, exploring the central roles of insurgency and counterinsurgency in the creation of the Village Scout movement. After sketching the historical development of the guerrilla movement in Thailand, I locate the BPP—in which Somkhuan Harikul was a high-ranking officer—against the backdrop of other relevant government agencies. In the ongoing war of position, Somkhuan Harikul's role as the founder of the Village Scout movement reflected a confluence of structure, events, and agency (Braudel 1980; Sahlins 1985).

The Official Genesis

According to Somkhuan Harikul, the bloody battle that proved so important in the development of the Village Scout movement began on December 3, 1968. The setting was a remote mountainous region in northeastern Thailand, where three provinces, Petchabun, Phitsanulok and Loei, come together.[1] That day communist insurgents set fire to a hill tribe village school run by Border Patrol Police.[2] As part of a strategy to encourage villagers living in remote areas to trust government officials and share information about local political developments, BPP officers often doubled as village elementary school teachers. When communist guerrillas threatened the two BPP teachers assigned to this village, they fled; shortly thereafter the school was burned to the ground.

At the time of the fire Somkhuan Harikul was already a high-ranking BPP officer. He was superintendent of Border Patrol Police Region 4 and was stationed at Camp Seni Ronnayuth in Udon Thani, an important northeastern province. As soon as he was notified of the attack, he sent in BPP and provincial police forces. He set up a base of operations at Daan Saaj District in Loei Province. There was intense fighting for more than seventeen days. Somkhuan Harikul's men were pinned down and unable to retreat. The government had to call in additional forces, both police and military. More than a hundred men were killed or wounded.[3] On some days as many as two Dakota airplanes (DC-3s, small transport planes), supplemented by Bell helicopters, were filled with dead and wounded (Somkhuan Harikul interview 1991). This battle was significant for two reasons: it was the most serious military encounter between guerrillas and government forces to date, and it marked the spread of guerrilla insurgency to a new area: fighting had hitherto been restricted to provinces along the borders of northeastern Thailand and one province of the North (Kerdphol 1986:180).

Somkhuan Harikul flew back to headquarters in Udon Thani aboard a helicopter carrying the dead out of the area. The only place to sit was on the corpses. Surrounded by death, his heart heavy with the weight of his responsibility to the men who had been under his command, Somkhuan Harikul began to reflect on the situation, asking why Thailand had turned into a battlefield and why Thais were killing each other instead of living in peace and harmony. En route to headquarters he spent the night in Lomsak. Unable to sleep, he stayed up all night and wrote eight pages reflecting on the causes of the fighting and contemplating solutions. That night marked the start of his concerted efforts to find a way to end what he described as the beginnings of a civil war (*songkhram prachachon*).

During the following year, 1969, Somkhuan Harikul attended a Wood Badge–level scout training session for senior Boy Scout officials held in Sakhon Nakhon Province.[4] He was interested in scouting because he had been a Boy Scout and later a Boy Scout leader. Also, BPP officers routinely promoted scouting among the children in the villages in which they worked. The weeklong training session impressed him deeply,[5] particularly for the way strangers from all walks of life came to form close bonds while working together. He left the session with the notion that he would promote scouting among his BPP troops. Because he would need others familiar with the program, he began to encourage police officers, police instructors, and border school teachers, both in the Northeast and elsewhere, to undergo scout training. He helped arrange some training sessions in the northeastern provinces of Udon Thani and Nong Khai.

Meanwhile conflict continued in the area where the school had been burned. Ever since he began as superintendent for Region 4 in 1963, Somkhuan Harikul had experimented with getting people to cooperate in border patrol work. He felt that even with modern technology his forces could not defend Thailand's long frontiers alone; effective defense required the cooperation of villagers living along the borders.[6] In 1965 he started an association for border villagers to which every household sent a representative. Membership cost 1 baht (then about 5 cents). The goal was to have villagers develop their own communities and improve their standard of living. Villagers also were to watch out for strangers entering their villages. They were to defend their villages, taking turns serving guard duty (VS history 1984:17). But the village associations proved insufficient; communist infiltration continued. Somkhuan Harikul increased the number of border teachers. He also sent more troops into the area. Originally each station had seven police officers. As problems

Figure 2.1 Provinces by Region in Thailand.

(University of Wisconsin–Madison Cartography Laboratory.)

intensified, the number increased to one platoon (*muat*) and later to a company (*kongroi*); even these increases did not ease the situation.

Contemplating the deteriorating security situation, Somkhuan Harikul decided to try holding a special training session for villagers, combining his earlier village work with ideas he had gained at the Wood Badge training session. One of his superior officers, concerned about further politicizing the peasantry, initially opposed Somkhuan Harikul's ideas. However, after this officer was transferred, Somkhuan Harikul was finally authorized to proceed with his experiment. Scores of people became immersed in developing the initiation rite, drawing on a range of skills. Core planners included members of his staff and representatives from the local district office. They spent months writing lyrics and music for the scout songs, conceiving appropriate skits and lessons, and handling the logistics of organizing an event expected to involve hundreds of people.

The pilot session was held in 1970 at a BPP camp in Loei Province, in one of the key insecure areas (see figure 2.1). Despite some initial difficulties when villagers wanted to be compensated for their participation, the pilot session proved to be largely successful. About 120 villagers, 30 from each of four villages, attended.[7] During this training session Somkhuan Harikul tested many techniques he had observed during the Wood Badge session. When I spoke with him, Somkhuan Harikul emphasized the following as the most important ideas he tried: forming groups, engaging in competition, team problem solving, working together, eating together, sleeping together, and sharing other activities as a group. According to Somkhuan Harikul, the session was so moving that instructors and participants alike wept when it was time to leave.

With the basic design tested, the BPP scheduled the first official Village Scout initiation session for August 9, 1971. Sessions followed in villages along the Thai-Lao border, in Udon Thani, Nong Khai, Sakhon Nakhon, Nakhon Phanom, and Loei provinces. Where initiation rites were held, villagers began to cooperate with officials, and Somkhuan Harikul found he could withdraw many of the additional BPP troops.

The State of Thai Communism

Because Somkhuan Harikul was a commanding officer in one of the primary government agencies entrusted with suppressing communism, he obviously was concerned with any new development in guerrilla tactics. Yet appreciating the significance of the battle of December 1968 involves

Somkhuan Harikul with royal regalia. *(Photo courtesy of Somkhuan Harikul.)*

understanding the early history of the Communist Party of Thailand (CPT), the dramatic escalation in communist military capability during the latter part of the 1960s, and Somkhuan Harikul's interpretation of the 1968 battle as a portent of civil war. These factors explain the pressure mounting on Somkhuan Harikul and others like him to devise more innovative approaches to counterinsurgency.

The Rise of the Communist Party

Because its designers were engaged in counterinsurgency, the genesis of the Village Scout movement is inextricably linked with the growth of the CPT. Opinion differs regarding the extent of popular support for communism in earlier decades. Many scholars have complacently assumed that the Thai peasantry was traditionally self-sufficient and therefore content. George Tanham, a leading counterinsurgency expert and the head of American counterinsurgency operations in Thailand from 1968 to 1970, goes so far as to suggest that "the relative economic well-being of the peasants and the lack of strong and impenetrable class distinctions have contributed to a society considerably free of the kind of tensions that communism utilizes in its drive for power" (1974:38–39).[8] Based on their presumption of economic abundance, many scholars also assume that the Thai peasantry has traditionally been conservative, apolitical, politically passive, and even "incapable of large scale organization" (Hindley 1968; Phillips 1965; D. Wilson 1962). Such assumptions imply that the CPT had little popular support historically and that its rise was a recent phenomenon.

Other studies challenge this assessment, noting significant and long-standing poverty, class stratification, and rural indebtedness (Andrews 1935; Bowie 1988, 1992; C. Zimmerman 1931). Certainly by the 1930s the peasantry was faced with "a rapid rate of population growth, closing of the land 'frontier,' a steep rise in rural indebtedness to professional usurers holding land as collateral, fragmentation of holdings and thorough-going commercialization of rice production" (Caldwell 1976: 138). In key areas of the central plains "over a third of peasants were landless by the 1930s" (Caldwell 1976:138). Thus Caldwell suggests that by the 1930s communist activity was evident "not only in the urban Chinese community, but also in the depression-ravaged rural areas among the poor Thai peasantry" (1976:138). Writing in 1935, a Soviet commentator described the Thai countryside as "pregnant with revolutionary possibilities" (cited in McLane 1966:197–200).

Peasant discontent surfaced from time to time in a series of uprisings. Throughout the nineteenth and early twentieth centuries resentment over the implementation of new taxes, efforts to amend existing taxes, or the intrusion of government monopolies into such traditional areas of village production as the manufacture of liquor spurred revolts.[9] History also records more isolated incidents, such as burning down government buildings, particularly police stations and courthouses.[10] Yet none of these earlier peasant protests evolved into a sustained national movement that threatened the stability of the Thai state.

The CPT was the first national organization to develop sufficient strength to threaten the government. The party grew slowly during the course of several decades. Although King Chulalongkorn is said to have expressed his concern about the danger of communism as early as 1881 (Buntrigswat n.d.:82), according to an official statement of the CPT,

Marxist groups in Thailand began political work only in 1927 (Turton, Fast, and Caldwell, eds. 1978:158). The Thai government wasted no time in repressing the nascent movement, enacting its first anticommunist law in 1927.[11] However, as Tanham summarizes this early period, "By the beginning of World War II, the communists had made very little progress in Thailand either ideologically or organizationally" (1974:31).

During World War II, when Thailand was ruled by a pro-Japanese government, communist partisans became active in anti-Japanese resistance. The CPT dates its origins to its first national congress, held on December 1, 1942. The anti-Japanese resistance, together with the brief period after December 1946 when the anticommunist law was lifted, enabled the party to operate more openly.[12] Nonetheless even after the repeal of the anticommunist laws there seems to have been little increase in communist activity (Thompson and Adloff 1950:63). The CPT acknowledges that at this time its membership was small (Turton, Fast, and Caldwell, eds. 1978:159). Party activities appeared to focus on fund-raising to relieve the suffering in China, and what domestic communist activity existed had an urban rather than rural focus (Thompson and Adloff 1950:60; Wongtrangan 1984:178).

Anticommunist repression resumed shortly after the 1947 coup by Field Marshal Phibun Songkhram. Suspected communists were arrested on a variety of charges, and some leading critics of the government were murdered (e.g., Chaloemtiarana 1979:84–90). The CPT held its Second National Congress in February 1952. At this congress the party made a clear shift from a focus on urban activities to a Maoist approach that emphasized that "the rural areas are the base of our forces" (Turton, Fast, and Caldwell, eds. 1978:162). No doubt this shift was in response to Mao's victory in China. Communist organizing was complicated by the passage of the anticommunist act of 1952 and another wave of arrests (see Snitwongse 1985:250 for details of act). Tanham describes the party of the early 1950s as "small, weak and composed primarily of Chinese. . . . Its primary activities seemed to be issuance of manifestoes and publication of leaflets" (1974:32).

A major change in the direction of the CPT occurred when the party decided to undertake armed struggle. According to a CPT statement, after Field Marshal Sarit's second coup of October 20, 1958, "the Party was then definitely convinced that the only path to be taken for the liberation of the nation and the people was through armed struggle, using the countryside to encircle the cities" (Turton, Fast, and Caldwell, eds.

1978:164).[13] In the 1958 coup Sarit declared martial law, suspended the constitution, dissolved the National Assembly, closed down the newspapers, and banned all political parties. In September 1961 the Third National Congress of the CPT passed a formal resolution declaring armed struggle as the proper political strategy.[14]

The next few years saw the implementation of the resolution. Sometime between 1962 and 1963 the guerrilla forces established headquarters in northeastern Thailand from which to direct the planned insurgency; they planned to develop similar headquarters in the west-central and mid-southern regions as well. Beginning sometime in July 1962 cadres were sent to Vietnam, Laos, and China for training (Race 1974:94; Tanham 1974:48). The CPT's radio station, Voice of the Thai People, began broadcasting in 1962 (Tanham 1974:34). The first shot was fired in Baan Naabua, Tambon Renuu, That Phanom District of Nakhon Phanom Province in northeastern Thailand on August 7, 1965, a day known since as the Day Gunfire Erupted (*wan ying arun*).

Assessing the reliability of government figures regarding the membership and activities of the Communist Party of Thailand is fraught with serious problems.[15] Nonetheless counterinsurgency experts generally agree that, even as late as 1965, the CPT was "still small and weak," with a total membership that probably was less than one thousand (Tanham 1974:42). Although opinions differ about the degree of latent peasant discontent, most observers agree that organized communism posed no real threat to the country. Thai politicians used the charge of "communist sympathizer" mainly to smear their rivals (Thompson and Adloff 1950: 59–60).

Armed Struggle Begins

With the institution of armed struggle the CPT entered a new phase. Its military strength grew slowly but surely. The initial armed attacks on Thai police and other government officials occurred in northeastern Thailand, primarily in the provinces of Nakhon Phanom and Sakhon Nakhon. The size of the guerrilla bands had increased noticeably by 1966, expanding from groups of five to ten to groups as large as fifty members or more (Tanham 1974:49). Tanham describes the growth of communist strength during this period: "The best estimates are that there were 200 or so guerrillas in the Northeast in 1965 and that this rather vague number rose to perhaps 600 in 1966. . . . These few hundred guerrillas were involved in perhaps fifty to a hundred incidents in 1965 and the figure rose in 1966 to over 500 reported" (1974:51).[16]

Although the CPT was clearly developing a significant military capacity, its strength remained uncertain. Violent incidents increased in February and March 1967, but the number tapered off thereafter (Kerdphol 1986:180). That year (1967) was a drought year in much of the Northeast. Because villagers suffered from food shortages, they were less able to support guerrilla forces. In 1967 the government also made some important arrests of ranking communist leaders, including members of the Central Committee. In early 1968 the number of incidents initiated by the guerrillas dropped, and the number of defections from the party increased sharply (Tanham 1974:53–54).

These difficulties notwithstanding, by 1968 the CPT had nonetheless opened new fronts in Nan and Chiang Rai provinces, marking the beginning of insurgency in northern Thailand (Kerdphol 1986:180). The total number of incidents and the total number of armed guerrillas were increasing steadily (see figure 8.1 and appendix, table A1.14). By the end of 1968 the CPT was demonstrating significant military strength. The December battle in which Somkhuan Harikul was involved provided dramatic confirmation. Concern about developments in Thailand was compounded by concern about events in Vietnam. The Tet Offensive, when an estimated seventy thousand communist troops in Vietnam attacked more than a hundred cities and towns and the U.S. Embassy in Saigon, had occurred in January 1968. Although the offensive ultimately failed militarily, the feat stunned U.S. and world opinion (Karnow 1983: 525).

CPT military strength grew steadily. Although 1969 showed a decline in the total number of casualties and incidents, the CPT was emphasizing political rather than military work (Tanham 1974:55). Communist strength increased steadily in all regions of the country. Units became active in the northwestern region of Thailand, in Tak and along the Burmese border, and in several provinces in southern Thailand (see Kerdphol 1986:181). Communist forces were also becoming more effective militarily. According to the Chinese press, during 1970 the insurgents "wiped out more than 1,100 enemy men, downed or damaged more than 50 aircraft and took more than 20 strongholds" (cited in van der Kroef 1974:118). In March 1972 at Hin Longkla, a guerrilla mountain stronghold near Lomsak, a band of communist insurgents estimated at several hundred seasoned guerrillas fought ten thousand Thai troops. In January

1973 more than three thousand Thai troops, supported by fighter bombers and heavy artillery, were arrayed against guerrilla forces in the South, concentrated in the mountains of Trang Province. "Several battalions of the Thai Second Army were said to have been involved in anti-insurgent drives in the northeastern province of Kalasin" (van der Kroef 1974:123). The number of guerrillas was estimated to be as high as five thousand (Kerdphol 1986:48–49).

The overall trajectory of the figures between 1965 and the early 1970s demonstrates the growing strength of the Communist Party of Thailand. According to General Saiyud Kerdphol, the head of the Communist Suppression Operations Command (CSOC), the number of clashes between guerrilla and government forces increased from a low of 154 in 1965 to 680 by 1972. The number of government casualties increased from 87 killed and 72 wounded in 1965 to 592 killed and 1,296 wounded by 1972 (see appendix, table A1.14), and by the early 1970s there was a growing consensus that new strategies were needed.

Assessing the Growth of the CPT

A growing number of officials believed the Thai government should deal with the guerrilla movement because it was gaining strength. However, they disagreed about the factors responsible for this and, consequently, what they should do. Academic explanations for the rise of the CPT have focused on three factors: external factors relating to foreign policy, the increased militarization of the counterinsurgency effort in Thailand, and the failure of Thai government development policies in the countryside.

Foreign Policy

The inception of the armed struggle of the CPT can be attributed to transnational factors, most notably the spreading war in Indochina and the resulting American military buildup in Thailand. Preparations for armed struggle intensified in response two new developments in Thailand's international relations. First, beginning on May 17, 1962, the Thai government agreed to allow U.S. troops to be stationed in Thailand (Turton, Fast, and Caldwell, eds. 1978:164). Second, it allowed the United States to use Thai airfields to bomb in Indochina (Tanham 1974:33). Several scholars, including Graham Martin, a former U.S. ambassador to Thailand, have suggested that a "direct causal relationship existed between the development of American air bases and the launching of the northeastern insurgency" (Randolph and Thompson 1981:14). Apparently as a result of increased Thai involvement in the Indochina war, Chinese assistance to the CPT increased.[17] As Randolph and Thompson explain this view,

> Insurgency was undertaken primarily to deter Bangkok from maintaining or expanding its alliance with the United States; the message was that an expansion of the U.S. role in Thailand would be met by an intensification of Chinese-supported domestic turmoil. The insurgency, in other words, may have been triggered more by the growth of U.S. activity in Thailand than by any internal political considerations.
>
> (1981:14)[18]

The U.S. military presence in Thailand had been escalating gradually throughout the 1950s and 1960s. In 1962 the Thanat-Rusk agreement was signed. Dean Rusk, then U.S. secretary of state, and the Thai minister of foreign affairs, Thanat Khoman, agreed that the United States "could, essentially without the concurrence of other SEATO members, come to the assistance of Thailand" (Tanham 1974:21). By 1965 the United States had about eighteen thousand troops stationed in Thailand, and by 1967 the number approached fifty thousand (Lomax 1967:83). The first major bombing raid of North Vietnam from a Thai airbase took place on February 7, 1965 (Lomax 1967:82). As U.S. involvement in Vietnam escalated during the 1960s, the American presence in Thailand also expanded. Just how pervasive the American presence became is revealed by Peter Bell, a British political economist:

> By the late 1960s Thailand had much of the appearance of an occupied country. It was literally a garrison. The combined strength of Thai military and police forces, trained and equipped by the US (over 15,000 Thais received military or police officer training in the U.S. and another 30,000 in Thailand) numbered around 260,000. Additionally there were some 50,000 U.S. troops stationed there on seven major air bases (including one that could handle B-52 bombers), nine major strategic communications centres, six special forces headquarters and one naval base. . . . There were U.S. advisers everywhere; they occupied choice residences in the best districts of Bangkok (usually with four or five servants per household); sat in the highest positions in Thai government Ministries and in the military; and were seen at the best golf and country clubs. In the

towns where the military had bases, shantytowns sprouted, of bars, brothels, tailoring establishments, and off-base housing for the GI's to house Thai mistresses.

(1978:64)19

The decision of the Thai government to align itself so closely with American foreign policy had serious internal repercussions. The U.S. presence in Thailand spurred foreign support for the CPT and aroused internal discord. Many Thai resented the American presence and were opposed to becoming embroiled in the Vietnam War. Furthermore many Thai believed that the American presence and the war were creating significant social dislocations that were contributing to the rapid spread of communism. Whether they blamed the overwhelming U.S. presence in Thailand or claimed that communist infiltration from Laos, Vietnam, and Cambodia was increasing, those who believed that turmoil resulting from the Vietnam War was the factor most responsible for the growth of Thai communism generally denied that the guerrillas had much popular support.[20] The holders of this view insisted that "the communists had no popular support and that they had to use terrorist tactics to force the peasants to cooperate with them" (McGehee 1983:100).

Internal Military Policy

In contrast to those who emphasized the role of international factors in the rise of the CPT, others focused on internal factors, primarily Thai economic development policies and Thai military suppression campaigns. Beginning in 1965 and 1966 counterinsurgency approaches gave way to large-scale military operations. Battalion-size units conducted "search and clear" operations, combined with air and artillery attacks (Snitwongse 1985:256). The use of direct military force escalated after 1968, when the Royal Thai Army decided to take over operational responsibility for counterinsurgency from CSOC.

With the growth in military force the government presence in the villages necessarily diminished. General Saiyud Kerdphol, then head of CSOC, complained bitterly of this change in the direction of the government's counterinsurgency policy. Before the military takeover General Saiyud Kerdphol and others involved in psychological warfare operations felt that significant progress had been made in halting the growth of the CPT, citing the arrests of high-ranking CPT members and the general slowdown in CPT activity. The BPP had been responsible for operating in the upland areas of

Thailand. As Jeffrey Race explains, the BPP "were specially trained and equipped for jungle operations, had individuals who spoke the tribal languages, and employed small-unit tactics which emphasized patrolling and engaging opponents outside of village complexes" (1974:103). By contrast the army was not trained for small-unit jungle operation and had no speakers of hill tribe languages. The problem, as Race notes, "was aggravated by the army's preferred tactic of napalming entire villages suspected of harboring enemy personnel" (1974:103). Removing BPP personnel from the upland villages further served to reduce government knowledge of what was happening (Race 1974:106–107).

Not only did government intelligence suffer but military attacks on villages were pushing the people "further towards the communist side" (Wongtrangan 1983:6–7). These operations were both "ineffective as well as counter-productive as the rural people became antagonized and turned to aiding the guerrilla cause" (Snitwongse 1985:256). In a particularly notorious attack on a village in northeastern Thailand in 1966 "women were raped, two men (one later found not to be a communist) were tortured, and an unknown number of villagers summarily executed" (Kerdphol 1986:16; see also van der Kroef 1974:106). Military patrols wrought further havoc with villagers' lives as they "raced through the rice paddies in half-track personnel carriers and tanks, tearing up the fields" (McGehee 1983:108).

Direct military operations began in northeastern Thailand. By 1967 the government was also conducting military operations in northern Thailand, primarily against hill tribe villages. The hill tribes' resentment of the government intensified further when, in April 1968, the government ordered them to come down and live in government settlements. As Race explains, "Many of the hill tribes refused to move" (1974:106–107). As the army continued to use napalm, artillery, mortars, and aerial bombing, villagers sought refuge in the jungle rather than resettle in the lowlands. Government efforts to force resettlement, combined with attacks on upland villages, "had the effect of creating enemies where formerly there were none" (Race 1974:103).[21]

Across the country military attacks on villages led to a rapid growth in the number of insurgents. In northern Thailand guerrilla strength increased tenfold or more, from fewer than two hundred fighters to about two thousand armed insurgents in 1970 (Race 1974:98, 109, 111; see also Kerdphol 1986:116–17). Guerrilla strength showed similar increases in northeastern and southern regions of Thailand.[22] Thus as Tanham writes, the government's military responses "harmed villagers and tended to make them more sympathetic with the insurgent cause" (1974:50; see also Kerdphol 1986:16, Race 1974:86).[23]

Internal Economic Policies

Although many criticized the Thai military campaigns, others also faulted the Thai government's economic policies. Because government officials designed development programs from Bangkok, villagers were not involved in their planning and implementation. Because of bureaucratic rivalries projects overlapped and government resources were not allocated optimally. Although some villages received good schools, good roads, electricity, and other benefits, other villages were totally ignored. Not surprisingly, the neglected villagers were resentful.

Government programs fostered the development of rural inequality in a variety of ways. Some programs contributed to inequality across villages, whereas others exacerbated divisions within communities. For example, the Accelerated Rural Development Program (ARD) introduced a rural credit program, but it benefited only those who could produce proof of land-ownership and excluded the chronic debtors. Consequently feelings of relative deprivation grew.[24] Some programs actually left villagers worse off. For example, ARD's first priority was building roads.[25] The all-weather roads were intended to provide access for armed forces and police to sensitive areas and to serve as supply routes for the U.S. airbases. However, villagers had little interest in having roads at this time, and implementation of the road-building projects was frequently mishandled. One key problem was the government's failure to pay for the valuable rice-paddy land it took for the roads. Furthermore, as Thak Chaloemtiarana explains, "To add insult to injury, taxes were raised two to seventeen times the previous rates on land near the ARD roads" (1979:266–67).

As the government came into more and more direct contact with villagers, problems of corruption and other abuses of power became more obvious. As Kusuma Snitwongse writes, "The traditionally supercilious attitude and indifference on the part of the central authority and those who represented it did little to endear them to the villagers. Abuses of power were not uncommon" (1985:255). As a result of the emphasis placed by the U.S. Agency for International Development (USAID) on expanding the provincial police forces, the government officials with whom villagers came into increasing contact were the police. Villagers' frustration at police demands for food and bribes grew. Thus, as Snitwongse observes, "Development by itself might even increase a village's propensity to come under the control of the CTS [communist terrorists]" (1985:153).

For those who emphasized economic grievances as the major factor in the growth of the CPT, the overt military activity of insurgents was simply a visible manifestation of the party's underlying political support among the peasantry. Although some counterinsurgency experts viewed government development programs as creating new grievances, others saw these programs as exacerbating widespread and long-standing rural poverty. The closer the experts lived to villagers, the more likely they were to hold the latter view. As one local policeman living in northeastern Thailand explained, villagers "were hungry, poor, and all but naked. . . . They were neglected; all Bangkok did for them was to send in special police to arrest the villagers for gambling and brewing homemade whiskey. This is why so many young men have gone up in the mountains to join Rassamee [a CPT guerrilla leader]" (Lomax 1967:9).

Those sensitive to economic grievances of the peasantry were more likely to view the peasantry as highly susceptible to communist appeals. Thus Frank McGehee, a CIA analyst who based his estimate of communist support on village studies, concluded, "The CIA estimated there were 2,500 to 4,000 Communists in all of Thailand. But our surveys showed the Communists probably had that many adherents in Sakhon Nakhon Province alone" (1983:109).

Somkhuan Harikul's Interpretation

Somkhuan Harikul saw the battle of December 1968 as a portent of civil war because he believed rural poverty was widespread. Although he would not deny the importance of escalating U.S. involvement in Thailand or the overmilitarization of Thai counterinsurgency in the growth of the CPT, Somkhuan Harikul believed rural economic conditions and achieving the cooperation and participation of villagers were more significant. One of his first comments to me in explaining his motivation in founding the Village Scouts noted the lack of educational opportunities and health care for villagers. He also expressed his concern about abuses of power by corrupt government officials (1991 interview).[26]

Unlike many other high-ranking government officials, Somkhuan

Harikul did not come from a wealthy urban family. He was born in the southern province of Krabi; his father was a low-ranking government official who usually was assigned to posts away from home (VS history 1984:13). Because the family had five children, Somkhuan Harikul's father had told him that it would not be possible to receive much schooling. However, Somkhuan Harikul's grandfather was a temple abbot, so he was able to live at the temple for free while attending elementary school. Because he was a good student and his father had some connections, Somkhuan received a partial scholarship that enabled him to receive his secondary schooling. He earned additional money for school by working as a manual laborer.

These early life experiences gave him a greater awareness of the difficulties of poor people in Thai society. Indeed because of his background and because of the low regard in which ordinary people held police, he was reluctant to become a police officer (VS history 1984:16). His perceptions of poverty, the abuse of power by police and other corrupt government officials, and other rural grievances were reinforced in the course of his work, most notably during his years as a paratrooper when he lived and traveled extensively throughout villages in remote parts of the country. Thus for Somkhuan Harikul the escalation of communist guerrilla strength represented by the battle of 1968 and the years that followed was not merely a military complication or an indication of increasing foreign infiltration but a political omen. The battle of 1968 marked for him the beginning of what he explicitly described as a civil war, a war not between Thais and outsiders but among Thais over who should have the power to determine the political character of the Thai state.

Communism and the Shaping of the Thai State

For Somkhuan Harikul the only way to avoid civil war after the battle of 1968 was to devise radically new strategies. As a high-ranking officer in a government agency that occupied a strategic position in the Thai state, Somkhuan Harikul had opportunities for experimentation that others elsewhere in the government with new ideas for combating insurgency lacked. Understanding both the pressures and opportunities facing Somkhuan Harikul requires an overview of the structure and rhetorical orientation of the Thai state.

Long before the actual outbreak of violence in 1965, many government agencies and civilians were already involved in suppressing communism. As early as 1927—even though communist activities were minimal at the time—the Thai state enacted anticommunist laws. The rhetoric of anticommunism and national security intensified dramatically after World War II in the wake of the victory of the Chinese Communist Party in 1949. The Thai state continued to use anticommunist rhetoric to justify everything from coups to debates over budget allocations even long after the end of the Vietnam War and the collapse of the CPT. The military character of the Thai state and its rhetoric of anticommunism have shaped the government and contributed to a proliferation of agencies claiming a role in counterinsurgency.

Since the ouster of the absolute monarchy and the establishment of a constitutional monarchy in 1932, Thailand has been ruled by a succession of military administrations. Continuity has been provided by the "bureaucratic polity" (Riggs 1966). The bureaucratic elite has emphasized stability as "the desirable mode of existence, order as the desirable mode of behaviour, evolution as the desirable mode of change" (Samudavanija and Paribatra 1987:192). The rhetoric of anticommunism proved useful to the new Thai state both in its efforts to extend its domain and to delimit internal rivalry. As Samudavanija and Paribatra suggest, counterinsurgency was useful in "extending the central government's role and presenting bureaucrats with opportunities for individual and group advancement" (1987:192–93). Kusuma Snitwongse, arguing that the bureaucracy sought stability and "the right to rule unchallenged by the extra-bureaucratic forces," comments that "the communist label has been used as a means by which the bureaucracy has kept out or silenced its opposition" (1985:248).

The military has had a long-standing role in Thailand. During the coup of 1932 military officers played a key role in the overthrow of the absolute monarchy and the establishment of a constitutional monarchy (Mokarapong 1972), and the military has played a major role in Thai politics ever since. The latest military coup occurred in 1991. Partly because the military controls considerable firepower and partly because Thailand has no tradition of parliamentary supervision of the military, the Thai military has been able to exert considerable influence in the government. In addition to defense budgeting the military has been involved in "the formation, development and operation of security apparatus, paramilitary units and security-oriented grass-roots programmes and organizations"(Samudavanija and Paribatra 1987:195). The threat of communism has long provided justification for military coups and budget allocations.

Even social welfare programs were justified on the grounds of suppressing communism and bolstering national security. In addition to the BPP, one of the first institutions created to respond to the threat of insurgency was the Department of Community Development, founded in 1962. ARD was established in 1964. Preexisting branches of the government transformed their priorities to give greater emphasis to counterinsurgency. The Department of Local Administration became increasingly involved in counterinsurgency because it is responsible for rural administration from the village up to the district offices (Tanham 1974:75). The Public Welfare Department established areas in which to resettle hill tribes in an effort to remove population from insurgent areas. The Public Relations Department engaged in some propaganda efforts, designing special radio broadcasts to reach hill tribe populations (Tanham 1974:77). Related work was also done by the ministries of education, health, and national development; as Tanham comments, "The programs of these ministries have significant implications for counterinsurgency. . . . Drawing the line between programs that are highly useful to the people and programs created to counter the insurgency is difficult" (1974:78).

More directly involved in suppression was the Communist Suppression Operations Command (CSOC), which was organized in December 1965. The Psychological Operations Division of CSOC, the Public Relations Department, and the National Information Psychological Operations Organization, established in 1969, conducted psychological operations (Tanham 1974:77).[27] The Thai National Police Department (TNPD) had five sections involved in suppression and intelligence: the Provincial Police, BPP, Marine Police, Special Branch, and the Police Air Division. Within the Ministry of Defense the Royal Thai Army was the dominant force and it played an important role in counterinsurgency. The navy and air force also played supportive roles. The National Security Command was formed within the Ministry of Defense to coordinate counterinsurgency work; the Mobile Development Units and several radio stations were under the jurisdiction of the National Security Command (Tanham 1974:82).

Thus to a remarkable extent the Thai state was highly militarized and oriented toward counterinsurgency long before the Communist Party of Thailand was ever a significant challenge. Many agencies were formed even before the outbreak of armed struggle, and the anticommunist rhetoric was in place even before the founding of the modern Communist Party of Thailand in 1942. This anticommunist stance enabled the Thai state to suppress opposition to its policies. As Samudavanija and Paribatra astutely observe, "Security came to be defined in terms of regime-maintenance, and any type of dissent, let alone armed communism, was seen to be a security threat" (1987:193). The state's counterinsurgency orientation was used to justify a growing military and paramilitary apparatus; it also affected the broader shape of society as well. Probably the single most important manifestation was the character of the Thai legal system. Crucial political freedoms, such as freedom of the press, assembly, and speech, were subject to suspension and control. Tanham acknowledges that much of what the Thai government did in the name of suppressing communism was in fact a way to suppress criticism of its policies, noting that "the times of repression were reactions to periods of considerable opposition to the government: however, the communist threat was also often used as an excuse for action against other forms of dissidence" (1974:40).

Communism, U.S. Pressure, and the BPP

The emphasis the Thai state placed on counterinsurgency was also a response to pressure placed upon it by the United States. As Snitwongse writes, the Thai government's responses to the armed communist movement, at least in the initial period up to approximately 1969, "cannot be properly understood without taking into consideration the involvement of the United States" (1985:250).[28] She continues:

> The American Mission in Thailand thus provided significant input into Thai counter-insurgency thinking and policy. While the Thais did not indiscriminately accept American advice as pointed out by George K. Tanham (1974:150), American aid which increased significantly from 1961 no doubt helped to create a vested interest among certain Thai military leaders in counter-insurgency operations and made them more easily persuaded to accept American advice.
>
> (1985:251)

Although Thailand and the United States have had diplomatic relations since the nineteenth century, U.S. involvement in Thailand expanded dramatically after World War II as an increasingly interventionist and actively anticommunist U.S. foreign policy took hold. In response to growing U.S. concerns about communist victories in Eastern Europe and China, and the insurgency confronting the British in Malaya, the United States provided assistance for the development of the Thai police forces, beginning in 1951 (Lobe 1977).[29] The BPP was created in response to U.S. pressure. Through the "Anti-Communist Committee" secret negotiations took place between Phao Siyanon, the director general of the Thai National Police Department (TNPD), and the CIA in 1951. As Lobe explains the rationale:

> The U.S. representative explained the need for a paramilitary force that could both defend Thai borders and cross over into Thailand's neighbors—Vietnam, Laos, Burma, Cambodia, and China—for secret missions. Phao's police were thought to be more flexible, more open to new roles and responsibilities than Sarit's bureaucratically entrenched armed forces. The CIA's new police were to be special: an elite force outside the normal chain of command of both the Thai security bureaucracy and the TNPD.
>
> (1977:20)

In a U.S. National Security Council (NSC) directive the United States detailed the CIA to build a paramilitary police force that would have both a defensive and offensive capacity. Such units would operate in small-unit patrols, parachute behind "enemy" lines, commit sabotage, and engage in espionage and surveillance (Lobe 1977:23). To implement the NSC order the CIA created a front organization in Miami called the Overseas Southeast Asia Supply Company, or Sea Supply for short, which contracted with the Thai government to train and equip the new police units.[30] Two paramilitary units were organized: the Police Aerial Reconnaissance (Resupply) Unit (PARU) and the larger Border Patrol Police (BPP). The United States, through its Sea Supply/CIA advisers, "continued to exercise almost complete control, both in training and operations—the PARU and BPP were 'their' units" (Lobe 1977:24). This dramatic development of BPP and other police capabilities took place in the early 1950s when "there was no evidence that an incipient insurgency existed in Thailand" (Lobe 1977:42).

In the 1960s the newly elected Kennedy administration also placed considerable emphasis on developing counterinsurgency capabilities (Blaufarb 1977; McClintock 1985a:12–27; Tanham 1974; Lobe 1977: 33). John F. Kennedy thought police and paramilitary groups could assist a government's development programs by maintaining law and order. The emphasis on police resulted from the prevailing theory of effective counterinsurgency. The British had succeeded in overcoming a strong communist movement in Malaysia during the 1950s by emphasizing the use of police rather than the army for counterinsurgency (see R. Thompson 1966; Stubbs 1989). This idea was taken up by American counterinsurgency experts as well, leading to the establishment of the Office of Public Safety (OPS) in the United States in 1962 (Blaufarb 1977; Lobe 1977). The OPS in turn took as its mission the establishment or upgrading of police forces in noncommunist countries throughout the world. In Thailand the newly created OPS channeled its assistance to the BPP and the Provincial Police, with the BPP receiving the lion's share (Lobe 1977:41).[31] Selected BPP officers went abroad to U.S. Army installations and paramilitary training camps in Malaysia and the Philippines to become more proficient in advanced counterinsurgency techniques, jungle warfare, and intelligence (Lobe 1977:42).[32]

With the military escalation in Vietnam and the declaration of armed struggle by the CPT, many senior U.S. officials believed that Thailand was the last chance for counterinsurgency—the only strategy that could effectively halt that spread of guerrilla warfare (Lobe 1977:46). In 1965 counterinsurgency became the highest priority of the United States Operations Mission (USOM), the agency that oversaw all USAID programs in Thailand (see Lobe 1977:17, 21; Tanham 1974:120–22): "Now all AID [USAID] projects were selected or rejected on the basis of assisting the Thais in defeating the guerrillas" (Lobe 1977:48). Beginning in 1965 the United States earmarked additional funds for the Provincial Police. Altogether 47 percent of all USOM aid to Thailand during the next four years was given to the Thai National Police Department (Lobe 1977:49). Between 1967 and 1972 the United States trained almost thirty thousand Thai police and army officers (Shawcross 1976:59).[33]

The Border Patrol Police and the Battle Against Insurgency

Given this background of the national and international history of counterinsurgency in Thailand, it is easier to understand why the Village Scout movement originated within the ranks of the BPP. There are three main reasons. First, although anticommunist rhetoric was useful in intrabureaucratic competition, the military and other key political players were generally more concerned with political machinations within the capital than with the growth of communism up-country. Many in the Thai elite never accepted the urgency of the threat that the United States articulated (Lobe 1977:74). Furthermore, as Lobe and Morell comment with regard to the army,

> It was in the army's own interest to let the BPP play a leading role in certain areas. The BPP was assigned those difficult and dangerous tasks for which the army had neither the capability nor the commitment. Why should army leaders decide to dissipate their own troops on possibly futile attempts to provide security in remote border areas? These leaders saw their principal personal and institutional objectives in terms of Bangkok's power politics, rather than of village or border operations. . . . Border Policemen could risk their lives and their agency's reputation in counter-insurgency activities and cross-border raids, while army units remained intact, ready to carry out a coup—or a counter-coup.
>
> (1978:170)[34]

In part because of its mandate and largely because of the differing priorities of other agencies involved in counterinsurgency, the actual hands-on responsibility for coping with "border" problems was relegated to the Border Patrol Police. Consequently the BPP was the agency most heavily involved in countering the guerrilla threat.

Second, because of this hands-on involvement the BPP had the most incentive to minimize the need for combat and the casualties it would likely incur. The BPP was also closer to the villagers than other agencies and so more aware of the importance of gaining villagers' trust, cooperation, and even loyalty. As Somkhuan Harikul explained to me, the Thai border was far too long to patrol effectively without villagers' cooperation. Lobe and Morell explain the BPP philosophy in greater detail: "If villagers were to be relied on for information and cooperation, they would have to accept this paramilitary organization as a friend rather than a foe. Antagonizing villagers was to be avoided at all costs. From the early 1960s, BPP directives and training sessions underlined the necessity of acting as the benefactor of the border peoples" (1978:161).

Third, the BPP was the agency within the structure of the Thai state that was in the best position to innovate because of its relative autonomy and its close relations to the palace.[35] Lobe and Morell also credit BPP leadership, noting in particular the work of Lieutenant General Suraphon Chulabrahm, the BPP commander for many years (in 1977 he became deputy director general of the Thai National Police Department). General Suraphon attracted subordinates "dedicated to the same kind of performance ethic and provided the leadership cohesion around which an unusual organization could emerge and thrive" (Lobe and Morell 1978:170). As Lobe and Morell write, "With leadership from General Surapon and potent linkages to the army, palace, and CIA, the BPP had the freedom to be different, to devise innovative relationships between an armed component of the government and the Thai people" (1978:171). The idea for the Village Scout movement might well have been stillborn had Somkhuan Harikul been involved with some other government agency. Because the BPP was directly involved in counterinsurgency on a day-to-day basis, because the BPP was conscious of the importance of gaining villagers' cooperation and had some familiarity with village life, and because the BPP was less bureaucratic than other government agencies, its higher-level officials were more likely to be receptive to innovative experiments such as the Village Scouts.

Innovation and the Individual

An age-old question of historiography involves assessing the relative weight of agency and structure, free will and determinism, the individual and his or her society. As Marx wrote, "Men make history, but not in circumstances of their own choosing." Somkhuan Harikul conceived and initiated the Village Scout movement as a result of several quasi-fortuitous events: his ride in a helicopter so crowded that he was forced to sit on the corpses of his men, his attendance shortly thereafter at a Wood Badge training camp, and the transfer of a certain superior officer who was opposed to his experiment. However, these more fortuitous events must be understood in the context of Somkhuan's biography.

Because Somkhuan Harikul came from a lower-middle-class family and had traveled extensively throughout the countryside, he was familiar with poverty and the everyday problems facing villagers. Consequently he was more likely to view the growth of communism in broader political terms rather than from a more narrow military perspective. Furthermore as a high-ranking BPP officer he had considerable psychological warfare training, which further reinforced his tendency to find political rather than military solutions to the appeal of communism.[36] His position as a commanding officer also placed at his discretion both budget and considerable personnel resources. Once he conceived the idea, Somkhuan Harikul could and did charge his subordinates with carrying out various phases of the work. Thus the specific shape of the Village Scout movement owes much to the skills of Somkhuan Harikul and the team of designers he assembled.[37]

However, even broader social forces shaped the context in which Somkhuan Harikul innovated. The pressure to find new solutions was escalating with the dramatic growth of the CPT and the growing realization that military policies alone were failing. As a high-ranking member of the BPP, an agency with a primary role in counterinsurgency, Somkhuan Harikul and his officers were under double pressure to innovate. The state of insurgency and the structure of counterinsurgency converged to create an atmosphere in which the Thai elite became receptive to new ideas. Biography merged with history in the enactment of an experiment. The Village Scout movement was conceived in a specific historical context, in the midst of the escalating class struggle, by a man whose profession made him a partisan. As Plekhanov writes, "It has long been observed that great talents appear everywhere, whenever the social conditions favorable to their development exist. This means that every man of talent who actually appears, every man of talent who becomes a social force, is the product of social relations. . . . Were it not for that trend they would never have crossed the threshold that divides the potential from the real" (1940:52).

King Bhumiphol, the queen, and other members of the royal family give chapter
flags to Village Scout leaders.

(Photo used by permission of Somkhuan Harikul, director of Village Scout Operations Center.)

3

The Expansion: The Monarchy and the Middle Classes

From the hellish helicopter ride bearing corpses away from battle to the first initiation, the course of events was at once fortuitous yet overdetermined. If Major General Somkhuan Harikul was the major figure in the genesis of the movement, King Bhumiphol Adulyadet was clearly the single most important personage fostering the movement's expansion. Royal patronage facilitated support from both the government and the private sector. Accordingly, understanding the expansion of the movement also involves an appreciation of the intricate dynamic between the monarchy—viewed both as an individual and as a symbol—and the shifting coalitions of class fractions and state factions within the broader society. Many scholars of Thailand have simply assumed the institution of monarchy to be inherently powerful. However, this assumption is ahistorical and underestimates King Bhumiphol's own role in turning the monarchy into a powerful political force. The significance of royal support was not constant but was historically constituted.

During the late 1960s King Bhumiphol (Rama IX) served as a unifying symbol of hope for the lower and middle classes; by 1975 he had also become a lightning rod for the conservative reaction of the elite. The ambiguity in the symbolic meaning of the royal family is a crucial factor in explaining the dramatic success of the Village Scout movement in the mid-1970s. To the extent that the king symbolized hope among his poorer subjects, his involvement with the Village Scouts attracted the lower classes to the movement. To the extent that the king was transformed into a symbol of conservative reaction against progressive reform, he catalyzed the financial contributions of the upper classes and conservative elements in the middle classes. Thus the king played an important role in the expansion of the Village Scouts, initially as a powerful symbol of unity and later as a multivocal political symbol motivating an intricate fusion of class fractions and state factions. This chapter focuses on these two phases of royal involvement in the expansion of the Village Scout movement, the first phase dating from 1972 to 1974 and the second phase from 1975 to 1976.

The Importance of Royal Patronage

Royal involvement in the Village Scout movement began early, with the visit of the king's mother to the ninth Village Scout initiation. The princess mother had long been active with the Border Patrol Police in its efforts to improve public welfare and the security of Thailand's borders. This initiation was held in November 1971 in a village in the northeastern province of Nakhon Phanom.[1] As a token of her approval of Somkhuan Harikul's initiative, the princess mother gave him a book entitled *The Long, Long War* by Richard Clutterbuck, a counterinsurgency theorist and expert in the suppression of the Malayan Communist Party (1991 interview). The king became involved a few months later, after he and the queen attended the thirtieth Village Scout initiation, held on March 19, 1972.[2] Favorably impressed, a week later the king invited Somkhuan Harikul and Charoenrit Chamrasromrun, his superior officer, for an audience at Chitrlada Palace.[3] At this meeting the king formally offered the movement his patronage. He donated 100,000 baht (about U.S.$5,000) to help underwrite the costs of expanding the movement across the country.

Thereafter King Bhumiphol and other members of the royal family became closely identified with the Village Scout movement. In addition to financial assistance the king provided the distinctive maroon scarves that each and every Village Scout received upon initiation. The king was also credited with having established the overall policies guiding the administration of the scout movement (see appendix, table A1.1). Furthermore members of the royal family attended many scout functions in person and during the initial years personally gave each Village Scout chapter its chapter flag. Increasingly, as members of the royal family traveled to the countryside, Village Scouts would be seen forming the front ranks of those gathered to greet them.

The king's role in the movement was both personal and symbolic. To understand the significance of the king's complex role it is important to appreciate just how extraordinary the expansion of the Village Scout movement was. To grow from an idea in the mind of its founder to a nationwide movement involving as many as 20 percent of the country's adults, the Village Scout movement had to overcome three major sets of difficulties. First, the state had to determine how to staff, budget, and logistically support the scout movement. Second, given the financial costs of the movement, the government needed to motivate individuals to contribute. Third, the organization needed to generate popular interest in membership.

Facilitating Interagency Cooperation

The multi-agency effort that the Village Scout movement entailed was quite remarkable. Crude figures shed light on the magnitude of the administrative obstacles. At its peak in 1976 the movement held 2,387 initiation sessions involving 1,897,540 initiates. Each initiation session required at least forty staff members, not including the personnel needed to take care of administrative matters before and after the initiations.[4] Because each of these forty people spent at least five days in each initiation, approximately 477,400 labor days were involved in simply staffing the initiations. This figure represents an annual staff of 1,836 people working around the clock (instructors were on duty for twenty-four hours a day throughout the five-day initiation). Were the labor days recalculated on the basis of a normal workweek, an annual staff of 5,508 people would be involved—for the ritual alone.

Not only did the Village Scout movement represent a tremendous commitment of personnel, it required considerable interagency cooperation. The staffing needs alone far surpassed the capabilities of a single government agency. Although the BPP, which came under the Interior Ministry, provided initial administrative support, by 1976 cooperation with other government agencies had become essential. As more and more different departments within the ministries of the interior and education and to a lesser extent the Ministry of Public Health became increasingly involved with various aspects of the Village Scout administration and oversight, the opportunities for bureaucratic conflict increased. The larger the movement became, the more remarkable was the level of cooperation that the Village Scout movement demanded of the bureaucracy.

Royal patronage provided the political pressure to facilitate intrabureaucratic cooperation. From the beginning the Village Scout movement involved the collaboration of officials from the ministries of education and the interior. Interagency links had initially been facilitated by the personal bonds of high-ranking members of the BPP leadership with various influential figures, but these connections were ad hoc and localized.[5] On October 25, 1972, the royal secretary wrote to the deputy minister of interior asking that all provincial governors be encouraged to cooperate with the BPP in holding Village Scout initiation sessions.[6] The Ministry of Interior was the most significant of all the various agencies involved in the Village Scout movement. Important functions ranging from provincial administration to village elementary schools were under its jurisdiction. On October 8, 1973, the working relationship between the BPP and the Ministry of Interior as a whole was formalized in an official directive that ordered every provincial governor to become personally involved in organizing Village Scouts in his province and to act as the provincial head (*Daily Times*, June 14, 1976). Because the ministry had a much larger staff than the BPP, its involvement in handling the bureaucratic minutiae of staffing and arranging each initiation contributed significantly to the movement's development.[7] The royal directive provided the political incentive to establish a working relationship spanning several national agencies and provided the Village Scout movement with the tremendous personnel and fiscal resources of the powerful Ministry of Interior.

Encouraging Financial Support

Royal involvement also facilitated fund-raising. The initiation rites were expensive. Depending on the lavishness of the props and the quality of the food provided the staff, an average session cost 15,000 to 40,000 baht (U.S.$750 to $2,000). This sum did not include staff salaries, food costs, or the expenses borne by the initiates.[8] Accordingly, the 2,387 sessions held in 1976 alone represented a cost of some 35 to 95 million baht

(U.S.$1.8 to 4.8 million). Thailand's first countrywide wage law, enacted in October 1974, established only 10 baht per day (50 cents) as the minimum wage. This law was rarely enforced, and most villagers working as agricultural laborers earned even less. Some families earned as little as $25 a year (Morell and Samudavanija 1981:209; see also Turton 1978:113 and Phelan 1975:14). Nonetheless, using the figure of a laborer earning the official minimum wage as an indication, the minimum costs of these initiation rites represented the combined annual incomes of 13,000 to 26,000 people working 365 days per year. Although scout staff members were not paid an official salary, virtually all were government officials and therefore were receiving their regular monthly salaries while serving as scout instructors. If staff salaries were included, the figure for the initiation cost would be even higher. For a country with only a meager social welfare program the basic financial commitment entailed in the Village Scout movement was considerable.

Staff salaries notwithstanding, the king pressured the Village Scout movement not to use government funds for scout events and increased its need to develop independent sources of revenue. At the same time royal patronage greatly facilitated fund-raising efforts in the private sector. Furthermore, although the stingiest of businessmen would have found it awkward to avoid making at least a minimal contribution, the fact that the mainstay of Thai businesses are in the hands of Chinese-Thai had special implications for fund-raising. Because the Chinese-Thai have periodically been the victims of xenophobic persecution, the king and these businessmen have developed a mutually advantageous relationship. Chinese-Thai businessmen often donate generously to royally sponsored charities, and the king often rewards their generosity with awards and titles, providing them with a kind of royal protection that helps to vouchsafe public goodwill (Girling 1981:142).

Generating Popular Support

The problems involved in overcoming village hostility toward government-supported projects should not be underestimated. The Thai state has supported scores of programs, and many programs fail despite government support. Since 1950 government counterinsurgency efforts had generated no less than 120 development projects, 12 security projects, and at least 20 initiatives for different types of paramilitary forces[9]; none had caught on like the Village Scout movement. The problems that developed during the pilot initiation, held in 1970 in Loei Province, illustrate the obstacles and the extent of village antagonism to the government.

Only two or three days into the pilot session the participants refused to cooperate, threatening to return home unless their demands were met. These demands included a per diem of 20 baht per day, free meals, uniforms, weapons, ammunition, and elephants, the last to be used to transport goods. Quick thinking by Somkhuan Harikul averted the imminent collapse of his experiment. He met with the villagers from 11 A.M. until 9 that evening, arguing that they were receiving far more benefits from the government than they were giving in return. He asked how many present had paid taxes. Of the 120 participants, only 25 had. The total tax paid by all 25 villagers amounted to only about 100 baht. However, the government had built a road 14 kilometers long at a cost of 500,000 baht per kilometer and a school building (150,000 baht) and paid the salaries of two schoolteachers, about 1,300 baht each per month. Using this logic, he was able to persuade the villagers to participate.[10] According to Somkhuan Harikul, by the end of the session the villagers had become eager participants and the pilot was deemed a success.

Although Somkhuan Harikul was able to overcome villagers' objections on a case-by-case basis, royal support greatly facilitated villagers' cooperation and their willingness to join without persuasion or direct coercion. At the very least, because of the threat of lèse majesté, it would be difficult for villagers to avoid joining the movement.[11] However, when the Village Scout movement was founded, the king's standing was high. Many villagers hoped that by joining what they saw as a royal organization they would gain direct access to the king or members of his entourage for assistance with their problems. Furthermore the monarchy's association with the Village Scout movement facilitated its drawing upon the vast lore of amulets and sacred powers that circulates in Thai society. Protective amulets are a favorite topic of conversation among urbanites and villagers alike.[12] Most Thais traveling any distance—and many as part of their daily attire—wear one or more amulets around their necks. An object may be sacred in its own right (as a relic of the Buddha or famous monk) or by having been blessed by someone holy. Because villagers were already predisposed to believe in amulets, scout instructors did not find it difficult to convince villagers that the kerchiefs presented by the king and blessed by the nation's most revered monks had protective powers. The king's personal stature reinforced the belief that the scouts' royal kerchiefs were sacred (*saksit*).

The Creation of Symbolic Power

The political position King Bhumiphol had attained when the scout movement began facilitated both state and popular participation in the Village Scouts. By the early 1970s King Bhumiphol had achieved a level of political respect greater than that of any Thai king of the twentieth century. To appreciate King Bhumiphol's position at the time the Village Scout movement was starting, it is necessary to place the Thai monarchy in its historical context and understand the effect of King Bhumiphol's own actions as king over the course of the 1960s and early 1970s.

The Thai monarchy was extremely weak throughout most of the twentieth century. As John Girling writes, "Even the awe and reverence evoked by the 'King' among Thai people, especially in the countryside, is only dimly reflected in the actual experience of the dynasty in this century" (1981:140). In recent years many scholars have noted the presence of pictures of members of the royal family in villagers' homes. However, Konrad Kingshill, one of the first anthropologists to describe village life in the 1950s, records that in those days photographs of U.S. President Dwight Eisenhower typically hung "in many bamboo huts, sometimes being the only picture on the wall" (1991:244, 246). In his 1954 survey of rural political opinions Kingshill notes that 61 percent of his rural informants were uncertain of the meaning of *monarchy* (1991:245).[13]

Early History of King Bhumiphol

Thailand was ruled by absolute monarchs until 1932. The revolution of 1932 established a constitutional monarchy, and the power of the Thai monarchy suffered a major blow. However, the signs of a weakening monarchy had been evident even earlier, most notably in the coup attempt of 1912 (for discussion of this period see S. Greene 1971; Mokarapong 1972; Ratanapat 1990; Vella 1978). From the abdication of King Rama VII in 1935 until the coronation of Bhumiphol in 1950 Thailand did not have a reigning adult monarch in residence. By the time Bhumiphol ascended the throne the monarchy had become quite weak. He became king upon the tragic death of his brother King Rama VIII in 1946, a death still mired in rumor (for discussion see Morell and Samudavanija 1981:n72). King Bhumiphol was only nineteen and had lived most of his life outside Thailand, in the United States and in Switzerland. Immediately after ascending the throne the young king returned to Switzerland for further schooling. Four years later, in 1950, he returned to Thailand for the coronation ceremonies. By then the army was again in control of the nation's political process.

Until the mid-1950s the young king was kept under restraint and removed from politics (see Chaloemtiarana 1979:309–34, Girling 1981: 140, Keyes 1987:80). In 1956 he was temporarily ordained as a monk at Wat Bovornives.[14] As Willard Hanna writes, "For a period of years King Bhumiphol and Queen Sirikit [Bhumiphol's wife] were apparently content to lead a life of royal detachment, appearing in public on state occasions, but devoting themselves mainly to the palace and to their growing family of children" (1964:280).

The King Begins His Ascent

Nonetheless during the 1950s the king and General Sarit Thanarat, the commander in chief of the army from 1954 on, began to develop a mutually beneficial relationship. Their relationship was facilitated by concerns growing among a core of royalists and members of the army staff over aspects of then-prime minister Phibun Songkhram's foreign and domestic policies. They opposed Phibun's plan to open foreign relations with Communist China as well as his domestic liberalization, which allowed party and legislative politics to resume (Morell and Samudavanija 1981:65).[15] Evidently, royalist supporters also believed they would be able to advance royal interests by working with Sarit. Their support ultimately contributed to General Sarit's seizure of power in 1957.

Because Sarit's coup displaced a somewhat more democratic and open government, many questioned the new government's legitimacy (Keyes 1987:80; for more on this period see Chaloemtiarana 1979; Darling 1960, 1962).[16] Sarit saw an opportunity to enhance his own legitimacy and status by providing the palace with a more prominent role. An anonymous official from the office of the prime minister stated explicitly that the decision to revive the monarchy as a political force was "a conscious act" by Sarit (Morell and Samudavanija 1981:65). According to Hanna, "The king and Sarit, surprisingly, hit it off quite well. . . . Sarit seemed to have decided that a popular, indeed even a powerful king might be advantageous to the nation and himself. He removed many of the remaining obstructions, therefore, to the king's freedom of movement" (1964:285).

After the 1957 coup the royal family began to travel widely. Between 1959 and Sarit's death in 1963 the king made state visits to twenty-three countries.[17] In return royalty from Malaysia and Great Britain visited Thailand. These various visits helped establish an international reputation for the Thai monarchy (Chaloemtiarana 1979:313–14). In addition members of the royal family began to travel throughout the country, demonstrating their concern for the victims of drought and other natural calamities, for the poor in rural villages and tribal communities, and for wounded soldiers and policemen. In the cold season the royal retinue often distributed blankets to needy villagers. As a further sign of royal concern, the retinue often included medical personnel. The royal family paid particular attention to the remote mountain regions, in part because the hill tribe minorities were believed to be especially vulnerable to communist appeals. Although many looked down upon the tribal minorities, the royal family popularized hill tribe handicrafts; the queen often incorporated tribal textiles in her attire.

Beginning with Sarit's regime, the royal family became active in various charities, educational institutions, welfare organizations, and other public interest groups. In addition the king became increasingly active in a variety of development projects, especially in the agricultural sector.[18] Royal activities were increasingly publicized in the newspapers, over the radio, and in TV news broadcasts (Keyes 1987:209). Thus even villagers who had never received a royal visit nonetheless appreciated the evidence of royal concern for the plight of the poor and less fortunate. Such activities did much to win the hearts of villagers, creating an image of the royal family as compassionate and caring.

Members of the royal family began participating more and more in both religious and secular ceremonies. Demonstrating the renewed grandeur of the Thai monarchy to the public at large, ceremonies neglected since the 1932 revolution were restored. The plowing ceremony to ensure a good harvest, discontinued in 1936, was reinstituted. The gilded royal barges, used in the nineteenth century for the royal kathin ceremony, were refurbished and the ceremony revitalized.[19] Sarit also adapted older traditions and created new ones. He staged public spectacles of military allegiance to the throne. The royal bestowal of ceremonial flags (*thong chaichalermphon*) flags on regiments, an occasion when troops swore allegiance to the throne and flag, became a major military ceremony (Chaloemtiarana 1979:319). With state support the king presented Buddha images to each province of the kingdom (Keyes 1987: 209). To further the association between state and monarchy Sarit changed the National Day of Thailand from June 24, the anniversary of

King Bhumiphol accepts flower garlands from schoolgirls dressed in their Girl Guide uniforms at the annual Kathin ceremony at a Buddhist temple in Bangkok on October 24, 1973. *(Photo by Neil Ulevich; used by permission of AP / WideWorld Photos.)*

the 1932 revolution that ended the absolute monarchy, to December 5, the king's birthday (Chaloemtiarana 1979:311).

Although many royal rituals were grandiose public occasions, others were more private and served to foster more personal bonds between the monarch and various members of the Thai elite. Thus during this period royal sponsorship of wedding and cremations, including those involving military officers, increased markedly. The king presented awards, decorations, and titles to military and bureaucratic leaders and their wives and to business leaders who donated money to these royally sponsored causes. The king also bestowed names on babies and gave new surnames as a mark of special favor (Chaloemtiarana 1979:324–27; Morell and Samudavanija 1981:66).

Thus through the use of both public and private rituals King Bhumiphol succeeded in establishing links with virtually all sectors of the Thai public, from ordinary villagers and remote hill tribes to various members of the Thai bureaucracy and middle classes. Beginning during the Sarit regime the BPP and other government agencies began distributing free pictures of the king, queen, and other members of the royal family to be hung in homes throughout the country (Lobe and Morell 1978:162). Films, sports events, and other public occasions opened or closed with the playing of the royal anthem. While the anthem played, movie theaters began showing special films of the royal family traveling throughout the nation and visiting ordinary villagers. Through ritual and media popular awareness of the monarchy became greater during the reign of King Bhumiphol than it had been earlier in the century (Morell and Samudavanija 1981:18). Benedict Anderson goes so far as to suggest that the interaction between state and king begun during the Sarit regime "sacralized" the monarchy. As he explains,

> Shortly after seizing power, Sarit began a systematic campaign to "restore" the monarchy, and, in giving it new luster, to fortify his own positions. . . . One could almost say that under Sarit a strange displacement of traditional roles occurred: the field marshal playing the part of the ruler (punisher of crimes, collector of taxes, deployer of armies, and political power-boss in general), and the ruler that of the Buddhist hierarchy (consecrator of authority and epitome of disinterested virtue). We need not be surprised, therefore, that in some ways the monarchy became more "sacred" as the dictatorship entrenched itself.
>
> (1977:22)

The King's Growing Dissatisfaction with the Military

Ironically, although the king's close association with the military aided his rise to prominence in the countryside, it was his break with the military that assured the respect of the Thai urban middle classes and intelligentsia. Although initially limited to a symbolic role, after Sarit's death in

1963 the king's role in politics became increasingly overt. He held private meetings with military leaders and businessmen and traveled more frequently to rural areas. He became increasingly concerned with the failure of the army suppression campaign in the border regions and also with the growing corruption of the government of field marshals Thanom Kittikachorn and Praphat Charusathien. By 1968 and 1969 he was making public statements insinuating his sentiments. In 1968 he told Thammasat University students that it would be the last year they would meet without Thailand's having a constitution (Morell and Samudavanija 1981:66). In March 1969 the king gave an address at Chulalongkorn University in which he expressed his concern about the government's interaction with villagers.[20]

The king was also becoming increasingly public in his criticism of the military. Having developed considerable knowledge of hill tribe issues, he shared the concerns of those who felt that the military's policies of bombing hill tribe villages and relocating hill tribe populations to refugee centers were counterproductive. Of all the hill tribe ethnic groups, the Hmong (Meo) were the most affected. Speaking to three thousand students and teachers at the College of Education (Prasarnmitr), the king commented, "There are very few Meos who are really reds. If we make mistakes, the whole Meo tribe will turn red and cause incessant trouble for us later." He said he thought the use of force was self-defeating and warned the military to use more "discretion in carrying out suppression operations." The king also called on the government to start telling the truth about the seriousness of the problem rather than continue to hand out propaganda that served only narrow political interests (Race 1974:105). Speaking in September 1971 at Chulalongkorn University, the king encouraged students to continue protesting corruption so that there would be no corruption in Thailand in twenty years (Morell and Samudavanija 1981:67).

By 1971 the public saw the military regime as ever more arbitrary, corrupt, incompetent, and complacent. The military coup of November 1971 provoked a groundswell of popular opposition. This coup dissolved the National Assembly, annulled the constitution, and banned political parties, returning Thailand to direct martial law and concentrating power even further in the hands of field marshals Thanom and Praphat (for a discussion of this coup and its context see M. Mezey 1973; Morell 1972). In addition to the prime ministership Thanom took over the portfolios of minister of defense and minister of foreign affairs. Field Marshal Praphat, in addition to serving as deputy prime minister, added the powerful offices of minister of interior and police director general (Heinze 1974:n495). This internal coup prompted the king to speak out even more explicitly. He cited a foreign observer who had suggested that having an elected parliament would continue an ancient Siamese tradition whereby the common people could petition the king to redress their grievances. The king added, "So I say to the generals, for them to understand, that we have this tradition of petitioning the government, and that they must learn to listen to the people" (Morell and Samudavanija 1981:69).

The demand for constitutional government grew in all strata of Thai society, from the king to professionals, students, merchants, and ordinary people. A series of events contributed to the popular uprising that led to the ouster of the hated military government. Inflation hit in mid-1972 after a long period of price stability. Mismanagement of rice supplies led to shortages and the unprecedented development of long queues to buy rice in Bangkok. Inflation also contributed to a spate of labor unrest and strikes. Student organizations across the country began to organize protests on a variety of issues, ranging from campus concerns, such as tuition increases and school administration, to national concerns, such as Japanese involvement in the Thai economy, the American military presence, government corruption, and rice shortages (for details see Heinze 1974, Darling 1974). With the election of Thirayut Boonmee as secretary general of the National Student Center of Thailand (NSCT) in August 1972, the relatively uncoordinated association of student groups was forged into a powerful organization of approximately 100,000 members, including students from engineering and vocational schools, teacher training colleges, and high schools (Heinze 1974:492).[21]

Popular anger intensified when, on April 29, 1973, a Thai army helicopter crashed in what became known as the Thung Yai Affair. The helicopter was returning from an illegal hunting expedition in the Thung Yai game preserve laden with the carcasses of protected animals. Six high-ranking military and police officers were killed and five injured. Field Marshal Thanom immediately announced that the group had in fact been on a secret mission. This claim contributed to further public outrage. In June 1973 nine students were expelled from Ramkhamhaeng University for publishing satirical articles about the Thung Yai Affair. Their expulsion prompted the largest student demonstration held in the country as of that time. Thirty thousand students participated in a protest march that tied up Bangkok's traffic for two days. The government was forced to back down. The expelled students were reinstated, the rector resigned, and an investigation was launched to determine who had hired the thugs who had beaten students during the demonstration. This demonstration was followed by another in July 1973 by students at Chulalongkorn University who organized a major protest against government rice policies.

A Rallying Symbol of Democratic Reform.

Throughout this period the king indicated his support for the prodemocracy movement in a variety of ways. During the massive student protest of the Thung Yai Affair in June the king instructed the police not to use violence against students and had tents and food prepared for the demonstrators on the palace grounds (Heinze 1974:494). So great was the tension between the government and the monarchy that rumors proliferated that the regime was even planning to establish a republic and eliminate the monarchy. During the summer of 1973 the military junta was rumored to have plotted an assassination attempt against the crown prince (Reynolds 1978:138). In a speech in late September at Chulalongkorn University the king stated that the public was ready to support the students whenever they saw that student activities were beneficial to society. Newspaper columns by M. R. Kukrit Pramoj in Siam Rath, considered by many readers to represent the views of the king because Kukrit was a close member of the royal family, were strongly sympathetic to the protest movement. These columns culminated in an editorial calling for the government's resignation (Reynolds 1978:146).

Events came to a head in October 1973. Early that month students began circulating leaflets in support of a petition, signed by one hundred prominent national leaders, demanding the promulgation of a new constitution. On October 6 thirteen activists were arrested for passing out leaflets; they were charged with treason. Student leaders demanded the release of the arrested activists and crowds of students grew. On October 13 they held the largest demonstration in Thai history; a crowd of 400,000 marched from Thammasat University to Democracy Monument. The demonstrators bore Thai national and Buddhist flags and carried large pictures of the king and queen. A delegation of nine NSCT student leaders went to the royal palace for an audience with the king at 4 P.M. The king informed them that the government had agreed to release

Woman mourns slain brother at the national cremation rites on October 14, 1974, sponsored by the royal family for the October martyrs. Behind her is a placard with the names of the dead.

the imprisoned activists and to allow the promulgation of a new constitution within the year. The delegation returned to Democracy Monument to inform the people gathered there. Although most of the crowd then returned home, mistrust of the military's promises was widespread, and tens of thousands remained through the night. Student representatives had a second audience with the king from 3 to 5:30 A.M.

Somehow shooting broke out in the early hours of the morning of October 14. As word spread, the popular uprising grew. Within hours battles were raging at several points in the city, with the army and police units using machine guns, tanks, and helicopter gunships to fire on the demonstrators (for detailed accounts see Heinze 1974 and Punyodyana 1975). During the day about seventy demonstrators were killed and one thousand injured.[22] Those killed became instant national heroes.[23]

The king's actions on October 14 placed him firmly on the side of the people against the military dictatorship, further solidifying his position as an icon of the prodemocracy movement. As the military opened fire, many fleeing students sought refuge on the palace grounds. By throwing open the palace gates to the fleeing demonstrators the king won a firm place in the students' hearts. At 7:15 that Sunday evening King Bhumiphol went on national television and, in what has been described as "a short, highly formal, but intensely emotional speech," expressed the sorrow and shame of the nation concerning the violence and killing that had occurred that day (Reynolds 1978:143). He then went on to announce that the military government had resigned and that he had appointed Sanya Thammasak as interim prime minister until a constitution could be written and elections held. Sanya was widely respected. He had served as chief justice of the Supreme Court of Thailand, as rector of Thammasat University, as head of the Buddhist Association of Thailand, and was at the time of his appointment serving as a member of the king's privy council (Keyes 1987:86). The princess mother also broadcast a plea for nonviolence. The fighting in the streets continued. The king met with the student leaders and the military triumvirate. Shortly thereafter, at the official request of the king, the three military dictators and their families were escorted to the airport where they boarded a plane for Taipei. Calm was restored only after their departure was made public.

In the days that followed these dramatic events the king began to set in motion the machinery needed to institute a constitutional democracy and begin the healing process. In well-publicized visits the king and queen went to see hospitalized students (Marks 1977:54). In addition to appointing an interim prime minister the king developed a mechanism for replacing the discredited national assembly appointed by the military government with a new interim parliament. With the counsel of trusted advisers he appointed 2,436 members to a national convention and charged them with selecting the 299 members of an interim national assembly. Unlike previous assemblies, the convention members included many rural leaders and few military or police officers (Keyes 1987:87).[24] Furthermore in an unprecedented speech King Bhumiphol urged students to remain unified in fighting dishonest practices, so that one day all corrupt people would disappear from Thailand (Mudannayake et al. 1975:B49).

Thus during the course of the 1960s and early 1970s the king gained tremendously in public estimation. After he helped to usher in a long-awaited civilian government, the king's popularity could not have been higher. Indeed M. Rajaretnam called this "the King's finest hour" (1975:174; see also Darling 1974:16; Van Praagh 1977:294). Morell and

Samudavanija note that "King Phumiphon [King Bhumiphol] had become the most powerful figure in his nation's political system" (1981:68–69). By 1973 he had reigned twenty-seven years; he had survived seven constitutions, half a dozen elections, and a score of cabinets. More important, he had become a unifying symbol of popular aspirations. In his speeches he had expressed his concern about military and government corruption, the misplaced use of force, and the lack of meaningful channels for villagers to express grievances. In his actions he had demonstrated his commitment to assisting with the development of the countryside, particularly of the border regions.

The King and the Village Scouts

Why did the king became involved with the Village Scouts? His motivation in patronizing the movement can be understood both as a way to support government counterinsurgency efforts and as a way to establish a popular base from which to counter certain factions in the Thai state. He had long-standing relations with the Border Patrol Police dating to the 1950s. As Lobe explains the historical development of this relationship,

> Whereas in 1951 both units [BPP and the Police Aerial Reconnaissance (Resupply) Unit, PARU] had recruited proportionally from the Army, Navy and the police, by 1953, Sarit's Army was excluded. Members of the Navy and the police came to dominate BPP and PARU. They were extremely loyal to Phao and also to the Thai King, who had traditionally favored the Navy and police. Sea Supply/CIA advisors encouraged and nurtured this royalist influence. These elite police were seen by their supporters and themselves as protector of King and country, giving them an *esprit de corps* not found in other security forces in Thailand.
>
> (1977:24)

BPP personnel frequently acted as royal bodyguards, and the king, queen, and princess mother usually visited remote hill tribe villages in the company of BPP units (Lobe and Morell 1978:157). Physical proximity reinforced the personal links between the king and his royalist police protectors.

The BPP troops identified closely with the king, and the king demonstrated his preference for the BPP over the army in a variety of ways. As Lobe and Morell write,

Nevertheless, by the early 1960s it was clear to all politically aware Thais that the King's heart was with the BPP rather than the army. Often His Majesty traveled to remote tribal villages to dedicate a new BPP school, or would spend time visiting the PARU camp near the royal summer palace at Hua Hin or the BPP installations near the northern palace at Chiang Mai. The mutual focus of the royalty and the BPP on remote tribal areas was not accidental for either of them, and clearly brought palace and BPP into close accord. From the army's point of view, these remote areas were the ideal ones in which these two institutions could be allowed to operate. Here they were less of a threat to continued army dominance.

(1978:172)

Thus on the one hand the close relationship between the BPP and the king helps to explain the king's willingness to provide royal patronage to a BPP undertaking. His patronage can be seen as wholly consistent with his general support of BPP counterinsurgency efforts. Because his key advisers included counterinsurgency experts such as Saiyud Kerdphol and high-ranking BPP officers, his concerns for the future stability of the kingdom were reinforced, especially in light of the growth of the Communist Party of Thailand (CPT). On the other hand the king's decision to bring the Village Scout movement under royal patronage can be read more broadly, as a bold step in the months shortly after the November 1971 coup to build an antimilitary, anticorruption, prodevelopment, and popular grassroots organization. The king may have been quite consciously building a power base from which to do battle with the corrupt military government that was still in power. Kershaw's perspective lends support to this interpretation:

King Bhumiphol, 40 years old in 1967, abhorred his exploitation by a self-interested and self-appointed power-group. Certainly he saw it as his duty to help preserve Thailand from revolution, but a monarchy which was identified with corrupt, military regimes would simply have guaranteed its own early extinction. Bhumiphol therefore set himself the task of fostering respect for religion and love for a monarchy which, while relying mainly on its traditional assets in relation to the peasantry, would be forward-looking like that of Bhumiphol's august grandfather and earlier Chakris. However, after three decades in obscurity the monarchy could hardly be a source of dramatic initiatives. . . . Rather, he appealed to

the patriotism and social responsibility of the university students.
. . . The university students and those recently graduated may be
seen as a "constituency" if not exactly a "power-base" of the King up
to about 1974, as he sought to escape military domination and free
himself for a more effective contribution to national unity.

(Kershaw 1979:257)[25]

Whatever the king's immediate motivations, his support of the Village
Scout movement played an important role in the movement's expansion.
When the king offered royal patronage to the movement, he had the
admiration of many villagers and the support of broad sectors of the middle and upper classes. This popularity eased villagers' suspicions of gov-
ernment-initiated projects and encouraged financial contributions from
the private sector. The king's broad base of support also increased his ability to pressure the government to carry out royal projects.

Although royal support clearly contributed to the initial expansion of
the Village Scout movement, it is important to recognize that the movement experienced dramatic growth only after 1975.[26] Royal patronage
was granted in 1972. In the ensuing years the number of initiation sessions
increased steadily but nonetheless relatively slowly. Only 8 sessions were
held in 1971 and 113 sessions involving 16,137 initiates in 1972. By the
end of 1974 the movement still had fewer than 100,000 members.
Membership began to expand significantly in 1975. The next year alone
saw almost two million members initiated (see figures 1.1 and 1.2 and
appendix, table A1.4). So rapid was the escalation of Village Scout activity that one Thai observer summarized the first years of the civilian government, 1973 and 1974, as "the years of the students, workers and farmers," whereas 1975 and 1976 were "the years of the Village Scouts" (cited
in Morell and Samudavanija 1981:245). Thus, although the king's support
was important, other factors explain the movement's sudden growth.

The Polarization of the Civilian Period

Understanding the explosion of the Village Scout movement in 1975 and
1976 requires an understanding of the changing significance of royal
patronage in the context of a volatile political economy. The civilian government was facing growing economic difficulties, which in turn intensified the political polarization of left and right. The fall of the regimes in
Vietnam, Laos, and Cambodia in 1975, and the withdrawal of U.S. troops
from Thailand in 1976, heightened domestic tension.[27] As the peasantry

and workers increasingly moved to the left and the elite moved to the right, the middle class split.

Whereas the leftward drift fueled the growth of liberal, socialist, and even communist movements, the rightward shift of a section of the middle class combined with the upper class fueled the growth of the Village Scouts. Some conservatives felt that change was happening too fast or was of the wrong kind; others wanted to see no changes at all. As the middle class was polarizing, the king was viewed, certainly by the urban classes, as moving to the right. Terrified by the domestic upheavals and events in Indochina, conservatives loosened their purse strings. Money poured into the Village Scout movement. If the lower classes were willing simply to join before, many actively sought membership as greater material resources became available through the organization's channels. With this shifting balance of class forces, the orientation of the Village Scout movement also changed, from its focus on rural counterinsurgency to an increasingly nationalist and even quasi-fascist urban movement.

Changing Conditions of Peasants

With the establishment of a democratic government popular grievances—long suppressed under years of military dictatorship—finally began to be heard. From 1973 on rural political activity increased dramatically. Agriculture is by far the dominant sector of Thai society. More than 80 percent of Thailand's population lives in rural villages or small rural towns. Although this figure is somewhat lower now, about 75 percent of the country's working population was engaged in agriculture in 1975 (Turton 1978:106). Thus it is not mere political rhetoric to refer to the Thai peasantry as the "backbone of the nation."

Despite agriculture's long-standing economic importance, the military governments had paid little attention to its improvement. The development policies of the military governments were oriented to the nonagricultural private sector. To the extent that government agencies addressed agricultural development, "their primary purpose had been national security rather than the economic growth of the agricultural sector" (Keyes 1987:91; see also Roth 1976:1059, Turton 1978:117). So nonchalant was the government about the agricultural sector that "the highest tariff protection was given to luxury consumer durable industries benefitting a middle class, while imported agricultural goods were allowed free entry" (Turton 1978:107). Government policies during the 1960s resulted in a decline of agriculture's share of gross national product from 50.1 percent in 1950 to 32.2 per cent in 1975 (Turton 1978:106, Ping 1978:41). The gap between urban and rural wages grew.[28]

Long-standing problems of poverty, indebtedness, and landlessness continued unabated during the 1960s and early 1970s. A 1968 survey conducted by the National Statistical Office reported that four million of Thailand's five million farming families were in debt. Interest rates ran as high as 5 to 10 percent per *month*.[29] A 1971 study showed that 63 percent of northern and 74 percent of northeastern rural households were living in poverty (Turton 1978:108, Ping 1978:42). A 1975 government survey revealed that 48 percent of Thailand's 5.5 million agricultural households owned only 16 percent of the cultivated land (Phelan 1975:14). As Girling notes, "Three-quarters of a million well-off farmers and their family members (the rural 'elite') cultivated as much land as ten million poor villagers" (1981:69).

The extent of agrarian poverty was and remains even greater than mere figures on landholding patterns suggest, because landless villagers—both tenants and wage workers—are not included in land-ownership surveys. Tenancy rates are highest in the central and northern regions of Thailand; in some districts in the central plains area the rates are as high as 90 percent (Turton 1978:113, Tomosugi 1969).[30] Some sense of the skew in land-ownership in the central plains region can be seen in the fact that three landowners with the largest holdings owned more than 120,000 rai (2.5 rai equal 1 acre), whereas another 82 people owned 1 to 2,000 rai each (Girling 1981:70). In the northern region the best irrigated paddy lands were often owned by absentee landlords and worked by local tenants. In this region rent was especially high, with landlords often taking as much as two-thirds of the harvested crop as rent.

Figures on the numbers of landless agricultural workers are difficult to obtain. A survey of 1,437 village households in one district of the northern province of Chiang Mai in 1974 found 37 percent of households were completely landless (Phelan 1975:15). My research in another district of the same province corroborates this figure. Landless villagers worked as hired laborers whenever possible; at other times of the year they caught fish and collected bamboo shoots, mushrooms, or other forest products; some were reduced to begging. Accounts by other anthropologists reveal similarly grim situations in other villages.[31]

That the effects of previous government policy, together with growing land pressure, mounting indebtedness, and declining real wages, were taking their toll became clear as peasants began to agitate politically. When the civilian government lifted the restrictions on freedom of assembly in May 1974, hundreds of farmers demonstrated to protest the dispossession of their land by money lenders. In response the civilian prime minister established a national committee to investigate the grievances. In its first month of operation (June 1974) the committee received an astonishing 10,999 petitions from farmers. By the end of September 1974 the committee had received 53,650 formal petitions (Morell and Samudavanija 1981:216). Other major farmer demonstrations occurred in June and November of that year.[32] These gatherings culminated in the formation of the historic Farmers' Federation of Thailand (FFT) on November 19, 1974. Because farmers' organizations had always come under direct government supervision, the creation of the independent FFT was a new phenomenon for rural Thailand.

The growing popular pressure prompted the newly formed parliament to enact the Agricultural Land Rent Control Act on December 6, 1974, and the Agricultural Land Reform Act in January 1975.[33] The FFT was particularly active in publicizing the provisions of the new acts and in supporting those farmers who pressed for their implementation. The FFT's activities grew rapidly, especially in the North.[34] As the FFT continued to grow and even began to publish a newspaper, tensions intensified. Because the FFT was independent of government regulations, government officials accused it of being illegal (Morell and Samudavanija 1981:224). The FFT's efforts to hold village meetings to inform villagers of their new rights under the laws were branded as communist agitation.

Meetings of FFT members were subject to increasing harassment. Red Gaurs threw bombs at a May Day gathering. In June 1975 campaign workers for Dr. Boonsanong Punyodyana, the secretary general of the Socialist Party of Thailand and an active supporter of the FFT, were attacked and vehicles belonging to supporters set afire (see chapter 5; for more on this election see Bowie 1975a). A wave of assassinations occurred, with twenty-one FFT leaders murdered between March and August 1975 (Morell and Samudavanija 1981:225; see also Bowie and Phelan 1975 and Karunan 1984). As Morell and Samudavanija write, noting the highly professional character of these killings,

> These murders seem to have been part of an organized plan of political intimidation. . . . Some suspected that *Nawaphon* was responsible for at least some of these killings. . . . A number of students, among others, alleged that members of the army's hunter-killer

teams or the Border Patrol Police were the professional hit men for these killings, acting under contract to Nawaphon, local officials, or local land owners.

(1981:225)

No arrests were ever made.

Changing Conditions for Urban Workers

Conflict was also increasing in the urban sector as Thailand industrialized. The process of accelerated economic transformation began during the 1950s, when the Phibun government began to play a role in developing the manufacturing sector by establishing several state industries. The inefficiency and corruption of these enterprises made them a net drain on government revenues. After Sarit's coup in 1957 economic policy underwent a major shift. In response to advice from the World Bank and the United States the Sarit government began to promote private investment in the nonagricultural sector (Keyes 1987:152). The Board of Investment was created in 1959 to promote investment, both domestic and foreign (Ingram 1971:288). The new policies had a significant effect on the structure of the Thai economy.

The 1960s saw extraordinarily rapid industrial expansion, particularly in the textile and food-processing industries. Growing numbers of villagers sought employment in factories and urban centers. From 1960 to 1970 the nonagricultural labor force increased by more than 1 million, from 2.12 million to 3.19 million. Unprotected by labor legislation, conditions for workers were often Dickensian and wages were low.[35] A Labor Department survey in 1972 found average *monthly* income for workers aged 20 to 29 was about 480 baht, or $24, and for workers aged 30 to 39 the average income was about 830 baht, or $41.50 (Morell and Samudavanija 1981:194.

The Thanom-Praphat regime passed a new labor law in March 1972 as a concession to workers. As a result a minimum-wage law went into effect in 1973, setting the minimum wage at 12 baht (60 cents) per day; however this wage law applied only to the capital city of Bangkok and the immediately adjacent provinces. Not until October 1974 was a countrywide wage established for the first time: 10 baht (50 cents) per day. However, neither the minimum-wage laws nor any other labor protection laws were actively enforced.[36] Furthermore the rate of inflation rose to 15 percent in 1973 and reached 24 percent in 1974 (Neher 1975:1098).

Consequently, the purchasing power of low-income groups was cut almost in half.[37] As Nikom Chandravithun writes, "Workers, whose wages in many cases had not changed for a period of 20 years, suddenly saw the prices of basic commodities, especially food, rise by 50 or even 100 percent" (1982:82). Before 1973 the increase in the cost of living had been 1.5 to 2 percent per year; in 1973 and 1974 prices rose an average of 5 percent per month (Chandravithun 1982:82).

These rapidly deteriorating conditions provoked a dramatic surge in workers' political activities. From 1958 to 1972 labor unions were illegal. Despite the ban some strikes did occur, but the average number of strikes from 1966 to 1972 was fewer than twenty per year. In March 1972 the new labor law enacted by the Thanom-Praphat government allowed the formation of worker associations, albeit with restrictions in size and function (Schut 1975:7–8).[38] Labor unrest escalated as a result of the new labor legislation, inflation, rice shortages, and other economic changes. In 1972 there were 34 strikes. In 1973 alone there were more than 500. Seventy-three percent of the strikes occurred after the October 1973 uprising, when government repression had been ended. One of the largest strikes was in June 1974, involving about twenty thousand workers in six hundred textile factories (for details see "Labour 3" 1975:26; Keyes 1987:91; Morell and Samudavanija 1981:189). In response the Sanya government agreed to raise the minimum wage. By 1975 the government had also passed the Labor Relations Act of 1975 (see Chandravithun 1982:81–87 for details).

Labor unions grew rapidly in strength and number throughout the years of the civilian period. After the Thanom-Praphat government allowed the formation of labor associations, about 60 groups registered by the end of 1974. By late 1976 Thailand had 185 registered labor unions (Morell and Samudavanija 1981:189). Furthermore in May 1976 a major federation of unions was organized under the leadership of the state enterprise unions. This unregistered federation was called the Labor Council of Thailand and claimed to include 80 percent of the registered unions (Mabry 1977:939).[39] Although the governments of Sanya and later Seni and Kukrit were willing to respond to organized labor, many in the military and business sectors looked upon the numerous strikes as further evidence of growing chaos. Although the last two years of civilian rule saw a decline in the total number of strikes, their average duration grew noticeably and the average number of days lost per strike increased about threefold (Morell and Samudavanija 1981:188).

The Country Polarizes: Growing Violence

On October 14, 1973, the country was essentially united under the spiritual leadership of the monarchy to expel the military triumvirate, but after three years of civilian government the country had begun to polarize. The earlier consensus fractured as people disagreed about the direction political and economic reform should take. The schism ran so deep that even the Buddhist monkhood split (see Jackson 1989). After years of silence imposed by military censors, the groundswell of debate was welcomed by many; others found it a cacophonous din. Entrenched interests, concerned about the growing popular demands for reform, began to resort to a variety of tactics in order to halt or hinder the process of change. Counterorganizations were formed to parallel and divide the worker, farmer, and student movements. In some cases the divisions were based on internal philosophical differences; in other cases the divisions were the result of external manipulation. New right-wing groups emerged, each for different reasons and with different targeted constituencies. In addition to the Village Scouts the two most influential organizations were Nawaphon and Krathing Daeng, also called the Red Gaurs.

Nawaphon was founded by Wattana Kiewvimol, who claimed to have developed close ties to U.S. intelligence agencies during his period of study in the United States (Morell and Samudavanija 1981:239).[40] Although Wattana was not a member of the Internal Security Operations Command (ISOC), as the Communist Suppression Operation Command (CSOC) was renamed in 1975, at least initially ISOC contributed money to the organization. He also received the support of leading individuals in the army and police (Morell and Samudavanija 1981:239).[41] Using a cell structure parallel to that of the CPT, Nawaphon cadres identified potential leaders for special political and motivational training at district, provincial, and national levels. As of late 1975 Nawaphon claimed a membership of more than 150,000, drawing primarily from members in the provincial bureaucracy, from governors on down, as well as monks and influential businessmen (Sangchai 1976:361; for a rare account of the revival-style meetings, see Morell and Samudavanija 1981:240).[42] Although its activities were clandestine, Nawaphon was thought to be responsible for inciting the anti-Vietnamese riots in northeastern Thailand at about the time that the civilian government was negotiating diplomatic relations with the socialist government of Vietnam (Flood 1977a:39). Nawaphon was also rumored to have masterminded the nationwide assassinations of the FFT leadership.

Whereas Nawaphon was a right-wing organization of the elite, the Red Gaurs was a right-wing organization of hired vigilantes. Unlike Nawaphon, which was only associated with isoc, the Red Gaurs were directly organized by a leader in isoc, Colonel Sudsai Hasadin.[43] Intended primarily as a means to divide the student and labor movements, the key cadres were "ex-mercenaries and men discharged from the army for disciplinary infractions, while their followings were mainly composed of unemployed vocational school graduates, high-school drop-outs, unemployed street-corner boys, slum toughs and so forth" (B. Anderson 1977: 19; see also Sangchai 1976). Unlike Nawaphon, the Red Gaurs recruited "by promises of high pay, abundant free liquor and brothel privileges," not primarily on the basis of ideological commitment (B. Anderson 1977:20).

The Red Gaurs became notorious for their violence, and their mandate soon expanded to include intimidating all kinds of gatherings. They were used as strikebreakers. They also were involved in an attack at Thammasat University in August 1975 (Anderson 1977:25). In February 1976 they firebombed the headquarters of the liberal New Force Party in Bangkok. At a demonstration by thirty thousand people on March 21, 1976, to demand the withdrawal of U.S. troops from Thailand grenades and plastic bombs were thrown into the crowd. Four people were killed and 85 injured. Red Gaurs were seen in the area at the time of the bombing (Morell and Samudavanija 1981:167). The Red Gaurs were rumored to have been involved in many other attacks. As Morell and Samudavanija write, "Red Gaurs frequently were seen carrying walkie-talkie equipment obviously borrowed from the metropolitan police, and they were constantly being transported in police vehicles from one part of Bangkok to another" (1981:167). They also participated in the massacre at Thammasat University on October 6, 1976.

Tension was escalating. The polarization had become so extreme that by the time of the parliamentary elections in April 1976, the head of the Thai Nation Party, General Pramarn Adireksan, was using his powers as both deputy prime minister and minister of defense to launch such slogans as RIGHT KILL LEFT over state-controlled media (Anderson 1977: 24). Right-wing radio stations played such songs as "Nak Phaendin" (Burden on the Earth), which attacked students and others interested in social reform. Hundreds of thousands of leaflets were distributed throughout the country accusing progressive parties and their candidates of being communists who wanted to abolish monarchy. Posters reading ALL SOCIALISTS ARE COMMUNISTS appeared in many public places around Bangkok.

The campaigns for the elections of April 1976 were the bloodiest in Thai history. On February 28, 1976, Dr. Boonsanong Punyodyana, the secretary general of the Socialist Party of Thailand, was assassinated near his home (for more on his life see Trocki 1977). Ten people were killed when a grenade was lobbed into an election rally of the New Force Party in Chainat on March 25, 1976 (Anderson 1977:13). More than thirty people died during the course of the campaign, many of them rural precinct captains affiliated with progressive candidates (Morell and Samudavanija 1981:263). Dozens more were injured, often by grenades thrown into political rallies.

The violence showed no signs of easing after the elections.[44] From the perspective of many members of the Thai elite the process of change was out of control. The demands for reform seemed to them synonymous with a call for a communist government. The concessionary policies of the civilian government appeared to some as heading in the direction of socialism.[45] That socialist political parties had captured 15 percent of the seats in Parliament during the 1975 elections was evidence of the country's leftward shift in the eyes of many conservatives (Morell and Samudavanija 1981:113). As Marks observes, "In the minds of the conservative upper echelons, of which the king was the leading member, the distinction between Thai socialism and communism was at best one of semantics" (1977:55).

The growing fears of conservatives were augmented by the developments in Indochina. In the space of a few weeks in the spring of 1975 the governments of Laos, Cambodia, and South Vietnam all fell to communist forces. Although communist guerrilla attacks had dropped noticeably in Thailand during the early civilian years of 1974 and 1975 the Communist Party of Thailand continued to be a political presence. The departure of U.S. troops began in March 1976, causing many members of the elite to panic even more.

The Shift in the Symbolic Significance of Monarchy

Not only did sectors of the Thai bourgeoisie shift to the right, but so did King Bhumiphol.[46] He was concerned both by the changes in Indochina and by the growing internal discord. As Shawcross noted at the time, the king "is said to have been personally horrified by the deposition of the king of Laos in December last year, and can have been no less concerned at Prince Sihanouk's 'retirement' in April this year" (1976:60). The down-

The crown princess dances the traditional lamwong with a Village Scout as the king
and other members of the royal family look on.

(Photo used by permission of Somkhuan Harikul, director of Village Scout Operations Center.)

falls of the Laotian and Cambodian monarchies "raised the alarming
specter that King Bhumiphol might prove the last of his line" (Anderson
1977:23–24; see also Morell and Morell 1977:338–39). Furthermore
the king was worried about "the steady drift to the left of student and
labor groups" (Marks 1977:55). Increasingly, the king and his followers
came to feel that "student violence, firebombing, labor violence, unbri-
dled corruption, rocketing inflation and crime rates" were undermining
faith in parliamentary forms (Marks 1977:55). As Morell and
Samudavanija write, the king was "becoming increasingly convinced that
the results of an open political system threatened the very foundations of
the monarchy, that student, labor, and farmer leaders were 'communist
agitators' themselves or were influenced by such elements, and that the
demise of the Chakri Dynasty was a distinct, foreseeable possibility"
(1977:338).[47]

The king's political shift was signaled in a variety of public gestures. In
addition to making their customary visits throughout the kingdom the
royal family became "conspicuous in activities supporting government
forces in their struggle against subversives" (Marks 1977:58). Although
most of these activities involved attending such events as funeral rites for

troops killed in clashes with communist guerrillas, the king went so far as to visit a Red Gaur training site in 1976 to test-fire weapons (Marks 1977:58–59). Conspicuous use of portraits of the king and queen during demonstrations by various rightist groups such as Nawaphon, Krathing Daeng, National Vocational Student Center of Thailand, and the "Free Thai Army" was also interpreted as evidence of the tacit royal support for the right (Marks 1977:58). Increasingly, the king took a "back-to-the-wall conservative anti-communist line in his public statements" (Anderson 1977:24). As a result "the royal shift was noted duly by a whole gamut of right-wing groupings, who were thereby encouraged to go violently on the offensive" (Anderson 1977:23–24).

The polarization of Thai society, together with the rightward shift of the king, combined to fuel a period of spectacular growth in the Village Scout movement. Conservatives terrified by international developments in Indochina, and the seemingly never-ending demands for greater internal reforms within Thai society, were eager for a new approach. The Village Scouts presented a perfect option. Some who joined may have found the simplicity of the Village Scouts' appeal to all Thais to unite and love each other an attractive antidote to the escalating divisiveness of Thai society. For others the movement was an alluring potential power base from which to affect future developments in the country. Whatever the specific motivation of individual members, the Village Scouts, nonviolent and under royal patronage, became the collective hope of conservatives to prevent "another Vietnam."

In the first two years of royal patronage the Village Scout movement grew because of the image of the king as a progressive symbol of democracy; in the final two years of the civilian period the Village Scouts grew because the king was increasingly being identified by the upper and middle classes as moving to the right. For many of the peasantry and the urban lower classes the king's earlier image remained intact. For yet others the lure of the growing resources now being channeled through the Village Scout organization provided an immediate material interest in joining. Appearing at once progressive and conservative the person and symbolism of King Bhumiphol contributed greatly toward creating the impression that the Village Scout movement could unify factions and fractions of an increasingly divided society. Through the ambiguity of his position he was able to facilitate the temporary merging of segments of society whose interests were highly divergent, uniting the fears and financial resources of a sector of the middle classes and the elite with the hopes and needs of the peasantry and urban lower classes.

Rural to Urban: Shifts in the Character of the Movement

The intensifying involvement of the elite and middle classes resulted in a significant change in the character of the Village Scout movement's membership. During the early years the initiation rites were held in up-country provinces and hence had a rural counterinsurgency orientation. However, as the movement grew, Village Scout initiations sessions began to be held in provincial towns and capitals across the country. Beginning in January 1976 Village Scout initiations were even held in Bangkok with the active support of the Bangkok metropolitan government. The governor of Bangkok, a conservative Democrat named Thammanun Thienngen, developed close ties to the Village Scout movement. By September 1976 the Bangkok government had held thirty-six training sessions, enrolling 19,828 members (Morell and Samudavanija 1981: 244). With the growth of the scout movement in the capital, members increasingly came from the higher echelons of Thai society. Wives of army generals, business leaders, bankers, and even members of the royal family participated in the scout training, together with street vendors and laborers (Morell and Samudavanija 1981:244).[48]

As the movement became more urban and middle class in its orientation, the character of the movement also changed, developing a more fascist overtone. Initially conceived of as an anticommunist rural security organization under government control, it became an urban middle-class phenomenon under the control of right-wing politicians. The public activities of the scouts became more overtly political. During the elections of 1975 and 1976 the Village Scouts campaigned heavily for right-wing and military candidates. Scouts were mobilized against progressive activists, intimidating and even expelling students who were trying to help villagers.

The urbanized Village Scout movement was not focused on winning the hearts and minds of villagers in the border areas but had set its sights on the center of the country, on changing the course of national politics. On October 5 tension within the civilian government had reached the point that the then-prime minister, Seni Pramoj, was forced to announce the formation of a new cabinet. When two right-wing Democrats were excluded, the Thai Nation Party and the conservative Democrats mobilized hundreds of Village Scouts to demonstrate at Government House. These protesters demanded the immediate ouster of three progressive members of the coalition government's cabinet.[49] The three ministers complied but to no avail. The ultimate demonstration of the might of the newborn urban-based Village Scout movement came on the morning of October 6, when it helped topple the civilian government and usher the return of military rule.[50]

Village Scouts mass at Government House in Bangkok on October 6, 1976.
(Photo by Mangkorn Khamreongwong; used by permission of AP/WideWorld Photos.)

4

The Moratorium: Fissures on the Right

❧

With the king as a symbol both of progressive reform for the lower classes and of conservative reaction for the upper classes, the polarization of Thai society fueled a logarithmic expansion of the Village Scout movement between 1971 and 1976. The coup of October 6, 1976, was a dramatic moment when the movement flexed its political muscle. Suddenly, without warning, just when the movement seemed all powerful, the new post-coup government halted further initiations. The royal decree ordering the moratorium was issued on November 12, barely a month after the coup. The moratorium was to take effect on December 11, and no date was given for the resumption of initiations.[1] Although some officials initially assured the public that sessions would resume in a few weeks, in fact initiations recommenced after May 15, 1977, some five months later.

The irony of a government's clamping down on its own creation—a movement that gave rise to popular enthusiasm that exceeded even its planners' wildest expectations—was yet another twist in the complex web in which the Village Scout movement and the state were now becoming entangled. With the victory of the right in the coup of October 6, it would be easy to conclude that a halt was called because the Village Scout movement was no longer needed. However, I argue that the moratorium was a consequence not of the right's strength, but of its internal weaknesses.

The very popularity of the Village Scouts had created a host of political complications. These problems included tensions within the bureaucracy, conflicts between scouts and officials, rivalries among politicians over access to the movement, divisions of public opinion regarding the monarchy, and rifts within the military. Although these problems were already surfacing during the civilian period, they became particularly acute for the new postcoup government. This chapter explores both why Village Scout initiations were stopped in December 1976 and why they resumed in May 1977.

The Right: The Appearance of Strength

The weeks and months after the October 6 coup were heady times for the right in Thailand. After the heated debates that had preceded the coup, the left fell silent, unable to speak. When the coup was declared on October 6, the military government immediately instituted martial law, abolished Parliament, and revoked the constitution. Those working or studying at Thammasat University were unable to return until weeks later. Dormitories, homes, and offices were searched. The authorities seized books and papers. More people were imprisoned across the country; the authorities detained about six thousand people during and after the coup.[2] Any discussion of politics was dangerous, and the government banned political gatherings of five or more people. The mood was tense and emotions were high, but the right was in control.

The government reinforced the quiet by muzzling the press. More than twenty daily and weekly newspapers were closed (Girling 1981:218). Bangkok residents who had obtained an early edition of the *Bangkok World* or other papers for October 6 saw horrifying pictures of the carnage; before the station was forced to stop broadcasting, those who were watching Channel 9 TV could not believe their eyes. Then the blackout descended. Authorities censored even the international editions of *Time* and *Newsweek*. People living up-country had difficulty finding out what had happened at Thammasat University. However, up-country political activists soon felt the pressure, as their homes or the homes of their friends were searched and the arrests began.

Anyone who had been politically active felt extremely vulnerable and alone. Although some went underground, the threat of arrest was enough to silence many others. Friends were often hesitant to contact each other, lest one cause problems for others. Villagers were often hesitant to talk to the families of those who had been arrested lest they too fall under suspicion. People now frequently repeated the old Thai adage "Kill a chicken to make the monkey afraid"; the meaning was clear to all. What had happened to a few at Thammasat University intimidated an entire nation.

The coup was staged by the National Administrative Reform Council (NARC). From a list of names submitted to the king by the NARC, the king appointed Thanin Kraivichien as the new prime minister. The junta announced his appointment on October 9. He had no prior political experience in government. Thanin was a former Supreme Court justice and an arch anticommunist, albeit with a reputation for honesty.[3] The new government was extremely conservative. It became, as Charles Keyes noted, "the most repressive in Thai history, surpassing in its authoritarian control of the populace even the governments of the various military dictators" (1987:100).[4]

In the weeks after the coup the new government announced a series of repressive orders and policies. Order No. 22 declared nine categories of persons "dangers to society," including "persons who stir up trouble" (Girling 1981:216). Anyone arrested under martial law could be held for six months without trial. All such cases could be decided by military tribunal with no right of appeal. Under the new Communist Suppression Act, anyone arrested in an area declared to have been infiltrated by communists could be detained for 480 days (M. Bunnag 1979:62). In these zones authorities could carry out searches without warrants at any time. The new constitution, promulgated on October 22, gave the king a prominent place, including the power to introduce legislation directly to the assembly (Marks 1977:62).[5] More important, the constitution handed virtually all power to the executive branch. The prime minister and his advisers had the power, "in cases where the Prime Minister deems it necessary to prevent, restrain or suppress any act subverting the stability of the Kingdom . . . to make any order or take any action," and all such orders and actions "shall be considered lawful" (see *Bangkok Post*, October 23, 1976, cited in Girling 1981:n216).

Other decrees followed. Political parties were outlawed. Strikes were banned and violators threatened with imprisonment. The State Universities Bureau announced the need for "greater supervision" of the universities. The bureau was empowered to restrain or stop the activities of educational institutions if they were "a danger to stability, national security, peace and order, or the good morals of the people" (*Siam Rath*, November 12, 1976; Girling 1981:216). From the countryside to the cities, from rural to urban activists, the right seemed to be in complete control.

Reasons for the Moratorium

To those unfamiliar with the internal dynamics of the Village Scout movement the announcement of the moratorium on new initiations came as a shock. The official reasons were various, vague, and unconvincing. Key government officials gave interviews in which they attempted to explain the initial dramatic announcement; they appeared to have faced a dilemma—they wanted to provide a plausible explanation without leaving the movement vulnerable to criticism. Yet the diversity of their explanations suggests that the government's decision to call a moratorium was made in haste.

As deputy minister of interior, Damrong Sunthornsarathun, gave to the press what may be considered a particularly authoritative official explanation. He confirmed that the order to halt further Village Scout initiations had been sent to all provincial governors but claimed that the ministry was merely acceding to a request from Major General Charoenrit Chamrasromrun, the director of the Village Scout Operations Center. Damrong implied that the Interior Ministry had no particular position on the issue. The official order halting further sessions asked that all provincial governors send by December 31 all missing reports for all sessions held thus far, call a meeting of the provincial scout leadership and scout instructors to standardize the instruction, and meet with provincial heads to strengthen the movement for the future (*Thai Rath*, November 16, 1976). According to Damrong, Charoenrit Chamrasromrun had expressed concern that Village Scout activities were getting out of hand (*yoonyaan*) and that the administration of the organization was too lax. Consequently, Charoenrit Chamrasromrun requested a halt to further Village Scout initiations until authorities could get a more accurate count of the organization's membership. Damrong also said there was concern about the cost of the sessions and the selection of candidates for initiation. Because he agreed with the concerns that Charoenrit Chamrasromrun outlined, Damrong issued the order to halt further initiation rites (*Daily News*, November 16, 1976).[6]

Charoenrit Chamrasromrun told reporters that authorities wanted to retrain all instructors and evaluate their overall procedures so that the initiation would be standard across the country (*Daily News*, November 16, 1976). The minister of interior, Samak Sunthorawej, made a similar point (*Daily News*, November 18, 1976). The deputy governor of the Bangkok Metropolitan Area, Dr. Ophaas Thamwanit, claimed that the only reason for the moratorium was the shortage of instructors to meet the demand for new initiations (*Thai Rath*, November 16, 1976). The governor of Nong Khai Province suggested that the moratorium would facilitate meetings with the provincial scout instructors to coordinate the many scout activities planned to honor the king's birthday in December (*Daily News*, November 18, 1976).

None of the official reasons seemed sufficient to justify a national halt to all initiation rites. The reasons given had four main themes: problems in the design and staffing of the initiation, difficulties in selecting members, dilemmas in recordkeeping, and potential budget problems. Any of these issues could have been dealt with on an ongoing basis. Somkhuan Harikul was more revealing in his explanations for the need for a moratorium, expressing his dismay that some people had joined the Village Scouts in order to create a political base of their own. Somkhuan Harikul believed that although most scouts were altruistic and sought only to do good on behalf of the country, a selfish minority was destroying the credibility of the movement (*Daily News*, January 8, 1977). He spoke of a "third hand" that had been infiltrating the movement up-country, seeking to use the movement for personal ends (*Baan Muang*, January 8, 1977). He faulted those who spread money around in order to get elected as troop leaders and, once elected, abused their influence with their followers (*Chaw Thai*, January 8, 1977).[7] Somkhuan Harikul told one reporter, "The matter that is of grave concern at present is that there are members of certain groups who disguise themselves as scouts but are waiting for their chance to damage the movement by using the movement for their personal ends. This is contrary to the intent and ideology of the Village Scout movement" (*Chaw Thai*, January 8, 1977). Somkhuan Harikul's comments hint at a more candid appraisal of the fissures that had developed within the Village Scout movement and with its relations with the right as a whole.

Government official participating in a Village Scout rally.
(Photo by Mangkorn Khamreongwong; used by permission of AP/WideWorld Photos.)

Fissures Within the Bureaucracy

The Village Scout movement created considerable tension within the ranks of the bureaucracy, not surprising considering the number of agencies and ministries involved. Tension between the Border Patrol Police (BPP), part of the Police Department, and other agencies within the Ministry of Interior was considerable. The tension became public after the coup when Charoenrit Chamrasromrun and Somkhuan Harikul both were transferred out of the BPP to at-large positions within the Ministry of Interior. However, some conflict had surfaced earlier. Thus a newspaper article published on September 14, 1976, claimed that the Village Scout movement in Bangkok was divided between those in the BPP faction and those in the Bangkok governor's faction, each under different departments within the same ministry (*Siam Rath*). The specifics of each point of disagreement aside, the ultimate problem was one of control. Each wing of the government wanted to bring the Village Scout movement under its jurisdiction. Power struggles were developing both across and within agencies.

From the beginning the movement had depended upon government officials to provide administrative and instructional staffing. The BPP provided the core instructors who served in the key roles involving political education; however, no more than one or two BPP officers were involved in any single session. Most of the staffing came from the ranks of district-level education officials and local schoolteachers, under the ministries of education and the interior, respectively. District education officials handled most administrative work. Schoolteachers, primarily from the village elementary schools, made up the rank-and-file instructors.[8] They oversaw the day-to-day needs of the initiates and provided the cast for the dramatic scenarios directed by the BPP instructors. In addition, cabinet ministers, provincial governors, district officers, police chiefs, and other high-ranking officials were routinely invited to serve as guests of honor at some portion of the initiation, either for the evening campfire sessions that lasted well into the night or for the closing ceremonies.

With the expansion of the Village Scout movement the demand for staff increased, placing greater burdens on the bureaucracy. At every level the heavy workload of scouting interfered with the performance of other routine government tasks. Some work was noticeably delayed and some work never got done. The absences of the district, provincial, and national heads meant delays in processing paperwork, because virtually all papers to and from their offices needed their signatures. One newspaper editorial complained that the governor of the Greater Bangkok Metropolitan Area was so busy with Village Scout activities that he was doing virtually nothing else (*Siam Rath*, July 23, 1976). The strain was also evident in the lower echelons, particularly in the schools.

Teachers received leaves of absence from teaching in order to participate in the initiation sessions. As a result their schools were understaffed, and other teachers had to take over extra classes. Some instructors participated in back-to-back scout initiations, which required them to be away from home and family for weeks at a time. One scout instructor I knew commented that he was gone so much that he barely had time to leave his clothes at home for his wife to wash. A letter written to the *Siam Rath* newspaper columnist known as Chankasem and signed "A Teacher with Two Classes," tellingly summarizes the nascent tension. The teacher wrote,

> I have a subject on which I would like your opinion, namely the Village Scout initiation session being held at——. Teachers from various schools will be helping out, a lot in some cases, a little in others. The teachers who go have a good time singing and dancing as is typical of the Village Scouts and in the manner introduced by the Border Patrol Police. Having the initiates working together, having

fun together and eating and sleeping together is a wonderful means to generate a wellspring of unity, and one of which I am in complete support.

However, those teachers who were going as support staff were absent from July 5 to July 21. They never once came back to visit their students. And the teachers who remained like myself had to cope with not only with our own classes but also the classes of those who went as Village Scout instructors. With each class having 37–38 students, that is over 70 students total. In the morning there is only time to teach one subject and in the afternoon another subject before the day is over. Together with homework, that is only two subjects a day. The fact that I am dying is not the issue. I'm old already. But the children are not being educated. The children's parents criticize me for not teaching their children, that all I'm doing is taking my salary. Some days the parents notice that I haven't graded their children's homework assignments yet and so they come and complain to the principal. The principal tries to explain the situation so they will understand. But some of them are not satisfied and threaten to take the matter up with officials higher up.

I myself am honestly in full support of the ideology and methods of the Village Scouts, and feel that they do many good things for the community. But taking teachers to work as staff is causing considerable damage to the education of our students. (Letter to the Editor, *Siam Rath*, July 23, 1976; translated by author)

Further exacerbating the tension was that, when the annual promotions in pay and rank were announced, the double and triple promotions tended to go to those officials who had been most heavily involved in scouting and not to those who had been left with the brunt of the work.

Furthermore differences of opinion were also developing in the ranks of government officials called upon to work for the scouts. Not all shared the same motivation. Some rank-and-file staff members were reluctant participants who had been informed that they were required to serve a minimum of five times.[9] Thus although some were involved because they believed in the ideology and purpose of the Village Scout movement, others participated because they had to, and still others did it because they had fun and enjoyed an escape from the everyday routine of teaching or other duties.

Between those motivated by fun and those motivated by duty, opportunities for tension were numerous. An important source of friction involved their differing attitudes toward sexuality. Scout leaders put considerable effort into assuring parents and spouses of trainees that loose sexual behavior would not be permitted. However, government officials generally were of much higher status than the ordinary people they trained as initiates; their standing was enhanced by the respect they acquired from their position as instructors during the initiation ritual. Because happily married instructors were more reluctant to be absent from their families for days at a time, a disproportionate number of instructors appear to have been single. Although sexual behavior between consenting instructors was essentially viewed as their private business, I met instructors who refused to participate in further training sessions because they were furious that some instructors had taken advantage of exhausted young female initiates. Tired and sheltered village girls were especially vulnerable when their favorite instructor, who had attained movie-idol status in their minds, paid attention to them. Although I heard of no scandalous incidents among the candidates during the initiation sessions, sexual liaisons did occur between instructors and between instructors and young female trainees.[10]

The tensions within the bureaucracy percolated through to the public at large. The families of instructors were not pleased to have relatives gone for protracted periods, and spousal suspicions of infidelity led to many domestic disputes. Parents of schoolchildren or citizens with business at the district and provincial offices were frustrated by staff shortages. Thus, rather than improve relations between officials and villagers, the heavy demand for staffing of the Village Scout movement often generated additional tensions, both within the bureaucracy and also between officials and citizens.

Tension Between Village Scouts and Government Officials

The rapid expansion of the Village Scout movement also generated a kind of grassroots activism that many government officials viewed as akin to anarchy. Both in the capital and up-country, government officials at various levels increasingly resented Village Scout interference in affairs that once had been almost entirely under their jurisdiction. Ironically, both honest and dishonest government officials had reason to be concerned about the uncontrolled expansion of Village Scout activities.

Because most members of the up-country elite were also scout leaders, they were influential in both local politics and scouting. Indeed it was often difficult to figure out which aspects of local events resulted from routine participation in local politics and which resulted from participation in Village Scouting. Scouting provided the local elite with many more occasions to meet and talk. Scouting also provided more frequent opportunities for the town elite to meet with the village elite. In addition, scouting provided members of the rural elite who served scout leaders with easy and ready access to their followers, who became in effect their new-found popular power base.

The interactions of scout leaders and government officials in one district in northern Thailand illustrate the tensions emerging at the local level. In this case events ultimately forced the government to transfer two of the highest-ranking district-level government officials, the district officer (*naaj amphur*), and the head of the district education office (*syk-saathikaan amphur*). Because I knew many of the participants in this incident, I can recount it in some detail. The problems arose over several months in 1977 and are representative of similar episodes elsewhere. In this case, as elsewhere, the district-level scout leaders were from the local elite, primarily the town and village merchants. These merchants, who had been contributing generously to scout events, were dissatisfied with how the district office was handling fund-raising for the scouts. The costs of an initiation had almost doubled, but when contributors asked to see receipts, none were available.

The local elite became even more displeased with what it saw as the district officer's general lack of cooperation. Even though the merchants were being asked to contribute generously to underwrite the costs of the scout initiations, the district officer refused their request to use the district hall for a scout event—a hall they had helped finance. Another petty event illustrates the deteriorating relations between the district officer and the town elite. One day some local merchants (also scouts) were sitting in a streetside restaurant near the district headquarters, treating several scout instructors to a cup of coffee. According to one local merchant who was present, the district officer walked by and made a comment to the effect that it looked like they were trying to gain face (*jaak ca daj naa ryy*). The comment upset the merchants, several of whom were scout chapter leaders. Disgruntled, they finished their coffee wondering why they should continue to make sacrifices, given how little they were appreciated.

However, as far as the local elite were concerned the district officer's fatal mistake came when a fire broke out at the district's town market-place. As soon as the fire started, people ran to district headquarters, where the fire truck was supposed to be parked. The fire truck was parked there, but no one who knew how to operate it was present. As he was in the habit of doing, the district officer had "borrowed" the fireman to serve as his chauffeur for the day. People managed to get the fire truck started and drove it to the market, but once there no one could make the gadgets work. So they resorted to the traditional bucket brigade. Before the fire was extinguished, the market had suffered considerable damage. People were outraged. A local leader and old school friend of the district officer suggested to the district officer that he mollify the merchants by leaving the fire truck parked at the market in full readiness, as the merchants were now demanding. But the district officer balked at this suggestion, saying that it was against the rules, that the fire truck had to be parked at the fire station.

After the fire, relations between the district officer and the town merchants were beyond repair. Rumors of the incompetence of the district officer spread from the town merchants to members of the village elite. The death knell for the officer's tenure in the district was sounded during the Thai New Year's celebrations in mid-April. Villagers traditionally pay respects to elders and community leaders, providing the former with offerings and the latter with a jovial dousing in buckets of water. At the annual dousing for the district officer a drunken celebrant snatched the microphone and began denouncing the district officer. The district officer, celebrating inside his office, grabbed his м-16 and began firing off rounds. After this and the fire, a delegation of local leaders-cum-scouts went to the provincial governor to complain of the district officer's behavior. His transfer was announced shortly thereafter.

The transfer of another district official, the head of the district education office, was announced at the same time. I spoke with several members of the local elite, and as far as they were concerned his transfer was wholly the result of a conflict that developed between him and certain influential Village Scouts. As education officer he had had primary responsibility for overseeing scout initiations. Unfortunately for him, a split had developed within the district's scout movement that was fueling intense interest in the election for district head of the scout movement. One faction was headed by a right-wing political candidate who wanted to involve the scouts more directly in anticommunist work. The education officer was opposed to what he saw as the politicization of the scout movement, arguing that the scouts were not to contribute to the division between left and right but rather to work to improve people's standard of living and safeguard the Nation, Religion, and King.

Most local scouts supported the education officer, and the conservative candidate lost the election. But the losing candidate was also a local journalist with considerable influence. Upset by his loss, he began to use his newspaper to attack the district education officer. The education officer's problems were compounded by his relationship with the district officer, who was already in trouble because of the fire. The district officer had become frustrated with the education officer. He felt that the education officer, who, given his position, worked closely with the district scouts, was responsible for fomenting the scouts' dissatisfaction with him. As a result both were transferred.

Similar conflicts between local scouts and government officials developed across the country in incidents large and small. In some cases the Village Scouts began to represent popular concerns of villagers at the local level; in other cases they were being manipulated to further the self-interest of local elites. As Morell and Samudavanija explain, "Influential businessmen, hoodlums, and gangsters in many provinces have found it rewarding to become Village Scouts in order to obtain greater protection and expand their influence over provincial officials. Several leaders of provincial extortion rackets and gambling operations, through their contributions to Village Scout training programs, apparently have become senior Scout leaders in their provinces" (1981:245).

One such example was the case of a teak logger who was charged with illegal logging by the government in Tak Province. A scout troop president, he rallied his troop to stage a demonstration demanding the charges be dropped. Although the Village Scout movement was in part intended as a check on government corruption, the movement sometimes was also used in efforts to force corruption upon government officials. In this case, perhaps because of national publicity, the scouts' efforts were to no avail. The man was arrested, fined, and his teak-logging equipment confiscated (see Muecke 1980:424).

Thus both honest and dishonest officials had reason to fear the unchecked growth of the Village Scouts. Because enforcing laws or violating them could make any official the target of scouts' energies, the movement seemed unpredictable and threatening. The events of October 6 only heightened a growing concern that the enormous movement could get out of hand and intervene in government matters in unforeseen ways.

It had the potential either to fall prey to narrow interests or come to represent grassroots interests against an entrenched bureaucracy. Although the mobilization of October 6 was an indication of the movement's ability to organize successfully, it was also a warning to an autocratic regime extremely wary of popular participation in government affairs.

Growing Partisanship

A third important fissure resulted from the intensifying politicization of the Village Scout movement. With the deepening involvement of the elite and middle classes in the last two years of the civilian period the character of the Village Scout movement had changed significantly. Royal guidelines stated that the Village Scouts should not be involved in politics.[11] Yet with the increasing involvement of the urban elite the movement was becoming embroiled in partisan intrigues. Although the movement was initially an anticommunist rural security organization under government control, by 1975 and 1976 scouts were becoming the "political tools of the business and landlord groups" (Ungphakorn 1977:11). A disillusioned scout instructor, a veteran of eighty initiations, described the developing dynamics:

> There are lots of people with money, with influence, even people who have broken laws, who have become Village Scouts. Very often it is these kinds of people who have become the heads or deputy-heads of the chapters. All they have to do is act like they are respectable and have money to help out with various activities of the scout chapters and they get elected as chapter heads. Even if it costs them hundreds of thousands of baht, they are happy to spend it to get the position, because they figure it will be worth it in the long run.
>
> (*Siam Rath Weekly*, April 30, 1978, p. 4)

Entanglement in vested interests took various forms. Although some sought to manipulate scout troops in support of private business interests, others sought to divert the movement to partisan politics. During the civilian period several newspaper columnists complained that the rightist organization Nawaphon was trying to infiltrate the Village Scout movement in order to divert scout membership to Nawaphon. In one newspaper interview a scout leader from Ubon Rachathani revealed that in some cases the instructors, including some from the BPP, were members of Nawaphon (*Siam Rath*, November 10, 1975). Citing the royal guidelines declaring that the Village Scouts were not to engage in politics, newspaper editorials complained that such efforts to move the Village Scout movement to the right were contrary to the royal mandate.[12]

Even more important in contributing to the politicization of the Village Scouts was its increasing involvement in electoral politics. During the elections of 1975 and 1976 the Village Scouts campaigned heavily for right-wing and military candidates. The Thai Nation (Chart Thai) and Protect Thailand (Phithak Thai) parties explicitly sought the support of the Village Scouts (Morell and Samudavanija 1981:244; see also Anderson 1977:28; Ungphakorn 1977:11). Members of the conservative wing of the Democrat Party also had close links to various scout troops.[13]

Newspaper editorials criticized the efforts of political parties and politicians to use the Village Scout movement as an electoral base. They complained that electoral candidates were underwriting the costs of initiation sessions, paying for dinners or presents, getting themselves elected as troop presidents, and generally using various opportunities during the initiation session to advertise and campaign for their political parties. In one particularly blatant incident, T-shirts bearing the name of Pramarn Adireksan, the head of the Thai Nation Party, were distributed at a scout initiation session in Bangkok.[14] In addition to campaigning for conservative candidates, scouts were involved in intimidating liberal and left-wing candidates (Ungphakorn 1977:11). The complaints of partisanship reached the point where there was discussion in the media of canceling all initiation rites during the election campaigns.[15]

Throughout the civilian period complaints mounted that influential scout leaders were using their position to attack the elected government. Major General Charoenrit Chamrasromrun, who often served as the primary BPP instructor for initiations in Bangkok, came under particular criticism. He had used the initiation sessions for virulent attacks on Thailand's communist neighbors,[16] and he apparently often used the sessions an an opportunity to make explicit political attacks on the policies of the elected civilian government. For example, he criticized the Kukrit government's policy of guaranteeing the price of rice to farmers, prompting one newspaper article to castigate him for spreading falsehoods and violating the goals and purposes of the Village Scout movement (*Siam Rath*, August 25 and September 3, 1976).[17] Furthermore Charoenrit Chamrasromrun tried to coordinate mass rallies. Scouts had frequently been involved in uncoordinated local acts of intimidation, even expelling students who were trying to help villagers (B. Anderson 1977:28; Lobe 1977:121; McNabb 1978). Under Charoenrit Chamrasromrun scout activities became better orchestrated. For example, on July 20, 1976, Charoenrit Chamrasromrun mobilized about two thousand Village Scouts from Bangkok and six other provinces (Chanthaburi, Prachinburi, Nakhon Sawan, Prathum Thani, Saraburi, and Lampang). They ostensibly had mobilized to clean up the streets and royal palace grounds in Bangkok. However, journalists suggested that the true purpose of the gathering was to keep tabs on members of the National Student Center of Thailand (NSCT) who were alleged to have some sort of activity planned for that day. The royal palace was not far from NSCT headquarters. As it turned out, nothing happened and the scouts returned home at the end of the day (see *Siam Rath*, July 21 and August 6, 1976).[18]

Critics also were pointing out that the movement as a whole had no checks on the activities of its membership. From the leadership to the rank-and-file some scouts engaged in activities that discredited the entire Village Scout movement. In the southern province of Surat Thani, for example, a governor and his entourage, returning from a Village Scout campfire session, were attacked by a group of men wearing Village Scout scarfs (*Thai Rath*, September 23, 1975). In another dramatic incident a gunman responsible for killing a police officer was found to be a Village Scout who had been active in local scout activities; he was killed by police and buried in his scout uniform (*Prachathipatai*, March 22, 1976).

Thus questions were being raised about the legitimacy of many activities associated with all levels of the Scout movement, from the rank-and-file to troop leaders. As one journalist summarized the range of problems, "Aside from communist infiltrators who join the Village Scout movement to damage it, there are also politicians seeking to take advantage of the opportunity, gamblers, brothel owners and influential merchants, each joining the Village Scout movement to further their own interests" (*Thai Rath*, September 23, 1975). The participation of hundreds of Village Scouts in demanding the resignation of cabinet members on October 5 and the bloody attack on Thammasat University on October 6 were dramatic evidence of how much the movement had changed.

Tarnishing the Monarchy

Given the king's close identification with the Village Scouts, the increasingly partisan and conservative character of the movement was beginning to tarnish the image of the monarchy. In the wake of the October 6 coup questions were raised about royal involvement in both the coup and the authorization for mobilizing the Village Scouts. The king's actions during the civilian period had demonstrated his growing ties not only to the conservative factions of Thai society but also, increasingly, to the military. From his popular rise to power as a symbol of antimilitary sentiment the king had, in the space of a few short years, come full circle. His shift in attitude toward the military was confirmed in his address to the nation two months after the October 6, 1976, coup: "At a time when our country is being continually threatened with aggression by the enemy, our very freedom and existence as Thais may be destroyed if Thai people fail to realize their patriotism and their solidarity in resisting the enemy. . . . Accordingly, the Thai military has the most important role in defense of our country at all times, ready always to carry out its duty to protect the country" (Girling 1981:215).

To this day the nature of the king's involvement in the return of military rule on October 6 is a matter of debate. Some scholars have suggested that the king and others on the ideological right were out-maneuvered by the generals (see Lobe 1977:122).[19] Others suggest that the king helped set the stage for the return of the military without necessarily being directly involved; as Morell and Morell write, "Once King Phumiphon moved to identify himself once more with the forces of stability (repressive if necessary) and against the elements demanding change (thereby threatening stability), the military could intervene respectably" (1977:337). Still other scholars suggest that the king authorized the military coup. Although some scholars have suggested that the king supported the coup as a lesser evil in order to preempt another coup plot by a more extreme faction of the ideological right (e.g., Mallet 1978:91; Van Praagh 1977:299–300), others have argued that the king felt the return to military rule was necessary to maintain internal stability. As Girling writes, "The king in effect approved the military coup of October, 1976, which he saw as necessary to prevent the country from succumbing to political chaos, internal subversion, and external aggression" (1981: 156).[20]

Debates on the nature of royal involvement begin with the matter of the return of a member of the hated exiled military dictatorship, Praphat Charusathien, in August 1976. Although Praphat was forced to leave the country shortly thereafter as a result of angry student demonstrations, the king received Praphat in a private audience before his return to exile.[21]

Similarly, the return of Field Marshal Thanom Kittikachorn, the exiled prime minister, in September was evidently organized with support "at a high level" (Ungphakorn 1977). Thanom stepped off the plane wearing the yellow robes of a novice, claiming he only wanted to see his dying father (Shawcross 1976:60). He traveled directly from the airport to Wat Bovornives, the principal royal temple, where he was ordained as a full monk. As Morell and Morell comment, "The ordainment, a controversial action which split the Buddhist Sangha, was a private ceremony, from which the public was explicitly excluded, in violation of an important Buddhist tradition which allows anyone to step forward to present evidence as to why a man should not be allowed to enter the monkhood. Under the Thai Buddhist structure, only one person had the authority to waive this stricture, the head of the church: the King" (1977:337).

The king also did nothing to intimate any displeasure with Thanom's return. The king was closely associated with Wat Bovornives because he had been ordained there. Two days after Thanom's return the king and queen personally visited him at the temple to "pay their respects" (Morell and Morell 1977:337). As Marks comments, "Campus criticism of his role or lack thereof percolated into the streets" (Marks 1977:60).

The actions of the crown prince raised further questions about the involvement of the royal family in the October coup. Although the crown prince had been studying in Australia, on October 2 he was summoned home for unexplained reasons (see Kershaw 1979:259; Ungphakorn 1977:12). Dr. Puey Ungphakorn suggests the crown prince was summoned by the king (1977:5). One of the prince's first acts was to visit and pay his respects at Wat Bovornives, where Thanom was living. Students were accused of hanging the crown prince in effigy at Thammasat University, a charge vigorously denied by students, who insisted the mock hanging was in memory of the student activists who had been garroted a few days earlier. On the afternoon of October 6 the crown prince was sent to meet with the Village Scouts who had congregated at the equestrian statue of King Rama V, ostensibly to assure them that he was all right and to encourage them to return to their homes.

Other connections between the royal family and the October 6 coup included a miscellany of events. The director of the Armored Division Radio Station (Yarn Kroh), which played a crucial role in mobilizing the Village Scouts and other right-wing groups during the hours before the coup, was Lieutenant Colonel Uthan Sanitwong na Ayuthaya, a close relative of the queen (Marks 1977:57). The Border Patrol Police units involved in the massacre at Thammasat University came from Camp Naresuan at Hua Hin; these units were closely identified with the king.[22]

Further compromising the king's position was the involvement of the Village Scouts, because they had come to be so closely identified with the royal family. In the days before the coup Village Scouts guarded Wat Bovornives, where Thanom was staying, on an around-the-clock basis (Mallet 1978:90). On October 5 they demonstrated to demand the ouster of members of the cabinet. Scout involvement on October 6 allowed the CPT's radio station, the Voice of the People of Thailand (VOPT), to describe photographs showing scouts "using their royal-presented scarves to strangle the students and drag their corpses around" (VOPT broadcast, June 15, 1977, quoted in Marks 1977:69). NARC tried to mitigate the tension created by October 6 by suggesting that the police had evidence that there were Vietnamese saboteurs among the students; they suggested that the Village Scouts, Red Gaurs, and others had thought that those they had garroted and burned alive were in fact Vietnamese agents. Another approach was that taken by Somkhuan Harikul when I interviewed him, namely, denying that "real" Village Scouts were involved in the atrocities and suggesting that Village Scout kerchiefs had been stolen and worn by people masquerading as Village Scouts. Regardless of the explanation, the actions of the Village Scouts appeared to compromise the status of the king.

Whatever the specific role of the various members of the royal family in the coup of October 6 and whatever the truth of the myriad rumors that circulated in the months thereafter, what is relevant is that, although the actions of the king on October 14, 1973, had won him praise, his actions on October 6, 1976, had raised questions. As Girling wrote, in the wake of the coup "the monarchy, hitherto the symbol of national pride and respect, has become intimately involved in conservative and even reactionary politics" (1981:287). The king's involvement in the coup of 1976, combined with his support of the rightist Village Scout movement and his participation in choosing the extremely unpopular and archconservative Thanin, politicized the monarchy (Keyes 1987:100, 210; Morell and Samudavanija 1981:313). Kershaw summarizes the damage to the king's reputation: "Yet however justified the apprehensions of the King, the manner in which the democracy of 1975–76 ended—with a massacre of university students which the King did not intervene to prevent, followed by an Army coup which he did not oppose—destroyed his standing with Thai liberals and the student movement. . . . The monarchy appeared to have become the willing tool of the extreme Right" (1977:259).

During the civilian period newspaper columnists had voiced fears that the growing partisan character of the Village Scout movement, if continued unchecked, would divide public opinion and damage the institution of the monarchy (e.g., see *Daily Times*, April 6, 1976). The bloodbath on October 6 made their worst fears a reality. Fear of further harm to the monarchy became yet another reason for the government to want tighter control over Village Scout activities.

Fissures Within the Military

Probably the single most important reason for the moratorium was the existence of major schisms within the military-backed government. On October 6 two military coalitions sought to stage coups. The successful bid of the military coalition calling itself the National Administrative Reform Council, or NARC, took place at 6:30 P.M. on October 6; however, this bid actually preempted another coup planned for 8 P.M. the same night (Race 1977:324). Only one, the losing faction, had developed close links to the Village Scouts.

Although Thai military factions are volatile coalitions, the two main military coalitions involved in October 6 and their civilian political affiliations are particularly important in understanding the immediate post-coup situation. The successful coup was headed by General Serm na Nakorn, then commander in chief of the army. General Serm was a member of the faction that had been headed by General Krit Sivara until his death in April 1976. After the ouster of the Thanom-Praphat clique with the popular uprising of October 1973, the Serm-Krit military faction remained dominant throughout the civilian period and the years after the 1976 coup.[23]

The failed coup coalition centered around members of the Thai Nation Party. The Thai Nation Party was headed by Major General Pramarn Adireksan and Major General Chartchai Choonhawan, who were also related through marriage.[24] Both formed a loose alliance with the head of Internal Operations Security Command (ISOC), General Saiyud Kerdphol, and General Chalard Hiranyasiri, a protégé of Pramarn's (Mallet 1978:84). Also part of this loose coalition was General Vitoon Yasawat, an ally of General Chalard's but tied to the conservative wing of the Democrat Party (Girling 1981:230).[25] Generals Vitoon and Chartchai were also linked to the Red Gaurs, who—it will be recalled—were associated with ISOC (B. Anderson 1977:28).

Ironically, it was this unsuccessful coup that did the most to mobilize the Village Scouts and set the stage for the coup. As Morell and Samudavanija, who have gone the furthest in analyzing the events of this fascinating period, conclude, the crisis triggered by the returns of Thanom and Praphat in mid-summer 1976 was engineered by "the Thai Nation party and the conservative faction of the Democrat party, together with the Thanom and Praphat factions in the military" (1981:270).[26] Girling essentially agrees, writing that "among the military, ambitious generals associated with Pramarn took advantage of the turmoil" (Girling 1981:214).

Although the machinations of the Thai Nation military-cum-political-party coalition became more obvious as October 6 approached, their rivalries with other electoral parties had long histories. The civilian period saw three different elected governments. After the first elections were held in January 1975, the Democrats formed the government with their party head, Seni Pramoj, as prime minister. Seni's major opponent for the position of prime minister was none other than Major General Chartchai (Morell and Samudavanija 1981:118). The first Seni government lasted only eight days, until it fell in a vote of no confidence on March 6. Seni's brother, Kukrit Pramoj, succeeded in forming the new government, which lasted until April 1976. Pramarn Adireksan, the head of the Thai Nation Party, occupied the positions of deputy prime minister and defense minister in the Kukrit government.[27] As minister of defense, Pramarn removed General Serm na Nakorn from the position of deputy army commander to an "innocuous staff position" (Morell and Samudavanija 1981:267). In Serm's place Pramarn promoted his protégé, General Chalard Hiranyasiri, in March 1976 (Girling 1981:n218, 229). However, with the ousting of the Kukrit government this situation was reversed when the second Seni government's new minister of defense transferred Chalard to an inactive post in the Supreme Command and General Serm became the army commander (Morell and Samudavanija 1981:n281).

The final events leading inexorably to the coup came with the escalation of conflict between the conservative and progressive factions within the then-ruling Democrat Party. The progressive wing of the Democrat Party was led by Damrong Latthaphiphat, Surin Masadit, and Chuan Leekphai. The conservative wing was led by Thammanun Thienngen and Samak Sunthorawej.[28] Thammanun became governor of Bangkok and during his governorship oversaw the dramatic expansion of the Village Scout movement in Bangkok. Samak Sunthorawej was deputy minister of interior in the second Seni government; by virtue of his position in the ministry he also had administrative links to the Village Scout movement. Furthermore Samak was closely associated with the Thai Nation Party and was considered an adviser to the queen (Girling 1981:206). Discord between the two wings of the Democrat Party had become public as early as 1975, when it was learned that money from the Thai Nation Party had been used to buy votes for election to the party's central committee at the time of its party convention (Morell and Samudavanija 1981:268).

The progressive wing had plans to remove several right-wing generals from important posts (Shawcross 1976:60). In response the party's conservative wing tried to discredit the progressive wing by appealing to the Village Scouts and other conservative groups. When the Democrats returned to power in the Seni government in April 1976, Damrong, Surin, and Chuan came under frequent attack, labeled leftists and communists in newspapers, posters, and army radio broadcasts (Morell and Samudavanija 1981:269). The attacks were greatly facilitated by the fact that the military owned more than half the radio stations in the country, and all but one TV station in Bangkok; by October 1975 it was clear that the military-led Thai Nation Party had influential links to the media (Girling 1977:394).

The Seni government had been uncertain how to respond to the return of Thanom in September 1976. The cabinet at this point was a coalition of the Democrat, Thai Nation, Social Justice, and Social Nationalist parties, with the Democrat Party, headed by Seni Pramoj, holding the prime ministership. The progressive wing of the Democrat Party supported the students' demands that Thanom either be arrested or expelled from the country. As Morell and Samudavanija explain, "The Democrat party's progressive faction supported the students' demand, primarily out of fear that the longer Thanom remained in the country, the greater were the chances that the Thai Nation party and the military would use the resulting unrest as their pretext for staging a coup. The progressive Democrats then sought the support of the Social Action party as a possible way to oust Thai Nation from the coalition" (Morell and Samudavanija 1981:272–73; see also Keyes 1987:98).[29]

According to Jeffrey Race, when the Thai Nation Party learned that the progressive wing of the Democrats "indeed did intend very shortly to dump the military coalition partners and join the business-oriented Social Action Party" (1977:325), the Thai Nation Party began to plan for a coup in earnest. A new Seni cabinet was announced on October 5, 1976. Even though the Thai Nation Party was still part of the cabinet, two conservative Democrats were ousted.[30] Their ouster became a rallying cause. Thai Nation Party members and conservative Democrats mobilized hundreds of Village Scouts to demonstrate at Government House. The scouts demanded the immediate resignation of the three progressive Democrats in the cabinet.[31] Because the situation was so explosive, the three ministers complied (Morell and Samudavanija 1981:273). On the eve of the October 6 coup the situation was volatile. The successful coup bid of NARC appears to have been a preemptive strike against the Thai Nation coalition. As Morell and Samudavanija explain,

> Thanom's return had threatened the late Krit's faction, by then identified in particular with General Serm Na Nakorn, General Kriangsak Chomanan, and Air Chief Marshall Kamol Dechatunka. This group, concerned over the possibility of a seizure of power by either military officers with personal and political ties to the Thai Nation party, by the Praphat/Yot contingents, or by some other combination of troop units, thus seized power itself in the wake of the brutality at Thammasat and the apparent threat to national stability and the throne.
>
> (Morell and Samudavanija 1981:276)

Although NARC staged its coup first, the Thai Nation Party and others in that military-civilian faction had played a major role in creating a political atmosphere ripe for a coup. In addition to rallying Village Scouts during the day of October 5, they were active all through the night. The Armored Division Radio Station, or Yarn Kroh, played a central role in rallying and coordinating the police and the Village Scouts throughout the evening before the massacre at Thammasat. This radio station had long publicized the activities of the Thai Nation Party members. That night the Armored Division Radio Station (Yarn Kroh) announced that the leader of the Thai Nation Party had telephoned the prime minister to demand action against the students (Shawcross 1976:60). Increasingly incendiary broadcasting continued through the night with speakers from Yarn Kroh, ISOC, the Village Scouts, and Thai Nation involved.

Thus, ironically, the faction that had done the most to create an atmosphere of crisis conducive for the rationalization of a military coup was not included in the new government. The Thai Nation Party was notably absent. Chalard and Vitoon were not part of NARC.[32] As Girling summarizes, "Chalard and General Vitoon Yasavat were the chief losers among the military in the October 1976 coup" (1981:229). However, the pre-emptive coup of NARC by no means ended the intense factional rivalries. Some jockeying surfaced in the media. As Norman Peagam wrote at the time, "Anonymous leaflets have appeared attacking the regime: a farmer was arrested in Bangkok for allegedly putting up anti-government posters, and the generally conservative local press has become increasingly outspoken in its criticism" (1977:8). Members of ISOC, such as Saiyud Kerdphol and Dr. Somchai Rakvijit, were especially bold in criticizing the new government in a variety of venues (Mallet 1978:95).[33] So unsettled were the times that the Thanin government closed down two right-wing newspapers. The editor of a paper with connections to ISOC was arrested for publishing an article about power conflicts within the government (Peagam 1977:9; R. Zimmerman 1978:106). In response Colonel Uthan Sanitwong launched radio attacks against the Thanin government on the Armored Division Radio Station, the same spokesperson and the same radio station that had been so important in coordinating the Village Scouts and other groups involved on October 6 (Peagam 1977).

The maelstrom swirling beneath the surface of the rigid Thanin government became manifest in the coup of March 26, 1977, a mere five months after October 6. This coup attempt was led by Chalard Hiranyasiri. Most Thai coups have been internally bloodless, but in the course of this abortive coup General Chalard shot another general.[34] In the months after the coup the Thanin government tried to consolidate its position. The failed coup of March 1977 made it possible to execute Chalard, thus removing one key player permanently. By early May the other co-conspirators in the failed coup had either been sentenced to prison or were in exile.[35] The Red Gaurs were "silenced or packed off to combat zones in the North, Northeast and South (where they reportedly suffered severe casualties)" (Anderson 1977:30). Colonel Uthan was removed from control of the Armored Division Radio Station, and its broadcasts were temporarily suspended (Anderson 1977:30).[36] Nawaphon was also silenced. As Keyes writes, "The new government was not made up of members of Nawaphon or, with perhaps few exceptions, of the military men who had backed Nawaphon" (1978:160).

Thus, despite the appearance of a rightist victory, the political realities facing the new Thanin government were far more complex.[37] Throughout the civilian period the Village Scouts had been most closely identified with the Thai Nation Party and with the right wing of the Democrat Party. These political parties and their military counterparts had played the key role in the mobilization of the Village Scouts (Race 1977:324; Darling 1978:155; Van Praagh 1977:302; R. Zimmerman 1978:52, 88; see also a fascinating column signed Sot Kromarohit in the newspaper *Sayamsaan*, November 21, 1976).[38] The military faction that had put the Thanin government in power was not the group with close links to the Village Scouts and other right-wing organizations. The faction's problem was how to put the genie back into the bottle, how to regain control of the various right-wing forces whose actions had helped create the stage for the coup. Hence calling a moratorium on the Village Scouts was a logical response by a government, albeit a rightist one, nervous about the potential of a national movement it did not wholly control. Making Samak Sunthorawej minister of interior—the government ministry with the closest direct ties to the Village Scout movement—can be construed as one way to bring the Village Scout movement under closer government control. The moratorium was another.[39]

Factors Ending the Moratorium

Given the social divisions generated by the Village Scout movement, all of which were thrown into stark relief by the coup on October 6, it is not surprising that the Thanin administration issued a moratorium. What instead becomes problematic is why the moratorium ended. The end of the moratorium was announced on April 8, to go into effect on May 15 (*Daily Times*, April 8, 1977). The Thanin government was hardly secure. On March 20, 1977, the government survived a coup attempt launched by General Chalard Hiranyasiri. Signs were mounting that the military as a whole was not satisfied with the Thanin government. As Kershaw suggests, "It was common knowledge in the capital that Thanin's government lasted a full year up until 20 October 1977—some six months beyond the point at which the Armed Forces leaders themselves had concluded that he was too inflexible—only with the protection of the Palace" (1979:259; see also Mallet 1978:91, 95–96). Given the unsettled circumstances, it is the cessation rather than the initiation of the moratorium that requires explanation.[40]

The Growth of the CPT

A major consequence of the October 6 coup and the bloody suppression of the student movement was the dramatic infusion of three or four thousand new recruits into the Communist Party of Thailand (CPT). In addition to those who joined the CPT, more and more Thais who had placed their hope in peaceful reform through the parliamentary process had become tacit sympathizers with those who had chosen the path of armed resistance. The CPT was increasingly coming to be seen as the only credible alternative to the status quo. People who had never before thought to listen to any radio station but local Thai stations now tuned in regularly for what they called "real news" on shortwave radios, listening primarily to the Voice of America (VOA), BBC, and VOPT, the CPT broadcasting channel. More than the BBC or VOA, the VOPT carried news about events in Thailand, frequently translating international newspaper accounts of October 6 and other events in Thailand.

Thus, although the voice of dissent had been silenced in the public political arena, the newfound strength of the CPT became evident quickly. Fueled by the CPT's rapid growth after October 6, armed guerrilla encounters increased steadily. A few statistics reveal the difference. According to CPT accounts, the CPT claimed 75 attacks in which 450 "enemies" were killed in all of 1975. In the one year between October 6, 1976, and October 6, 1977, the CPT claimed a total of 717 engagements, killing 1,475 government troops (see de Beer 1978:148–49). As Patrice de Beer comments, "Even if those figures are inflated, they do show a great increase in the CPT's military activities" (1978:149). By 1979 the CPT had about ten thousand armed guerrillas and was mounting company- and battalion-size combat units in the northern, northeastern, and southern regions of the country (Snitwongse 1985:259–60; see also Kerdphol 1986:114–20).

In general the armed encounters occurred in remote mountainous regions along Thailand's borders. Nonetheless the political advance of the CPT was becoming more noticeable in the districts closer to the urban centers. Government figures reveal a dramatic increase in popular support. In January 1975 a total of 412 villages were under strong or wholly communist control. More than 6,000 villages with a population of approximately 3.9 million persons were subject to some degree of communist influence. By 1977–78 CPT activity was at a peak, having spread to 52 of the 72 provinces (Wongtrangan 1984:136). Schoolteachers teaching in remote villages came back to their natal villages and described how communists worked in their areas. One teacher I knew recounted how guerrillas came into the village where he was teaching to help villagers with planting and harvesting their crops or with building a new home or other daily village activities. Ordinary villagers throughout the country were beginning to have firsthand knowledge of communist activities, unfiltered through government media.

The countryside was becoming increasingly politicized and could not safely be ignored if the Thanin administration was to combat the spread of communism. With the right comprised of politicized and unstable factions and the left threatening to mushroom in the countryside, the Thanin government faced a dilemma with regard to the Village Scout movement. To continue the movement unchecked was to invite trouble; to do nothing to counter the spread of communism in the countryside was to do no less.

Continuing Problems of the Legitimacy of the Thanin Government

The king's actions leading up to the coup of October 6 raised questions in the minds of many Thais who believed strongly in democratic government. Moreover his association and close involvement with the immensely unpopular Thanin government further undermined the reputation of the monarchy. As Keyes explains, "The King (or, some people believe, the Queen) chose Thanin Kraivichien to become the next Prime Minister" (1987:100). The king's evident support for Thanin alienated not only liberal reformers but even "the ruling elite's support for the monarch" (Mallet 1978:96). As Van Praagh comments, "Disappointment over the palace's role, expressed in different ways by extremist generals on the one hand, and educated young Thais on the other, caused one respected royalist to remark: 'I fear for the monarchy next time there is a change of government'" (1977:303).

Within a few months of taking office Thanin succeeded in alienating much-needed sources of support. His rural policies did nothing to increase village support for the regime. He stopped all projects in the rural areas initiated by the Kukrit government. Financial development grants to local communities were terminated and replaced by "voluntary labor" schemes in which villagers were "invited" to show their patriotism by contributing their labor to road building and other projects (Mallet 1978:92). Many believed his policies were aggravating the problem of insurgency. Under the Communist Suppression Act local officials had greater leeway to arbitrarily exercise power. As Keyes explains, the category of "endangering society (*phai sangkhom*) . . . gave local officials, police, and even ordinary citizens with grievances against their neighbors license to have thousands of people throughout the country arrested and detained" (1987:100). Summary justice, indiscriminate arrests, and the execution of communist suspects increased (for more on the legal situation, see M. Bunnag 1979; see also Mallet 1978:n101).

Economically, the Thanin government did not fare well. In 1977 the trade deficit hit a high mark. The balance of payments, which showed a large surplus of 8 billion baht in 1974, revealed a record deficit in 1977 of 7.5 billion baht (na Pombhejara 1979:316). Domestic investment in industry for example, was only U.S.$10 million in September 1977, compared with U.S.$900 million in 1974. Businessmen feared that the Thanin government's xenophobic policies were scaring away foreign investment. Although they appreciated the prohibition on labor strikes, they resented other government restrictions and interventions in economic spheres (Somvichian 1978:835). Moreover the flight of capital to Hong Kong and Singapore was reaching unprecedented levels (Mallet 1978:94).

Thanin's policies also undermined his support within the ranks of the bureaucracy. He summarily dismissed scores of civil servants, including senior officials (van der Kroef 1977:612). As part of his anticorruption and antinarcotics campaigns, he embarked upon a large-scale reshuffling of police officers serving in lucrative posts; Samak Sunthorawej, then minister of interior and seen as most directly responsible for the policy, suffered two assassination attempts (Mallet 1978:94). The Thanin government also launched an investigation against army general Tienchai Sirisamphan of the Special Warfare Center and a close protégé of Praphat's; the army rallied behind the general and forced Thanin to back down (Mallet 1978:94; Peagam 1977). Thanin was alienating himself not only from liberal and centrist support but even from other rightists: the Thanin government was becoming immensely unpopular. His ultimate downfall came when he also alienated the same military men who had helped put him in power. As Girling explains, military leaders "increasingly distanced themselves from an unpopular and largely discredited administration" (1981:218–19; see also discussion in McCoy 1991:416–23).

The unpopularity of the Thanin government jeopardized the king's reputation. Indeed several scholars have commented that the only reason the Thanin government survived as long as it did was because of royal support (Mallet 1978:91, 95–96). Furthermore the king, rather than dissociate himself from the horror of October 6 and distance himself from the government, the military, and the Village Scouts, continued to be seen in their company.[41] Even after the moratorium members of the royal family continued to visit numerous scout initiations; they were frequently shown on television surrounded by scouts during their visits up-country, and had formal photographs taken for national distribution in scout uniforms. Members of the royal family also regularly went to visit soldiers and police injured in combat with communist guerrillas. The queen and other members of the royal family were increasingly seen in public appearances in military uniform. As Dr. Puey Ungphakorn writes, "After the coup, newspapers carried daily photographs of the prince in the company of army and police officers. Both he and the king himself are also shown receiving the homage of Village Scouts who had gained so much 'merit' in the events of October 6. Finally, the two royal princesses have done their part by being photographed with wounded policemen in Bangkok hospitals" (1977:12).

Many Thais, including royalists, felt that the militarization of the royal family was a mistake. However, given the political climate, few dared speak out in public. Kukrit Pramoj, a former prime minister and of royal lineage, was a prominent exception. In a series of oblique articles implying parallels with the actions of monarchies elsewhere he made his views known, arguing that "the Royal Family must play a unifying role in relation to *all* their subjects, including the insurgents" (Kershaw 1979:261).[42] Although Kukrit did not deny the importance of military suppression, he felt that "the Royal Family must not be directly identified with it—their task should fall, so to speak, on the 'psychological warfare' side of the operation, offering hope of reconciliation and reacceptance into the national community for any who were led astray and are prone to have a change of heart. . . . The monarch must not take sides" (Kershaw 1979: 261).

Throughout this period a sense of doom about the future of the monarchy was mounting. Rumors of discord between the king and queen filtered out. Embroiling the royal family in the immediate politics of government severely damaged the reputation of the queen, provoking the "emergence of intense animosity" toward her (Kershaw 1979:260). The queen was alleged to be much involved in the behind-the-scenes intrigues. As Kershaw notes, "It is she (it is said) who determined the choice of the obsequious Thanin, she and her faction at court who caused the King's loyal, but brilliant and outspoken old servant, Kukrit Pramoj, to be ostracized" (1977:260; see also Girling 1981:n217; Keyes 1987: 100). During this period the queen's relatives were said to be exerting pressure on the bureaucracy to have liberals transferred out of influential positions, and certain summonses to the palace appeared to have been issued "without the authority of the King" (Kershaw 1977:260). As Morell and Samudavanija write,

> The growing influence of Queen Sirikit may also help explain the monarchy's actions in 1976. Some close associates of the king argue that His Majesty was, in fact, manipulated by the queen's close advisors, mostly extreme rightists. Reliable sources suggest that the king had preferred not to get involved in dealing with the return of Praphat and Thanom, but that the queen, for her own reasons, had initiated these moves and finally implicated the king in the situation. After the October 6, 1976 coup, several leaflets distributed in Bangkok argued that the Sanitwong family (the queen's family) was maneuvering to force the king to abdicate in favor of the crown prince, who was said to be under his mother's influence. According to this source of information, the palace was divided into two factions: the moderates (the king and his close advisors such as Kukrit Pramoj and Police Major General Wasit Dejkunchon), and the extreme rightists (the queen and her closest aides, including Thanin Kraivichien, Colonel Uthan Sanitwong, and Deputy Interior Minister Samak).[44]
>
> (1981:272)

Various other events contributed to doubts about the future of the monarchy. The sudden marriage of the crown prince to his first cousin, a niece of the queen's, struck many as a hastily conceived diversion from the coup. The first notification of the impending wedding, set to take place on January 3, 1977, came only with the crown prince's return from Australia in October 1976. Public confidence in the suitability of the bride was undermined by her failure to complete high school. To add to the inauspicious omens a few months after the wedding the crown prince's wife had a miscarriage. Her second pregnancy resulted in a daughter and hence no heir to the throne. Even before the ill-fated wedding took place, discreet doubts were expressed about the leadership qualities of the crown prince.[43] On his fiftieth birthday, December 5, 1977, the king changed the traditional rules of succession to the throne. Traditionally, only male heirs could accede the throne; the king's changes gave female heirs the right as well (see Kershaw 1977:261, n265; Mallet 1978:n102). He then made his elder daughter crown princess.[45] This change at once allayed and reinforced public doubts about royal succession. The rumor that the Chakri dynasty would have only nine kings continued to spread.

The perception of the monarchy's vulnerability was heightened by the initiation of attacks, both military and verbal, on the royal family. In February 1977 the convoy of the crown prince in Petchabun Province was fired on (Kershaw 1979:260). Shortly thereafter, on February 16, 1977, communist gunfire killed Princess Wiphawadi Rangsit, a secretary and emissary of the queen's who was traveling by helicopter in Surat Thani Province (Kershaw 1979:261; Marks 1977:63). On September 1, 1978, the crown prince was once again endangered when his helicopter was hit by ground fire (Kershaw 1979:263). These attacks on members of the royal family or entourage were simultaneously an indication of the increasing royal participation in military activities and of the growing military capabilities of the CPT. Neither served to instill public confidence in the strength of the monarchy.

Just how deeply vulnerable the monarchy had become was perhaps most tellingly revealed by the fact that the CPT now began criticizing the institution, referring to the king as the "great investor" or the "great feudal lord." The CPT had heretofore refrained from any direct criticism of the monarchy. Even radicals had had discussions about how socialism was not incompatible with monarchy, often citing the example of Pridi Panomyong who had supported many socialist policies even while serving as regent. However, in February 1977 increasingly direct attacks on the royal family began. In response to government editorials accusing the communist forces of being "savage terrorists" after the death of Princess Wiphawadi, the voPT responded with a piece called WHO IS REALLY THE CRUEL AND SAVAGE ONE? It labeled the princess as a "representative of the big feudalists who have been conducting psychological operations to deceive the people."[46] A discussion by Thirayut Bunmee, a former student leader, was broadcast on April 1, 1977, and is generally considered the first direct criticism of the Thai monarchy (van der Kroef 1977:620; Marks 1977:65).[47] Increasingly, the issue of the wealth of the Crown Property Bureau became a theme in voPT broadcasts, and the increase in security efforts to protect the members of the royal family was interpreted as indicating that the king was afraid of his own people (Marks 1977:65–68; see also de Beer 1978:152).

Thus the Thanin government had every reason to be concerned about its deteriorating position. The CPT was growing rapidly in the wake of the October 6 coup, while the government faced an internal crisis of legitimacy. By mobilizing the Village Scouts the Thanin government could hope to accomplish three objectives: fight communism, promote public support for the monarchy, and, given the king's support for Thanin, bolster support for his government. Whereas in the early years of the Village Scouts the movement grew because of the high regard in which the king was held, it could now be argued that the Village Scout movement was growing under government auspices to safeguard the reputation of the monarchy. With eroding popular support and intensifying guerrilla pressure the Thanin government needed a populist vehicle that shared its conservative vision in order to burnish the tarnished monarchy and foster the illusion of public support. The Village Scout movement appeared to be a ready solution.

PART TWO

Efficacy and the Peasantry

Mourners for Dr. Boonsanong Punyodyana, slain secretary general of the Socialist Party of Thailand, hold a mass rally near the Grand Palace in Bangkok.
(Photo by Neil Ulevich; used by permission of AP/WideWorld Photos.)

5

Setting the Agrarian Stage

✤

Throughout 1977 the Communist Party of Thailand (CPT) was expanding in the countryside and the Thanin government faced mounting domestic opposition. After several delays Village Scouts initiation sessions resumed on May 15, 1977.[1] The Ministry of Interior had grand plans to initiate five million Village Scouts over the next five years—one million each year (*Siam Rath*, December 14, 1976). Once the moratorium ended, new initiation sessions proceeded at a relentless pace, with subdistrict after targeted subdistrict being told to organize initiations. In the final months of 1977, about eighteen hundred sessions initiating three-quarters of a million recruits were held nationwide. The government used the moratorium to institute reforms in the administration of the Village Scout organization. Although the initiation rite remained essentially unaltered, bringing the movement under tighter administrative control wrought another significant metamorphosis. From its incarnation as a relatively autonomous, middle-class, and urban-oriented movement, it now returned to its original agrarian counterinsurgency agenda.

This new phase of the Village Scout movement affected ordinary villagers more than before. Although villagers had been targeted in the movement's first years, the organization was small and not many villagers participated actively. The new guidelines again targeted villagers but in much greater numbers. For example, in San Patong District, the district in Chiang Mai Province that is the ethnographic (fieldwork) basis of chapters 5, 6, and 7, only seven initiations were held from the organization's founding in 1971 to the coup in October 1976. In the eighteen months after the moratorium ended (June 1977 to December 1978) this district held fifteen new initiations. Furthermore before the moratorium these initiations were generally held in the larger and more prosperous town and subdistrict centers, not in remote villages. In San Patong District, two of the seven precoup initiations were held in the district town, and the other five were held in larger, more densely populated subdistricts. With the new policies in place more sessions were held in the poorer and more remote subdistricts; in San Patong District two initiations were held in Mae Win Subdistrict, a mountainous area inaccessible by car during much of the year.

With the communist victories in Vietnam, Laos, and Cambodia the stakes were increasing. The crucial battleground was to be the countryside, both because that was where the majority of the Thai citizenry lived and because the Maoist-based strategy of the CPT called for using the countryside to encircle the city.[2] On October 6 the scouts had proved capable of playing an important role in toppling a democratically elected civilian government and ushering in one of the most extreme right-wing governments Thailand had ever experienced. Bloodshed was increasing and the term *civil war* was used with growing frequency (e.g., Muecke 1980:427; Kerdphol 1986:135). In the increasingly militarized drama that was now being played out in the villages, what role, if any, would the refurbished Village Scout movement have?

The preceding part of this book focused on establishing the complex interplay of individuals, state factions, and class factions whose interests motivated the rise of the Village Scout movement. This part of the book explores the impact of the movement on the political attitudes of villagers in the countryside. It focuses on the postmoratorium phase of the movement, beginning with the resumption of Village Scout initiations in May 1977 and ending with the military coup that ousted the Thanin government on October 20, 1977.

From the Cities to the Countryside

Although I have lived in many villages in northern Thailand, I observed the Village Scout initiation in a village I shall call Samsen.[3] Samsen Village is located in San Patong District, a generally more prosperous district whose seat is about twenty-five kilometers southwest of Chiang Mai City (see figure 5.1). Chiang Mai City, the capital of Chiang Mai Province, was the second-largest city in Thailand at the time, and the province was one of the most fertile rice-growing areas in the country. Samsen Village was the largest of a dozen or so villages comprising Samsen Subdistrict and served as the subdistrict center. Its village headman almost invariably served as the *kamnan*, or head of the subdistrict, or *tambon* (see figure 5.2). Under the revised Village Scout guidelines, which ranked the "sensitive" areas by priority, Samsen Subdistrict was among the first subdistricts targeted for a Village Scout initiation rite in the postmoratorium period. Because I was living in this village when it was chosen, I witnessed this village's reaction to its initiation session in its entirety.

To interpret the range of views expressed by Samsen villagers and their neighbors it is important to place them in relation to those expressed by villagers elsewhere. How the political exigencies of the day contributed to the selection of Samsen Village as one of my field sites is revealing. In the course of my work as a freelance journalist I had become interested in understanding the factors that had led to the recent growth in the expression of rural grievances. Before the coup I had planned to conduct research in Doi Saket District, where Sithon Yotkantha, the vice president of the FFT, lived. After a bomb was thrown at his home he went underground. The difficulties of Sithon and other activist villagers, as well as the threats made against me, made me decide that I would be well advised to live in a "safe" village, one with no previous history of political activism.[4] The coup finalized that decision. Because San Patong was one of the wealthier districts in the Chiang Mai Valley and had no significant reputation for political activism, university colleagues advised me that this district would be more suitable.

When I began my research in San Patong District in December 1976, there were only a few early signs of communist activity. Only in Mae Win Subdistrict, a remote mountainous and forest-covered area with little population density, were there rumors of a guerrilla presence. FFT activity was reported in one or two other subdistricts. During the civilian period one

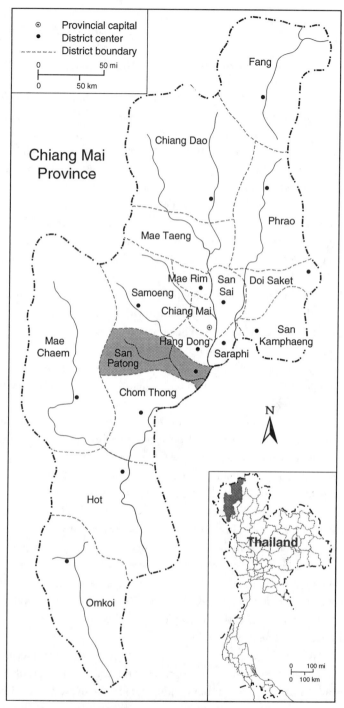

Figure 5.1. Chiang Mai Province.

(University of Wisconsin–Madison Cartography Laboratory.)

Figure 5.2 Thai Administrative Structure

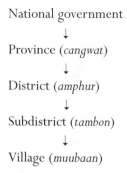

National government
↓
Province (*cangwat*)
↓
District (*amphur*)
↓
Subdistrict (*tambon*)
↓
Village (*muubaan*)

Each village is led by a village headman and one or two assistant headmen. Each tambon is led by a kamnan, a village headman selected from among the village headmen in the tambon to serve as the subdistrict head

FFT leader was shot but survived. In another cluster of villages residents were about to be evicted for trespassing in a "forest reserve" area. Aside from these few pockets San Patong had a reputation as a prosperous and contented area. Within San Patong District both Samsen Village and Samsen Subdistrict seemed as quiet and run of the mill as any other.

Although every village is unique, Samsen Village was not unusual. Located along a winding red dirt road, the village was the site of the tambon's (subdistrict's) main morning market, health station, and largest school. The village, nestled among coconut trees, banana palms, and a variety of other fruit trees, was more or less like any other lowland, rice-growing village in the area. Its four hundred families lived in homes that ranged from beautiful teak houses with tile roofs to simple bamboo huts roofed with thatch or leaves. Like other northern villages, about 60 percent of the villagers owned some land and the remainder were landless.[5] Those with land usually planted rice in the rainy season, followed by soybeans in the dry season. The landless worked, as best they could, as agricultural laborers. Because even most landholding villagers did not own enough land to make ends meet, virtually all villagers, landed and landless alike, supplemented their incomes with a wide variety of activities, from collecting forest products to producing handicrafts.

Assessing the impact of the Village Scout movement on peasant political consciousness necessarily involves trying to understand villagers' attitudes before and after the movement's inception. The next two chapters will describe the initiation ritual itself and its aftermath; this chapter sketches

A villager plows his fields at the beginning of the rainy season in the northern countryside.

the political landscape in northern Thailand prior to the resumption of scout initiations. After describing the major political events with which most villagers were familiar and outlining Village Scout activity in the area, the focus narrows to the villagers of Samsen as they receive the news that their village and subdistrict are expected to hold a Village Scout initiation. Because Samsen Village is an "ordinary" village, examining how the Village Scout movement played itself out in this village, this subdistrict, and this district approximates what was happening elsewhere in the countryside.

Political Polarization in the North

Under volatile conditions political consciousness is difficult to assess and document because villagers have learned to be wary of outsiders. However, events such as elections and some organizational activities of students, villagers, and laborers were common knowledge to a majority of villagers from listening to radios, reading newspapers, or word of mouth. Elections and political protests offer particularly good opportunities to gain insight into what was otherwise seemingly invisible.

After the overthrow of the military dictatorship in October 1973 the countryside soon heated up. Elections were called for January 1975. For the first time socialist parties fielded candidates. Significantly, left-wing candidates won 5 of 57 seats from the northern region in the National Assembly.[6] Their victories were momentous, considering the harassment they had experienced.

The election campaign of Dr. Boonsanong Punyodyana, the secretary general of the Socialist Party of Thailand (SPT), provides a good example of the political tension of the period. Because I covered the election for the *Bangkok Post,* I am familiar with many of the details of his campaign (see Bowie 1975a). Boonsanong was running in a by-election for a seat in parliament representing Zone 1 of Chiang Mai province. In the course of my research I was struck by the vague rhetoric of the campaign and the lack of specific policies proposed by most candidates. Unlike those of other candidates, Dr. Boonsanong's platform included land reform and land rent control. Not surprisingly, his campaign was rapidly gaining support in rural areas. Indeed many FFT members campaigned for him. His popularity was further enhanced by the fact that, as a northerner, he was able to campaign in the northern dialect. As his popularity grew so did the attacks.

One of the most vicious attacks on Dr. Boonsanong and his supporters occurred at a school in Hang Dong where a progressive organization of schoolteachers had organized a three-day seminar. Hang Dong is the district immediately adjacent to San Patong District, and schoolteachers from San Patong District were also involved. Dr. Boonsanong was a featured speaker. Other speakers included Intha Sribunryang, vice president of the FFT and president of its northern chapter; Insorn Buakhiew, another SPT member who had been elected from Hang Dong in the January 1975 elections; and Boonyen Wothong, another well-known SPT leader. On the evening of the second day, at about 10 P.M., a mob of about fifty men attacked the school. They threw bottle bombs and rocks at the schoolhouse, where about seventy seminar participants were gathered. They also set fire to three vehicles; two cars belonging to Boonyen and Insorn, respectively; and a motorcycle belonging to a local schoolteacher. Shortly thereafter, police arrived and arrested the seventy seminar participants who had been trapped inside the school. They were taken in trucks to the provincial office. Although initially charged with "agitating the masses" (*pluk kradom*), they were subsequently released. No effort was made to arrest anyone in the mob. One seminar participant, now a college professor and a friend of mine, told me recently that the terror of that night has never left him. The assailants were not local villagers but were thought to have been Red Gaurs, working with the support of members of Nawaphon.

This incident drew national attention to Bonsanong's campaign.

Ironically, the seminar was not directly linked with Dr. Boonsanong's election campaign; Hang Dong District was outside Zone 1, where Boonsanong was running. Seminar organizers had simply taken advantage of Dr. Boonsanong's presence in Chiang Mai. Although he was not in Hang Dong at the time of the attacks, many newspapers reported that it was his car that had been incinerated. The incident was used by his opponents as evidence of villagers' alleged contempt for his socialist ideas. During the campaign, Dr. Boonsanong also found himself battling charges of gun running; illegal guns were mysteriously found in the trunk of his car.[8] Although Dr. Boonsanong did not win the election, his candidacy demonstrated a base of support in rural areas. His assassination during the national election period in 1976 was a chilling example for other leftists contemplating electoral politics.[9]

Throughout the civilian period students from Chiang Mai University and the local teachers' colleges became active on behalf of the peasantry, as they were elsewhere in the country. In the North students were involved in many villages in the Chiang Mai–Lamphun area where the rate of tenancy was high. The students informed villagers of the 1974 law that limited rent to no more than one-third of the crop and often publicized rural grievances. One of the best known examples occurred in Mae Liang in Lampang Province, where villagers and a nearby mining company were in conflict. Villagers charged that the water used to wash the ore was damaging their rice crops. Between 1971 and 1976 villagers had tried on twelve occasions to seek government help, all to no avail (see *Jaturat*, September 1976; Vaddhanaphuti 1984:319). Finally, the villagers decided to blockade the mining company. As a result of students' reports, journalists investigated the conflict, and the government was eventually forced to close the mine. A similar mining dispute occurred in Mae Thaa District of Lamphun (see Bowie 1975b).

Student involvement almost invariably prompted a right-wing backlash. In the protest against the mining company in Lampang the government sent an anticommunist insurgency unit into the village and arrested several villagers (Vaddhanaphuti 1984:319). In other cases Village Scout leaders were asked to inform on students' activities. Village Scout initiations were often deliberately held in areas where increased political activism had been reported. For example, students from Chiang Mai University became involved in a project in a village in Mae Taeng District, Chiang Mai Province. In this project university students tried to bridge the gap between urban and rural culture by tutoring village schoolchildren while the students were learning about village life (see Vaddhanaphuti 1984:329). Although the Mae Taeng project was innocuous, its existence prompted the government to hold a scout session just across the river from this village in 1976 "to mobilize the villagers against the students" (Vaddhanaphuti 1984:330). After the 1976 coup village headmen were told to notify the district office of the arrival of any strangers. Although many villagers supported student involvement, others feared its consequences. Chayan Vaddhanaphuti, then a graduate student, records the challenge of doing fieldwork in the postcoup period in the wake of the "ideological campaign against the leftist/Communist elements":

> In the late 1970's, the rural areas of North Thailand were filled with fear and suspicion. On the one hand, the authorities tended to see intellectuals and university students as potential dangers that could cause unnecessary rural unrest. On the other, many villagers became unduly suspicious of any stranger due in part to their overexposure to the counter-insurgency and counter-intellectual campaigns. As a consequence it became a burden for me to convince both the authorities and the villagers in any area I might study that I was not an agitator.
>
> (1984:199–200)

The rapid spread of the FFT was perhaps the most dramatic evidence of the politicization of the countryside. Although the FFT was a national organization, it was particularly strong in the Chiang Mai Valley, especially in the districts that had high concentrations of lands owned by absentee landlords. The first vice president of the FFT, Intha Sribunryang, lived in Saraphi District. Saraphi District, only about ten miles from San Patong District, had one of the highest concentrations of tenancy in the entire Chiang Mai Valley. The FFT newspaper, *Chawnaa Thai* (Thai Farmer), was published from Intha's home in Saraphi. After Intha's assassination in August 1975 another FFT leader from the Chiang Mai Valley, Sithon Yotkantha from Doi Saket District, became the new FFT vice president (see Turton 1978:183–87 for interview with Sithon). Although no one in the FFT in San Patong District was killed, more than one assassination was attempted. Of the more than twenty FFT leaders killed between March and August 1975, eight were assassinated in Chiang Mai Province alone, all between June and August 1975 (see Bowie and Phelan 1975; Morell and Samudavanija 1981:227 for details).

Although the killers of these farmer leaders were never caught, there is little doubt that they were killed by the right. Morell and Samudavanija suggest that Nawaphon was responsible for "at least some of these killings," because "during this period *Nawaphon* was particularly active in trying to recruit new members in Chiang Mai and Lamphun, and its cadres had been placing great pressure on student activists throughout the North" (1981:225). Because of the assassinations villagers were afraid to discuss the FFT publicly. While writing an article on the FFT, I traveled to several villages where FFT representatives had been killed. Even in these villages—even when the person killed had been the village headman—villagers denied any knowledge of the FFT. After the rash of assassinations the FFT became a taboo subject and it was difficult to assess the extent of sympathy and support for it. Although no one in Samsen Village or Samsen Subdistrict was an acknowledged member of the FFT, some villagers hinted at their sympathy with the issues being pressed by the FFT, if not with the organization itself.

Most political organizing in the North focused on the countryside. Unlike Bangkok, the towns and cities of the North were small. Chiang Mai City had a population of about 100,000, compared to Bangkok's population of nearly four million (Mudannayake et al. 1975:E28). Consequently, relatively few large factories were located in Chiang Mai or the other cities of the North. The few factories that did exist were either small or agriculturally oriented. Nonetheless three conflicts between factory owners and villagers became particularly well known during the civilian period.

The first case to come to public attention involved village girls who were working from dawn to as late as ten o'clock at night in knitting factories under conditions of virtual slavery (see Samruam Singh's short story "Khunthong's Tomorrow" for a quasi-fictional account in Bowie, ed. 1991). After conditions were made public, a local member of the National Assembly who was also an active Village Scout successfully intervened on behalf of a group of girls who worked in one such knitting factory. With his intervention the girls were allowed to terminate their "contract" and return to their villages. The National Assembly member lived in San Patong, and one girl who was freed came from Samsen.

A second case involved the Thai Farming Factory, a foreign-controlled agribusiness accused of cheating farmers on prices for crops grown under contract. The factory, which planned to can and freeze various fruits and vegetables, was located in Lamphun Province, just across the Ping River from San Patong District. Villagers in San Patong District and elsewhere grew crops for this factory. The factory also purchased land in Chom Thong District, just south of San Patong District, with the idea of cultivating additional crops for its operation. However, the land in Chom Thong was acquired under hotly contested circumstances, and angry villagers resorted to various means of sabotage, including pouring salt in the wells used to irrigate the crops. Furthermore villagers under contract to the factory complained that the factory's buyers used underhanded methods to cheat them. As a result the factory was eventually forced to close and the military took over the disputed lands.

A third major arena of conflict involved disputes between northern tobacco growers and their buyers. Tobacco was grown for export throughout the Chiang Mai Valley, including by villagers in San Patong. Villagers sold the tobacco leaves to curing stations, many of which were owned by foreign tobacco companies. Farmers complained that the tobacco-curing factories were cheating them by undervaluing the quality of their tobacco. In at least one well-known dispute the factory manager succeeded in silencing complaints with the assistance of local Village Scout leaders.[10]

Throughout the civilian period villagers—whether farmers or workers—became increasingly vocal in expressing their grievances. However, as I have shown, virtually each time that villagers expressed grievances, the right, in the form of Nawaphon, the Red Gaurs, the Village Scouts, or some government agency, became involved in a counter-response.[11] Of the paragovernmental organizations, the Village Scouts had by far the greatest public presence. As elsewhere in the country the Village Scouts became increasingly active throughout the North during the civilian period. The majority of Village Scout activities involved various kinds of "development" projects such as street sweeping or canal cleaning, as well as visiting new scout initiates during their evening campfires. However, together with the other right-wing organizations such as Nawaphon and the Red Gaurs, the Village Scouts were also used for more direct political purposes.

In the North, as in Bangkok, the political tension between left and right climaxed on October 6, 1976. Like the students in Bangkok, students throughout the country opposed the return of the dictator Thanom and were angered by the garroting of the two students. Students at Chiang Mai University and the local teachers' colleges held rallies in support of the students at Thammasat University. In response the Village Scouts were mobilized in Chiang Mai. On October 6 Village Scouts massed at Wat Jedi Luang in Chiang Mai to attack the students. Students had been demonstrating during the previous few days, first at Tha Phae Gate, one of the four main gates to the old city of Chiang Mai, and later at the provincial office in the center of town. The scouts gave the students one hour to clear the provincial office (*salaklang*). The students were uncertain how to react, but they decided to leave in order to avoid a direct confrontation, planning to return later. At the end of the assigned hour the vocational students-cum-Village Scouts arrived.[12] One informed observer, an American consular official, commented to me that it was extremely fortunate the university students had decided to leave; had they not done so, he was convinced, at least thirty more students would have been killed in Chiang Mai as well.

The North, already tense during the civilian period, remained so after the October coup. Here as elsewhere, one side of the debate fell silent. Up-country activists were arrested, including several faculty members from Chiang Mai Teachers College, as well as candidates or campaign workers for progressive political parties. The repression touched nearly everyone; even a governor's son was among the students killed in the military attack on Thammasat University. As word of the coup spread in the North, more and more student, labor, and village activists fled to the jungle. Among the villagers who fled was Sithon Yotkantha, the newly elected vice president of the FFT; a bomb had been thrown at his house before the coup, and he had been living with extreme vigilance ever since. Sithon then became a founding member of the Coordinating Committee for Patriotic and Democratic Forces, which formed an alliance with the CPT (de Beer 1978:154).

Village Scout Activity

With the left forced underground, the right was ascendant. It was a difficult time to begin fieldwork, with political opinions polarized, intense, and volatile. I sought refuge in my ambiguous categories of "American" and "student." As is the case with virtually all researchers in Thailand, my entry into village life was from the top down, beginning with government officials and the village leadership. Because so many rural leaders were involved in the Village Scout movement, I initially felt quite nervous around them. I had been working at Thammasat University at the time of the October 6 coup, so the violence was etched in my memory. I was also aware of the difficulties Thai university professors and students faced in trying to conduct research in the villages after the coup. And, of course, the threats I had received had not slipped my mind. However, because so many in the rural elite were Village Scouts, they were impossible to avoid.

Although no official statistics are available, Village Scout membership in the North appeared to fit the national pattern of the pre-1976 coup period—overwhelmingly urban and rural elite. A disproportionate number of initiates came from the city of Chiang Mai itself, from the district towns, and from the elite in the surrounding villages. Townspeople I had met on earlier visits to Chiang Mai had gone through the initiation sessions and were now enthusiastically recruiting others to join. In December 1976 an American official stationed in Chiang Mai commented during a conversation with me that virtually everyone he contacted in town had become a Village Scout.

Because all the precoup initiations had been held either in the district town or in the larger subdistricts, a disproportionate number of those who became scouts early on in San Patong District were of elite backgrounds. This urban elite orientation was evident in the troop leadership. For example, one San Patong scout chapter had two merchants of Indian-Thai heritage, one Chinese merchant, and a wealthy villager as its four main officers. Considering that Thais of Indian heritage are less than 1 percent of the overall population in Thailand and are heavily concentrated in cities or towns, this high number is telling.[13]

In accord with normal research protocol and the requirements of village etiquette, the various opinion makers of the village were among the first villagers I met. In Samsen these included the school principal, the kamnan, and the owner of the largest store in the village—all of whom were already Village Scouts. The store owner was an especially serious and active Village Scout, himself a Wood Badge Scout.[14] Because many of the rural elite were Village Scouts, I quickly found myself being invited—indeed inevitably and even unavoidably—to a series of scout events.

My first night in a village (not Samsen) was an exploratory visit. I stayed with a tambon health official (*moh anamaaj*) who was a Village Scout. She could talk of little but her excitement about her work as a health officer for scout initiations. Health officers were always on duty for the last day so that they were on hand when initiates were carried to a first aid area on stretchers, and for some of the evening campfire events as well. On my second night with her we went off to an evening campfire. My hostess clearly enjoyed her socializing, but to me the whole thing seemed noisy and silly. Loudspeakers were blaring, innumerable vendors were selling all kinds of foods, and the scout initiates were all singing, dancing, and clapping. This was serious politics? What relationship could all this folderol possibly have with the insanity of October 6? When we finally returned home about midnight, I embraced the peace and quiet of my pillow and slept soundly. The following morning I was stunned to learn that a scout trainee at the session we had attended the night before had committed suicide—apparently because he had lost his scout kerchief. This session was the last initiation held in San Patong District before the moratorium took effect.

Although Village Scout initiations were not held during the moratorium, other Village Scout activities continued unabated. Within the first few weeks of my stay in Samsen Village, because I was hobnobbing with the village elite, I participated in a variety of Village Scout activities. One of the first important scout events I attended was the scout gathering held in Chiang Mai to honor the crown prince and his new bride. The royal couple had been married on January 3, 1977. The sudden wedding occasioned no less discussion in northern villages than it did in the country as a whole. Two weeks after the wedding, on January 17, the Village Scouts held a royal wedding reception in Chiang Mai City. It was not clear who had done the primary planning for this scout reception, but the local radio station announced the upcoming event. Scouts were told to dress in "traditional" Thai clothes and meet at the field grounds in Chiang Mai.

I traveled to the outdoor wedding reception with local schoolteachers who were also Village Scouts. The event was well organized. Cars and trucks were everywhere, with excited people pouring out of them. White lines framed the area where the scouts from each district were to stand. The district officials, who were also scouts, formed the front row. Most scouts were wearing customary northern Thai dress, men in indigo blue farmer shirts and waistbands (phaakhaamaa) and women in full-length skirts and long-sleeved blouses. Many of the women's skirts and blouses were made of silk. Some Lisu and Hmong hill tribes were also present, wearing their traditional dress. In addition there were columns of young dancers in matching costumes, complete with long brass fingernail extenders. Despite the heat and the dust the excitement was considerable.

Finally, the crown prince and his bride drove up. The welcoming reception had a genuineness and innocence about it that was touching. Although most of those present were government officials, primarily rural schoolteachers or members of the town and rural elite, few had had any prior encounter with a member of the royal family. No one was sure how to behave. As I recorded in my notes that day,

> After the royal vehicle arrived, the royal anthem was played. The scouts weren't sure how to act, whether they should get down on the

ground or stand at attention; they all stood straight. The dancing girls were in position and before any music played, they bowed; many scouts weren't sure whether this was part of the dance or not, and so many of them bowed as well. The crown prince made a speech, thanking people for coming and asking the people's help in seeing that things went well for the country and religion. He also encouraged everyone to preserve their native customs and traditions.

After his speech the royal anthem was played again, and the crown prince and royal consort walked through the crowds, receiving everyone's best wishes. After they made their way through the groups of scouts, the royal anthem was again played as the couple returned to their car and drove away. The rest of us tried to do the same but were caught up in the instant traffic jam created by hundreds of hot and thirsty scouts.

Scouts I knew were impressed with the friendliness of the consort, saying she had held her head and body in such a way as to indicate respect (*khawrop*) for the people kneeling before her. The Village Scouts left this gathering full of best wishes for the young couple.[15]

Nonetheless most villagers were not scouts. Thus, although Village Scouts were active in San Patong District, participation in scout events primarily involved an elite minority. In the months after the coup the royal family was extremely active, touring the nation and meeting with villagers. Many of their activities were on behalf of or in cooperation with Village Scouts. In San Patong District a series of events reaching down to the district and village levels gave villagers an ever-increasing number of occasions to come in contact with members of the royal family. However, because only a few villagers were Village Scouts and because Village Scouts were often given a particularly prominent role in royal visits, these were often occasions for some tension between scout and nonscout villagers.

For example, in February 1977 the king and queen visited San Patong District after presenting troop flags to eighty-seven newly initiated scout chapters in Chiang Mai. Because their visit was announced over the radio in advance, villagers throughout the area knew the king and queen were coming. Radio broadcasts encouraged Village Scouts to turn out to pay their respects to the royal couple and admonished the scouts to dress neatly and wear their neckerchiefs. On the day of the royal visit police lined up at various points along the route, with scouts and villagers waiting at the places marked for stops. One designated stop was a newly formed village that the king had assisted and was now under official royal patronage. The village was settled in the middle of scrub brush. Because Samsen villagers had relatives there, they decided to use the occasion to visit their relatives and pay their respects to the king and queen. I traveled with them, walking the six or seven kilometers. We waited from mid-morning until two in the afternoon. At long last the royal procession arrived, the king and queen driving a white jeep.[16] While the king went to inspect the new irrigation pump, the queen, accompanied by her ladies-in-waiting, greeted the crowd of villagers and local government officials. The villagers and officials had formed a circle, kerchiefed Village Scouts in the front rows. The queen graciously answered questions while her ladies-in-waiting distributed favors to the children. After perhaps fifteen minutes the procession, led by several police cars with lights flashing, continued up the dirt road to visit the owner of an orange orchard. Afterward, as we all returned home, villagers commented on how kind the king was and how beautiful the queen was. Those villagers who had heard that the king always traveled with a medical team were disappointed that they could not find any medical staff; some had been hoping to get treatment for a variety of ailments and diseases. The walk home passed quickly; people went over the queen's answers to the various questions the people had asked.[17] None of the villagers I walked with was a Village Scout. On the return trip several expressed resentment that the Village Scouts occupied the front rows and kept ordinary villagers from being able to talk with the queen.

Scout events often built upon traditional rural practices, sometimes in ways that nonscouts interpreted as cultural hijacking. For example, members of a local Village Scout chapter in San Patong became the core organizers for an abbot's funeral. Because the abbot was famous, the funeral was a particularly elaborate ceremony, and the funeral pyre was to be lit by the king's representative. The funeral was the most lavish funeral I had ever seen except for the cremation ceremonies held in Bangkok for the "Martyrs of October 14," the latter a funerary rite presided over by the king and queen in person.[18] As was customary, the celebration in San Patong lasted several days. Fifteen women were ordained as nuns (*mae chii*) in honor of his death. The final moments were spectacular. The royal flame raced along strings leading to the funerary urn, setting off sparklers and firecrackers. When the fire reached the urn, flames shot up, spewing clouds of billowing multicolored and scented smoke.

Although the funeral was not officially organized by the Village Scouts, there was considerable ambiguity and overlap among the planners. The master of ceremonies for much of the event was the secretary of the local scout chapter. He would make periodic announcements to the assembled throngs of villagers, telling those who were Village Scouts to be sure to wear their scout kerchiefs and insignia. He urged those who lived close by to go home and get their scarfs if they had forgotten them. He pointed out that scouts had taken a special oath to Nation, Religion, and King, and because this funeral was being sponsored by the king it was doubly important that the scouts wear their kerchiefs. Because few ordinary villagers were scouts at this point, Samsen villagers with whom I attended the funeral rites made disparaging comments about the arrogance of those who were.

Throughout the moratorium San Patong District's Village Scouts organized various local development and merit-making activities. The largest single project undertaken by a scout troop involved raising money to renovate the facade of a large and important district temple. Because rumors were rife that the king would attend the celebration for the new facade, local scouts, together with local villagers, put considerable energy into cleaning up the grounds, the roads leading to the temple, and the public areas in the nearby village. More commonly, scout activities were smaller, involving merit-making activities or development projects such as cleaning up roads and public areas in the district. Sometimes a local scout chapter would spearhead such an event, inviting other nearby chapters to join in. If funds were to be given to the designated temple, the scouts, wearing their kerchiefs, would organize a procession, headed by those carrying the ceremonial tree decorated with money. Someone at the microphone would announce the amount of each contribution and lead in singing scout songs. Sometimes a district official or other dignitary would be invited to attend. These activities followed established village patterns of village cleanup and merit making, except that now the scout chapter replaced the traditional organizing nucleus, the village or temple steering committees. However, because the members of these traditional committees were also likely to be scouts, the distinction was not necessarily clear-cut.

Scouts also assembled on other special occasions, the most significant of which were when death or disaster befell a scout member. On at least three occasions during my first year in the village, scouts in San Patong District were mobilized on behalf of other scouts; each involved exceptional circumstances. In one case a scout chapter helped rebuild a home destroyed in a fire. Scouts also attended the funeral of the scout initiate who committed suicide during the initiation; apparently, several thousand baht were raised by the scouts and contributed to his family to help pay for his funeral. A third time was the tragic death of a Village Scout chapter head. He had gone into a burning home to rescue a child; two other people were injured and he was somehow electrocuted. Because he was well known and well liked, his funeral would have been large anyway. Once word of the circumstances of his death were broadcast on the radio, scouts from as far away as the city of Chiang Mai came to the funeral (a distance of about thirty kilometers). Unlike normal funerals, where the family of the bereaved must provide food for all the guests (although the guests make financial contributions to the host), the scouts brought their own food, so as not to impose on the host family.

Although most scout activities built upon traditional village practices, a few occasions were unique to Village Scouts. Foremost among these were the scout anniversary celebrations, commemorating either the date of the troop's initiation session or the date on which it received its troop flag.[19] These celebrations varied according to the energy level of the chapter leadership but could include merit making, fund-raising, and a campfire to which other chapters in the area were invited, as well as their instructors and other government officials.

Thus, when the government authorized the resumption of Village Scout initiations in May 1977, San Patong District already had a clear Village Scout presence. Samsen Subdistrict and Samsen Village also had a limited Village Scout presence. In Samsen and in the district in general the overall reputation of the Village Scouts was mixed. Leftist villagers, familiar with use of the organization for the surveillance and harassment of activists, disliked the Village Scouts. Less politicized villagers believed that the organization was not doing any harm with its involvement in development and merit-making activities, although some resented the pretentiousness of many Village Scouts. Yet other villagers viewed the scouts positively, as a way for villagers to unite to struggle for justice and protect their interests.

Everyday Opinions on Communism

Despite my choice of a relatively unpoliticized village, it was clear that the overall process of politicization of the countryside was occurring here as well. In the wake of the coup official political culture and discourse had become increasingly militarized and focused on the "communist threat." On the radio and TV news broadcasts throughout rural Thailand the lead news item was always the public activities of various members of the royal family. A second regular news feature was the activities of the military, including accounts of real and alleged encounters with communist guerrilla forces. So much did communist suppression fill the news that I recall that one radio listener, an aspirant to the village elite, sighed after one broadcast; he said that he no longer found listening to the news enjoyable. He found the accounts of police and soldiers being killed or wounded to be depressing.

Outdoor movies, shown in a village paddy, village market, or school yard, were a favorite form of village entertainment. In the postcoup period these movies were often anticommunist in theme or subtheme. Movies shown during the first months I was living in the village in 1977 included a film in which Sombat, one of Thailand's most famous leading men, fought communist smugglers; in one subplot, communist smugglers raped a schoolteacher who was teaching poor children in a remote area. Another film shown in the village was called *Saam Nat* or *The Three Bullets*. This movie concluded with the father shooting his son three times for having betrayed the nationalist trio of Nation, Religion, and King.

One of my earliest encounters with the range of villagers' knowledge was a visit in one family's home, where a group of teenage girls was chatting while one girl worked busily on her knitting machine. A poster of Che Guevara hung over the machine. I asked the girls about the picture. Their answers were eclectic. One girl suggested he was a movie star. A second suggested he was a famous singer. Yet another girl knew he was a famous revolutionary who had been killed. In retrospect, as I learned more of the last girl's ordeal in a knitting factory, it is not surprising that the experience had radicalized her. This brief moment showed clearly just how varied villagers' knowledge could be. Villagers had quite different levels of familiarity with communism, depending on their experiences.

Given the frequent references to "communist terrorism" in the mass media and the expansion of armed communist struggle throughout this period, it is not surprising that villagers were using the phrases "communist," "communist terrorist," "comrade" (*sahaaj*), and communism in intense and emotion-laden ways. However, I heard villagers discuss the subject in a variety of contexts, and it was equally clear that they had very confused notions of just what communism was. The mass media—radio was the most relevant at this point in village life—used the term frequently and in a negative context but without necessarily being concrete about communist policies or goals. Consequently, many villagers with no firsthand knowledge of members of the CPT appropriated the term to refer to anything they disliked. Common negative targets in village culture were outsiders and nonvillagers in general—ironically, elites and urbanites, categories that often overlapped. Thus one villager informed me that "rich people are communists; they are too lazy to work." Another villager saw communism as essentially an urban plot to increase rural taxation: "Communists want town people and workers to pay less taxes and villagers to pay more taxes. Villagers now pay eight baht per rai in taxes to the state, but under communism, villagers would have to pay everything to the state and then just be given what they needed to live on day by day."

Villagers' opinions of communism also varied according to their economic situations. Some villagers, usually those with land, identified communism with government control of their lives. Thus a common comment that landed villagers made about communism was that if the communists won, villagers would have to sell everything to the state and receive rice day by day, liter by liter. However, landless villagers took this same idea, of the state's taking responsibility for feeding its citizens, not as an indication of government harassment but rather as a positive policy that they would like to see implemented. Landless villagers complained that rich people in the village were getting so lazy that they would rather sell all their rice to middlemen in the cities than to other villagers; thus landless villagers were now having to import rice into the village, a process that was time consuming and expensive because it involved transportation costs. To them, a government that allocated rice to all its citizens would be an improvement over their present situation.

However, even wealthier villagers were not necessarily supportive of existing government policies, and many felt that the government was forcing villagers to turn communist. For example, during the civilian period the government tried to extend low-interest loans to villagers, especially through the government cooperatives and groups under the Bank of Agriculture and Agricultural Cooperatives (BAAC). At the time interest rates of 5 to 10 percent per *month* were normal in villages, but BAAC charged only 12 percent per *annum*. According to BAAC's policies, villagers could form groups of up to fifteen people to guarantee each other's loans; thus landless villagers could borrow money if they could form a group with other villagers willing to use their land as collateral for the group loan. This policy was praised by many villagers—most notably those landless villagers who were able to join a group but also by those seeking lower interests rates.

However, some landed villagers, understandably reluctant to risk their land in a group venture, resented the pressure placed on them to guarantee loans for their landless friends and relatives. Other villagers disagreed with what they interpreted as a government policy of encouraging indebtedness. Many of these villagers then faulted the government for turning villagers into communists. As one middle-aged village man explained: "The government's BAAC cooperatives are just helping us get more in debt. It is stupid that a few villagers undertake the risk for all. If someone defaults, those villagers lose their land and then how will they make a living? It'll be no wonder that more people go into the jungle" (khaw paa, i.e., join the guerrillas). But even as some villagers faulted the government agricultural cooperatives for turning villagers into communists, other villagers were campaigning on behalf of the cooperatives, arguing that without the help offered by the cooperatives, villagers would have no choice but to join the communists.

Although most villagers in San Patong District did not seem to have had any firsthand familiarity with guerrillas or communist-controlled villages, some did. Such villagers generally had positive assessments of what life under communism would be like. As another middle-aged villager put it,

> Communism is good for poor people since they would have work to do and enough food to eat, but rich people wouldn't like it, or people that lived comfortably now. [He then paused, looked around and asked jokingly if any police were coming.] The soldiers are the hired forces (rapchang) of people trying to keep themselves in power. In the communist areas there are no problems with thieves or drug addicts. And look at China. China is exporting food and doesn't have all these loans from the World Bank.

With this motley kaleidoscope of political views it is difficult to make an easy generalization about peasants' political consciousness. The situation was much in flux. Villagers could combine pro- and anticommunist comments in the same conversation. In some cases villagers would argue opposite opinions from one conversation to another. Broadly speaking, landed villagers were more likely to be concerned about the possibilities of greater taxation, yet many were highly critical of existing government policy and open to the idea of a government with better centralized control of agriculture and subsidized crops. At first glance landless villagers seem to have presented a broader range of opinion, because of their idio-syncratic definitions of communism. However, once their private defini-tions of communism are reinterpreted in terms of what they defined as good and bad, the opinions of the landless were in fact somewhat less diverse than they initially appeared. The landless were united in their resentment of the wealthy and their desire for the government to provide them with greater assistance.

The multiplicity of views and definitions is testimony to the volatility of political opinion at the time. Both the left and right were making advances, and the countryside was undergoing intense politicization. A personal example illustrates the potential fusion and confusion of left- and right-wing propaganda. Villagers I met frequently asked me if I were a CIA agent or a communist, not necessarily even differentiating the one category from the other. In one case a villager asked me if it were true that I was a CIA agent. Before I even had begun to say no, a neighbor listening in asked if that meant I was a communist. Ironically, although the connotations of *communist* in these contexts were unclear, it was clear that—even among the anticommunist villagers—being a CIA agent was not a positive category.

The Moratorium Ends

Although some members of the Samsen Village elite, themselves Village Scouts, talked from time to time about holding a Village Scout initiation in their area, nothing had ever come of their talk. Even before the mora-torium ended, Samsen villagers learned that their subdistrict had been designated to hold an initiation. Unlike the civilian period, when initia-tions were held in response to local demand, initiations were now being organized in accordance with government objectives. To understand the metamorphosis of the postmoratorium Village Scout movement it is nec-essary to understand the changes in policy and administration that were being implemented nationally.

National Changes

During the moratorium previously initiated scouts were allowed to con-tinue with scout activities. The two main national events in which Village Scouts participated during this time were the king's birthday on December 5 and celebrations around the January wedding of the crown prince.[20] Meanwhile a series of meetings was held to discuss how to reform the Village Scout movement. Toward the end of December a Village Scout advisory board (*anukammakaan*) met in Bangkok to discuss future fund-raising. This meeting included prominent businessmen as well as high-ranking government officials. Because the cost of the kerchief and other basics awarded to each new initiate averaged 14 baht per person, the committee determined that if the movement were to grow by one million new initiates each year, it would need an annual sum of at least 14 million baht just for kerchiefs and other insignia. A steering committee comprised of prominent bank presidents and businessmen was elected to be in charge of fund-raising (*Siam Rath*, December 21, 1976).[21]

The next steps toward reforming the Village Scout movement began with the first of a series of national and regional meetings of officials from both the Ministry of Interior and the Border Patrol Police, held in Bangkok from January 5 to 7, 1977 (*Siam Rath*, December 14, 1976). Subsequent meetings were held in each of the four regions of the country.[22] Newspaper accounts of the various regional meetings suggest a rather diffuse pattern of brainstorming, with few of the announced recommendations actually materializing in the final policy changes made by the Ministry of Interior.[23] Although initial explanations for the moratorium had emphasized the need to standardize the initiations and improve the quality of instruction, no substantial changes were made in the content of the initiation rite.[24] Nor were changes made in the training or recruitment of the scout instructors. When I asked Somkhuan Harikul, the movement's founder, what kinds of changes were made to standardize the initiations, his response was vague. When I asked the same question of local scout instructors who had participated in virtually every initiation session, they could not recall any changes in the basic format of the five-day program.

The important planning meeting that resulted in the final policy occurred under the auspices of the Ministry of Interior on April 4, 1977. As a result of that meeting, the government announced that Village Scout initiation sessions would resume after May 15 (*Daily Times*, April 8, 1977). On April 7, a representative of the Ministry of Interior announced the following policy changes at a press conference:

1. Each province was to submit a complete plan for all the initiation sessions it intended to hold during a given year, detailing the dates and exact locations. Furthermore precedence was to be given to places that had not yet held an initiation session or

had held relatively few. Only those initiation sessions in the annual plan would be authorized.

2. No less than 200 and no more than 320 initiates were to attend a given session.

3. One important member of each household would be encouraged join the movement.

4. Sessions were not to be held in the same location more than twice and no sessions were to be held in scout camps.

5. Every candidate for initiation needed a guarantor. Candidates aged fifteen to seventeen who did not yet have an identity card were required to have their parents or some other respected member of the community serve as their guarantors.

6. Initiates were to bring their own rice and dried foods to the training session. Efforts were to be made to keep all expenses to an absolute minimum, and a committee should be appointed to oversee expenses.

7. Every province was to find space for scout leaders and instructors to work. Statistics regarding new membership were to be sent to the Ministry of Interior as quickly as possible.

8. Once a province had completed the first seven steps, it would be allowed to begin holding initiation sessions after May 15. (*Daily Times*, April 8, 1977)[25]

Hidden in bureaucratese were important policy shifts in recruitment strategy. In the early years of the scout movement the initiations sites were selected on the basis of counterinsurgency considerations; however, during the civilian era sites were chosen according to where the funding and popular interest were strongest. Thus a large number of initiations were held in Bangkok and other large cities and towns, rather than in remote sensitive border villages. The new guidelines specifically discouraged holding initiations in the same place, thereby discouraging repeat initiations in centers with high population density. This shift to the poorer and more remote areas relocated the Village Scout movement from the urban centers controlled by merchants and influential politicians to counterinsurgency terrain. As scout instructors with whom I spoke explained, the subdistricts designated to hold the first initiations after the moratorium were those that had come to be labeled either pink or red.[26]

The procedural changes also served to tighten administrative control on the rank-and-file membership. In the past the Village Scouts had mimicked the cell structure of the CPT; one scout initiate recruited two or three others. However, because earlier troops consisted of recruits from a wide range of places, it was often difficult for them to maintain contact. Sending messages by motorcycle or the other local forms of communication was inconvenient, often inefficient, and sometimes expensive.[27] Under the new procedures troop members were to come from the same area, where their moral character was known and where it would be easy to maintain oversight. Earlier sessions had as many as 500 participants and more (Lohachaala 1976; Vaddhanaphuti 1984:532, 558–59); the new restrictions limited the number of new initiates to no more than 250 to 300 people. This facilitated supervision, both during and after the initiations (Somkhuan Harikul 1991 interview).[28] The injunction to recruit from each household inoculated as many households as possible against the communist threat.

Changes in the administration of initiation budgets further assured government control. According to the scout rules, funds were to be raised independent of the government budget. This rule was part of the reason that initiations came increasingly to be held in urban and town centers where the merchants and other major donors lived. However, after the reformulation of the movement a central budget was allotted to the district officers under the Ministry of Interior. Approximately half the initiation costs were covered, leaving the remainder to be raised in the local community. I tried to determine the source of this central budget; local organizers with whom I spoke understood that it was coming through the BPP.[29] This change in the method of funding sessions was important in facilitating the shift of emphasis from urban power bases to rural counterinsurgency. Such underwriting made it possible to hold sessions in poorer areas where villagers were less likely to have the financial means to sponsor an initiation and were simultaneously more likely to be fertile grounds for communist organizing. Thus as a result of the moratorium a refurbished Village Scout movement under tighter control of the Ministry of Interior emerged.

In the civilian period the impetus for holding a Village Scout initiation was generally voluntary. In the postmoratorium period specific villages were targeted. Just how involuntary the new system could be was shown dramatically by the lengths to which organizers went to hold an initiation in a "red" subdistrict known to have an active communist presence. Before the initiation session began, soldiers were sent in three times to suppress the guerrillas. Tension was high and the instructors traveled under armed guard to the site. One instructor I interviewed described how terrified he was during this session: "I'm only human after all. We had to go in by motorcycle. I rode in there with two policemen carrying м-16s. We were all scared, watching for land mines the whole time." During the whole session, the BPP, the police, and the military were on alert.

The participants were hardly enthusiastic. According to comments made by the district officer, about 160 initiates had signed up. However, on the day the session was to begin, only 30 actually showed up. So the district officer went around asking everyone why they were not attending the session. The would-be participants pleaded illness. The district officer had a scout medic visit the villagers' homes to distribute sets of ten antisickness pills to all of them.[30] The next day, when the session was scheduled to begin, the district officer went around to see how the villagers were doing. When he saw that no one had taken the pills, he concluded that they were not really sick. He believed that between the time the villagers had signed up to be scouts and the time the session was to begin, the communists had gone around "propagandizing" (*pluk kradom*) to discourage villagers from showing up. Consequently, before the session could start, the scout instructors had to persuade more villagers to join. Eventually, they were able to convince another 100 villagers to participate. The session was held with 130 initiates. To add to the complications of this particular session, about 20 percent of the initiates were Hmong (Meo). Although the session had an interpreter, he provided only summaries, not word-for-word translations.

Clearly, this initiation was but a weak echo of those held in "pink" or "white" villages. Not only was this subdistrict rife with guerrillas, it was virtually inaccessible, located about fifteen kilometers over poorly maintained dirt roads from the nearest large village and about twenty-five kilometers from the district town. Hardly any senior scout troop members came to visit the evening campfires during the enforced initiation, and afterward the interactions between this chapter and other chapters in the same district were minimal.[31]

The Moratorium Ends in San Patong District

After the moratorium ended, an avalanche of government-designated initiations followed. San Patong District held three sessions in one month alone. Samsen Subdistrict was one of the first subdistricts targeted to hold an initiation session. Because several tambon leaders were already scouts, Samsen's elite had toyed with the possibility of organizing an initiation session. Nothing had come of their talk. However, in January 1977 the district officer informed the kamnan that Samsen Subdistrict had been designated as one of the next training sites after the moratorium. His subdistrict had been classified as pink and so was a high priority. Furthermore, the district officer informed the kamnan, under the new guidelines the local community would have to raise at least part of the money.

The news came as quite a shock to the kamnan and other members of the village elite. They were stunned that their tambon had been classified as pink. No one was aware of any overt communist activity in the subdistrict; the closest to left-wing activity was a village headman who had campaigned on behalf of the New Force (Palang Mai) Party during the elections. The only subdistrict that was actually red in their opinion was Mae Win, which was heavily forested and lightly populated. The kamnan consulted with three other influential villagers, who were also his closest friends, about how to proceed. They focused their attention on how to raise their portion of the costs of the initiation. The total cost was estimated to be about 15,000 baht, but it was not yet clear whether they would have to raise some or all of the expenses themselves.[32]

The Complications of Initial Preparations: Fund-Raising.

Fund-raising was a major problem. The subdistrict had two or three obvious options. One was a universal levy, but that would hit poorer homes harder than others. Another alternative was door-to-door fund-raising for voluntary contributions. A third possibility was to hold fund-raising events such as a movie or fair. The kamnan and his friends spent considerable time discussing each of these ideas and each met with criticism. The group was strongly opposed to the idea of a village fair and irritated with the district officer for even suggesting the idea. In Samsen Village fairs usually ended in trouble. Two years earlier a village fair ended in disaster when a feud erupted between local youths and youths from a neighboring village. Someone threw a bottle bomb, injuring several people. Given the consumption of liquor, violence was not uncommon. However, in the past youths had fought with fists and occasionally with knives; more recently, guns and even bombs were being used.[33] Because of the bombing incident the village had not held a fair for two years. Movies were somewhat easier to organize than fairs, but the problem of controlling violence remained.

The kamnan and the other villagers with whom he consulted agreed that the best option was to bring the issue up at the next village meeting. The village already had to raise money as part of its levy for building a secondary school in the nearby town; Samsen Village needed to raise 1,500 baht for that project alone. Community leaders decided that both issues could be brought up and discussed simultaneously. The meeting was held in mid-January and attended by about 150 villagers. By the time the public meeting was held, the village leadership had already decided to hold a fair, so there was little controversy or discussion. The store owner, a Wood Badge scout who was enthusiastic about the movement, spoke about the virtues of being a scout. And, as if to allay any doubts, he explained that scout membership carried many financial advantages. He, for example, had been able to buy a 200-baht ticket for the famous Saensak–Monroe Brooks boxing match for a mere 99 baht.[34] The schoolmaster expressed concern that the fair not be held while the students were having exams and that provisions be made that the school grounds be protected because the teachers and students had just planted scores of new flowers and saplings. Another villager commented that permission for the fair would have to be obtained from the district office. Everyone else was quiet. The vote was in favor of holding the festival, providing the district officer approved and that suitable precautions were taken with regard to the school grounds. The meeting then shifted to other topics.[35]

Shortly after the village meeting a delegation from the village traveled to the district office to seek permission for the fair. The delegates first met with the chief of police, who also expressed his concern for maintaining order. The village delegates assured him that they would ensure that nothing happened, that they would personally be involved in the supervision of the event. Once the chief of police had agreed, they talked to the district officer. Because the fund-raising was for the scouts and the school, he agreed to authorize the event.

The fair was held about two weeks later. It lasted three nights and drew hundreds of villagers from the surrounding tambons. Entry cost 5 baht each night for adults or 10 baht for all three nights. There were movies, female dancers for hire, boxing matches, and scores of villagers lined up selling all kinds of local treats and drinks. Every effort was made to ensure there would be no violence. Villagers established checkpoints to search for weapons on each of the four roads leading into the village and again at the only entrance to the school grounds. The school grounds in turn had been walled in with a bamboo fence. In addition the village headmen, their assistants, and other village leaders were on the alert inside the grounds.

These dance-for-hire girls were a new feature of village fairs in the mid-1970s. Although some villagers disapproved, many youths eagerly paid to dance with these nonlocal girls.

The checkpoints were effective: the guards confiscated a gun and several knives. There were minor skirmishes outside the grounds on the first two nights, but these were easily broken up. Trouble began on the last night when villagers found a gun on the person of a policeman out of uniform. He refused to allow the village guards to confiscate it. Because he was a policeman villagers were reluctant to insist. He was allowed to proceed to the entrance to the fair itself. At the entrance to the fair, despite his drunken state and his possession of a weapon, he was again allowed entrance. The inevitable happened. He soon got into a fight with some local village boys. The village elders who had been assigned to keep law and order inside the school grounds did not know he was a policeman because he was out of uniform. Seeing a brawl at hand, they responded as they usually did to brawling village youths—the elders beat all the participants over the head with their bamboo sticks in an effort to break up the fight. This so enraged the policeman that he drew his gun and began shooting. Six shots were fired and three village youths were wounded.

At the time villagers wanted to press charges against the unruly policeman. The following morning, however, they decided it would be wiser to remain silent. They did not want the village to become a target for police harassment in the future. Because various villagers supplemented their incomes with illegal activities such as making moonshine, logging teak, and operating an underground lottery, villagers did not want to encourage frequent police visits. Instead the episode was settled "out of court," with some form of compensation to each of the three families.

This event was important for another reason. It was the first time that an incident from Samsen Village made the radio news. Villagers were shocked to hear how the event was portrayed in the media. The journalists had only spoken with the police chief and had not bothered to travel to the village to interview any of the hundreds of eye witnesses, of which I was one. According to the radio account, a scout campfire was being held in Samsen Village. Some fighting broke out between youth gangs from Samsen and Baan Kaat Village. Police had been invited to keep law and order and tried to break up the fighting. According to the radio account, a policeman had been wounded in the fracas.

To add to the miseries the fair had not proved profitable. Although it grossed more than 20,000 baht, by the time the organizers subtracted the costs of the band, dancing girls, movies, boxing prizes, and hospital stay for the wounded youths, only 2,000 baht remained. Interest in fund-raising for a scout initiation session dwindled. The moratorium had not ended and no one in the village was eager to make any further efforts toward fund-raising. Indeed for months there was no further discussion of holding a scout session in the village. However, once the moratorium was lifted and initiations were being held again, the subject was raised again. The district officer informed the kamnan that his tambon would be having a session in mid-August. He also explained that the government would provide about 6,000 baht toward the session—less than half the cost. The tambon was responsible for raising the remaining amount.

The kamnan again informed the village leadership that their village was to be the site of an initiation and that they would have to raise the balance of the money. Their initial reaction was one of anger and frustration. They had not asked to have a Village Scout session in their subdistrict— why did they have to run around trying to raise money for it—especially in a subdistrict such as theirs, which was poorer than others in the district? Nonetheless they were sufficiently attuned to the national political culture to know that if they refused an initiation, they risked being accused of being communist sympathizers. Their subdistrict was particularly vulnerable because it had recently been reclassified as pink.

The village leaders decided to visit the district officer the next day. They politely suggested that, much as they were honored by this opportunity, their subdistrict was so poor that they did not think they would be able to raise the necessary funds. The district officer replied that, although he sympathized with their problem, there was nothing he could do—the decision to have an initiation rite in their subdistrict had already been made. Once again he suggested that they raise money by arranging a village fair.

The district officer also outlined the several factors contributing to the choice of Samsen Village for an initiation site. Their school was the largest in that subdistrict. Because it was the only school in the subdistrict offering grades one to seven (rather than grades one to four), it drew students from other lower primary schools in the subdistrict. Consequently, it had more of the facilities needed for the session: toilets, a water storage tank, a typewriter, a mimeograph machine, and electricity for microphones. Furthermore, as the largest village of the subdistrict, Samsen would be best able to provide sleeping quarters for the initiates. Finally, the village was also the most centrally located and most accessible of the twelve villages in the subdistrict, thus making travel for potential initiates easier.

Resigned to the inevitability of the initiation rite, the village leaders met again that night to discuss what to do. The village fair had been a disaster and no one wanted to risk holding another. Another complication was that a group of villagers had been showing a series of movies in the village as a private money-making venture. Over the past two years one of the wealthier villagers had allowed a traveling movie company to show movies on his land. The admission fee was 5 baht per person. Although poorer villagers generally allowed their children a special treat during the planting or harvesting season when work was plentiful, they could not afford such expenses often. When movies were shown too frequently, poorer village youths would stand around outside the canvas fence so they could at least listen to the movie. Fistfights increased. At the last movie some disgruntled villagers were so fed up with the continual tension in their families whenever a movie was shown that they slung wads of human feces wrapped in banana leaves at the sponsor's house.

For these reasons the kamnan and his advising friends decided that they would only be inviting more trouble if they held a fair or showed a movie to raise money. Instead they decided to pay a personal visit to each of the wealthier villagers, asking them to make generous contributions. There was no point in asking poorer villagers to contribute because they had no money anyway. Even for temple fund-raisings poorer villagers were hard-pressed to give just 1 or 2 baht. After several days' effort the village organizational "committee" raised 6,200 baht. They had appealed to each donor's love of Nation, Religion, and King, pointing out that the donor's name would be read aloud to all the scouts during the session and in the presence of the district officer. At this point the village's main scout committee, consisting primarily of the local leadership, started to get excited again. To generate contributions they had to convince the donor of the value of the undertaking. In the process they convinced themselves.

Finding Accommodations

The next problem confronting the village organizers was that of finding villagers whose homes were large enough to sleep twenty people, the average size of a scout subgroup, and who were willing to be hosts. Initially, no one wanted the bother of having people going in and out of their homes at all times of the day and night. After some persuasion the organizers lined up the sixteen hosts they needed, but not until the organizers had agreed to include their own houses. This last point is interesting because only one of the four who were doing most of the organizational work was already a Village Scout (he was a Chinese businessman who had moved into the village about ten years earlier and ran the only store of any size in the subdistrict). The others were not scouts and at this point professed no intention of becoming scouts. They were merely organizing the scout session as their duty as village leaders.

Although some people agreed to be hosts because they were flattered to be publicly reminded that their houses were among the largest and most beautiful in the village, and that it would be embarrassing to have guests to the village sleep anywhere else, one incident illustrates the extent to which some people were cajoled into being hosts. A former kamnan who was the son of the village abbot owned one of the most beautiful teak houses in the village. Because he had squandered his money on women, drink, and gambling, all that remained of his former wealth was his house. However, he had never publicly acknowledged that which everyone privately knew, namely, that he was broke and heavily in debt, having mortgaged his land and the house. So when he was approached to act as host, he magnanimously agreed. Had he been approached privately on a one-to-one basis, he might have acknowledged his dilemma. But because he was asked in the presence of several people, he agreed and appeared to participate in all the scout planning and preparations from then on. Two days before the session was to begin, he disappeared. There was great consternation as to when he was planning to return and just where he might have gone. He was known to go on binges for days at a time. Finally, one organizer went to speak with the man's wife. She explained that their toilet was not working and that they did not have any money to fix it. In light of this revelation the organizers found another host, and no further major problems developed in regard to housing.

Organizing the Initiates

The next problem was figuring out who would be initiated. Because Samsen was hosting the initiation and its leaders had done the most work in organizing the session, the organizers—most of whom were from Samsen—felt that they had the right to have a disproportionate number of initiates. The remainder of the places were allocated essentially in accordance with the size of the villages.

The organizers then had to determine who wanted to join. Of the primary village organizers, one was already a scout and the others did not want to join. They felt that becoming a scout was probably good fun for village youths. It might teach them a thing or two about love of Nation, Religion, and King, encourage them to become responsible citizens, and discourage the troublemakers. However, they felt it was not appropriate for women. They were concerned that the chastity and good names of their daughters would be threatened because males and females would be sharing sleeping quarters. Furthermore they thought it humiliating for their wives or sisters to be prancing about like adolescents—after all, dancing was only for teenagers or prostitutes. Nor would any of them be caught dead being addressed publicly before his peers as "boy-child" (*dekchaaj*), which was the case for all initiates during the rite.

However, district officials quickly informed them that all kamnan, village headmen and their assistants, were expected to join. Initial dismay soon dissolved into a feeling of camaraderie, of "Oh well, if I have to do it, let's do it together. Besides, it will probably be fun. Think of all the cute young girls there we can flirt with." With the main village opinion makers agreed that they would all join—after all, their houses were being used, they might learn something, have a good time, and serve the worthy cause of Nation, Religion, and King—numerous other villagers soon decided that they too would join. The opinion makers were related by blood or marriage to virtually everyone else in the village.

At this point the organizers had to strictly enforce the quota system for each village. The host village suddenly had many more villagers who wanted to join than there were spaces available. The list of names was recorded basically on a first-come, first-served basis. Close friends and relatives of the opinion makers tended to be among the first enrolled. The additional names were put on a waiting list in the event of cancellations or unused quotas.

The other eleven villages in the subdistrict all had fairly small quotas. These were easily filled as each village headman and his assistants convinced their friends and relatives to join with them. Only one village did not meet its allotted quota, a failure that led to some criticism of its headman. This village headman was already susceptible to accusations of communist sympathies because he had been an active campaigner for the New Force Party, one of the new moderately left-wing parties formed during the civilian period. However, according to this headman, his villagers were too busy to join the Village Scouts. Unlike other villages in the subdistrict, his village did not have a wide gap between rich and poor but was comprised wholly of small landholders, each of whom owned two to ten rai. Other villages used wage labor, but his village relied primarily on exchange labor. Because the initiation fell during the time of rice planting, the villagers were busy helping each other plant their crops and could not give up their farm work and make other arrangements in order to become scouts. Moreover, because this headman was young, he could not lean on senior villagers to help out in the same way the older organizers could. The extra initiation slots went to Samsen villagers who wanted to attend the session.

Women

Despite its efforts to the contrary, the Village Scout movement was viewed by many villagers—both male and female—as inappropriate for women who wanted to keep their good names. At the session I observed, women had to be pressured to join. Of the forty-five villagers who had signed up from one village, only five were women. In the host village some women who had initially signed up were now changing their minds. Several weeks before the initiation session was to begin, the scout instructors met with the village organizers to discuss why so few women were joining. The scout instructors assured the village leadership that they were well aware of villagers' concerns about hanky-panky during the initiation rites but that they made sure all the scouts were so busy all the time that they had no time for untoward goings-on.

After this meeting the organizers made a special effort to encourage women to join, even consenting to let their wives and daughters join. Although some women agreed, the majority remained firm, absolutely refusing to degrade themselves by public dancing, acting like harlots, and being addressed like little children.[36] One woman under pressure to join angrily exclaimed to me, "If the king thinks we should show our love to him by dancing and singing about, acting like drunken whores, then I want no part of it. If that means that people will say I am a communist, so be it!"

This woman's daughter wanted very much to join. Her reluctant father finally gave her permission over the opposition of her mother. The mother insisted, however, that the daughter would have to get her close girl-friends to join and the father would have to keep an eye on her. Although the housing assignments were supposed to be random, the mother also made the scout instructors agree that her daughter and her daughter's best friend would be assigned to sleep in the house of the mother's relative.[37] With the wives and daughters of the village leadership now beginning to join the initiation more wives and daughters of other village households followed. However, the problem of getting women to join was never really overcome, despite the active encouragement of the village organizers. In Samsen Village 19 of 75 initiates were women. Overall, 69 of the 300 initiates, or 23 percent, were women.

In the end the organizers had no problem finding enough people interested in becoming scouts, although they had the inevitable headaches from people changing their minds right up until the last minute. These three tasks—arranging accommodations, recruiting members, and raising funds—were the only preparations for the scout initiation with which villagers were involved. Other aspects of the session were organized by the scout instructors.

With the stage now set, we are ready to follow villagers through their initiation. The chapter that follows describes the five-day course of initiation in the Village Scouts. The initiation begins with a gauntlet of ants and nervous laughter and ends with a procession to receive the royal kerchief and sobbing hysteria.

A tiger mouth doorway into the initiation grounds of the Village Scouts; the budget for the Samsen Village initiation was too small to pay for a tiger entrance.

6

From Humor to Hysteria: Turning Villagers into Subjects

Even years later, as I reread my field notes of the intense five days and four nights of the Village Scout initiation rite, I am struck by its sophistication and subtlety. Taking a light-hearted approach to a deadly serious enterprise, the Village Scout initiation session beguiled villagers into accepting the movement's agenda of nation building through jokes, skits, songs, and moments of earnest solemnity. Viewing each of the five days of the initiation as a unit of analysis, the ritual becomes a psychological drama in five acts.

The initiation began with the classic phase of all rites of passage—villagers were transformed from their initial status as adults into Village Scout initiates. The second day, which had the most serious intellectual content, taught the history of the Village Scout movement and focused on key symbolic episodes from Thai history. The third day focused on unity-building exercises. The high point of the fourth day came as the initiates were tested on how much they had learned and encouraged to view themselves as virtuous subjects of a mythological kingdom.

The climax of the five-day ritual occurred on the final day, when the initiates received their royal kerchiefs, transforming them into full-fledged Village Scouts. During the closing ceremonies, which were held immediately after the bestowal of the royal kerchief, many initiates were overcome with tears. Some collapsed into sobbing hysterics and were carried on stretchers to a health station that was standing ready. Extra medical personnel (primarily *moh anamaaj*) had been called in to serve special duty. The four nights of sleep deprivation had their full effect. I can assure readers that the immediate short-term emotional effects of the Village Scout ritual should not be underestimated.

Although this account focuses more on the substantive aspects of the initiation, readers should bear in mind that episodes of comic relief were interspersed throughout. Psychologically no less important, the moments of silliness and light-heartedness maintained a festive atmosphere and kept the increasingly sleep-deprived initiates awake. The lead instructors were very professional and had tremendous stage presence. They often generated laughter just by rolling their eyes or acting coy.

The staff drew upon a repertoire of prepared gags to provoke laughter. For example, the instructors called each group and told members to shout in unison that they were present. Suddenly, the lead instructor shouted, "Will whoever is not here, please raise their hands?" Everyone laughed. Periodically, instructors asked initiates to raise their hands high, both to stretch and to keep time to the music. In the middle of explaining the arm movements the instructor added, "Whoever hasn't showered recently, don't raise your arms very high." Again everyone laughed. At another point the instructors asked the initiates if they would like a change of venue. The initiates were not sure how they should answer, but the instructors prompted them to answer affirmatively. Then the instructors told the initiates to pretend they were driving cars. The trainees put keys into the ignition of their imaginary car, put it in gear, gave it some gas, and pretended to steer right and left, according to the instructor's directions. Whenever they drove straight, they were to repeat "ning nong, ning nong." These antics met with laughter, in part because hardly anyone owned a car.

The day's heat only compounded the initiates' sleepiness, so the instructors also had a variety of games prepared for overcoming heat. From time to time the instructors asked the trainees whether they were feeling hot and wanted a fan. The trainees then played a fan game in which everyone waved their hands like fans. At one point initiates were pantomiming. One group was to act out the New Year festival of Songkhran, which includes throwing water on people. The scout instructors used the pantomime to rush in and pour water over as many initiates as they could.

The most common technique was simply to have everyone sing short songs such as "Smile, Smile" (*yym thy yym thy*), "Being on Time" (*trong waelaa*), or "Holiday in America" (*hohliidae amerikaa*). Other frequently used devices included telling initiates to stand up, sit down, dance in place, or chase each other for some reason or another. Instructors also told initiates to stick out their tongues, wiggle their eyebrows, or nod their heads in time to their songs. Sometimes rows of initiates were responsible for making certain nonsensical noises upon seeing a prearranged signal. Often these activities were the basis for competitions among the groups. The losers were then made to dance the duck-waddle dance or the crazy man dance, much to the laughter of all who were watching. When all else failed, instructors banged cymbals in the ears of individuals who had fallen asleep. Such moments were too numerous to include in the chronological account but occurred throughout the session.[1]

Day 1: From Villagers to Tiger Cubs

The most important ritual element of the first day was effecting the transition of ordinary adult villagers into young "tiger cubs," essentially children aged eight to ten (*dekying, dekchaaj*). Because age distinctions are an integral aspect of Thai language and culture, and respect is generally accorded to those of greater age, age reduction was a sensitive step that required some delicacy. The issue was introduced only after initiates were led to believe that something serious and of national importance was taking place. Age reduction was crucial to the initiation session, because it created a context in which the recruits would tolerate silliness and even humiliation. Restoration of age in the concluding phases of the five-day ritual was handled with similar care.

The first day began with registration shortly after lunch. Most villagers arrived by foot, bicycle, and motorcycle. Some villagers, especially those who lived farther away, arrived by truck. Each village initiate was to report in with enough clothing for the five days, toiletries, a blanket, pillow, length of bamboo, and some string. Candidates were also supposed to bring enough milled rice for the five days (four to five liters) and some cash to buy meat and vegetables (about 20 baht). By 4 P.M. everyone had arrived and registered.

Afternoon 1: Identity by Scarf

With registration complete the trainees were ready to be divided into six-teen groups identified by color and known as "color groups" (*muu sii*). The sixteen villagers who had agreed to lend their houses to the scouts for sleeping quarters formed a line. The initiates were sorted into the sixteen color groups in the following order: (1) male villagers and female vil-lagers, (2) male government officials (including village headmen), and (3) female government officials. One by one they sat on the ground behind their respective homeowner, each of whom was hosting a given color group. Each village was called separately to ensure the broadest distribu-tion. Instructors also ascertained whether members of any given color group were relatives; if they were, one relative-trainee was switched with a member of another color group.[2] The instructors explicitly made the point that they wanted the initiates to meet as many new people as possi-ble. To keep everyone's attention from wandering while forming into color groups, the scoutmaster from the Border Patrol Police (BPP) led the new initiates in clapping rhythms and simple Village Scout songs. In the end a representative color group was comprised of eighteen or nineteen people, four or five of whom were women and one or two of whom were government officials.

At this point the instructors distributed temporary scarves. There were actually only eight different colors: red, blue, green, purple, pink, yellow, dark blue, and dark orange. The initiates as a whole were divided into two major groups, Division A and Division B, each made up of the eight colors. For the exercises in the days that followed sometimes Division A was pitted against Division B, and sometimes color groups were pitted against each other, regardless of division. Two scout instruc-tors were assigned to each color group to ensure that everything func-tioned according to plan.

After the colored scarves were distributed, the main scout instructor, a mid-level Border Patrol Police officer, gave some preliminary explana-tions, all conveying a mood that something important and purposeful was occurring. He asked whether anyone had been forced to attend the initia-tion session. When no one responded, he moved on to the preliminary rules. He crisply explained that each member of each color group was to wear his or her scarf throughout the five-day training session. Members of the same color group were to do everything together. Furthermore these color-group scarves were important because only scout initiates could wear them. If they completed their training successfully, these scarves would be replaced on the last day of the initiation rite by the genuine scout scarf provided by the king.

To further heighten the emotional attachment and pride initiates took in their scarves the BPP scoutmaster made comments throughout the training session about how nice they looked as they stood at attention and how good they would look when they finally received their full scout insignia. From time to time passing villagers would stop to watch, especially the campfire sing-songs. The scoutmaster would say, "I notice there are people clapping in time from the sidelines. Too bad none of them will be receiving the royal kerchief." Thus from the very beginning of the session the scarf was the primary focus of attention, serving both as the main way to differentiate initiates from noninitiates and as the forerunner of the royal scarf the initiates would receive at the end of the session.

The Gauntlet: Humiliation and Subordination

After the color scarves were distributed, those government officials and village headmen who were also initiates were summoned for a meeting in the village school. The other trainees were lined up by color group and instructed to pass single file through a gauntlet of instructors holding leafy branches on which red ants had been poured from jars in great profusion. The instructors, who held the branches in both hands, beat the trainees repeatedly on their backs to make sure they were well bitten. As soon as the trainees had passed through the gauntlet, they were met by other instructors standing ready with bowls of flour paste that they smeared all over the faces of the unsuspecting initiates. At the end of the gauntlet was a big sign bearing the message WELCOME! and other placards with scout slogans such as SCOUTS MUST PERSEVERE!, although just how many initiates noticed these signs in all the confusion is unclear.[3] After the ordinary villagers went through the gauntlet, the trainees who were government officials and village headmen were instructed to follow suit.

The effect of the gauntlet can be interpreted in a number of ways. The scout instructors explained that the gauntlet was a fun (*sanuk*) way to say welcome while teaching the initiates that scouts must be able to endure pain and hardship. As Muecke notes, the practice of rubbing flour on the initiates' faces is "a custom adopted from the traditional New Year's celebration" (1980:414). In the New Year rituals water scented with jasmine blossoms symbolizes respect for and best wishes to village elders and leaders as well as government officials. However, people usually use the flour paste as a joke with their peers or younger people, not as a sign of respect for older people, people of higher rank, or strangers. Thus the gauntlet and the flour paste were a rude transition from the decorum that usually marked official functions to the world of the ritual, where everyone was to treat each other as equals, as age-mates. The flour paste made the initiates look comical. Although they laughed it off, many were quite mortified because they were wearing their best clothes.

The gauntlet was a technique for achieving a quick transition from the daily world of reality to the liminal world of ritual (Van Gennep [1909] 1960; V. Turner 1969). Degrading the villagers forced them to lose their individual identity and become scout initiates over whom the instructors had complete power. The gauntlet also paved the way for that evening's revelation: for the duration of the initiation the trainees were to view themselves as children. Putting government officials and village leaders through the gauntlet separately was a way to ease them onto a social footing that temporarily was equal to that of the villagers.

After the initiates had wriggled through the gauntlet, they resumed their places behind their hosts. The instructors led them through a welcome song and then dismissed them for supper. During the ninety-minute supper period they were supposed to get to know each other and choose their color-group leaders. Half the groups were to choose a male head with a female assistant, and the other half were to do the reverse. Specifically eliminated as candidates for positions of leadership were all government officials, village headmen, and the host household heads. Instructors explained that the scout movement would teach them to be both followers and leaders and that because government officials and headmen already were leaders, others should be given the opportunity to lead. The household hosts were declared ineligible for leadership positions to counteract the traditional tendency to choose them as leaders in a gesture of respect.

During the supper break the scouts were also assigned to make a pole on which to mount their color-group flag. The instructors gave them specific instructions that included how long the pole should be as well as how they were to walk to and from their sleeping quarters: the group head was to walk in front, and the rest were to follow in single file, with the assistant head bringing up the rear. The instructors explained that this arrangement was both to ensure that people would not get lost and to instill the scout virtue of orderliness (*khwaam riaprooj*). Finally, everyone was told to reassemble at the school grounds at 7:30 P.M. sharp. Thus the scoutmaster set a paternalistic tone even before the official age-reduction took place; the initiates were already being treated as if they were schoolchildren.

Night 1: Unity Against External Enemies

The evening session began with a series of songs and speeches that emphasized the need for political unity against external enemies. After some initial clapping rhythms the instructors led the initiates in a simple song about the closeness felt by brothers and sisters. The second song, sung as a bass solo by the BPP instructor, was a patriotic song about the role of Thai soldiers in defending the nation from enemies and their willingness to sacrifice their lives so that the nation might be free. Stirringly performed, this song set a melodramatic mood intimating that the initiates were somehow about to play a vital role in defending the Thai nation. The trainees learned another song, the refrain for which roughly translates as "It's nice to meet you, my friends. / We should join our hearts and love each other wholly as brothers and sisters. / My friends, let our hearts be joined." They sang this song several times, with all the initiates holding hands, creating a feeling that they were indeed members of one large family, united against the outside.

After teaching the initiates how to salute nicely, the instructors announced the arrival of the district officer and head district education official. The scouts saluted as the district officer walked up to the microphone. He began by welcoming the initiates and noting that they were following in the path laid out by King Rama VI (1910–1925), the founder of the scout movement in Thailand. The district officer encouraged an aura of exclusivity by commenting that the trainees were among the fortunate few who had been able to join this initiation session. He said he had been informed that, although there were three hundred trainees in this session, three hundred more had been turned away. He said that many who had been turned away cried, saying that if they could not join this session, they would surely die.[4] He noted that although he had made special inquiries of provincial officials, he had been told that the ceiling for each initiation could not be raised.

The major portion of his speech dealt with the current political situation in Thailand and its neighbors:

> Although Village Scouts are not to be involved in politics, politics comes to involve itself with Village Scouts. You probably know

already from the newspaper headlines that Cambodia has been invading Thailand, killing Thai people, burning Thai villages located on the border, killing innocent children and old people unable to fight and defend themselves in great numbers. The reason that Cambodia is attacking our people is because Cambodia has changed its form of government from a democracy to communism. Cambodia does this because they do not have enough to eat. Cambodia has no water buffaloes or oxen to plow their fields; they use people to plow the fields instead. Cambodia is a country without moral principles. Cambodia has been receiving rice from other countries. Iran has sent sixty thousand bags of rice to Laos. But the Lao people have not been able to eat any of it, not a single grain. They go hungry as they must give all their rice to the Vietnamese soldiers who have taken over their country. The Cambodians are not only attacking Thailand, but they are also invading Vietnam on their other border. The Cambodian government is invading Thailand because they need food, so that their people will be satisfied with their new government. Thailand has never given in or retreated, so now Thailand must take arms and fight back. This is the reason for the headlines you have been reading. This is the result of the fall of a democratic government which had a king as head of state.

Other countries are watching us now. Once the change has happened, there is no turning back. Look at Vietnam, Cambodia, and Laos. Before they lived in peace and quiet, now they live in turmoil. People are fleeing these three countries in great numbers, by the hundreds of thousands, coming across the Mekhong River. They tell us that people can't live there—dogs can't even live there. This is a fact that Thailand must face. Refugees now number more than one million people. If we were to become like Cambodia, Laos, and Vietnam, where would we and our dogs and animals flee to for refuge?

He concluded by saying that if the Village Scouts succeeded in unifying people from different backgrounds into a single force, they would help to ensure the survival of Thailand.

The theme of external threats to Thai security was repeated throughout the training session. On the last day the BPP instructor said that scouts and all citizens who loved their Nation, Religion, and King must unite to fight off those who sought to harm the country. He explained, "Right now in Laos and Cambodia, they are giving Lao men a potion that reduces their sexual desire and are having Vietnamese troops breed with Lao women instead. Soon there will be nothing left of Lao and Cambodian cultural traits. Soon the words *Cambodian* and *Lao* will no longer exist. Already enemy troops are infiltrating Thailand. This is why it is so important that the Thai people unite."

He went on to suggest that the violence on October 6, 1976, was caused by Vietnamese communist commandos ("sappers") who were trying to destroy the Nation, Religion, and King. The scout instructors were clearly trying to portray Thailand as a nation whose cultural survival was being threatened by external enemies who were infiltrating the country. For Thailand to survive Thais had to unite and not allow internal divisions to occur.

Unity Through Age Reduction

The suggestion of external enemies and the need to unite set the stage for the next major step in the scout training session. By far the most important event of that first night was the ritual reduction of all initiates' ages to that of children aged eight to ten. Easing the transition from village adults to scout children were the afternoon's gauntlet and such comments made earlier in the evening session as, "We must love each other like brothers and sisters (*phii nong*). Everyone here is equal, no high, no low, no rich, no poor." Between songs the BPP instructor encouraged the initiates to forget the differences in their backgrounds. He noted that they came from all over, from different walks of life, from different villages. Some might have known each other in the past and had conflicts, but they should forget such ill feelings.

The BPP scoutmaster introduced the problem of generating unity among initiates of such diverse backgrounds by explaining, "At present some of the initiates are old people aged seventy and others are young, aged fifteen. Some of you are high-ranking officials and others of you are not. Some of you are rich, and others of you are poor. The district education officer is now going to explain how we are going to reduce such differences." The district education officer made the formal announcement:

> Since all of you are from different backgrounds and ages, I would like to ask all of you to reduce your ages to that of children. I ask your cooperation in this. From now on, all of you, regardless if you are high-ranking police or government officials, are young boys and girls. We do this because we want all of you to feel as comfortable

as possible with each other. We want you to be as unselfish and caring for each other (*khwaam yyafya phyaphae chenkan laekan*) as possible and to feel united. Some of you are seventy and some of you are
fifteen years old. But from now on, we would like you to pick an age
between eight and ten. From now on you are all boys and girls. You
are all of equal age and equal status.

The BPP scoutmaster then took over the microphone and asked the initiates whether they were all willing to be children. If so, they were to
cheer in assent. A simple song about being on time followed. Then, to
impress upon the initiates that this transition had been effected, six older
initiates were summoned to the microphone and asked their names and
ages. Although these initiates would normally have been addressed as
Grandfather or Grandmother, they were now addressed as *dekchaaj* and
dekying, or Boy-child and Girl-child. The scoutmaster teased and chided
them:
"What is your name?"
"Grandmother Khamlaa."
"No, you're Dekying Khamlaa. So how old are you?"
"I'm forty-nine."
"No, you're ten."
"How many children do you have?"
"Six."
"No, you are ten, so how can you have so many children?!"
"Are you married yet?"
"Yes."
"What! At age ten!"
Because all had given their real ages rather than their new ages, the
scoutmaster chastised them by making them mimic a duck and perform
the duck-waddle dance back to their places. Everyone else laughed and
sang the duck-waddle song: "This is what a duck looks like, not a pretty
sight at all!" Indeed the scoutmaster used the duck-waddle dance for the
first time immediately after the age-reduction phase.

Rules: Reputation and Infiltration

With everyone back in place the BPP instructor went on to explain the
rules for the initiation. The rules were simple: no liquor consumption, no
smoking except during rest breaks, no weapons, and no flirting—"after
all, you are children, not adolescents." Everyone was encouraged to help

everyone else in everything they did. As the education officer explained, "We want you to sleep together, eat together—do everything together except shower together. If we are separated, we shall die. If we stay together, we will overcome. Unity is necessary for the prosperity of the nation, for the survival of the country."

The scoutmaster raised the specter of infiltrators and the importance of preserving the reputation of the scouts and their scout group to vouchsafe their behavior. He cautioned initiates not to do anything that would in any way damage the scouts' reputation, lest they fall victim to communist infiltrators and others who tried to pose as scouts and "do bad things to undermine the integrity of the movement." The BPP instructor was particularly concerned about the problem of flirtation: "If you meet someone at the session who interests you, you are welcome to flirt after the training session is over. If you decide to marry, the instructors would be delighted to attend the wedding. However, do not let anything happen here that would hurt the scout movement. The opposition tries to do things like this to us, so we will lose our reputations."

Guarding against infiltration was also the reason given for requiring all initiates to wear their scarves at all times. The instructors implied that any trainee who misbehaved was probably a communist, an outsider.[5] They also announced that anyone who created trouble by getting into fights or causing disruptions would be turned over to the local police.

The evening session concluded with a skit in which a few instructors demonstrated how good scouts kept their belongings neatly folded in their sleeping quarters and tried to find ways to help others. Bad scouts snored and strewed their belongings all over while others worked. As was to happen each night, the session closed with everyone chanting the Three Refuges of Buddhism in Pali and singing the Royal Anthem while facing south toward the royal palace in Bangkok.[6] The initiates then went to their respective quarters, where they still had to elect their color-group leaders.

Day 2: A Day of Lessons

On the second day initiates were about as mentally alert as they were going to be. Sleep deprivation would soon take its toll, so it is not surprising that most substantive lessons were concentrated on this day. The primary lessons included learning the scout oath, history of the scout movement, scout salute, ten scout laws, history of the Thai flag, and certain key episodes from Thai history.

Morning 2: Homage to King Rama VI

The instructors roused the initiates at 5 A.M. after about five hours' sleep. While some made breakfast, others prepared placards and a flagpole to decorate their sleeping quarters. After breakfast they assembled at the school yard at 7:30 A.M. The morning session began in the thatch-roofed meeting hall specially erected on one side of the school grounds. The trainees began by singing songs about smiling, being glad to meet each other (sung with hands held), arriving punctually, and not disdaining work. The initiates were then taught the threefold scout oath:

1. Scouts are to love the Nation, Religion, and King.
2. Scouts are to help others at all times.
3. Scouts are to follow the scout laws.

The initiates were then taught a special song in honor of King Rama VI, the official founder of the Wild Tiger Corps and the Boy Scouts of Thailand.

After these initial preparatory instructions and the formal introductions of the scout staff instructors, the morning session officially began. The instructors told the initiates to stand up and said that anyone wearing a hat should take it off. The instructors, all dressed in their full scout uniforms, led the group in chanting the Three Refuges, the threefold scout oath, and the singing of the Royal Anthem.[7] The district officer made a brief speech describing the statistical composition of this initiation session and its budget. He said that the total budget for the initiation session was 12,550 baht, with 5,000 baht from the district office and 7,550 baht from voluntary private contributions.

The provincial forestry official gave the keynote address, noting that the purpose of the scout initiation was to engender love for the Nation, Religion, and King:

> I feel it is a great honor to open this session of the Village Scouts being held at the Samsen Village School. In the name of the provincial governor I welcome you. Initiation into the Village Scouts is for the purpose of sensitizing the people (*chakchung citcaj khong pracha-chon*) so they will love the Nation, Religion, and King and to create unity among the people for the security of the nation. It is to create one heart among all members of the Village Scouts. You are probably well aware of contemporary events. I can think of nothing more

important than to create unity and encourage a willingness to sacrifice for the common good. If everyone will follow this principle, unity will definitely result. Everyone must show that they are generous and have concern for their fellow man.

In the next four to five days you will come to know each other well, so let me make one further point. Flirting is an important infringement of the Village Scout code (*vinaya*). To honor means to respect, to have integrity. Therefore one shouldn't do anything that one knows is wrong. The scout code states that Village Scouts are honorable and trustworthy. I'd like to thank you and entrust my best wishes to you and your instructors that this session be productive.

After the opening speeches everyone moved into the open area of the school grounds and formed a large circle, each group behind its respective color-group flag. A statue of King Rama VI had been placed in the middle, near the flag pole. While everyone stood at attention, an instructor walked forward and performed a full kneeling bow (*kraap*) before the statue. Everyone assumed a kneeling position and sang a song for Rama VI the initiates had just learned. Then everyone stood at attention again, and instructors assigned two color-group leaders to raise the Thai flag. As they raised the flag, the BPP instructor cried out, "Thailand is a free country, dominated by no one." All then sang the Royal Anthem and were told to salute. Because the initiates did not salute simultaneously, they had to repeat the salute several times until it was properly executed (*riaprooj*). The BPP instructor then led them in chanting the Three Refuges, followed by a long moment of silence in which they were to reflect on the good deeds of King Rama VI. The trainees shouted, "We will do good!" three times and recited the scout oath. All initiates then were dismissed for a five-minute break during which they were free to smoke a cigarette, get a drink of water, or use the restrooms.

The special ceremony paying homage to King Rama VI was particularly interesting, given that the Village Scout movement did not start during his reign but during the reign of the current king, Rama IX. King Rama VI started the Wild Tiger Corps (*sya paa*) and the Thai Boy Scouts (*luuk sya*). However, paying homage to King Rama VI served as more than mere recognition of his role in founding these related but different organizations. The homage was also an indirect way to affirm the nationalistic ideas Rama VI propounded in his speeches and writings. Furthermore linking the Village Scout movement with King Rama VI contributed to the legitimacy of the Village Scouts by giving it a longer history, implying that the movement did not begin in the early 1970s but at the turn of the century.

The Importance of Thai Traditions

After the break the scouts reassembled in the meeting hall, and those who were late were made to dance the duck-waddle dance. Although the second half of the morning sessions was larded with silliness to recapture wandering attentions, the thrust was nonetheless patriotic. The instructors taught the trainees a slow song of tribute to the royal family, each verse in honor of a different member. As they were singing the song, some initiates began to clap in time. The instructors reprimanded initiates, saying that because this was a royal song, they were not to clap. This admonition thereby set royal songs apart from other scout songs. At the end of the song everyone shouted, "Chaiyo!" or "Hurrah!" three times, raising their right hands to their chests.

In this session the instructors gave a talk on how to dress in a manner that reflected the best of Thai tradition and culture. They told the men to keep their hair clean and short, their shirttails tucked into their pants, and not to roll up their shirtsleeves or pant legs. One instructor told the women never to wear Bermuda-length shorts. The woman who gave this presentation was wearing customary dress, a fitted long-sleeved blouse and a long straight skirt (for a discussion of northern Thai dress see Bowie 1992). The fashions demonstrated included variations on how to dress when meeting a member of the royal family. The instructor admonished women to continue the practice of wearing flowers in their hair because it was so feminine. She encouraged villagers to keep neat homes and plant many flowers. She reassured villagers that they should not feel embarrassed about speaking the northern dialect in front of government officials because it is a lovely language. Concluding her presentation with a discussion of the proper way to dance, she summarized her talk by observing that "if Thailand is to maintain its independence, Thais must keep their traditions and culture alive."

The next presentation explained various whistle patterns. A long whistle meant that all scouts should stop instantaneously and listen for further orders. Another pattern meant they should get into formation. A third call indicated an accident had occurred. Another call, a series of three long blows and a short one, was used during the flag lowering, also done in four stages.

The Scout Salute and Social Connections.

The BPP instructor next explained in greater detail the symbolism of the scout salute. The three fingers are a reminder of the threefold oath taken by all scouts.[8] The little finger is a reminder that junior scout troops must listen to senior scouts (ranked according to who was initiated first). The thumb represents the 108 countries of the world that have scout troops and hence are brothers and sisters.[9] He noted that there are two styles of saluting—the British style, in which the arm is kept closer to the body, and the American style, in which the arm is held away from the body. The Village Scouts used the British style. Scouts were to salute while the flag was being raised, when the Royal Anthem was being sung, or when they met other scouts.

The BPP scoutmaster then went on to say that the scout salute was an important signal. He suggested that by joining the scout movement, the initiates were entering a useful network of connections; he even suggested that otherwise illegal activities might be overlooked. He implied that the scout salute was like the secret sign of an elite group. He explained how one night he was returning from the city of Chiang Mai alone at about 12:30 A.M. He was carrying a gun for which he had an owner's license but no permit to carry it on his person. He was stopped by a police officer and was worried that he would be charged with violating the gun control laws. So he greeted the police officer with a scout salute. It turned out that the officer was a scout. Although he had noticed the gun, the police officer decided that because the scoutmaster was a scout, he would not misuse it. So the officer did not press any charges and sent the scoutmaster on his way with best wishes for a safe journey home.

The scoutmaster went on to say that he knew of another case that had occurred during World War II. It seems a Thai soldier was fighting in hand-to-hand combat with a Japanese soldier and ended up pinned to the ground. Believing his death was certain, he decided he would like to die in a scout salute position. He raised his hand in the scout salute. The Japanese soldier was startled; he recognized the salute because he too was a scout, and he spared the Thai soldier's life.

During the morning of the last day, the BPP instructor further encouraged the association of special privileges and being a scout. In discussing the membership cards that the initiates would receive the BPP instructor commented on their importance. He suggested that if, for example, a police officer stopped scouts on the road and was about to ticket them for failure to carry their driver's license (a common complaint because most villagers drive without licenses), they could show their scout identification cards. The officer might then be willing to show leniency and not press charges. The BPP instructor did caution the initiates to do this only once and not as a matter of habit. He noted that some scouts had abused their privileges by trying to get into movie theaters free and creating scenes when denied free passes. He admonished them not to abuse the honor of being a scout but nonetheless suggested that there might be times when scout membership might stretch the limits of the law. This was not lost on villagers, who after the session commented that they would be sure to carry their scout cards with them when they left the village to go into town.[10]

Afternoon 2: The Scout Laws

The afternoon session was more games and songs, interspersed with the teaching of the ten scout laws:

1. Scouts are persons who are trustworthy.
2. Scouts love their Nation, Religion, and King.
3. Scouts have a duty to help others.
4. Scouts are friends to everyone, including other scouts all over the world.
5. Scouts are well mannered and polite (suphaab riaprooj).
6. Scouts are kind to animals.[11]
7. Scouts respectfully follow the orders of their parents and superiors.
8. Scouts persevere in the face of difficulty.
9. Scouts are thrifty.
10. Scouts are well behaved (phraphyyt choop).

In discussing kindness to animals the BPP instructor explained that scouts, unlike the enemies of the nation (i.e., communists), do not kill or harm other people. In regard to perseverance in the face of difficulty he commented that no matter how poor or despairing scouts are, they never give up trying and never commit suicide. In regard to thrift he admonished the initiates to buy goods produced in Thailand rather than in foreign countries, lest the balance of trade be upset. He encouraged them to spend their money wisely and to try to save money in a bank to use for emergencies such as illness or accidents. Rather than spend their money on the latest fashions, they should give their money to the temple or the Village Scout movement so it could help develop the nation, religion, and monarchy. The last scout rule was interpreted as meaning that scouts should not argue or criticize others but should try to do and say only that which benefits society. Scouts should have no false cravings (*kilesa*) or attachments to things that belong to others.

The interpretations of these scout laws reveal much about the intended thrust of the Village Scout movement. The scouts were to be dutiful, uncritical, undemanding members of society who solved their own problems. Implicit was a suggestion that if they were poor, they had not persevered sufficiently or had not been frugal enough. The movement did not encourage the independent thought or reasoned debate necessary for a pluralistic democracy but instead encouraged an orderliness and a passivity compatible with an authoritarian government. During the rest of the afternoon the trainees learned to tie rope knots and played games and sang songs designed to keep everyone awake.

Night 2: Where to Flee?

The evening session began with lighthearted singing and dancing. The mood changed dramatically when the BPP scoutmaster sang a moving patriotic military song. His voice, a rich resonant bass, captured everyone's attention. There was complete silence. The instructors admonished the initiates to listen carefully to the words and think about their meaning. The song asks,

> How many wounds have been stabbed into the Thai nation?
> How many generations of our forefathers have died before the Thais settled in this peninsula?
> How many bones have been crushed and cremated?
> How many heads decapitated until the Thais ruled this land?
> How much blood has been shed?
> How many times have hearts broken?
> Tears fall in the eyes of all Thais each time we lose our land.
> Why do we kill each other?
> We are all Thais together.
> If Thais kill each other, other nations will rule us.
> Then the souls of our forefathers (*winyan puu*) will cry out,
> "You descendants are damned (*canraj*)."

The instructors then gave a presentation on the history of the Thai flags, beginning with the flag of King Rama I. Thailand's current flag was designed during the reign of King Rama VI, the same monarch who founded the scout movement in Thailand. The instructors pointed out that earlier flags had been reserved as a symbol of royalty, but this flag belonged to the nation. The white represents the Buddha, the blue the monarchy, and the red the blood of the nation. The instructors also explained that "the flag demonstrates the independence of a nation. Whichever country has a flag is a country sure to have its independence."

After a few songs and jokes a schoolmaster from another district gave a stirring lecture on Thai history. He told of how the Thai people originally lived in southern China but that because of fighting the Thai had migrated slowly southward, following the Salween and Mekhong Rivers. Using an enormous map specially prepared for his talk, he showed where the Thais had formed small city-states in northern Thailand.[12] He showed the vast expanse of territory that had been part of the Thai nation during the thirteenth-century Sukhothai period, an area that incorporated much of present-day Burma, Laos, Cambodia, Malaysia, and even southern China. He explained how Thailand had fought to maintain its independence throughout history, noting the efforts of Phra Naresuan in 1590 and Phrayar Taksin in 1767 to reunify the country after it had fallen to the Burmese.

Beginning with the vast territories under Thai jurisdiction during the reign of the Sukhothai king, King Ramkhamhaeng (1275–1317 A.D.), the schoolmaster described when, how, and to whom these territories had been lost. He explained how land in present-day Burma and Malaysia was lost to the British and how land in present-day Laos and Cambodia was lost to the French. He noted that Thais have been willing to sacrifice smaller portions of land in order to preserve the integrity of the core of Thailand. The last land lost was the famous temple of Khaw Phra Wiharn, given to Cambodia as the result of a World Court decision in 1962. At this point the schoolmaster cried out through the night air in a deep powerful voice, "How much more land are we willing to lose?" The schoolmaster then went through the number of square kilometers sacrificed at each juncture. He concluded his dramatic presentation by crying, "And now the twelve provinces of the Northeast want to separate from Thailand. Four provinces of the South want to separate and join Malaysia. This is Thailand's last stand. We cannot afford to lose any more land. We have nowhere to go now but into the sea." The BPP instructor then took the microphone and sang a slow song: "Whoever invades Thailand, Thais will fight on to the end of our abilities. / We are willing to sacrifice our blood and our lives because even if one dies, one's names will live on in honor. / If Siam survives, we will also live. / If Siam collapses, how can we hope to live on? / It would be the end of our lineage."

The Fall of Ayuthaya: Of Traitors and Unity

After the schoolmaster's lecture set the historical stage, instructors performed two plays.[13] Virtually the entire staff had a role in the cast or stage crew. Each play began with the traditional formalities in which the actors pay tribute to their drama teachers and beg forgiveness from them and their audience for any aspects of their performance that might be inappropriate. Stagehands moved in the set for the first play, and the actors, beautifully costumed, took their positions as other instructors sang a song about the bravery and daring of Thai ancestors. The chorus was "Get ready, my brothers and sisters. / We are the blood of free Thais and will not let ourselves be conquered by our enemies." The set was stunning. Replicas of village houses, made of bamboo and thatch, were built on the periphery. A white Styrofoam temple and stupa , located in the center, cut a stark contrast against the night sky. (A stupa is a moundlike structure in which a Buddha bone or other relic is said to be buried.) Over the microphone came this announcement: "This is the story of the city of Ayuthaya, once the prosperous capital of Siam. It was a city which had met with many obstacles and survived. But ultimately it collapsed. Tonight we consider why it fell."

The background for the performance was given by the actor playing the role of the acting ruler of the city of Ayuthaya:

This city has been well built. The bridges and foundations of the city are strong, and we are now fortifying the gates to the city. We must hurry as the Burmese are now preparing to attack us. We must make absolutely sure that our fortifications will hold. The Burmese have already captured our ruler, Phrayar Chakri, and his close advisers. We don't know if he is already dead or if he is still alive and can be ransomed. Still our people are united and in the meantime have asked that I be their leader. Burma has started its invasion. Soon they are going to be starting another onslaught. The women are heating

The set of the ancient city of Ayuthaya.

up the gravel and sand.[14] The men are walking guard, two by two. Some men are helping the women boil water. When the Burmese try to come through the city gates or climb over the walls, we will pour the hot stones and water over their heads. The first to break through our defenses will be the first to get it.

In another corner of the area that served as the stage the "Burmese" were discussing their strategy. A Burmese soldier noted that Burma had surrounded Ayuthaya many times but had never succeeded in taking the city. The Burmese decided they would never be able to storm the city by sheer force and had to devise an alternate tactic. Another Burmese suggested that there must be some way to deceive Ayuthayan soldiers into unwittingly joining forces with them. The Burmese then settled on a plan to convince Phrayar Chakri, whom they had captured, to help them take the city. They sent for Phrayar Chakri and suggested to him that, in exchange for his help in capturing the city, they would reinstate him as ruler of Ayuthaya. At first Phrayar Chakri refused, saying, "I am a Thai. Even though I have been living in Burma, Thai blood runs in my veins. Even if you threaten to kill me, I still will not help you. My Thai blood won't let me." The Burmese then tried to persuade Phrayar Chakri's advisers, at first to no avail. However, in a "private" consultation with

Phrayar Chakri, one adviser suggested that he could trick the Burmese by appearing to agree and then kill them later. So Phrayar Chakri told the Burmese that the Ayuthayan forces on the northern side of the city were strong and the weaker forces were at the southern gate. He would go into the city and have the two divisions switched. As proof of his good faith he agreed to be whipped fifty times by the Burmese.

Phrayar Chakri then returned to the city of Ayuthaya and was greeted by all his concerned followers. Some Ayuthayans argued that the position of leadership should not be returned to Phrayar Chakri because he might be a traitor. They thought it strange that after four to five months in captivity he would be allowed to return at this time. However, the majority decided to reinstate Phrayar Chakri, and the leader of the dissent was executed. Once reinstated, Phrayar Chakri informed the Ayuthayan soldiers that he overheard the Burmese plans and knew that they planned to attack from the south. Therefore he ordered the stronger troops to stand guard at the south gate, while the weaker forces stood guard at the north.

The Burmese attacked, complete with gunpowder set off in bamboo rockets. The Burmese soon won and arrested all the Ayuthayans, including Phrayar Chakri. The Burmese commander admonished Phrayar Chakri, saying, "Did you really think you would rule here? If you could sell the country of your birth, then you could also sell us out later." Phrayar Chakri was then taken away to be executed, while the temple and homes were literally set on fire. As the set burned amid the oohs and aahs of the onlooking initiates, a mournful song was sung:

> To listen to the story of our ancient city of Ayuthaya
> > Makes the heart heavy.
> Once it was a famous golden city of all Thais.
> Now it lies in ruins, making us feel a sadness 100,000-fold over.
> It was destroyed by enemies. Every Thai heart is pained.
> The soldiers burnt it completely. We who are the descendants
> > Are sad to listen to its demise.
> It is a memorial to us that we must be firm and united,
> > So no one will ever dare to destroy the Thai nation again.

The BPP instructor then spoke solemnly:

> My brothers and sisters. This is the story of the first fall of Ayuthaya. Ayuthaya fell a first time and then a second time because Thais themselves were traitors. But in the end, the traitors died with the

city of Ayuthaya. Fellow brothers and sisters, when Ayuthaya was destroyed the second time, its temples and palaces were destroyed, burnt by the soldiers. If you ever have a chance to travel to Ayuthaya, stop and see the ruins. See first hand the ruins that pain every Thai heart.

Ayuthaya fell for the second time because of the greed for power. Tonight we saw just a reproduction of what happened, but imagine how you would have felt if you had had to see the real thing. Fathers separated from children, children separated from their mothers, husbands separated from their wives. Those who survived were taken to be slaves of Burma. On the long walk from Ayuthaya to Hongsawaddi (Burma), they met with a hundred thousand difficulties but still they survived.

The major message of this performance was not only that the Thais should stand united but also that they should not betray one another, lest they fall prey to agents of foreign powers trying to undermine the unity of the nation.

Burmese and Thai "soldiers" fighting.

Valiant Thai Villagers

The second play also dealt with the wars between Burma and Ayuthaya. In this scene the Thais knew in advance that the Burmese would attack before help could arrive. The men prepared to fight to the bitter end. One man summoned his wife and children and told them of the decision. He explained that fighting would soon erupt and it was likely that he and all his comrades would be killed. He asked his wife to raise their children well and not to let them forget what happened in this village, so that one day their children would take revenge on his behalf. The wife replied that she would rather kill herself and their children if anything happened to him. Finally, however, she tearfully agreed to fulfill his last request.

The women and children repaired to a safe distance as the men prepared to do battle. The Burmese attacked, but despite the valiant efforts of the Thai villagers, the Thais were all killed. The commander of the Burmese troops stood over the corpses of the Thai villagers and praised them for their bravery. Even though they were untrained villagers, they dared to fight his trained troops. Consequently, he forbade his soldiers to ransack the town and told his troops to take a lesson from the unity and bravery of these noble villagers. After a song on the importance of loving the nation, the master of ceremonies called out the names of the Thai villagers who died in battle, assuring them that their descendants would never forget their sacrifice. One by one each slain villager stood up and assumed a fighting pose, holding his wooden sword outstretched. The women then joined the men and performed a graceful sword dance in slow motion.

The BPP instructor then brought the evening session to a close, reviewing what the initiates had learned and seen that night. He reviewed the lands lost to foreign countries and the current threats to the provinces of the far south and northeast. "Where," he asked, "can Thais flee to now? Now only the sea is left to flee to. We can no longer retreat. We must fight. Are we willing to fight?" The initiates cry back, "Yes, we will fight." In a scene reminiscent of the mass rallies in film clips from Nazi Germany, the scout initiates repeated several times, "Yes, we will fight." They raised their right arms in the air, their hands clenched in fists. The evening concluded with the singing of the Royal Anthem at about 1 A.M.

Day 3: Developing the Theme of Unity

By the beginning of the third day of the initiation ritual the initiates were feeling the effects of sleeplessness. Although the previous evening's drama ended about 1 A.M., the initiates still had several activities they had to complete before reconvening at the school grounds again the following morning.[15] They had to make posters to help them memorize the ten scout laws and fill in personal data forms for the scout instructors. The earliest any initiate got to sleep was about 2 A.M. Consequently, when they were awakened at 5 A.M., they had had only about three hours of sleep. In the morning, in addition to marketing and preparing breakfast, they had to dig holes for garbage and make such things as toothbrush holders from lengths of bamboo.

Whereas the second day was filled with considerable historical content, the third day was much lighter and primarily oriented toward the theme of unity. The highlight was to be the evening campfire session for which Village Scouts from other chapters throughout the area would visit. The language used to refer to these chapters was kin based, suggesting that older siblings, those initiated earlier (*run phii*), were visiting their younger siblings, or those initiated later (*run nong*). The implicit ideology was that of a family in which seniors helped their juniors. Hence the senior troops were coming to visit their new junior siblings as a gesture of moral support. Thus the trainees devoted considerable attention to preparing for the evening campfire, planning skits, choosing the flower bearers to welcome the visiting troops, getting the firewood, and the like. To heighten the contrast between familial support and internecine strife, instructors also staged a big fight in mid-afternoon.

Morning 3: Skits and Self-Reliance

The morning session began at 8:30 with the initiates facing south while they sang the song of homage to members of the royal family. Next came the flag-raising ceremony and the Pali chant of the Three Refuges. The district education officer then had the scouts stand at attention while he gave the cleanliness reports.[16] As he called different color groups forward, two scout instructors stole some of their color-group flags, forcing the group members to chase after them. The education officer announced that the instructors had visited all the living quarters the night before and had found that only one initiate had resigned and returned home. He praised them for being exceptionally strong in their resolve, for persevering, and for being willing to cooperate so fully.

After a brief break the initiates reassembled in the meeting hall and sang a few songs. The assistant scoutmaster then discussed the tradition of campfires and skits. He explained that the campfire circles began as a way to ease the loneliness of long-distance travelers.[17] Travelers endured great difficulties in those days. He further explained that each group was to perform a skit at the campfire that evening and spoke of the importance of learning to perform in public without embarrassment. He said that working out the skits was an exercise in communal problem solving. The skits were not to involve political ideologies. The scout movement would not tolerate bad language, and the trainees were to maintain respect for religious institutions. The skits were to be about some aspect of Thai history or culture. The instructors then demonstrated how the trainees were to present their skits.

During this discussion the initiates were fighting sleep, many unsuccessfully. Consequently, instructors provided several intermissions for wake-up songs and chants. From time to time the instructors also threw water on initiates' faces and clashed cymbals in the ears of those who were falling asleep.

In addition to preparing skits the color groups had to collect firewood for the campfire and select three women from each color group who were to dress as nicely as they could. These women were to dance in during the opening campfire ceremonies, carrying garlands of flowers to give to the campfire's master of ceremonies. The initiates were told that when the campfire began, everyone should think of all the other scouts all over the world. An initial cheer would be followed by the women dancing out with their garlands. After presenting the flowers the first woman would ask the emcee to dance with her, and the other women would ask the other guests of honor, such as the heads of the visiting senior scout troops, to dance with them.

The assistant scoutmaster, who usually performed the lead male roles in the instructors' skits, then went on to explain the art of pantomime.[18] He noted that pantomime could prove an important skill for scouts, for example, as a way to inform their neighbors that a thief is robbing their house. The trainees were then given fifteen minutes to figure out how to act out assigned topics. The last topic pantomimed was of water throwing at New Year's. As the color group was acting out this sequence, the instructors threw buckets of water on everyone. Amid squeals of laughter, the soaking wet initiates were dismissed for lunch.

Afternoon 3: Brothers Should Not Argue

After a song about holidays in America a district agricultural official gave a talk on the use of insecticides and fertilizers and urged villagers not to cut down teak trees or kill fish by throwing bombs into the water.[19] This was followed by a discussion of medicinal herbs and other useful products that could be gathered from local plants. After these presentations the instructors told the initiates to build a platform from bamboo and rope, testing out the knot-tying techniques they had learned the day before. Each color group then marched into the schoolyard carrying their bamboo platforms overhead. On each platform sat a girl wearing her color scarf over her head; flowers had been tucked into the scarf as decorations in a kind of mock beauty pageant.

Divisions A and B ended up on opposite sides of the school grounds. The instructors organized a relay. Two members of each group pulled the platform forward, while a third hung onto the back end. The point was to test the strength of the platforms they had made, as well as the strength of the division's members. The race was quite chaotic. Suddenly, an instructor announced to the out-of-breath trainees that a certain group had won. An instructor assigned to another color group screamed out, "That's not true. That's a lie!" He yelled his group was there first, and he accused the other group of cheating.

A fistfight broke out among the instructors. The BPP scoutmaster ordered them to stop fighting, saying the fracas was disgraceful. Meanwhile many village bystanders fled the area, fearful that greater violence might soon follow. The BPP instructor ordered the initiates to remain in formation. The instructor who began the fight ran off. Some instructors started to go after him, but others grabbed them and told them to let him go. The BPP instructor, dismayed, intoned:

> Never in the five thousand or more scout training sessions in the country and never in all the sessions I have been involved with has anything like this ever happened. We are all brothers and sisters, whether we come from the North of Thailand or from the Northeast like the instructor who has just run away. Whatever part of the country we come from, we are all part of one big family under the king and queen. The king and queen are the father and

mother of all Thais. How, since we are all members of the same family, can we get into fights with each other?

At this point the troublesome instructor returned, his head low, and apologized. The instructor with whom he fought also apologized. The trainees agreed to forgive the two for their bad behavior, at which point the two instructors performed a happy song and dance. This event created quite a flurry of discussion in the village, because many bystanders had run home and spread news of the fracas. The scenario had been utterly convincing. Everyone was quite relieved to learn that this too had been a staged event and commented on how clever the instructors were to find so many ways to teach. All agreed it was wrong for Thais to fight each other because all Thais were members of the same family and should love each other as brothers and sisters.

Night 3: Zulus and Peace

The evening program began at 7:30 P.M. with songs, followed by a talk by the district education officer on the history of the scout movement. He outlined the founding of the international scout movement by Lord Baden-Powell (*Than Bii-Phii*, or his excellency B-P, as he was thereafter called) and the establishment of the Thai scout movement by King Rama VI. The education officer then explained how the Village Scout movement was started by the Border Patrol Police in northeastern Thailand. He noted that scouting is an international, peace-loving movement involving 108 countries. Because scouts love peace, scouts shake with their left hands as that hand is unbloodied by killing.

The BPP scoutmaster then took over the microphone and welcomed the visiting senior scout troops. The senior scouts saluted the instructors as they marched in.[20] Any who had forgotten their kerchiefs were specifically forbidden to join the campfire circle. All the initiates were told to note the support shown them by their seniors and to make similar efforts to visit the training sessions of scout juniors in future.

After everyone sat on the ground, the BPP instructor led a circular cheer. The cheer was "I will do good things, things that the government wants. Whooooooo." Then instructors with bootblack on their faces, wearing hula skirts, and carrying swords in mock representation of Zulu warriors came leaping and whooping into the center of the campfire session. After lighting the campfire they performed a skit reenacting Lord Baden-Powell's making peace with the Zulus. The skit concluded with

A "Zulu" lighting the campfire.

their decision not to fight but to be friends, and as a sign of their friendship they shook hands with their left hands.

After this the three women chosen from each color group earlier in the
day, usually the youngest and prettiest in each group, formed a line and
danced in bearing the flower garlands.[21] The dancers then presented their
garlands to the honorary emcee, the district-level scout leader, and the
district education official. Then each dancer chose a partner and danced
the first song. Everyone joined in for the second dance. The scoutmaster

Master of ceremonies clowning.

then asked the senior scouts if they had brought any presents for the initiates. The visiting scouts then presented flowers to the instructors and puffed rice candies to the initiates.

Then it was time for the color groups to perform their skits, interspersed with songs and cheers to keep everyone awake. Rain began to pour as the last skit was being performed, but the scouts had to stay to prove their endurance. Despite the downpour they sang the Royal Anthem and finally were dismissed. Thoroughly drenched, they raced to their hosts' homes to sleep. Once again it was well after midnight.

Day 4: Setting the Final Structure in Place

The first three days had tended to focus on the past, on the history of Thailand and the history of the scout movement. The fourth day began the reintegration of the initiates into the present and set the tone for the attitudes that scouts were to hold toward the structure of their society. As usual the day began with the raising of the flag at 7:30 A.M., singing the Royal Anthem, and inspection reports. Then the group repaired to the meeting hall where the election of permanent troop officers began. The trainees were to choose a president, two vice presidents, a troop secretary, and a treasurer. One vice president was to be male, the other female.

In the afternoon session the male president and female vice president of the scout troop were crowned king and queen of their village kingdom, thus making the parallel between the microcosmic realm of the village and the macrocosmic kingdom of the nation. The evening campfire was similar to that of the night before, with many senior scout troops coming to show their support. Thus the initiates were slowly being integrated into an "imagined community" that included them in a network far beyond their village—to other subjects around the country and ultimately to the royal court in the nation's capital.

Morning 4: Elections of the Status Quo

Whereas the first three days had stressed equality among the trainees, the criteria for the election of troop officers stressed more pragmatic considerations. The candidates were to be people who had sufficient time and financial resources to coordinate scout activities. Government officials were specifically excluded from consideration because they already had so many demands on their time. Furthermore the president was to be someone who lived fairly centrally, so troop members could travel to consult with him with as little difficulty as possible. The candidates were to be literate and have a reputation for being unselfish. They were to be well-connected and comfortable meeting people from all backgrounds, from monks to district officials, rich to poor. Village headmen were eligible for consideration.

These criteria, although understandably pragmatic, eliminated most initiates from consideration and restricted eligibility to members of the local elite. Thus it is not surprising that the choice for president was at once the richest man in the subdistrict and headman of a neighboring village. One vice president was the second-richest man in the subdistrict and the richest man from the village in which the session was held. The assistant kamnan (subdistrict head) was chosen treasurer, and the head of the subdistrict agricultural cooperative was chosen as secretary. The female vice president was a former contestant in a local beauty pageant and well-known singer. Her troop regarded both her beauty and singing ability as assets that would be important to the troop in future scouting events. The elections reflected traditional gender stereotypes, namely, that the man be wealthy and the woman beautiful.

No one gave nomination speeches, and the votes were lopsided. The nomination of the preferred candidate was generally quick. It took longer to get the mandatory alternate nominations, and their names were generally put forward for the sake of appearance. The election results came as no surprise to anyone and had been decided by the session organizers before the initiation rite began. The election was just a matter of confirming the decision that had been reached earlier. Any chance of a surprise candidate's being elected was effectively stopped by the restriction of candidates to wealthier members of the subdistrict.

The rest of the morning consisted of an uneventful talk by the district police chief, who encouraged villagers to report suspected criminals to the authorities, a discussion of birth control by a health official, a demonstration of first aid, an explanation of how to use the scout kerchief as a bandage, and a talk on the importance of good posture. After some games consisting of relays between stretcher bearers, the scouts returned home for lunch. Before the beginning of the afternoon session each group was to make a bamboo airplane and dress up as members of different ethnic groups, such as Indians, Burmese, or any of the hill tribes. Although the initiates did not know why they were to do these things, these last steps were preparation for the main event of the afternoon session.

Afternoon 4: On Criticism and Gossip

In the afternoon everyone reassembled on the temple grounds. After some initial songs the instructors asked five initiates—in fact all government officials—to leave the area while they told the remaining initiates a story. The instructors then selected a trainee to repeat the story to one of the absent officials, who in turn was to repeat it to the second, and so on. Given how tired all the initiates were by this point, it is not surprising that by the last retelling the story was virtually unrecognizable. The point not missed by the villagers was that if government officials, who were already the best educated among the trainees, could distort a story so completely, the gossip and rumor mills of villagers must garble accounts even more. The instructors concluded by saying that when people tell stories critical of the government villagers should wonder what basis the story has in fact.

The story was interesting because its plot portrayed government officials in a favorable light. According to the narrative, a fictitious flood in the village of Baan Khaa in 1973 swept away a village home. The husband of the family was in Panang Village at the time. When he heard his family was in trouble, he rushed to help, as did the district officer and two other district officials. The man had a wife and seven children, but they could save only four children. Because the district officer felt sorry for them, the four children had lived with him ever since. According to the story, the district officer was now trying to locate homes for these children, so the storyteller said that anyone interested in raising the children should contact the district office.

Journey to a Royal Kingdom

Just as this parable was ending, a messenger dressed in the traditional garb of a royal attendant arrived at the temple carrying a large scroll. He explained that he was bearing an important message from the king and queen of the kingdom of Samsen, a kingdom that lay "over yonder, past the Kingdom of Kukii."[22] The instructors opened the scroll but said they could not read it. It was in a strange language, which must be the language of the people in the kingdom of Samsen. The messenger explained that he was the commander in chief of the royal guard and that he would translate the message.

The letter explained that the king and queen of the kingdom of Samsen were getting old and wanted to retreat to meditate in the forest. Therefore the king and queen invited the recipients of the letter, the scouts, to come to the kingdom because the king and queen had looked far and wide for good subjects and good leaders to ascend the throne in their stead. They enclosed a map to their kingdom. It was now clear why the initiates had made bamboo airplanes during the lunch break. The stage had been set for the journey on which the trainees were to embark.

The mood was humorous and fanciful. Although the messenger punctuated his speech with royal language, he was nonetheless cavorting flirtatiously with various girls, asking them if they would please join him in the kingdom of Samsen and pouting when they shyly turned him down. In the end they all decided to go and the journey started. As they rounded the main building in the temple compound, they encountered a meditating ascetic (*rrysii*) who asked where they were going. Informed that these were Village Scouts who had been asked to visit the king and queen of Samsen, the ascetic explained the four directions, gave them his blessing, and sent a crazy man (*phii baa*) to guide them on their way. The lunatic led the way, trailing tin cans and chasing laughing village children out of the

The cast of characters for the journey to the royal kingdom included Rysrii, Royal Attendant, Angel, Terrorist, and Crazy Man.

way. The initiates were led by their color-group heads, who held the mock airplanes.

Just past the temple grounds en route to the school they were stopped by a sorceress (*mae mot*) dressed in black and wearing a skull face. She refused to let them pass until everyone told her who they were. The scout instructors explained that these were Village Scouts en route to the kingdom of Samsen. The sorceress wanted proof of their identities. The instructors explained that the scarves they were wearing identified them as scout trainees. The sorceress countered that if they were really scouts, they would know the ten scout laws. She demanded that they recite the ninth scout law. The initiates repeated the ninth law, and the sorceress agreed to let them pass but not without first administering a taste test and warning that if they failed to recognize all the tastes, she would turn them all into dog turds.

On they went with their journey until they were stopped by three daughters of the goddess of the oceans. These water spirits were delighted to learn that the Village Scouts and not an impending storm were coming. But they too wanted proof that these were truly scouts. They asked the trainees to repeat the fifth scout law and pass a memory test. At this point the scouts learned that they had run out of airplane fuel, but the water spirits solved the problem by offering to show them a short-cut to the kingdom of Samsen.

Next the traveling scouts were attacked by bandits who exploded fire-crackers and pointed wooden guns at the encircled scout troop. The bandits demanded that the scouts turn over their money. The scout instructors protested, "We are Village Scouts and we have no money." The dialogue continued:

> "Who are Village Scouts?"
> "We are people who represent all the different nationalities, races, and religions in the world."
> "Well if that's so, then what's so special about you?"
> "Scouts are special because of their unity, their kerchiefs and their special scout salute. Furthermore we have a Nation, Religion, and King. These are all things that you don't have."

The bandits became jealous and asked if they too could become Village Scouts, saying, "We have lived in the woods for years, no wives, no children, no family." But the scout instructors pointed out that they could not become Village Scouts because they had not been doing good deeds. However, if they agreed to reform their ways, they could become scouts and join them. If so, they should come down from the mountains and form into straight lines and salute. The bandits decided to join, and the scout trainees taught the bandits how to salute properly.

Their ranks swelled by the addition of ten bandits-turned-scouts, the group finally arrived at the kingdom of Samsen. Here they were met by the guardian angels of the kingdom, who asked who were these people all dressed up in strange clothes. The messenger replied that these were Village Scouts and—because scouts don't care about class, ethnic background, nationality, or religion—they dressed according to their customs. "These scouts," he continued, "come from the province of Chiang Mai." The angels asked the scouts if they were sure that they had sufficient knowledge to be deserving of entering the city. To make sure the initiates were asked to listen to various sounds because it was important that scouts be able to recall everything they heard.[23] The scout initiates were then declared welcome to the city of Samsen.

Thus the scouts finally arrived at the city of Samsen—in fact a meeting hall located on one side of the school grounds. Two royal attendants asked everyone whether they were thirsty and whether they should throw some imaginary coconuts for everyone to drink.[24] All repeated, "How refreshing!" Then the travelers were told to put their heads down and close their eyes. In swept the king and queen of Samsen, singing a song of welcome. They expressed their gratitude to the scouts for coming and explained that they were planning to give up their throne and go off to meditate. Therefore they had asked the commander in chief of their troops to find suitable candidates to ascend their throne, people to whom they could entrust the care of this city.

The commander in chief announced to all that worthy candidates for the throne must be people who have good memories, are observant, and are farsighted. He reported to the king and queen that he had succeeded in fulfilling their royal wishes and announced that "the most worthy person to accede to the throne of your majesty the king is someone born on the fifth of January 1925." The individual with that auspicious birthday was none other than the president of the scout troop, elected that morning. The auspicious birthday for the new queen matched that of the female vice president.

The king and queen expressed their joy at being able to entrust the care of their kingdom to such worthy individuals and informed the new king and queen that they would receive their trusted officials and all their royal treasure. They then took off their royal clothing and insignia and dressed the new king and queen in the royal regalia.

At this point there was a little comic relief as two royal attendants ran up and asked to be paid their back salaries. The old king gave one of them a 100-baht bill but told the other to collect his salary from the new king. The new king had only a 20-baht bill on him, so the attendant accused the new king of being stingy. The commander in chief then intervened and sent the two attendants scampering, while everyone laughed.

The afternoon journey imbued the villagers chosen as the troop officers with a certain mythological legitimacy. Having the scouts wear different types of ethnic dress reminded the scouts that a nation is a coalition of people from diverse backgrounds. The journey also gave the scouts a sense of completion, that they had been trained in the preceding three days, tested on the fourth, and were now ready to receive their scout kerchiefs on the following day. Furthermore there was a sense that, although the scout session might be drawing to a close, the magic would live on and that their troop officers had a special responsibility to see to the well-being of all scout members in their subdistrict.

However, lest the royal metaphor be taken too far, and to ensure that no one would dare put the king and queen of Samsen on the same pedestal as the king and queen of Thailand, the Samsen king and queen were made the subject of gentle ridicule and mock respect. The attendants who demanded their salaries (money that, incidentally, was not returned but was spent for a feast by the scout instructors that night) were part of the ridicule. And the king and queen were no sooner crowned than they were made to dance the bump, a dance reported to be popular in the United States at the time but that the villagers viewed as quite vulgar.

The afternoon journey suggested an interesting relationship between politics and religion, because the journey began at the temple and ended in the palace. The first character the wandering scouts met was a meditating ascetic and the last were bandits, who in fact shared many characteristics usually ascribed to communist guerrillas—they lived in the woods; had no Nation, Religion, or King; and survived by harassing the passing citizenry. The various tests and dramatic episodes conveyed the impression that Village Scouts make good citizens and that a stable political environment that kings and queens can trust is fostered by passive, law-abiding subjects who keep a watchful eye and ear out for any potential troublemakers or dissidents.

Night 4: The Beginning of the End

The evening campfire session of the fourth day was essentially fun and games. Each color group performed a skit; the skits alternated with songs and dancing. The evening began with the instructors, males in one row and females in the opposite row, dancing in. They were wearing traditional peasant dress and carried lit tapers. It was a beautiful sight. Then young women from each color group danced with flower garlands in their arms.

At the conclusion of their dance the women presented the flowers to the guests of honor at the evening ceremonies, the district officer and the district chief of police. The new president and female vice president were also invited to receive garlands. Members from six other scout troops were present; in all the visitors numbered about one thousand. After some general dancing and singing more skits were performed. Each visiting troop also performed special dances, such as a drum dance and dances typical of other regions of the country. The performances lasted well into the night, ending about 3 A.M.

The official evening program concluded with the singing of the Royal

Anthem, with all the scouts facing south. Then the scouts formed a large circle, joined hands, and sang a melancholy song about friendship to the tune of "Auld Lang Syne." The intent was to heighten the sense of camaraderie among the initiates and their awareness that soon they would face the sadness of separation.

After the district officer and chief of police took their official leave (just after 3 A.M.), the scouts assumed their former positions in the camp-fire circle. The oldest woman trainee, who had been the brunt of many jokes, was then told to come forward. As a gesture of the instructors' appreciation for the good sport she had been, she was dressed in a cape, paper crown, presented with a garland of flowers, and told to parade around the campfire as a beauty queen. She was too tired to walk straight. She was also given a box wrapped in decorative paper. She thought it was a real present and opened it. Finding she was the brunt of yet another joke, she threw the box to the ground in a mix of anger, frustration, and disappointment.

The instructors outlined the next day's events to the scout initiates and then dismissed them to return to their sleeping quarters. Just as the initiates were departing, the instructors expressed their hope that, because the trainees had already endured many hardships, nothing would happen to disqualify them from receiving the royal kerchief the following day.

Once at home the initiates had to complete their homework assignment, which was to write down as many of the sights, sounds, and tastes they had encountered in the afternoon journey. This assignment kept most initiates up for the rest of the night, and few got more than one hour of sleep before being awakened at 5 A.M.

Day 5: Building to the Climax

The last day culminated in the afternoon when the initiates received their royal kerchiefs, and many collapsed in hysteria. Because the initiates had had no more than an hour of sleep, they were exhausted. The morning began with an incident that, as the scout instructors explained it to me, was intended to heighten the significance of the kerchiefs the initiates were to receive in the afternoon; it would suggest to the initiates that the kerchiefs were not being given out to everyone who participated in the five-day initiation session but had to be earned.

After the cleanliness awards were given, the finishing touches were put on the permanent organization of the scout troop assigning each initiate a permanent role. From then on, in preparation for the final afternoon ceremonies, the instructors focused their attention almost exclusively on the kerchief, its symbolism, and its magical powers. After the royal kerchiefs were distributed, one final piece of important business remained before the transition from ritual to reality could be completed, returning the children of the ritual to their normal adult ages. When this transition was complete, the initiates were ready to be declared full-fledged Village Scouts.

Morning 5: Heightening the Meaning of the Kerchief

The initiates reassembled at the school grounds at 7:30. After the flag-raising ceremonies, the district education official gave a talk on the importance of cleanliness. He noted that at first only a few color groups had received cleanliness awards. However, as the color groups had learned how to cooperate with each other, by the fourth day all the color groups had received awards. Such cooperation, he noted, showed the importance of unity for the nation and its continued survival. The BPP instructor then asked which color group had received the most cleanliness points overall. An instructor said that Group A Orange had won the most points. Another instructor disagreed, saying that this group had received the lowest number of points. A third instructor said that he had also been informed that the members of this group did not cooperate well. "What?" cried the BPP scoutmaster. "Their score is this low? They were not cooperating with each other? Out with them. They are not eligible to receive their royal kerchiefs."

Members of the orange group were ordered to leave the grounds, pack their belongings, and return home. The BPP scoutmaster announced that only fifteen of the sixteen color groups would be receiving their scarves in the afternoon. Although he was sorry about what had happened with the orange group, those were the rules and there was nothing he could do, other than suggest they try again at the next initiation rite. Looking somewhat dumbfounded, the orange group got up and began moving toward the gateway until another instructor, who was waiting there, said they should wait a moment to make sure that no mistake had been made.

The BPP instructor then asked for a recount of the scores and drilled the members of the orange group. He had them stand at attention and repeat the three-point scout oath and various scout laws. He asked them whether they had done their own breakfast shopping and cleaned their host's house well. One initiate answered in the affirmative and said they had also made a sign over the house door that read WELCOME. They had also fixed the door hinge for their hosts.

When the recount was finished, the instructors announced that in fact this group had received the highest number of cleanliness points and its members were truly deserving of becoming full-fledged scouts. They and another group received prizes (bags of snacks), and the tension broke as the instructors stole various color-group flags and forced the group heads to run about trying to retrieve them.[25]

Division into Permanent Subgroups

After a short break the initiates reconvened in the meeting hall. At this meeting the trainees were divided into twelve permanent groups of twenty-five members each. These groups were in turn broken down into five subgroups of five members. Each group was to choose officers: a group head, two assistant group heads, and a secretary. Each of the five subgroups in turn elected each of its five members to one of five positions, leader, public relations officer, communications officer, activities organizer, and safety official. It was privately explained to me that the election of every initiate to a position in the organizational hierarchy was intended to ensure that each would feel a sense of responsibility and involvement. It was part of an effort to counteract the tendency observed in earlier sessions for scout trainees to lose interest in scouting activities.

The twelve royal policies of the scout movement were then explained to the initiates (see appendix, table A1.1). These points were emphasized:

> Scouts should not become involved in politics.
> Scouts should help government officials perform their duties.
> Scouts must honor the Nation, Religion, and King.
> Scouts should not wear any uniforms other than the royal kerchief, lest rich be separated from poor.
> Scouts should not spend large sums of money for presents when they visited junior scout troops, either for the instructors or the trainees.
> Scouts should not accept political monies, and they were to be hardworking upright citizens of their community and set a good example for others to follow.[26]

The Royal Kerchief

The instructors then explained the symbolism of the scout insignia—the kerchief, pin, and clasp—to the initiates. Throughout the initiation session instructors had periodically mentioned that the scout kerchief was something that no amount of money could buy. Although the scarf cost only 15 baht, it could not be purchased, not even for 1 million baht. Only individuals who completed scout training could receive this royal gift, and then it was given free of charge. The instructor mentioned that some people had tried to obtain the scout scarf by lying to the district office, claiming that they had lost theirs. However, the district offices were aware of such tactics, and they investigated each case of a missing scout scarf to determine whether the individuals concerned really were scouts or impostors.

The scarf, along with the gold-colored pin and clasp, were the only official insignia of the Village Scouts. There were no official uniforms, for the simple reason that having or requiring uniforms would have made it too expensive for most villagers to join the movement. The kerchief was a maroon cloth edged in yellow, blue, and black piping. The yellow symbolized religion; the blue, the monarchy; the maroon, the blood of the nation; and the black, the memory of those who died to protect the nation. On the back of the kerchief was a circular emblem with a map of Thailand woven in yellow. It was explained that the emblem originally was designed with a Buddha image woven in yellow, but this was later changed lest the scout movement be viewed as intolerant of other religions. On the clasp fastening the scarf at the throat was a tiger face with the slogan *sia chaat, yaa sia satya* (It is better to lose one's life than one's honor). Ten lines representing the ten scout laws radiated from the tiger's face. The three-pronged design on the pin represented the threefold scout oath. The insignia were donated by the king. They were blessed at a famous temple and then sent to BPP headquarters in Mae Rim, Chiang Mai, for distribution.[27]

The scouts were admonished to keep the royal scarves in an honored place in their homes, preferably next to their family altarplaces, because the royal scarves were so special. The scouts were not to wear the scarf lightly but only on special occasions. They were not to wear it to show off but reserve it for scout activities, such as visits of members of the royal family, scouts' funerals, and scout development projects. The scarf was not to be worn by an individual scout but only when many scouts were involved.

The instructors reminded the scout initiates of the difficulties they endured in order to receive their kerchief and warned them not to let anyone borrow their scarf. The BPP instructor explained that people who were not scouts had not been properly trained and they might do things that would harm the reputation of the scout movement. True scouts do not drink or create trouble. The initiates were told that those who do so are clearly not true scouts but private individuals, probably communists posing as scouts to undermine the integrity of the scout movement and with it the Nation, Religion, and King. The scoutmaster noted that untrained individuals would not know how to salute properly and commented that such impostors brought disgrace to the movement. He also observed that in the event of a scout's death no one else was to use the kerchief; it should be kept as a memento of that person. In other words, being a scout was such an important aspect of a person's identity, it should be remembered even after a scout's death.

Afternoon 5: Personal Confrontation with Nation, Religion, and King

The momentous occasion had finally arrived. The initiates gathered at the school grounds dressed in their best clothes. They formed lines outside the meeting hall, roped off to keep nonscouts at a distance. To capture everyone's attention the initiates danced in place (*lamwong*) and then filed in, color group by color group, to the meeting hall and took their seats. The abbot from the local temple was sitting on a large red and gold wing chair on the platform in the front of the meeting hall. The district officer, in his official uniform, bowed to the abbot and lit the candles on the altar set up behind him. The abbot then recited the Three Refuges in Pali and gave a brief sermon on the importance of unity, noting how all five fingers are necessary to make a fist. He thanked the district officer and the scout instructors for their selfless efforts to foster unity in order to protect the nation from danger and assist in its future progress and development. He then lit a candle floating in a bowl of scented water, blessed it with a Pali chant, and then, still chanting, sprinkled holy water on everyone gathered in the meeting hall.

From the distance we could hear the rhythm of cymbals and drums, typical of processions in which villagers carry offerings to the temple. Three scout instructors, one carrying a picture of the king, the second a Buddha image, and the third the Thai flag, led the procession. Behind

The mock king and queen (scout troop president and vice president) with royal attendants.

these three were other instructors carrying ten trays bearing the scout kerchiefs. The trays were the same ones villagers used when making offerings to the monks. Behind the instructors were the color-group heads, each carrying a money tree, also typical of religious ceremonies, which the scouts had made during the lunch hour.

The procession arrived at the school grounds and entered the meeting hall from the front, the candidates having previously entered from the rear. The instructors holding the royal kerchiefs formed a line at the front. At other times during the initiation the instructors had deliberately worn gaudy pink or green jackets; now all the instructors were formally dressed in official khaki scout uniforms. Everyone then stood and sang the Royal Anthem. The instructors placed the ten trays with the scarves on a raised bench that ran the width of the platform. The instructors then saluted, and the color-group heads went to rejoin their groups.

The initiates were then instructed to remove their old training scarves. The mood was solemn, with an aura of anticipation. The district education official then informed the district officer that group number 333-CM10-988[28] had completed its training:

I, in the name of the scoutmaster, instructors and members of scout troop 333-CM10-988 would like to thank you for accepting to be the officiant for this training session. The members of scout troop 333-CM10-988 of Samsen Village have completed their initiation at the Samsen Village School, in the subdistrict of Samsen, district of San Patong, province of Chiang Mai, during the dates of— in 1977, a total of five days and four nights. There are two hundred ninety-nine candidates, of which two hundred thirty are male and sixty-nine are female, together with myself serving as training supervisor, joined by instructors from the Border Patrol Police Division Five, and assisted by a total of forty-two scout instructors from the district of San Patong and two from the district of—.

This session received support from all involved. I am proud to inform you that all participated wholeheartedly in this session. All members are strong and healthy. All members have passed the training successfully and have earned the right to become Village Scouts. The initiation rite has now been completed and I offer my praise to all of you involved.

Unlike earlier phases of the initiation, which were punctuated with comic routines, this sequence was carried out in utter solemnity. A large picture of the king now was placed on a tripod at center stage, replacing the abbot's chair. In a somber tone the scout instructors described the protocol the initiates were to follow in receiving their scarves. The initiates were to present themselves at the platform, ten at a time. They were to remove their shoes, but because it had rained and the ground was muddy, they could wear their shoes until just before they knelt to receive their scarves. They were supposed to stand before the platform, salute the picture of the king, and reflect on the magnanimity of his majesty. They were then to kneel on a padded bench that ran the width of the stage, make a complete bow (kraap), and then reach up with their right hand, take a scarf, and place it over their heads. Then they were to stand, look at the picture of the king, salute, and walk off to the left.

The official high point of the ceremony passed quite quickly, as row after row came forward to receive the new kerchiefs. The room was generally hushed, except for the shuffling of feet and rustling of clothes. The back rows came forward first, forming a long line down the aisle to the right of the stage. The initiates filed silently into position, ten at a time, in front of each of the ten ornamental trays bearing the maroon kerchiefs

Scout instructors bearing the royal kerchiefs.

and followed the ritual as instructed. One Village Scout recounted years later, "I had always loved the king, but never as intensely as I did that moment. That moment I felt it through the core of my being (*saabsyyng*)." Many initiates shared her intense euphoria.

After receiving the kerchiefs people in each row filed from the platform to return to their seats as another row filed in. They were now officially Village Scouts. As the new scouts were returning to their seats, scout instructors somberly admonished some to get a haircut and helped others to tie their kerchiefs properly. Once all were back in their seats, the BPP instructor asked the initiates to "think for a moment of the kindness and generosity of his majesty the king. Reflect on the importance of the Nation, Religion, and King. Think of the oath that you have taken and follow it." Then he asked everyone to stand, salute, and repeat the threefold scout oath.

The district officer was then invited to speak:

I feel it is a great honor to have been asked to serve as the guest of honor at this initiation session. I serve as guest of honor at the request of the governor of this province, in my capacity as overseer of initiation rites for this district. I have observed that all three hundred members present at this session have completed their training successfully and noted the moral support given by the visits paid by members of senior scout troops. This session was made possible by funds received from numerous sources, of which seven thousand seven hundred fifty baht was given by the government's budget.

I hope that each of you will cherish this beautiful experience and opportunity for the rest of your lives. I hope that your troop will lend other junior troops the same moral support that your senior troops gave to you and visit their campfire sessions. You have been well taught by your instructors, and I am confidant that you will take what you have learned away with you and practice it. The scarf which you have received today will be a bond between your hearts, uniting you. Before we part today, I ask that all the sacred forces in the world will watch over and protect each of the three hundred scouts and your instructors, and that you will have much happiness and good fortune in the future.

The district officer concluded by saying that Village Scouts were a glory and honor to their country (*pen phuu prasert*). He said he would meet with the presidents and vice presidents of each troop at the district office at least twice a month and with the group heads at least every four months. He also said that he looked forward to meeting all the scouts at reunions.

Begging Forgiveness of Elders: Return to Normal

The BPP instructor thanked the district officer for his talk and asked that all the scout trainees older than fifty-five, male and female, come forward and sit on the stage in front. Twelve men and two women came forward, and they were joined on stage by all the uniformed instructors. The BPP instructor then explained that on the first day of scout training they had reduced the ages of all initiates to that of children, "not because they wanted to do anything nasty or be disrespectful, but because it was necessary to find a way to bring people from diverse backgrounds and experiences together. We reduced your ages in the interest of unity, and so we ask for your forgiveness for any disrespect you may have felt."[29]

Newly initiated Village Scouts.

At this point the instructors, seated at the feet of the village elders, bowed down before them, asking their forgiveness. The elders now no longer were being addressed as Boy-child or Girl-child but as Grandfather and Grandmother (*poh ui, mae ui*; *phuu thaw phuu kae*). In a gesture that evoked the New Year's ritual blessings (see also Muecke 1980:471), the instructors sprinkled water on the palms of the village elders. The elders, now assuming their traditional roles, responded by chanting Pali and other traditional blessings and in turn sprinkled water on the instructors' heads. The instructors bowed again before the village elders and politely requested that they return to their seats.

Tears of Separation

Even as the trainees regained their social positions of everyday life, they had acquired a new identity as fully initiated Village Scouts. Participants were feeling complex combinations of emotions. The color groups had developed a feeling of friendship.[30] Many new scouts also felt a sense of gratitude and veneration for the instructors at this point in the session, particularly after their humble apology to the village elders. The symbols of the Nation, Religion, and King had become quite intimate and immediate to each scout as she or he received the scarf. The initiates, for whom family bonds were already of profound importance, now had a sense that they had joined the larger family of the Village Scouts and the Thai nation.

The BPP instructor encouraged such feelings, saying, "We are all Thais and, like all Thais, respect our elders. Like all Thais, we are children of their majesties the king and queen. We want to see unity among our fellow Thai brothers and sisters to prevent bad things from happening to the villages, subdistricts, districts, and provinces of the nation." At this point the instructors sang a sad slow song about how all Thais are members of the same family, with the same mother and father in the king and queen. Therefore all Thais should love each other and be united. They should not fight or argue, for doing so is like a knife tearing through the hearts of their mothers and fathers, making them hopeless in the face of the future, for who then will dry the tears?

A heavy sadness spread throughout the scouts. Many were fighting back tears, but the BPP scoutmaster said softly over the microphone that "it is good to cry as long as one cries from a pure heart, so don't be ashamed to let the tears flow." He was casting a spell. The instructors began crying first, some of the better actors emitting a weeping sound and dabbing at their eyes. Soon heartfelt tears were flowing from the eyes of many initiates and instructors, especially the female instructors. Some nonscout villagers were watching. One made some kind of a catcall but was quickly glared into silence by scout instructors.[31]

The instructors continued with another sad song, prefaced by the BPP instructor who said, "Even though we must now go our separate ways, don't be sad because we will still have occasion to meet one another again." The lyrics said in part, "Even though the body was far away, our hearts remain with you. / Oh my darling, though the time has come to part, the heart still dreams of you." Throughout this song, which had numerous verses, the instructors went among the scouts, hugging them and handing out bits of tissue. A growing number of scouts became hysterical. Sobbing uncontrollably, their arms and legs flailing, these scouts were carried out on stretchers through a corridor that had been roped off.

Instructors begin the tearful finale.

A group of scout instructors had been detailed to carry the stretchers back and forth between the meeting area and the first aid center. Scores and scores were carried off in a seemingly unending procession. A room in the school building had been furnished with mattresses. Health officials from around the area staffed it, giving smelling salts and fans to the relatives of the hysterical scouts. Many relatives, looking stunned and overwhelmed themselves, continued to patiently fan the exhausted scouts long after they had cried themselves to sleep.

The scouts who remained then filed out of the meeting hall and formed two concentric circles on the school grounds around the flag. Staff members formed the inside circle and initiates were on the outside, so that the circles faced each other. Speaking for all the instructors, the BPP scoutmaster said, "Although we, the instructors, must go now, we won't forget any of you. We look forward to the time when we can meet again. If anything bad has happened during this session, we ask you to forget it and remember only that which was good and useful." He asked the other instructors to remove their caps, and then he led everyone in chanting the Three Refuges in Pali. He then invited "the blessed spirit of each of the kings of Thailand, the ancestors and heroes of the Thai people, and all the

Newly initiated scouts in tears. Some sob uncontrollably and are removed to holding centers by stretcher.
(Photo used by permission of Somkhuan Harikul, director of Village Scout Operations Center.)

sacred forces in the world to protect each of you from danger and misfortune. May the royal lineage continue into eternity." Everyone saluted and the flag was lowered.

All the scouts and their instructors then crossed their arms across their chests and joined hands while they sang a song to the tune of "Auld Lang Syne." The district officer, followed by the district education officer and the scout instructors, then walked around the circle, shaking hands with each new scout and wishing them all the best. After each scout's hand had been shaken, the scouts formed into four rows facing south toward the flagpole. The instructors then formed another line facing them.

The BPP instructor then announced, "We must go now and wish each of you the best." He hoped that each would be a good scout and reminded all to be careful while traveling home. He admonished them to be sure to thank their hosts and hostesses. With that the instructors sang another song; part of the lyric was, "We go now, but we will meet again." On the third verse they slowly began to walk backward, moving farther and farther from the new scouts, who remained in position. The instructors were moving southward, in the direction of the central government and the royal palace. During this period one more scout collapsed and had to be carried away on a stretcher.

The scouts then went back to their hosts' homes, thanked their hosts and hostesses quite uneventfully, and took their leave. Many had relatives who came to pick them up. The instructors had suggested that anyone who felt unable to travel should ask the host families for permission to stay another night. So far as I know, no one did so. Most scouts returned home safely. One tired girl walked into a passing motorcycle and had to be hospitalized for two days with head injuries.

District president of the Village Scouts for San Patong and other Village Scouts present supplies to needy schoolchildren.

(Photo used by permission of Mae Liang Inthong Suriyasak.)

7

Mixed Metaphors: The Class Struggle Unmasked

From initial humor to concluding hysteria the Village Scout initiation ritual was an attempt by the elite to deploy symbols in the Thai war of position. The primary appeal was to the emotive rhetoric of the family. The villagers sobbing hysterically as they were borne away on stretchers are evidence of the immediate efficacy of the ritual's emotional appeal. The ritual drew upon the overarching symbols of the nation as a loving family in which the king and queen were presented as national parents. Yet the family imagery reflected contradictory class perspectives. For the elite the imagery reinforced hierarchy and an authoritarian vision of the ideal society; for the hopeful villager the imagery appealed to the ideal love of parents for their children. Thus through the powerful imagery of family the elite sought to maintain its domination by generating support from its subalterns. However, this symbolic strategy created expectations of benevolence that the national urban elite never meant to satisfy and the local village elite could not. This chapter focuses on the contradictions between the ideology of the Village Scout movement and the realities of village life.

The Ideology: The National Scout Family

The five-day rite can be analyzed both in terms of the vision of society it encouraged and the issues it ignored. Villagers were initiated into an imagined national family, with the king and queen as the nation's parents and all scouts their children. Its vision was not that of an egalitarian society but of an authoritarian paternalistic government presiding over orderly, obedient, and passive childlike subjects. Communism was not presented, as it often is in the United States, as a repressive totalitarian political system that curtails freedom of speech but as chaos, conflict, and anarchy. Ironically, the change the Village Scout ritual sought to bring about in the minds of its initiates was, in effect, no change at all. Upon the completion of the five-day session the new Village Scouts were to embrace the status quo. No significant economic or political reforms were suggested. The movement's mantra of Nation, Religion, and King was intended to render the status quo enchanting; it was not an agenda for meaningful social reform.

In Praise of Hierarchy

The instructors repeatedly reinforced the family metaphor, beginning with the first day when age reduction transformed villagers into children. Scout initiates were portrayed as younger members of the extended royal family. On the fourth day, as the climax approached, the initiates became subjects of a mythical village kingdom, a microcosm of the nation. The ritual ended with the initiates formally restored to adulthood but as children in the national family and subjects of the nation. Villagers associated the family ideology with self-sacrificing parents and caring siblings, with the moral bonds of mutual support and love that bind families into a cohesive whole.[1]

However, the ideology of the national family contains a conflict between the illusion of equality and the reality of hierarchy. On the one hand scout instructors said repeatedly that they were trying to foster equality. After all, the purpose of reducing all initiates to the age of children was to minimize the awareness of class and other differences in their backgrounds. On the first day one instructor said, "We must love each other like brothers and sisters (*phii nong*). Everyone here is equal, no high, no low, no rich, no poor." The idea of reducing class differentiation (*lot chong wang rawang chon chan*) was in part an incorporation of critiques made of Thai society by a range of social reformers. As one scout explained, "Thailand will only survive if the gap between rich and poor is reduced. That is why the scouts are good. There are no class distinctions in the scouts—everyone is equal, everyone is a child just the same. There are no lords (*chawnaaj*) or officials, just little boys and little girls."

On the other hand siblings do differ in age and ability; parents supervise and discipline children, and children are not given an equal say with their elders. Hence the image of the family easily becomes hierarchical. In fact, the phrase *phii nong*, although it is generally translated into English as 'brothers and sisters', is more accurately translated as 'older and younger siblings.' Rather than eliminate class differentiation, the Village Scout movement offered a class-stratified society modeled on the idealized but nonetheless implicitly hierarchical relations of the Thai family.

Despite the protestations of nominal equality, the initiation rite carefully maintained the distinctions between villagers and government officials. Officials and village headmen went through the gauntlet separately, and they were never called upon to dance the humiliating duck waddle. Similarly, other important village figures and generous financial contributors were never singled out for such public humiliation.[2] The initiation reinforced the sense of villagers' subordination to authority by addressing them as Girl-child and Boy-child (*dekying dekchaaj*). The trainees tolerated this form of address because virtually all instructors were government officials, whereas most initiates were villagers.

In the Thai context family ideology suggests that younger siblings (*nong*) should listen to their older siblings (*phii*). The scout movement drew upon this assumption, saying that junior scout troops should listen to senior scout troops (*run phii run nong*); seniority was determined according to which troop was initiated first. Hierarchy was thus transformed into a primordial reality of nature. Using the anatomical structure of the hand, instructors informed initiates that the thumb crossing the little finger in the scout salute was a reminder of the kinship hierarchy.[3] The generational hierarchy and injunction to respect seniors mirrored the broader society; senior scouts were more likely to be of higher social status than junior scouts because those initiated as scouts earlier were more likely than those who joined later to have been wealthy urban middle-class people and higher-ranking government officials. Thus the scout hierarchy paralleled the status quo with its stratification into rich and poor, older and younger, royalty and commoner, government official and peasant, and urbanite and agriculturist.

Of Mutual Support and Patronage

The scout movement appealed to villagers' long-standing practices of mutual cooperation, their tendency to view the village as one large family or support network. For generations villagers have exchanged labor for house building and agricultural work. Most villages have funeral societies in which all villagers contribute to the costs of members' funerals. Scout instructors encouraged villagers to believe that by joining the scout movement they were becoming part of a large social insurance program, a nationwide mutual assistance association. They cited examples of scouts' helping with funerals, rebuilding homes that had burned down, and providing generous contributions to local temples. Initiates' hopes of a large social insurance program were fueled by rumors that Village Scouts received free or less expensive medical care. In the Northeast, according to one news report, Village Scouts received a discount for government health care that ran as high as 25 percent (Muecke 1980:423).[4]

However, in addition to tapping the more egalitarian belief in mutual support the Village Scout instructors encouraged villagers to believe that by becoming scouts they had joined a network of connections and privileges. Villagers believe that the way to get into police training school, avoid military duty, or get a job depends heavily on a person's *sen*, or connections. In Thailand villagers have long safeguarded their future, not by agitating for equitable laws but by ensuring that they are personally linked to influential people who can unobtrusively circumvent the laws. Thus on the morning of the second day and again on the afternoon of the last day the scout instructors gave various examples of how police and other government officials might overlook occasional violations by other scouts. By suggesting that the Village Scout movement facilitated such connections, the movement was essentially condoning a political machinery based more on extralegal patronage and privilege than on championing universal laws equally applicable to all.

Protection and Obedience

The family imagery also masked authoritarian agendas. The ritual encouraged villagers to see government officials as older siblings in the national family, as people who are naturally motivated to care for and protect their younger and more vulnerable siblings, the villagers. As the scoutmaster from the Border Patrol Police (BPP) explained to initiates on the morning of the last day, "No one should be allowed to divide Thais from Thais, to divide officials from the people, be those officials policemen, teachers, or whomever. Do you feel exploited or oppressed? The government officials are here to help you. If any problems develop, you should notify the authorities."

According to this reasoning, just as parents have a moral obligation to care for their children, the government has a moral obligation to its subjects. Conversely, just as children have an obligation to obey their parents, citizens have an obligation to obey their government. As filial children villagers were expected to honor and obey their parents, the king and queen, and by extension their surrogates, government officials. The seventh scout law specifically states, "A good scout respects and listens to the wishes [literally, 'orders', *chyafang khamsang*] of his parents and superiors." Thus whereas the villagers were to obey, the government officials were to be trusted to use their positions wisely.

The scout appeal to the family motif reversed the belief characteristic of democratic societies that government officials should obey the wishes of the people—that the people, not the government, should be the force determining government policy. The good citizen follows the laws of the nation without question because those who make the laws "know better" than the citizenry; the citizen does not participate in setting the laws. The tacit ideal is that of a passive citizenry far removed from the affairs of state. In the family motif the citizens are infantilized and subordinated, passive subjects and not active participants in society.

Unity, Not Criticism

Khwaam samakkhii was a term used repeatedly in the ritual and political rhetoric of the day. Although the phrase is often translated as 'unity', in the context of the Village Scout movement it might better be translated as 'harmony.' Thais were not simply to be united against an external threat but were to have harmonious relations among themselves. A good citizen and a good scout would not speak ill or find fault with others. The fight scenario between the two instructors was intended to underscore this point. As one scout instructor explained this scenario to me, "Thais should not argue or fight among themselves as they are all brothers and sisters under the parentage of the monarchy."

The ritual portrayed criticism of the government as divisive. It disrupted harmony, contributing to anarchy and the vulnerability of the Thai nation. This theme was the primary lesson to be learned from the historical dramas performed on the second night; because the people of Ayuthaya (ironically, in fact, the members of the ruling elite) had not been united, the kingdom had fallen to the Burmese. Similarly, in the scenario dealing with gossip on the afternoon of the fourth day the initiates were taught that rumors critical of the government were likely to be distorted, untrue, and even could be creations of communist agitators. Gullible villagers who believed rumors critical of the government left the country vulnerable to communist infiltration, division, defeat, and ultimately destruction.

In emphasizing the ideals of unity and harmony the Village Scout movement reinforced an authoritarian Utopia, not a democratic and pluralistic society. The belief that differences of opinion are evil is in direct opposition to the ideal of a pluralistic democracy, which sees divisions of opinions and heated debate as vital checks against the abuse of power. Not only were villagers to obey government officials but, just as filial children were not to argue with or criticize their parents, villagers were not to argue with, criticize, or make demands of the government.

Followers Versus Leaders

Instead of encouraging independent expression and grassroots leadership the Village Scout movement reinforced a preexisting attitude among villagers that it was better to remain anonymous and part of a group than be singled out as a leader. At no time during the initiation rite was an initiate singled out for a unique personal ability or praiseworthy accomplishment. Instead villagers were singled out only in a negative light—for having done something wrong. Those wrongdoings involved arriving late or walking out of order, or contrived violations such as being the last to stand at attention because a scout instructor had run off with the color-group flag.

Although being made to dance the duck waddle was not a grave punishment, it was nonetheless humiliating, especially for older villagers made to dance in front of a generation that otherwise addressed them as Mother, Father, Grandmother, or Grandfather. In every case in which villagers were made to dance the duck waddle, once they got near their color group, they broke the duck posture and scurried back into place, clearly quite relieved to be back with their group. Villagers have traditionally believed in safety in numbers, and they are reluctant to become embroiled in conflicts that might alienate them from the consensus.

Thus the Village Scout movement based its ideological appeal upon the rhetoric of the family. The ideology was "naturalized," the scout hand salute serving as an appeal to hierarchy that was reinforced by the natural shape of the hand. Family provides an ideal imagery for conservative or fascist movements to draw upon. Intrinsically hierarchical, the family imagery can be used to rationalize and naturalize hierarchy—and hence social stratification—by disguising it in the emotional cloak of love, protection, and mutual support.

Agrarian Issues Ignored

Although countering insurgency was a primary motivation of the Village Scout movement, the ritual included no serious discussion of communism or the factors underlying its spread. Communists were presented primarily as foreigners recruiting Thais willing to betray the country by destroying its unity. Whether the designers of the ritual were unaware of agrarian problems or whether they were unable to find solutions that did not jeopardize established interests, the five-day ritual never included discussion of the real economic and social problems villagers were facing or appropriate ways to address such difficulties.

Communists: An External Threat

To the extent that communism was discussed explicitly in the course of the five-day ritual, the emphasis was on hostile external forces seeking to invade Thailand. Throughout the session instructors referred to the past, when Thai kingdoms fell to the Burmese. These historical references served as allusions to the contemporary alleged enemy, the Vietnamese. During the civilian period the government already had directed significant propaganda campaigns against the Vietnamese. In northeastern Thailand, where there is a concentration of Vietnamese, violence had broken out against Vietnamese shop owners. As I mentioned in chapter 1, much of the propaganda had sexual undertones. Beginning in the civilian era the media were reporting rumors that certain Vietnamese-made foods caused impotence. Throughout this period a rash of hysterical men sought medical help at hospitals, reportedly suffering from shrunken penises. The scout session played upon these fears, with one instructor suggesting during the first day's evening session that the Vietnamese were giving men in Laos a potion that reduced their sexual desire.[5] Thus the threat to Thailand was portrayed as an intrusive and intimate penetration by foreign agents.

The initiation skits insinuated that communists operated like the Burmese of the Ayuthayan period who were able to manipulate internal dissension for their own ends. Just what the communists' goals were and why they might want to take over Thailand was never clearly stated. In one skit performed during the evening campfires the villagers were portrayed as neatly dressed men, women, and children helping each other in the fields and minding their own business.[6] Suddenly, they were attacked by unruly, dirty, bearded men who were slovenly dressed and carrying guns. Yelling and shouting, they started killing the villagers for no reason. Unlike bandits, they did not want money. After the attack the villagers sought help from the government. The Border Patrol Police arrived, neatly dressed, clean shaven, and speaking politely to the villagers. With the next communist attack the police killed the communists and restored peace. Similarly, the Zulu skit portrayed scouts as an orderly, civilized, peaceful force pitted against a dark, wild, savage, warlike body of jungle dwellers. The contrast between democracy and communism was portrayed as a simplistic distinction between order and chaos: neatly dressed clean-shaven citizens against dirty bearded wild men; village community members against nomadic forest dwellers with no family or community ties; families against single men; peace-loving passive citizens imbued with moral principles of law and order against gun-toting, aggressive, amoral anarchists who sought not the betterment of society but its destruction.

Communism was not portrayed as a form or philosophy of government but as a state of nongovernment, of anarchy and lawlessness. The Village Scout movement did not appeal to moral principles of justice or equality. Instead it sought to remind villagers of their desire to live in peace with their homes and villages unmolested by intruders.[7] The ritual never confronted why some Thais were becoming communists. The implicit suggestion was that Thailand had no real internal problems, only imaginary problems created by communist propaganda. By suggesting that criticism of the government was bad, the scout movement portrayed all leftist criticism of government policy as false agitation. By defining communists as outsiders and non-Thai, the scout movement was able to imply that all critics of the government were in collusion with outsiders seeking to undermine the government. Non-Thais were not loyal to the Thai nation, religion, or king. Equating critics with non-Thais transformed the quest for social change or social reform into a plot to undermine the Nation,

Religion, and King. The difference between left and right was not presented as a legitimate acceptable difference of opinion but as a difference
between Thai and non-Thai, harmony and discord, order and chaos.

No Recourse for Grievances

Unlike citizens of a Western democracy who are admonished to participate in the political process, the scout initiates were repeatedly told that
scouts do not engage in politics. Although the scout instructors never
specifically broached the issue of demonstrations, strikes, or petitions to
the government, their injunction that scouts were not to be political was
understood to mean that villagers were not to demonstrate, strike, or file
petitions. Muecke notes that the staff training manuals state that Village
Scouting was intended as "a means to strengthen Thai society against
instability and political abuse" by, among other things, trying to "avoid and
prevent labor disputes to preserve national security, to nourish peace and
prosperity" (1980:423).[8] Scout instructors I interviewed confirmed their
view that good citizens did not strike or demonstrate.

When I asked the scout instructors how model citizens were to voice
their grievances, I was informed only that they should notify the appropriate authorities. When I asked what a citizen was to do if the appropriate authority failed to take action for whatever reason, the instructors
responded with a smile and shrug of the shoulders. Although the issue of
corrupt officials was broached during the session, the instructors never
explained to whom and how scouts should report such complaints. The
exhortation to the initiates was less to report corruption to a given
authority and more that villagers should not help corruption by paying
bribes. Thus it would seem that just as children have no way to force their
parents to be good and wise, so too the Thai citizenry was offered no
legitimate channels to ensure that the government be "good and wise."[9]

Order, Thrift, and Self-Reliance Lead to Prosperity

Given the extent of economic grievances manifested during the civilian
period, it is remarkable that the designers of the Village Scout movement
paid so little attention to economic issues. Poverty, landlessness, indebtedness, and conflicts over land rent were all major problems facing villagers.
These unresolved issues contributed to both the growth of the Farmers
Federation of Thailand and to the strength of communist guerrilla forces.

The scout view of the state of the Thai economy appears to have assumed underlying natural abundance; the much-quoted thirteenth-century inscription of King Ramkhamhaeng, "In the fields there is rice and in the waters there are fish" was accepted as a twentieth-century truism (see Bowie 1992). The Village Scout movement suggested that if citizens abided by the laws, the country would have peace and order and everyone would prosper (*thaa thuk khon tham taam kotmaaj, prathet thai ca caryyn*). Thus the scouts were reproached and admonished to keep other villagers from logging teak, making illegal liquor, and killing fish with bombs because such activities were said to harm the nation's economy (just how was never specified). Although they chastised villagers for undertaking illegal activities, the instructors never confronted the economic forces driving villagers to engage in such behavior or suggested alternative sources of income.

The Village Scout philosophy thus began by assuming that Thailand had no significant economic issues that needed to be addressed. Its ideal paradigm was that of a government presiding in the capital while the citizenry peacefully went about making a livelihood. To the extent that economic issues were addressed scouts were encouraged to be thrifty (scout law nine) and to avoid buying foreign goods because this hurt the balance of trade. The scouts were also prompted not to be idle because leisure time leads to time wasted on "thinking evil thoughts or doing useless things like playing cards, gambling, cockfighting, making illegal liquor or getting into fights," as the BPP scoutmaster told them on the fifth morning. This last injunction was perhaps based on the prevalent urban ideology, which assumed that people were poor because they were lazy, drank, or gambled. Scout philosophy took the burden of solving economic problems away from the government and placed the onus on the individual citizen. Because good scouts always persevere, impoverished villagers who had lost hope of being able to support their families had evidently not tried hard enough (i.e., scout law eight). The message to the Village Scouts discouraged them from making demands of the government and actively participating in policy formation; rather they were to follow the laws, be thrifty, persevere, and all would be well.

Underestimation of Rural Poverty: Insulting Poor Villagers

In an effort to mitigate the traditional tension between villagers and government officials, the special lessons for initiates were clearly intended to familiarize villagers with the kind of assistance they might receive through various government offices. However, the subjects the initiates were "taught" were often so simplistic and out of touch with village realities as to be insulting. For example, one lesson taught knots for binding lengths of bamboo. Although this information may have been novel to urbanites, villagers use bamboo in a wide variety of ways in daily life; they were already experts in finding, cutting, splitting, flattening, and tying bamboo together. A more useful lesson was first aid. The lesson in family planning was useful, but villagers, virtually without exception, already practiced birth control. Yet another discussion dealt with the importance of having short fingernails and other such issues of personal hygiene; because village culture already valued personal cleanliness, the lesson was essentially superfluous. Apparently, the scout instructors thought that they were imparting new information, an indication of the extent to which a common urban attitude—that villagers are poor because they are ignorant—influenced the design of the initiation rite. Although villagers might agree that they were ignorant, their ignorance lay more in the area of knowing their legal rights than in areas such as knot tying or hygiene.

Other talks, especially that given by the district police chief, also highlighted irrelevancies and ignored village issues in implicitly more controversial ways. In a district beset with growing crime, particularly theft and heroin addiction, the police chief's decision not to talk about these problems was remarkable.[10] Instead he explained that the duties of the police department are to maintain law and order, enforce the laws, protect religion and religious institutions, and enforce the traffic laws. He focused on this last issue, explaining in considerable detail that drivers should stop at stop signs and red lights and drive on the lefthand side of the road. Pedestrians were to walk on the righthand side so they could easily see oncoming traffic and to cross streets at marked intersections (most villages are comprised of dirt roads, so intersections exist only in towns and cities). After this talk the scout initiates sang about looking to the left and right before crossing the street and taking care not to walk in front of cars. Because most villagers went to town only rarely and villages had few cars at this point, the discussion and song were quaint.

Even more controversial—again for what was not discussed—was the talk given by the district agricultural officer. In Samsen Subdistrict as much as 80 percent of the population of some villages was comprised of landless wage laborers. Given the prevalence of landlessness, the agricultural officer broached a sensitive topic by assuming that farming was the way of life of all villagers. He told the villagers that teak logging was illegal because it caused erosion problems. He told them not to throw bombs into the water when they fished, because bombs killed both young and old fish. He told them not to use fertilizers and insecticides in overly great amounts because too much could be just as harmful as too little. He also recommended that villagers join the government agricultural cooperative so that they they could buy tractors at lower prices and obtain lower interest rates. The district agricultural officer then led the initiates in singing, "Let's smile, let's smile, a big, broad smile," as the scout instructors sprinkled water on everyone to help them stay awake.

Poorer initiates must have found it difficult to smile cheerfully after hearing this talk. Everyone knew that teak logging was illegal. Everyone was also well aware that throwing bombs into the water killed small and large fish alike and thus would lead to a shortage of fish in the future. However, poverty forced them to live from day to day, and they could see no alternatives other than starving or continuing with what they were doing.[11] They also knew about the inexpensive loans available through the government agricultural cooperatives. However, before people could borrow money there, they needed a land title as collateral. The growing use of tractors by wealthier villagers had already become a tremendous source of tension between rich and poor villagers. Poorer families traditionally tried to keep buffalo in order to hire out to do plowing for the wealthier villagers. These poorer villagers would hardly have been sympathetic to the the officer's endorsement of tractors.

Thus an analysis of the content of the five-day initiation ritual reveals no serious channels for the expression of political or economic grievances. The lectures revealed a remarkable lack of knowledge or unwillingness to confront the complex social problems besetting villagers. Given the avoidance of the difficult issues, what influence did the Village Scout movement have on peasants' political consciousness? As the remainder of this chapter will show, the movement had different consequences for the village elite, the village middle class, and the poor.

Effect on Village Initiates over Time

Emotions ran high in the days immediately after the Village Scout initiation session. Many initiates felt empowered by their membership in a transvillage organization. One village teenager, from one of wealthier families, even dared to invite several scout instructors to her birthday party.[12] Not only were the bonds among scouts heightened in the days afterward, but the consciousness of communism as an evil threat to the Thai nation intensified. The newly initiated villagers teased nonscouts about it with varying degrees of seriousness. I overheard one new scout joking with a friend who had not been initiated, "Hey, you communist, aren't you afraid to come into my house? This is a tiger den, you know."

The headman of one small village, who had campaigned for the progressive New Force Party, bore the brunt of this newfound self-righteousness and vigilance. Because of his support for the New Force Party he was already suspected of being a communist sympathizer. As discussed in chapter 5, scout organizers blamed him when only four of his villagers signed up to become scouts, unconvinced that the rest were so busy planting rice in the fields.[13] After the initiation some scouts began to ostracize him, even though he had been elected to the chapter's leadership. When I planned to visit his village during a religious festival there, a few Samsen villagers cautioned me not to visit him—they said his house had a smell (*mii klin*). The headman in turn complained that when members of the Samsen scout chapter went to visit their "junior siblings," no one informed him of the times and places, even though he was one of the seven chapter officers and they always came to his village to pick up one woman who was a well-known local singer. Furthermore the growing discussion about holding another session put him in a difficult position. Although they had declined to attend, families in his village had reluctantly agreed to donate money for the initiation. He did not feel that the wealthier families would appreciate being asked for further contributions again so soon, and the poorer families really did not have the money to give. However, he worried that he would be under an even deeper cloud of suspicion if he failed to raise the expected amount of money. Within a few weeks of the initiation he began to contemplate resigning as headman.

Although the Village Scout initiation encouraged some scouts to ostracize and intimidate others in the community, many other new initiates voiced critical or skeptical comments. As one new scout remarked, "The government makes all this big to-do about the scouts. It thinks that this way it will keep us from becoming communists. But really it is like tiger balm [camphor salve] on a wound—it doesn't cure it, but it makes the hurt go away for a short time. All that you really get from the scouts is the scarf. And what good is that? You can't eat it and you can't sell it."

The Village Elite: From Euphoria to Apathy

The Village Scout ideology generated moral pressure toward unity, toward treating other villagers as members of the family, and toward making sacrifices for the well-being of the entire village family. This ideology placed considerable pressure on the rural elite to be generous toward less fortunate community members. The obligation of the rich to help the poor is inherent in the elite ideology of patron-clientship and reinforced by the Buddhist exhortation to give (*dhana*; see Bowie forthcoming).[14] In effect this ideology shifted the burden of helping villagers from the central government to the local elite—a Southeast Asian anticipation of U.S. President George Bush's "thousand points of light."

Right after the initiation session the predominant mood of the village organizers was enthusiasm. The village elite was swept away by a kind of euphoria. Scout philosophy reinforced the preexisting village ideals that the wealthier should help the poor. In their evening chats members of the village elite vowed that they would visit their junior scout troops whenever possible. They were eager to arrange for another initiation session in their subdistrict for those who had been unable to attend the first, bandying about a date in late November. They were aware that government funds were available only for the first initiation rite in a given subdistrict. Nonetheless they argued that raising the money would not be a problem. They reasoned that if ten villagers in each of the twelve villages gave 100 baht, they would already have 12,000 baht.

However, the enthusiasm soon palled. Scout activities were numerous and all involved financial outlays by the wealthier villagers. When scouts made merit at any one of the dozens of temples in the district, the organizers always contacted the local elite for contributions. Although members of the village elite had always been expected to make substantial contributions for merit-making ceremonies, the scout network dramatically increased the number of occasions on which scouts in one village or another, from one troop or another, were engaged in merit-making activities. Although I do not believe the total number of merit-making ceremonies held by village temples increased significantly, the scout elite was being solicited for a far larger percentage than when contributions were solicited primarily within the immediate community.

When scouts met to clean up the district office grounds, to pull weeds from the canals, to make merit at another temple, to visit a junior scout troop, or to engage in any other of the myriad scout activities, the village

Village Scouts participating in a Buddhist religious festival.
(Photo used by permission of Mae Liang Inthong Suriyasak.)

elite was invariably asked to provide transportation. Every time a truck was borrowed for scout activities, its owner lost money: money in income not earned, money for gas, and often money to pay for a round of friendly drinks. Over time the Samsen Village elite came to resent the financial burden. At first the truck owners didn't mind being good sports, but after a few trips they began to complain. Finally, on one occasion they decided to charge their scout passengers 2 baht each. Poorer scouts believed the truck owners were being greedy. Resentful poorer scouts felt that the truck owners were already wealthy and more easily could afford the expense of gas. At the time 2 baht equalled the cost of a liter of rice. Poor villagers were earning only 5 baht a day weaving bamboo mats.

Conflict surfaced again when members of the village elite disagreed about who was to pay for scout-related expenses. In one case scouts had come from neighboring villages and subdistricts to make merit at the village temple some months after the training session. The scout merit-making event was organized by a village merchant who was also a scout. Supposedly, the kamnan had told the merchant that the temple committee would pay for the soft drinks, but communications broke down. The bill for soft drinks came to 200 baht. The temple committee refused to pay. The total funds raised for the temple amounted to little more than the cost of the soft drinks. The committee countered that it had assumed that the merchant-scout was donating the drinks. If they had known that the money was to come from temple funds, they would have served just ice water. A drawn-out debate followed about whether to ask wealthier local scouts to defray the cost of the soft drinks or whether the cost should be deducted from monies contributed. The bickering then fueled a movement already underway to force the kamnan to resign, with his critics claiming that the incident provided further evidence of the kamnan's alleged incompetence.

Planning scout activities involved considerable effort and could provoke tremendous frustration. The complications that developed in the case of a scout troop's first anniversary celebration provide a dramatic example. This case did not involve the Samsen Village anniversary but that of a neighboring scout troop. Because this troop had been founded earlier, some of Samsen Village's elite had been initiated with this neighboring troop. The meeting to plan the anniversary was to be held in a village not far from Samsen, the site of that troop's initiation. Because this meeting exemplifies the everyday ramifications of the movement, I shall describe the debates and ensuing events in some detail.

The meeting got off to a bad start because only seven of the ten leaders expected were present; of the seven, four were substitutes, so they were more observers than active participants. Initial discussion centered on whether the anniversary celebrations should include a morning merit making and/or an evening campfire. If both were held, what would everyone do for the rest of the day? And given that all the troop instructors had to be invited and feasted, how were they going to raise the 3,000 baht they figured it would cost? They decided to hold a fund-raising event and use the amount of money they raised to guide how elaborate the anniversary celebration would be.

This decision then led to a lengthy discussion of how best to raise money. The scout officers decided that having a band was too expensive and consequently too risky. After much discussion they decided to organize an all-night film festival, showing five films in succession. They initially thought to ask for volunteers from each subgroup to handle ticket taking and other organizational work. They calculated that they would need about twenty people. However, because they weren't sure they could get twenty volunteers, they decided that they would hire people for 20 baht each. Discussion of the various alternatives for maintaining order was considerable. The military and the BPP were both ruled out as too expensive. One participant said that at an event in Chiang Mai City the military police were paid 100 baht each, but they also ran up a 1,000-baht restaurant tab that the sponsors had to cover. Although organizers were worried about using local police, especially in light of what had happened in the village where I lived (see chapter 5), they decided that the police were the best option under the circumstances. Trying to check for weapons themselves would only cause problems because they wouldn't be able to confiscate the weapons carried by plainclothes police.

They figured the film festival would cost about 6,000 baht: 4,000 baht to rent the movies, 400 baht for hiring help, 800 baht for the outdoor canvas wall-tent, the cost of security, printing tickets, and other miscellaneous expenses. Prepaid tickets were to cost 3 baht, increasing to 5 baht the night of the event. They then discussed where to show the film. Various people volunteered for different jobs, but the bulk of the work was to fall on the shoulders of my friend, a shopkeeper.

With the fund-raising plans settled, they returned to planning the anniversary day. They decided to contact various village hosts to see whether they would be willing to open their homes during the day. They spoke at length of how meals should be arranged (whether the scouts should bring their own food or host families should be paid to cook); who should serve as master of ceremonies for the evening campfire; which monks, which dignitaries, which scout chapters should be invited; and how the publicity should be handled.

Given the amount of effort involved in coordinating and planning a single scout activity, my friend, the village shopkeeper, was upset by the thanks he received for his labor. He had agreed to be the main organizer for the movie fund-raiser. He put in hours contacting various film representatives. Using his own capital, he paid the 500 baht deposit and signed a contract for five films at a cost of 4,000 baht. Everything looked to be in order, but everything went wrong despite his best efforts. The company brought four films instead of five, it didn't start showing the films until 10:30 instead of the agreed-upon time of 8:30 P.M., and instead of a big outdoor screen the company brought video monitors. The turnout was better than the shopkeeper had dared dream. But when the moviegoers saw the video monitors, they became angry and many demanded their money back. There was nothing the shopkeeper could do but apologize profusely to everyone and return their money. As if that wasn't enough, some irate moviegoers urinated on his car before they left.

Nor did the nightmare end that night. The shopkeeper refused to pay the film company its money, and the company threatened to sue him. In the end he reached a compromise with the company, and the fund-raiser realized a profit of 2,000 baht. On the occasion of the first anniversary elections were also held for new officers of the scout chapter. The shop-keeper was voted in as president; not surprisingly, he turned the position down, saying it was more work than he could handle.

Aside from supporting Village Scout events, the village elite initially also felt pressured to help other villagers. I recall being shocked when I heard one notoriously selfish member of the village elite discussing fund-raising strategies for future scout events. With uncharacteristic compassion he said that it would not be right to ask for contributions from poor peo-ple because the intent of scouting was "to reduce the gap between rich and poor" (*lot chong wang rawang ruaj kap con*). Still the enthusiasm of the rural elite for helping poorer villagers was uneven and often short lived. Within days of his noble declaration of sensitivity to the poor the aforementioned villager got into an argument with a poor neighbor who was unable to pay his portion of an electricity bill (because electrification was progressing slowly in rural Thailand, many villagers shared electric lines). As a result of the dispute he cut the electricity to the poorer neighbor's home.

In another case a generous villager was criticized for his largesse to the poor. This villager and scout troop leader had gone so far as to sell rice somewhat less expensively to poor villagers.[15] Other members of the vil-lage elite resented his beneficence because they were unwilling to match it. As one of them said, "It's all right for him. He was an only child and received a large inheritance. He only has two children. On top of that he is already a village headman and is looking to become kamnan. But me—"

Even among the most charitable of the rural elite the pressure to help poorer kinsmen and other villagers took a mounting toll. The poor out-numbered the rich, so it is not surprising that richer villagers felt hard pressed when asked repeatedly for loans of money and rice. Nor was their willingness to provide loans always met with the measure of gratitude they felt appropriate, because the gratitude of the poor for a loan was often tempered by resentment of the high interest rates of 5 to 10 percent per month. Thus, although the village elite cooperated with the Village Scout movement initially and justified the sacrifice of time, money, and effort in patriotic terms, scout activities presented a continual series of petty obstacles to be overcome. Influential villagers had insufficient incen-tive, whether financial rewards, power, prestige, or religious merit, to continue to overcome such obstacles indefinitely.

The Poor and Middle Classes Who Joined

Of the landless poor and smallholding peasantry who joined the movement, reactions to the Village Scout initiation varied widely according to their motivations for joining. Some joined because they had heard the five-day initiation was a lot of fun. Some joined because they had heard of the magical properties of the royal kerchief and wanted to obtain one. Some villagers joined under duress, fearing that if they did not join they would be labeled as communist sympathizers. Still others joined because they hoped that they would become part of a broader network of mutual support for times of need.

A common belief of villagers was that people get ahead in life less on the basis of their abilities and more on their social connections. Thus many villagers joined in hopes of developing closer ties to wealthier villagers and townspeople who might then be more willing to help them in times of need; such needs included providing loans or access to a car to take sick relatives to the hospital. Many also hoped to develop connections with government officials in order to facilitate requests for licenses or to ward off harassment for violations of seemingly endless bureaucratic regulations. Some also joined in the vague hope that, should overwhelming problems arise, they might have a better chance of having their letter read by the king and thus receive special assistance.[16]

Those who participated in the five-day session because it was fun and they wanted to meet people generally had their expectations fulfilled. Those who sought the magical scarf proudly placed it high upon the altar with the family's ancestral spirits and Buddha image. However, those who had joined with the expectation of material benefits became increasingly disillusioned. The initiation session had reinforced moral expectations of generosity. As wealthier scouts became less and less willing to assist their less fortunate neighbors, the hopes of the poorer and middle-class villagers, ironically aroused by the Village Scout movement, were increasingly disappointed.

The Village Scouts over Time

Although the Scout movement generated an initial camaraderie among scouts and provided the momentum to ostracize dissident members of the rural community, the euphoria soon dissipated. In addition to temple merit makings and the like, scouts were enjoined to attend the initiations of their *run nong*, or junior sibling chapters. In the euphoria immediately after initiation Samsen scouts had vowed to attend every initiation of their younger siblings. The following month Samsen scouts visited the initiation of a neighboring tambon (subdistrict). Despite the initial excitement, only about one-third of the Samsen chapter went. When the next initiation was held two weeks later, no one from Samsen attended.

The plans for a second training session in Samsen Village never materialized. Despite the scout leadership's initial proclamations that fundraising would be easy, a new consensus developed in subsequent, more private discussions. Several village headmen and other members of the subdistrict elites commented that their village elite had made substantial contributions to the last scout session and subsequent events, concluding that they probably would not be pleased to be asked again so soon. Poorer families were clearly unable to contribute. Initial talk was for a session to be held in November. The date was delayed until February, and by December the date had been postponed to March. After December all talk of holding another session ceased.

On October 6, 1977, not coincidentally the anniversary of the coup of the previous year, the Samsen scout chapter joined with scores of other scout chapters in Chiang Mai for the scout reception welcoming combat troops home from battle with communist guerrillas in the jungle. It was a politically charged day, with thousands of scouts rallying to welcome two to three thousand soldiers.[17] Samsen scouts also participated in two "development" (*patthana*) projects in the district with other scout troops, cleaning up a graveyard and a public road. In November the Samsen chapter members received their identification cards and organized a campfire to celebrate the event. Scouts contributed 10 baht each in order to feast the scout instructors who had been invited to attend, and local village girls performed a traditional dance in costume as the evening's entertainment. On the night of the campfire at least one fight broke out between a local village nonscout and youths from the neighboring village who were scouts. In late February 1978 Samsen scouts went into Chiang Mai to receive their chapter flag. It was presented by the king and the crown princess. Thereafter my field journal notes no further scout activities by members of the Samsen scout chapter.

Given the additional financial burdens and disagreements emerging for wealthier scouts, it was not surprising that more and more of them found excuses not to attend or organize further scout functions. Similarly, poorer villagers failed to attend scout activities, although their problem was often one of not having free time. With the exception of the only villager in the subdistrict who was a Wood Badge Scout and hence had many scout meetings to attend, the most active of the new scouts attended at most two or three junior scout troop initiations, a scout funeral, and two scout functions held in the provincial capital. A matter of a few months separated the euphoria of the initiation from the ensuing apathy.

Of Communism and the Poor

The primary motivation for the development of the Village Scout movement was countering the communist threat. How effectively did the initiation achieve this goal? The reformed Village Scout movement that emerged after the moratorium explicitly stated that it wanted at least one member of each household to be initiated as a scout. Although they never publicly said so to the initiates, the Village Scout leaders were particularly eager for the movement to reach the "alienated riff-raff" of village society before the guerrillas did. This policy was explicitly explained to me by one scout instructor who said, "The communists appeal to the alienated riff-raff of society. If we can get to them before the communists, then the communists will have a harder time winning recruits. The scouts is a non-military way to fight against communism, the 'hearts and minds' of it all."

The goal of reaching the rural poor was a response to prevailing theories of counterinsurgency. According to these theories, guerrillas sought first to create a small core of sympathizers that preferably included one or two notable personages from the community, such as prominent farmers, retired officials, or Buddhist clergy. However, the rank-and-file supporters were made up of "the landless and relatively destitute, the petty criminal element, and especially the unemployed youth" (van der Kroef 1974:120).[18]

A Skew in Membership

Although the Village Scout movement tried to recruit the alienated "riff-raff" of society, an examination of the movement's membership in Samsen reveals a clear bias toward the wealthier, not the poorer, villagers. I asked a village school principal and a kamnan to categorize the initiates from their village and the villages nearby. Of the 145 villagers they ranked, 33 percent were wealthy (owned more than 10 rai and had money in the bank); 37 percent were middle class (owned 5 to 10 rai and may have had some money in the bank), 23 percent were poor (owned 1 to 5 rai and had

Table 7.1 Economic Standing of Scouts Versus Nonscouts

| | Samsen Scout Chapter | | | | | | All Samsen Villagers | |
| | *Chapter Totals* * | | *Non-Samsen Scouts* | | *Samsen Scouts* | | | |
Economic Category	NUMBER	PERCENTAGE	NUMBER	PERCENTAGE	NUMBER	PERCENTAGE	NUMBER	PERCENTAGE
Wealthy: Own more than 10 rai & have money in bank	48	33	29	31	19	38	24	8
Middle Class: Own 5–10 rai & may have some money in bank	53	37	38	40	15	30	78	25
Poor: Own 1–5 rai & have no savings	34	23	22	23	12	24	60	19
Landless Wage Laborers: No land, no savings	10	7	6	6	4	8	148	48
Total	145	100	95	100	50	100	310	100

*All chapter members for whom I was able to obtain data. Data for scouts from outside Samsen Village and for the Samsen scouts were provided by a school principal and a kamnan. Data for all Samsen villagers was obtained from interviews of all Samsen Village household heads (interviews conducted by school principal as part of an official government survey).

A poor, landless villager weaves a bamboo mat in the shade near her home.

no savings), and 7 percent were landless wage laborers (see table 7.1).[19] Complete data for land-ownership in the subdistrict as a whole is not available, although some villages in this subdistrict had landless populations as high as 80 percent. More detailed economic data are available on the village of Samsen. Although only 8 percent of the village as a whole owned more than 10 rai, 38 percent of the village's initiates fell into this category. Whereas 48 percent of the village was landless, only 8 percent of the initiates were (see table 7.1). Thus the proportion of landless scouts is remarkably low.

To a certain extent the ratio of wealthier to poorer villagers in the Samsen scout chapter reflects the time of year that the initiation was held: the middle of the rice-transplanting season. Consequently, only wealthier villagers who hired wage laborers to plant their fields were really free to attend the session. Smallholders generally practiced exchange labor. Therefore only those smallholders whose fields were already planted and who had fulfilled their labor exchange obligations, or who had sufficient family labor otherwise, were able to join. For landless wage laborers transplanting and harvesting were their best opportunities to earn money during the year, so they could least afford not to work at this particular time. However, I believe that the bias in the membership of the Samsen chapter was characteristic of the movement as a whole, regardless of the time of year. Wealthier villagers could afford not to work, whereas poorer villagers were always working to make ends meet. When agricultural labor was in less demand, the workers logged teak, pursued cottage industries, or undertook any other of a number of sidelines.

In addition to the problem of not being able to afford the time away from work, most poorer villagers could not afford the actual cost of the initiation session. In fact, the costs of the scout session were relatively low. Initiates paid no membership fees and brought their clothes, toilet gear, pillow and blanket, a length of bamboo, some rope, four liters of milled rice, and some cash to contribute to the cost of meals. Most initiates spent 15 to 20 baht during the five-day period, apart from whatever voluntary contribution they made to the temple on the last day. Nonetheless landless villagers, who worked today to pay for what they ate yesterday, could not afford five days of leisure and did not have four liters of rice to spare in advance. Despite announcements that Village Scouts were to wear no uniforms, and despite efforts to keep costs at a minimum, becoming a scout was too expensive for many villagers. Several landless villagers I interviewed suggested that they would have become scouts if they could have afforded the time or money, a point intimating the profound lack of comprehension by the designers of the Village Scout movement of the degree of poverty in rural Thailand.

Tension Between Scouts and Nonscouts

This analysis of the intravillage class differentiation in Village Scout membership clarifies the isomorphism between tensions occasioned by scout and nonscout interaction and those that resulted from resentments between rich and poor. Far from incorporating the "alienated riff-raff" of society, the core members of the Village Scouts were members of the village elite and their subordinates. The privileged role that many scouts assumed at public gatherings only reinforced the preexisting tensions between the class fractions within village communities.

Among the most frequent public gatherings in village communities were the temple festivals. Traditionally, villagers from one village would join in the temple celebrations of their friends' villages. One of the most common such temple celebrations occurred around the end of Buddhist Lent in about September or October. At this time a series of different kinds of temple celebrations such as *kathin* and *kin salak* took place in the North. Such festival exchanges combine merit making with fun before the hard work of harvesting begins. As the Village Scout movement expanded in the district, scouts formed their own temple processions. In Samsen's temple merit making for that year, scouts from two different chapters formed two separate processions to carry their merit-offering trees into the temple. In previous years these villager-scouts would have participated in the festivities with other village kin or friends' families, joining them in their procession to bring trees to the temple. Similarly, after the initiation, temple contributions that villager-scouts would have made anyway were often presented to the temple in the name of their scout troop. As scouts they were participating as before, but instead of joining in as family and friends they were now marking themselves off as Village Scouts. This separation caused some comment and resentment among nonscouts.

Similarly, the funeral of a respected elder and a scout leader in a neighboring village caused comment when it was coopted as a scout activity. Another occasion was the housewarming celebration of the deputy head of the Samsen scout chapter. Villagers and scouts from throughout the village and subdistrict attended. Because he was a well-known villager and because the custom was to attend housewarming celebrations, villagers were doing this as much in their capacity as villagers as in their role as scouts. Thus nonscouts felt that they had become second-rate guests at the festivities, with scout guests more important. As Muecke also notes of her conversations with nonscouts, villagers complained that "scouts often take over ordinary local activities such as temple fairs, and claim them as Scout endeavors" (1980:423).

During the initiation the scouts were instructed in appropriate ways to dress and bow before members of the royal family. They also rehearsed the words to several songs of homage. Because of this training scouts were more likely to be confident about how to behave in formal social situations. In many cases this confidence was reinforced by the scouts' wealthier village backgrounds, which gave them more occasions to practice proper etiquette. Thus Village Scouts were quite assertive about taking the front rows at official gatherings. This presumption of preeminence was another cause of resentment, particularly on occasions for paying respects to members of the royal family.

Idiosyncratic Village Definitions of Communism Continue

Although no one explicitly stated at the initiation that the Village Scout movement was intended to counter communism, it was clear to everyone that this was its major objective. The failure to confront the issue explicitly meant that villagers continued to be confused about what communism was. The call to fight against communists was perhaps more of a double-edged sword than the scout instructors realized. From external saboteurs to members of the nation's elite, from money lenders and merchants selling on the black market to police officers, corrupt government officials, and a prime minister, a whole array of people fit villagers' definitions of a communist.[20] For many villagers *communist* was simply another term for a bad person. A few examples provide some sense of the ambiguity and complexity of villages' responses. Ironically, in some of these cases poor villages accused scouts of being communists.

Within a month or so of the initiation I overheard a loud argument at the kamnan's house. It was a dispute between a borrower and a lender; the parties involved had been called to the kamnan's house to straighten out their misunderstandings. The lender was the president of the local scout chapter, a wealthy villager with a reputation for generosity and a willingness to help those less fortunate. It seems the lender had not asked the borrower to sign a contract, and now the borrower was trying to evade repayment of the loan by denying that any loan had ever been made. The borrower was a poor villager and evidently had no means of repaying the money. As I passed by, the scout president was walking down the front steps of the kamnan's house, with the borrower calling after him that he was a communist.

A similar incident took place about the same time. Police were checking villagers for motorcycle licenses on the main road leading into the village. Few villagers were licensed in those days. The police stopped one motorcycle and asked to see the driver's license. As the police officer was about to write out the ticket, a passenger muttered something about the officer's being a communist. He arrested the passenger on the spot, and the kamnan had to go to the district police station to arrange the passenger's release the following morning.

Further complicating village understandings of communism were a series of conflicting developments. On the one hand villagers heard with increasing frequency reports of the atrocities committed by the Khmer Rouge in Cambodia and alarming accounts of those fleeing from Laos, Cambodia, and Vietnam. On the other hand the Communist Party of Thailand (CPT) was continuing to grow throughout this period. Underground pamphlets describing the events of October 6 and criticizing government policies began appearing in the villages. Growing numbers of villagers were coming in contact with communist cadres. Poor villagers who went into the forest for food and lumber increasingly encountered villagers who were in direct contact with the guerrilla forces in the area. Slowly, word of actual guerrilla activities and guerrillas' efforts to help the poor was spreading. The cadres the villagers met were Thai and not Vietnamese, as suggested by the scout instruction.

The tactics of the guerrilla movement were oriented to helping villagers solve local problems. In the initial process of wooing villagers the guerrillas appealed to economic grievances to mobilize villagers' opposition to the government. For example, a cadre traveling about the villages dressed as a pig merchant might start a conversation about the low price of pigs compared to the high price of pig food. From there the conversation could easily be turned to a general discussion of the problems faced by villagers and the government's failure to solve them. The villager who suggests that the government helps by building roads may well find the counterargument more persuasive:

> Oh, do you have a truck? Do you have a car? Do you have a motorcycle? You sold your bicycle to buy medicine when your daughter was sick, you said. So why do you care if the road is wide or narrow, tar-topped or not? Aren't roads built by the government to help rich people get richer? Don't they just make it easier for middlemen to come? Then there is no surplus rice left in the village, and then there are rice shortages before the year is over. Don't they just make it easier for soldiers and officials to come and demand your chickens?[21]

As political organizing by the CPT cadres continued apace, the view expressed by one villager was becoming more common: "The government is afraid of communists because then they, the rich people, would have to work. Right now, only poor people do all the work."

Because the Village Scout initiation never defined what communism was, the ritual seemed to have had little effect in changing attitudes toward communism. My sense was that in the initial aftermath of the initiation session those inclined to be communist sympathizers remained so; those who were hostile to communism continued to be hostile, albeit with more enthusiasm; and those who were wavering continued to waver, although with a greater sympathy for the government's perspective. The major overall change was to shift the spectrum of acceptable public discussion further to the right, forcing those who were sympathetic to leftist criticisms of the status quo to be more circumspect in their public comments.

Continuing Economic Difficulties

However, as time went by villagers became less and less circumspect in their criticism of the Village Scout movement and of the government. With the guerrilla presence growing in the surrounding mountains sympathy for the guerrilla movement was on the rise. By far the most important issue contributing to the growth of leftist sympathies among villagers was their worsening economic plight, namely, the growing shortage of land and the lack of alternative employment. The issues of land reform and land rent control had fueled support for the Farmers' Federation of Thailand and the socialist parties during the civilian period. The economic distress of the North intensified in 1978 when the region faced significant rice shortages. Rice doubled in price in the villages, and milled rice sold for as much as 5 baht per liter. There were shortages of villagers' staple, glutinous rice, and many villagers had to buy the less popular nonglutinous varieties.[22] The high price of rice provoked considerable frustration with the government, and more and more villagers were becoming sympathetic to the left.[23]

The wealthy, who felt burdened by the demands of their poorer relatives, became increasingly frustrated that the government was doing nothing to ease the plight of the poor. For landless villagers, who worried each night where they would find money to buy rice for the following day, the rumor that rice was rationed in communist societies offered appealing security. The promise of free medical care was also attractive because illness was a primary cause of indebtedness. Free education would mean that more of their children might have a chance for advancement. The threat that everyone might have to work for the government posed little terror to poor villagers. Their response was, "If you have ever carried a length of teak for four days and nights through the forest, you would never be afraid of a little work in the paddy fields." In response to the idea that communism offers no freedom, such villagers concurred with the villager who said, "We have no freedom now. All we ever do is work and worry." More and more villagers were coming to believe that without major changes their situation was not going to improve.

These comments were no doubt as much an expression of frustration as serious comments about political preferences. Nonetheless they point to the ambiguous outcome of the scout movement with regard to fostering an anticommunist ideology. The initiation session did not reach the key group ostensibly targeted in the Village Scout movement, the alienated poor. The Village Scout movement gave no clear alternatives to villagers frustrated by their daily problems and attracted by the promises of communism. Increasingly, as time passed with little improvement in their economic situation, more and more scouts came to share the view of a landless villager who never became a scout:

> I wouldn't become a scout even if I had the time. What good is there in it? All you get is a cloth scarf. Villagers are small fry (*phuu noi*). If the government is left, the people are left. If the government is right, the people are right. We are like trees that bend in the wind. That is the only way for us to survive. If I opened my mouth and talked too much and got myself arrested or killed, who would care for my family? It is better to say nothing and agree with everything, and just go on minding one's own business. To say things, you have to have money. So there is no point in becoming a scout. It won't change anything. Rich people are still rich and poor people are still poor.[24]

Aftermath at the District Level

The Village Scout initiation encouraged a paternalistic model of government with no real agenda for political, economic, or social reform. As this analysis of the aftermath of the Village Scout initiation in Samsen Village has shown, the movement generated heightened expectations of assistance for the poor. Given the national policy vacuum, these expectations placed increased pressure on the local elite to solve the problems of the nation's poor. Thus it is not surprising that over time the local scout elite began to avoid further involvement with the movement. Poorer villagers also lost interest; their hopes, raised by the movement, were not fulfilled. Albeit for different reasons, the various classes and class fractions within the village began to drift away. I believe that the overall trajectory demonstrated by the Samsen chapter can be generalized: an initial burst of enthusiasm immediately after the initiation session, followed by ever-diminishing participation. Thus, as this analysis demonstrates, the issue of efficacy is complex and must be considered over time. Although national statistics reveal a movement that was mushrooming overall, particularly in 1976 and 1977, a microlevel analysis reveals a more subtle trajectory. Underlying the national explosion in numbers of new members was a pattern of ebbing enthusiasm within the ranks of the older members.

San Patong District held eight initiation sessions from June to

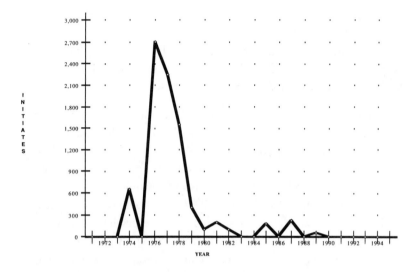

Figure 7.1. Number of New Village Scout Initiates, San Patong District, 1971–1995 *(Source: Data supplied by District Education Office, San Patong District.)*

December 1977.[25] Most of the staffing problems that had contributed to the declaration of a moratorium remained and were clearly visible at the district level. With the flurry of scout initiations in the district in the latter half of 1977 the district office was forced to devote much of its time to preparing for scout sessions. The district officer was involved in all the sessions, attending at least one or two segments of each initiation. In Samsen he was present for the first evening's program, the campfire of the fourth night (which ended about 3 A.M.), and the final day when the kerchiefs were distributed. The police chief also attended various portions of the initiation sessions, presenting one lecture on the fourth morning and attending the virtually all-night campfire that evening. The police, given their security concerns, were even more heavily involved in the initiation in Mae Win Subdistrict.

Throughout the country by far the most heavily involved official was the district education officer (*syksaathikaan amphur*). In Samsen the San Patong District education officer was present for the first evening and most of the third day and night. In addition to whatever time he spent attending initiations, this officer processed all the paperwork for each of the hundreds of initiates of each chapter. He was also responsible for staffing each initiation. Because most scout instructors were drawn from the ranks of the rural schoolteachers, this department was heavily bur-

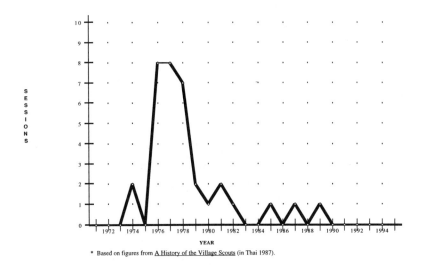

Figure 7.2. Number of Village Scout Initiations, San Patong District, 1971–1995. *(Based on figures from VS history [1987].)*

dened. As was occurring elsewhere in the country, the schoolteachers who were left behind in the village schools became increasingly frustrated. These teachers, with many of their colleagues on leave to staff the initiations, found they had to handle several classrooms at once. The quality of teaching was suffering. Furthermore they were becoming increasingly resentful that the teachers involved in scouting were developing closer and closer ties to district officials, increasing their chances of receiving promotions and pay increases. Their district-level superiors, also involved in scouting, saw scout participation as a special sacrifice, so they awarded the coveted "double step" salary increases to many scout instructors–teachers. The teachers left behind were perceived as performing only their ordinary tasks and so were not as likely to be considered as candidates for double pay increases.

In addition to individual initiations, district-level scout activities also had to be organized. In the months immediately after the moratorium San Patong District officials were involved in organizing a districtwide scout merit-making at a temple in the district town. The district officer spoke at this gathering, as did other scout officials. District officials were also involved in coordinating the October 6, 1977, reception for returning troops. In mid-October the officers of the scout troops attended a district meeting to discuss scout participation in a nationwide effort to wipe out the *topcawaa* weed, which was clogging many irrigation canals and river-ways.[26] Thereafter district-level scout activities fell into a lull.

The overall pattern of scout activities in San Patong district reflected a convergence of dual pressures, those from the village and those coming from the national bureaucracy. Unlike the expansion of the civilian period, in the months that followed the lifting of the moratorium, government orders, not local demand, provided the impetus for new initiations. Thus, given the increasing discontent of the village elite and many local government officials, it is not surprising that without outside pressure and resources the movement waned over time.

The course of the movement in San Patong District shows a notable decline after 1977. In 1976 about 2,670 new members were initiated in six sessions. In the seven months in which sessions were allowed in 1977, 2,295 new members were initiated in eight sessions. By 1978 the total number of new members in seven sessions had dropped by 30 percent, to 1,602. By 1979 this trend was greatly exaggerated; only two new sessions were held, initiating a mere 418 new members. Between 1980 and 1986 only seven more sessions were held, each with an average of only 150 new members. The last session was held in 1989 and had only 58 participants (see figures 7.1 and 7.2). There are no current plans to hold additional sessions in the district.

The declining interest in Village Scout activities coincided with significant changes at the national level. On October 20, 1977, a new government headed by General Kriangsak Chomanan seized power. By 1979 it had become increasingly apparent that the CPT was torn by internal divisions. Nonetheless the decline in the Village Scout movement was not entirely inevitable. Had the CPT continued to provide a meaningful challenge to the government, the national Thai elite would have been more motivated to continue to pour money into the movement. With the provision of funds to aid the rural poor, participation in the Village Scout movement would have appeared more attractive for a longer period of time. Thus to completely understand the decline of the Village Scout movement, we must return to a consideration of changes occurring at the national and international levels.

Conclusion

Prime Minister Chartchai Choonhavan at an award ceremony for Village Scout leaders in 1990. Chartchai, formerly a member of the Thai Nation Party, has had a long-standing relationship with Village Scouts since the 1970s.

(Photo used by permission of Mae Liang Inthong Suriyasak.)

8

Declawing the Tigers

✤

From the opening gauntlet of ants to the closing ceremony of the magical royal scarfs and the stretchers bearing away initiates who were sobbing hysterically, the initiation ritual of the Village Scout movement underwent little change. Its very stasis has helped throw the drama of this period into stark relief. The Village Scouts traversed one of the most tumultuous periods in Thai history, a time when armed opposition to the Thai state was growing. The Village Scout movement began with a man sitting on corpses in a helicopter flying out of the thick of battle and grew until it exploded in the frenzied gruesome atrocities of October 6, 1976. Although stopped short by the postcoup moratorium, the movement appeared to regain momentum. However, as more villagers were drawn into the postcoup movement, disenchantment spread. If in 1976 a gas station attendant could be arrested for criticizing the Village Scouts, by 1977 discontented moviegoers had no hesitation in urinating on a scout leader's van.

Waning village support for the scout movement dovetailed with dwindling support at the national level. The pattern of declining interest among Samsen villagers was paradigmatic of the pattern in village after village around the country at the time. The number of new Village Scout initiation sessions and the number of new members showed a steady decline after 1978.[1] A comparison of the number of new members for 1976 and 1978 shows a dramatic 70 percent drop in the number of new initiates nationally. This trend continued, and in 1981 the national movement initiated only 38,850 new members, or 2 percent of those initiated in 1976. Since 1981 Village Scout initiations have held steady at about two hundred sessions annually, with new membership averaging 30,000 candidates each year, according to Somkhuan Harikul (1991 interview).

The decline of the Village Scout movement dates to the coup by General Kriangsak Chomanan on October 20, 1977. The Kriangsak government represented a new coalition of state factions that for a variety of reasons sought to rein in the Village Scout movement. With the demise of the Communist Party of Thailand, Kriangsak's successors had even less reason to maintain the organization. This last chapter explores the interplay of events in the late 1970s and 1980s that led to the movement gradually fading from the national political stage.

Updating the National Movement

Shortly after he assumed power on October 20, 1977, General Kriangsak Chomanan, the new prime minister, began to declaw the Village Tiger Cubs, as the name of the Village Scout movement is more literally translated. It was widely known that Kriangsak was not sympathetic to the Village Scout movement; he never appeared in more than a simple Boy Scout uniform.[2] However, the tension between Kriangsak and the Village Scouts was not personal but structural. The new Kriangsak government came to power in a coup that ousted the Thanin government. Not surprisingly, the Kriangsak government faced internal problems of stability not unlike those that beset Thanin's.

The new prime minister had been secretary general of the National Administrative Reform Council, the faction that successfully staged the 1976 coup that brought in the Thanin government. Recall that two major groups had plotted separate coups for October 1976. The losing group, which included the conservative wing of the Democrat Party led by Samak Sunthorawej and the Thai Nation Party led by Pramarn Adireksan and Chartchai Choonhavan, had particularly close ties to the Village Scout movement. Thus General Kriangsak was not allied with factions close to the Village Scouts, either in the coup of 1976 or in his subsequent coup in 1977. Consequently, when he assumed power in 1977, he faced the same problem that Thanin had had with regard to the Village Scouts: he had no real control over a group able to mobilize significant popular pressure.

Kriangsak, moreover, had poor relations with several individuals and factions closely affiliated with the Village Scouts. One factor in the coup of October 20, 1977, was the insistence of the leaders of the armed forces that Samak Sunthorawej, minister of interior under the Thanin government, be dismissed. The military saw Samak as "both embarrassing and a potential threat" (Girling 1981: 219). With the coup of 1977 Samak was ousted from power, but he remained a potent figure. One reason for his continuing influence was his status as a trusted adviser to the queen (Morell and Samudavanija 1981:272). Another reason was his considerable base in the urban Village Scout movement (Morell and Samudavanija 1981:269). The magnitude of the political threat to Kriangsak that Samak posed became clear later, in Samak's landslide victory in the 1979 elections.

The other major political party with close ties to the Village Scout movement in 1976 was the Thai Nation Party headed by Pramarn Adireksan and Chartchai Choonhavan. After the 1977 coup powerful military factions, including that of Pramarn and the Thai Nation Party, remained uncommitted.[3] As Morell and Samudavanija write, "Though they lacked adequate leadership to oust Kriangsak, they were unwilling to really support him either" (1981:278). The estrangement between members of this party and the Kriangsak government became even more apparent after the 1979 elections, when the Thai Nation Party refused to join the government and instead formed one of the strongest opposition parties.

Further complicating Kriangsak's political position was that, unlike Thanin, he had at best only "grudging support from the monarchy" (Keyes 1987:102).[4] In addition, as part of the justification for the ouster of Thanin, Kriangsak had promised that popular elections would be held within a year.[5] Lacking both the clear support of the monarchy and the backing of other political figures with connections to the Village Scouts, Kriangsak had to bring the scouts under tighter administrative control in order to consolidate his position for the upcoming election campaign when politicians again would be free to mobilize public opinion. As Girling explains, Kriangsak sought to neutralize his adversaries and "to broaden his political support (against rivals to the Right) by making some overtures to the Center and Left" (1981:220).[6]

One of Kriangsak's first steps was to implement national changes to bring local Village Scout leaders directly under government control, thereby reducing the likelihood that they would initiate actions without official approval. This new national policy administrative took effect in the district in which I was living on December 23, 1977. The reorganizational meeting was held at the district office, and the leaders of all scout chapters in the district were invited. At this meeting the district officer announced the formation of a district scout center (*suun amphur*). All current leaders and deputies of the individual scout chapters would serve as their chapters' representatives to the district scout center. The district officer announced that he would serve as president (*prataan*) of the district scout center for the first year, the chief of police would be the vice president (*rong prataan*), and the district education officer would act as treasurer (*heranyik*). Then, if no problems arose, the scouts would be allowed to elect new officers.

An earlier meeting had been held for the senior heads of scout chapters at Border Patrol Police headquarters in Mae Rim, where they were informed of the decision to bring the scout movement under direct administrative control, at both the district and provincial levels.[7] In explaining the new policy the officer in charge noted that the scouts had been manipulated for political purposes in the past. He cited the example of October 6 when the scouts in Chiang Mai had been called up to counter the students who were occupying the provincial headquarters (*salaklang*), adding that scouts could easily have been hurt if violence had broken out.

Many local scout leaders bitterly criticized the decision to rein in the Village Scout movement. They felt that allowing government officials to serve in scout leadership positions violated the royal guidelines. As one senior scout, a village merchant who believed strongly in the importance of Village Scouts as an independent check on wrongdoings by government officials, commented to me, "Who is one to complain to now if government officials are corrupt? To the officials in question themselves?" Such objections notwithstanding, the Kriangsak government was more concerned about eliminating the possibility that the Village Scouts would act independently.

In March 1978 the Kriangsak government took another major step intended to curtail the movement's independence; the head of the Village Scouts, Major General Charoenrit Chomrasromrun, was transferred out of the BPP. He was demoted to a regular civil service position as an "inspector" in the Ministry of Interior in an effort "to deflate his power"

(Muecke 1980:409). The transfer did not go uncontested. When it was announced, mysterious leaflets appeared encouraging Village Scouts to gather at the scout headquarters in protest. Newspaper editorials attacked the leaflet campaign as a sign that the scout movement was once again being manipulated by political interests (see *Siam Rath Weekly*, April 30, 1978, pp. 4–5). On March 24 national Village Scout leaders went on the radio to denounce the leaflets as counterfeit, adding that they were being distributed in order to cast aspersions on the integrity of the movement. These events were indicative of both the growing divisions within the movement and the weakening political position of the Village Scout leadership.

Both as an inducement to soften the transfer and as a tacit nod to the power of the movement, on April 18 the government announced the formation of the Village Scout Operations Center (*Suun Batibatkaan Luuk Sya Chawbaan*). A national center had been established by Major General Charoenrit Chomrasromrun in 1974, but it had never received official recognition (Muecke 1980:409). Kriangsak now agreed to recognize the center. Charoenrit Chomrasromrun was officially recognized as the director, and Somkhuan Harikul, the movement's founder, was made the deputy director (*Saanprachachon*, May 1, 1978, pp. 7, 16). Located at the headquarters of the Border Patrol Police, the center was to coordinate Village Scout activities throughout the country, organizing initiation sessions, keeping track of scout membership, and planning future activities.[8] Although giving it its own center strengthened the scout movement, it also adroitly brought the movement under tighter administrative supervision. Whereas the Village Scouts had previously come under the powerful Ministry of Interior, the new center came under the overall jurisdiction of the National Boy Scout Council of Thailand. This shift to the national Boy Scout organization brought the Village Scout movement under the jurisdiction of the far less powerful Ministry of Education. Unlike the Village Scouts, the Boy Scouts were a long-established and far more politically neutral organization.

Newspaper articles criticizing the Village Scouts gradually grew bolder. Because the media were still subject to strict supervision, any criticism was usually an indication of the sentiments of at least a faction of the government.[9] Some journalists even went so far as to raise the highly sensitive issue of Village Scout participation in the October 6 massacre and a host of other vaguely phrased but apparently questionable activities by scouts and the scout leadership (*Siam Rath*, April 30, 1978, pp. 4–5). The

Thai media also began reporting conflicts between Charoenrit Chomrasromrun and Somkhuan Harikul. The media generally praised Somkhuan Harikul for his efforts to keep the scout movement "free from politics," whereas they portrayed Charoenrit Chomrasromrun as some-one "seeking power for himself through the Village Scouts" (Muecke 1980:409).[10]

The prime minister began criticizing the scouts, explicitly warning them against interfering in state affairs (Girling 1981:213). In April daily newspapers had headlined a story about a Village Scout leader who had been arrested in Mae Sot District, Tak Province, for illegal teak logging. Because he was facing the possibility of a death sentence under Emergency Decree 21, one thousand scouts gathered to ask the prime minister to reduce the charges. Newspaper columns suggested that the protesters were not bonafide Village Scouts, and the prime minister took the opportunity to denounce such activities as inappropriate: "This kind of activity is political involvement and interference with the administration of the country. It is wholly inappropriate. Such activities must be changed" (*Siam Rath*, April 30, 1978, p. 4).[11]

From this period on the Village Scout movement faded from national view gradually but surely. However, the changes in the administration of the Village Scouts implemented by the Kriangsak government were only part of a complex series of events that contributed to the demise of the movement. Popular conservative support for the movement also diminished in response both to an improving economic environment and the declining political power of the Communist Party of Thailand.

State of the Communist Party of Thailand

Although Kriangsak needed to curtail the Village Scouts to stabilize his own position, international events helped seal the movement's fate. A major cause for the long-term decline of the Village Scout movement was the dissolution of the movement that had catalyzed its formation, the Communist Party of Thailand. The CPT had grown rapidly after the October 6, 1976, coup, in terms of both armed guerrillas and sympathizers. However, the Vietnamese invasion of Kampuchea in January 1979, followed by China's attacks on Vietnam a month later, had serious repercussions for the CPT. The CPT had tried to avoid being drawn into the conflicts developing among Vietnam, Cambodia, and China. The party avoided making any official comment on the Khmer Rouge, China's border skirmishes with Vietnam, and Vietnam's invasion of Cambodia (Girling 1981:246, 283). Despite its caution, the CPT found itself being dragged into the conflicts emerging in these neighboring communist countries.

Although the CPT had been oriented toward China, it needed support from the Soviet-supported countries of Vietnam and Laos. Many of its cadre had trained in Laos and Vietnam. Vietnam, Laos, and Cambodia had all provided safe areas for the CPT. As a result of the continued pro-Chinese policy of the CPT, the CPT radio station VOPT (Voice of the People of Thailand) in Laos was closed in July 1979.[12] United Front committee members in Laos were ordered to leave the country. Kanok Wongtrangan details the disastrous consequences for the CPT of this deterioration in relations between Vietnam and China: "Its sanctuaries in Vietnam and Laos were withdrawn and this necessitated an evacuation of CPT training schools, hospitals, supply stockpiles and personnel stationed in those areas. Additionally, the main external supply line from China running through Laos was abruptly terminated. These set-backs effectively forced the CPT to relinquish its permanent base areas in Tak province, Chiengrai province and in the north-northeast sector" (1984:136).

Furthermore the split within the Chinese leadership and the attack on the Gang of Four complicated relations between China and the CPT.[13] The disastrous state of affairs under the Chinese-supported Pol Pot regime in Cambodia created doubts in the minds of many in the CPT about whether the Maoist form of revolution was an appropriate model for Thai society. As the Chinese government undertook to strengthen its relations with the Thai government, it became doubtful that the Chinese government would continue to support the CPT.[14] The CPT began to splinter under the pressure of the strife between rival communist powers. Girling identifies three factions that emerged in the party: "the old-style pro-Peking leadership; those who are prepared to go along with the Vietnamese; and the 'nationalists,' represented especially by the socialists and democrats from the younger generation, who insist on an independent course" (1981: 285–86).

Meanwhile the Thai government was changing its policies toward the CPT. Beginning in 1978 the Kriangsak government offered amnesty to students and intellectuals who had gone underground because of the events of October 6, 1976. About four hundred students decided to take advantage of the amnesty and were allowed to complete their education (Morell and Samudavanija 1981:304). Many of these students criticized the pro-Chinese bias of the CPT leadership (Wongtrangan 1984:136). As Morell and Samudavanija write, "Because of their desertion from the party and their vehement attacks on it, other radical students were expressing increasing skepticism about the party instead of uncritically accepting it as in the past" (1981:305). Kriangsak's successor, General Prem Tinsulanonda, expanded the amnesty policies. Under what became known as the "66/23" policy (because it was the sixty-sixth order announced in the Buddhist year 2523, or 1980), Prem Tinsulanonda promised immunity from prosecution to guerrillas and supporters of the CPT who surrendered to the government. Thousands took advantage of this amnesty, with groups as large as several hundred turning in their weapons together (see McKinley in Sivaraksa 1985:397).

By early 1980 the CPT was in severe disarray (see figure 8.1). The desire of the Chinese government to work with the Thai government toward a withdrawal of Vietnamese forces from Cambodia led to China's decision to reduce its support to the CPT in February 1981 (Wongtrangan 1984:161). The CPT's Fourth Party Congress in 1982 proved to be a watershed (Keyes 1987:111). The CPT made an effort to change its long-standing Maoist line, which was oriented toward the countryside. Although the party decided to place more emphasis on cities, the changes seem to have been insufficient to sustain the party (Wongtrangan 1984:137; Keyes 1987:111). Many members became alienated from the party and large-scale defections continued. By late 1982 guerrilla strength was estimated at "no more than 4,000" nationwide (Keyes 1987:111). The beginning of the end occurred on July 3, 1984, with the arrest of a number of high-ranking members of the CPT (Keyes 1987:111; McKinley 1985:394). Thus if administrative changes initiated by the Kriangsak government curtailed the independence of the Village Scout movement, the fear of communist insurgency, which had initially inspired the development of the scout movement, was also dissipating.

The Political Ambiguity Remains

Thus the political decline of the Village Scout movement can be traced to the changing alliance of fractions within in the Thai state represented by Kriangsak's rise to power and the changing balance of forces within the country as a whole with the collapse of the CPT. If economic conditions had worsened and if the Kriangsak government had not reached out to students, labor, and farmers, the CPT might have continued to grow.

Figure 8.1 Strength of the Communist Party of Thailand, 1965–1985

VIOLENT INCIDENTS

(ATTACK, AMBUSH, CLASH, HARASSMENT, ARMED PROPAGANDA, AND SABOTAGE)

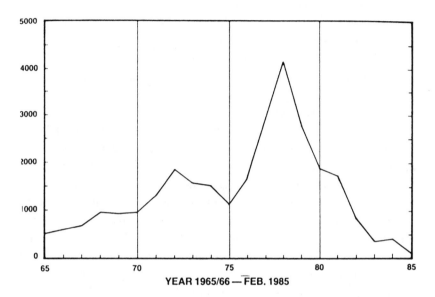

YEAR 1965/66 — FEB. 1985

NON-VIOLENT INCIDENTS

(PROPAGANDA, SUBVERSION, RECRUITMENT, SIGHTINGS, AND OTHERS)

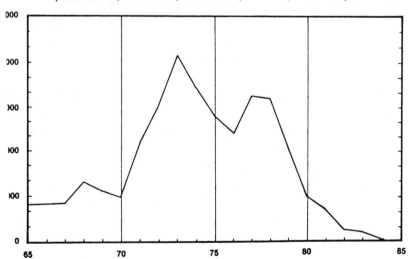

From Kerdphol (1986:187).

Instead the administrative changes initiated by the Kriangsak government allowed it to suppress the Village Scouts. Under Kriangsak the scouts "became less conspicuous" (Girling 1981:213).[15]

However, even if the Village Scout movement did not have much overt political significance, it was not without an ambiguous political presence. By the time the elections were held in April 1979, so many candidates had become scouts that it is difficult to assess the role that scout connections played. That so many candidates were scouts insinuates the movement's continuing potential while suggesting its irrelevance as a factor that was influencing voters' choices. Nonetheless during the elections of April 1979 Kriangsak felt it necessary to caution the scouts not to become involved in the elections, reminding them that they were "not to be involved in politics." A number of candidates expressed concern about the role of the scouts. District education officers, who had considerable inter-action with local scout leaders, came under considerable pressure from a variety of candidates, each hoping to obtain their tacit endorsement and thereby their influence over the local scout movement.

Of the four political parties receiving the greatest number of seats in the 1979 election, to varying degrees three had bases in the Village Scout movement; the fourth, Social Action (*Kit Sangkhom*), established its pop-ulist base with the tambon development funds of the civilian era.[16] In Bangkok Samak Sunthorawej's newly created political party, Thai Citizen, captured 29 of 32 Bangkok seats in the National Assembly. This victory was attributed in part to Samak's "demagogic personality, with his ability to mobilize the village scouts and other 'patriotic' groups" (Girling 1981:n223). Thus, although Kriangsak's reforms clearly had taken some independence and initiative from the Village Scout movement, in 1978 and early 1979 it was too soon to declare the scout movement moribund. The Village Scouts remained a political uncertainty with which whoever was in control would need to reckon.

The Kriangsak government, never firmly grounded, collapsed in March 1980. Another reformist military government soon followed, led by General Prem Tinsulanonda. Prem did nothing to revitalize the Village Scout movement. However, his government courted key politicians influ-ential in the scout movement, appointing generals Pramarn Adireksan and Chartchai Choonhavan of the Thai Nation Party as deputy prime minis-ters (Girling 1981:n226, n318).[17] Nonetheless in 1984 Village Scouts, apparently opposed to the amnesty policy and what they saw as the gov-ernment's "soft treatment of left-wing subversion and communism," participated in an effort to topple the Prem government (J. Williams, quoted in Sivaraksa 1985:375). On July 26 about one thousand Village Scouts rallied in front of Government House to demand the prosecution of a famous intellectual, Sulak Sivaraksa, on charges of lèse majesté (Sivaraksa 1985:438).[18] Thus the Village Scout movement took one of its last gasps immediately after sixteen suspected members of the CPT, including several members of the central committee, were arrested on July 3 (Sivaraksa 1985:358, 394).

Although initiations have continued, the Village Scouts have received public attention on only a few occasions since.[19] The most recent occasion was during the uprising against the military government in May 1992, when Somkhuan Harikul intervened to prohibit the government from mobilizing the scouts.[20] Nonetheless Village Scouts continue to organize or participate in local parades from time to time, and politicians ranging from prime ministers to candidates running in local elections continue to meet with representatives of the Village Scout movement. The current Village Scout leader in San Patong District is most proud of a photograph that shows her receiving an award in recognition of her outstanding service to the Village Scouts. Presenting the award was none other than General Chartchai Choonhavan, then prime minister of Thailand (1988–1991; see photograph on p. 268).

Today the Village Scout movement appears to have become part of the background of Thai society, no more noticeable than the Boy Scouts or Girl Scouts. What the movement's political potential is or might be in the future is unclear. Some observers consider the movement as moribund; others deem it a sleeping giant that can awaken when summoned. Some attribute the low initiation figures to lack of interest; others suggest that everyone who wanted to become a scout already has and consequently the nation is in a state of constant preparedness. Thus some scouts I interviewed made such comments as, "The scouts are in the past. People just lost interest in it. After all, what was there in it except a scarf?" One prominent scout leader lamented that the organization in her district would die when she dies, because no one else was willing to undertake the financial burden. Yet others held a different view. As one scout leader said, "The movement lives on. We are all trained and in readiness. Should the need ever arise, we could be mobilized in a flash." Today the Village Scout movement has little political vitality. However, the right set of circumstances could resurrect the Village Scout movement. In 1995, when the king's health was uncertain and concerns about succession were emerging, the government had its village headmen report on the numbers of Village Scouts in their villages. A certain ambiguity remains.

Hegemony and State Rituals

Assessing the long-term effects of the Village Scout movement is not easy. The movement can be declared neither dead nor fully alive. Nor is it possible to offer a simple conclusion about its success or failure. It played an ever-shifting role with varying effects. The movement appears to be on the wane as a specific organization as of this particular historical moment. Ironically, it lost much of its effectiveness at the same moment it succeeded and became embroiled in partisan political machinations. The Village Scout movement was one of a few state-sponsored initiatives of the 1970s to win some level of support from the citizenry. The controversial Tambon Development Fund, which channeled additional government resources into rural areas, was no doubt the other single most important state effort. A path-breaking program launched by the Kukrit government during the civilian era, it allocated funds to subdistricts to spend on grassroots development initiatives.[21]

Nor was the Village Scout movement the only initiative of the Thai state to develop state-controlled and populist conservative organizations as a strategy for mobilizing government support. Although Kriangsak mothballed the Village Scouts, he supported the development of several related paramilitary organizations.[22] More recently, the Thai government has initiated another conservative popular movement called the Oh. Phoh. Poh. (*ongkaan asaa phattana lae pongkaan ton eng*, the Development and Defense Association). The latter is remarkably similar to the Village Scout movement. It uses teachers, police, and soldiers as instructors and puts villagers through an orientation program that lasts several days; members receive such insignia as kerchiefs and armbands upon the successful completion of the program. However, unlike the Village Scout movement in which several ministries were involved, this program is administered entirely by the Ministry of Interior. Thus avatars of the Village Scout movement live on, albeit in ever-changing forms.

This book has argued for the need to consider agency, efficacy, cross-class symbolism, and dynamism in understanding state rituals. Part One explored the issue of agency. At the time Somkhuan Harikul conceived of the basic idea for the Village Scouts, class struggle was escalating into armed conflict. Forced to experiment, state agencies, beginning with

Village Scouts marching in a 1991 parade in Chiang Mai in honor of the king's birthday.
(Photo used by permission of Mae Liang Inthong Suriyasak.)

Border Patrol Police and other departments of the Ministry of Interior, allowed a conception to become a social reality. The monarchy, at once an individual, an institution, and a symbol, facilitated the expansion of the movement. The Village Scout movement benefitted from King Bhumiphol's simultaneous mobilization of progressive hopes and conservative fears. The genesis and persistence of state rituals necessarily involves more than a few individuals; it is best understood as a complex interaction of individuals, state factions, and class fractions.

State rituals in a class-stratified society must be understood not only from the perspective of their agents but also from that of their intended audience. Accordingly, Part Two explored the complex ways in which the Village Scout movement played out at the village level. Although assessing the political consciousness of the peasantry is complicated by villagers' recalcitrance and idiosyncratic usage of language, I have argued that different class fractions within the peasantry varied in their responses to the movement. The elite and middle-class villagers joined, whereas the poor and landless did not. The elite, although generally anticommunist, joined with some reluctance, whereas the middle-class villagers were more eager, hoping to receive economic and political benefits. Immediately after the initiation most participants felt euphoric. Over time that euphoria dissipated into apathy, the village elite perhaps most disenchanted of all.

Numerous scholars have argued that ritual is a symbolic medium of communication. A class-based analysis of state ritual encourages an appreciation of the extent to which specific symbols may carry different meanings to different classes. As Moore and Myerhoff suggest, the deployment of certain symbols by the state may indeed be intended to "mask [deep contradictions], to deny and disguise them and gloss the difficulties they present" (1977:16). Symbols mediate both agency and efficacy. The Village Scout initiation rite combined royalist and family imagery. In portraying the king as the father of the nation the two symbols merged. Yet the symbolism of the family is inherently contradictory; it is at once a progressive symbol of altruism and a reactionary justification for hierarchy and privilege. The ambiguous medium of symbolism allowed the real differences between planners and participants to be masked in a temporary imaginary convergence.

A Historical Bas Relief

The Village Scout movement, whether considered since its inception or in light of its precursors, reveals the dynamism inherent in state rituals. As noted in the first chapter, earlier state rituals were by and large intended to impress their peasant audiences by displays of grandeur. In its effort to reach the hearts and minds of villagers with an approach grounded more in persuasion than public spectacle the Village Scout movement represented a dramatic departure from the state's former strategies. Yet the novelty of the government's approach bespoke the volatility of the period. Old techniques of governance were failing. Viewed over the "longue durée" (Braudel 1980:25) the constant transformation of state rituals can be understood as an inevitable aspect of the war of position between the classes. Once a state ritual is no longer efficacious, it is reformulated and revived, or it wanes and is eventually discontinued. New approaches are deployed.

The relative stasis of the Village Scout initiation rite contrasts with the dynamism of the movement it initiated, illuminating the shifting alignments of Thai society. At its inception in 1971 the movement was primarily a counterinsurgency strategy deployed by the Border Patrol Police in politically sensitive, remote border regions. With the fall of Indochina and the heightening of a sense of domestic crisis in 1975 and 1976, the

Village Scouts metamorphosed into an urban-based movement funded by economically and politically nervous fractions of the middle and upper classes. With high political and economic stakes generating ever-intensifying conflict, warring state factions and class fractions sought to manipulate the movement for partisan advantage. The movement increasingly took on a fascist character, its emotionalism and potential vigilantism not under any single person or agency's clear control. Ultimately, the state was forced to find ways to rein in its creation. The faction that emerged victorious in the military coup of October 1976 imposed a moratorium and reprioritized the organization. The postcoup movement had a quite different character, again taking rural counterinsurgency as its primary emphasis. Sensitive rural areas, not urban centers, again became its focus. Thus the movement underwent major transformations as the historical context changed, and the consequent alignment of state factions and class fractions shifted.

It is also important to understand how a ritual plays out at the microlevel. Given the power of the state to force participation, the starts and stops in the movement's overall trajectory give little insight into its popular reception. As the village-level discussion revealed, the effect of the movement varied over time. The short-term efficacy of the movement was obvious to anyone who observed the five-day initiation session and saw the steady streams of stretchers carrying the hysterical initiates off to nearby health stations. The ritual's immediate effect was emotionally overwhelming and all encompassing, engendering a kind of hysterical euphoria. As I noted in chapter 7, one elderly village woman recalled, "I had always loved the king but never as intensely as I did [at] that moment. That moment I felt it through the core of my being (saabsyyng)." Nor can there be any question that during the mid-1970s, at the height of the political polarization, the Village Scout movement served to intimidate many people into refraining from embarking on development projects in many villages lest they be harassed as suspected communist agents. Political activists from this period vividly recall the difficulties of working under those intensely polarized conditions.

However, the immediate effectiveness of the initiation soon gave way to more complex realities. The ideology of the movement was inherently contradictory. The Village Scouts was a conservative movement that paradoxically sought to generate popular support among the poorer majority of the society, not for social change toward a more egalitarian society, but against social change in favor of the existing social hierarchy. Not surprisingly, the Village Scout movement played out in ironic ways because, although the village elite generally favored the status quo, the village poor did not. When the Village Scout movement failed to achieve any changes in their basic living conditions, any sympathy poorer villagers had for the movement faded into apathy. Thus the targeted audience of the movement, villagers susceptible to the lure of communist propaganda, were captured only temporarily. Furthermore even members of the village elite who were progovernment and anticommunist came to avoid and even actively dislike the movement when it became clear that any assistance to the poor in their villages would be coming primarily from their pockets. Here the movement even backfired. Thus within a matter of months the initial euphoria dissipated and support waned across the spectrum of agrarian class fractions.

Because the struggle between the elite and the subaltern is never static, the issues of the agency, efficacy, and symbolism of state rituals are necessarily dynamic. Their discussion must include a historical perspective. During the life cycle of the Village Scout movement elite support for the movement waxed and waned. The apparent false consciousness of the initiates, buoyed by unfulfilled promises, was elusive and transitory. Time served to unmask the contradictions behind the symbolic appeals of the movement, the mirage of optimism giving way to the harsh reality of class stratification.

State Hegemony and Populist Organizations

The Thai government is not the only government to attempt to create populist conservative organizations to buttress its position. Similar organizations have been created in South Vietnam, the Philippines, Indonesia, Japan, and Nationalist China.[23] Ultimately, comparisons can be made with fascist organizations that developed in Germany, Italy, and elsewhere. Even the original Boy Scout organization developed in the context of an insecure England that feared German expansionism (see Rosenthal 1980, 1986 for a fascinating discussion). Far more research needs to be done on conservative, antireform movements in general.

As I suggested at the beginning of this book, I believe such right-wing movements evidence a different character from those of the left. The goals of a movement seeking social reform in the interests of a majority are fundamentally different from those of an elite minority seeking to maintain the status quo. Whereas the left generally attempts to form alliances based on an intersection of reason and real interests, the right stalls for time, to delay the formation of an organized opposition. To do so the right seeks to forge an alliance based upon misapprehensions and illusions that mask the underlying cross-class contradiction. As this book has suggested, the right in Thailand used the ideology of the monarchy and family in order to mask the elite's interest in maintaining the hierarchical status quo. To do this the right appealed to the emotional desire of the poor for a loving, supportive, nurturing, and caring government. In the long run this appeal must fail; in the short run it can be an effective strategy.

This book, then, has explored the history of an experiment in using ritual in nation-state formation. States rely on a variety of means to establish their hegemony, but attention thus far has generally focused on social and cultural institutions such as schools, the media, religion, and the arts. The Thai state, like many other governments in underdeveloped countries, could not rely on such institutions to affect the political consciousness of its citizenry. Until the late 1970s the Thai educational system required villagers to attend only four years of school; even today villagers are not required to attend school for more than six years. Hence the state's opportunities to affect villagers' perceptions of the world around them through education are weaker than they would be elsewhere, where mandatory schooling covers more years (see Vaddhanaphuti 1984; Keyes 1991). The Thai media have expanded only recently (see overview in Mudannayake et al. 1975:sec. O, 1–19). During the 1970s, when most of the events described in this book take place, most villagers had access to only radio. At most one or two village households had a TV, and not even schools had a regular subscription to a daily newspaper or weekly newsmagazine. Furthermore, given that control over radio and TV has been overwhelmingly in the hands of the government and military, it is uncertain how much credibility the media held in the minds of villagers.

Buddhism in Thailand, although administered through a national bureaucracy, still maintains considerable village autonomy. Unlike conventional Christian denominations in which priests or ministers receive years of specialized training before preaching, Buddhist monks are usually village youths reciting Pali texts that they often only barely understand. Thus Buddhism has proved to be an uncertain instrument for the consolidation of the state, having nurtured as many revolts against the state as it has discouraged. Similarly, the cultural arts of the elite cannot reliably serve to instill state values in villagers. Although film is perhaps one of the most effective cultural media, during the 1970s most villagers had never seen the inside of a movie theater. They were likely to see only the occasional movie shown during the dry season in someone's paddyfield. Even then many villagers could not afford admission.

Because the Thai state lacked the social and cultural avenues typically available to stronger states, it was forced to seek an alternative avenue for shaping popular political consciousness. The ritual of the Village Scout movement became that alternative. The Thai state sought to use initiation in the Village Scout movement to establish its legitimacy in the minds of its citizens. The use of ritual by the state is not new. However, whereas most earlier uses of state ritual sought to impress through spectacle, the Village Scout initiation sought to win people's hearts and minds.

As I have shown, the creation of a populist conservative movement carries significant risks. Because such a movement involves popular participation, it poses the constant threat that it may develop beyond the state's control. Various Thai administrations feared the Village Scouts because they lacked effective control over the organization. Developing a populist conservative movement presents an inherent contradiction: the generation of mass support for the perpetuation of elite advantage. Because states fear that the balance of power in such organizations may shift toward the popular will and beyond their control, states are not likely to open a Pandora's box of right-wing conservatism lightly. I submit that they are most likely to do so when the existing institutions for the establishment and maintenance of state hegemony are weak, either because they did not exist before or because the state is under siege from a growing opposition.

Appendix

Table A.1	The Royal Policies for Village Scouts of Thailand*

1. Do not involve village scouts with politics.
2. Do not show off the power of village scouts.
3. Do not use government official system in village scouts.
4. Village scouts do not have uniform. They have only symbol, that is scarf, woggle and scout badge. Avoid using all other kinds of uniforms and symbols.
5. His Majesty wishes that village scout affairs are of the people by the people and for the people.
6. The village scouts are leaders in self development, vocational and local dvelopment.
7. The village scouts are leaders in the building of discipline and thriftiness.
8. Do not spend the money excessively in the training and camp fire activities. And do not drink any alcoholic beverages during the training.
9. To abide by and propagate group system of village scout to the people to promote unity, readiness and oneness.
10. Do not use political budget in village scout affairs.
11. The village scouts are to be leaders in the use of Thai goods and to consume food produced in Thailand.
12. The village scouts are to be leaders in the restoration and conservation of the good traditions and culture of each locality.

*Reprinted without corrections from VS history (1983); official publication of Village Scout Operations Center, Bangkok).

Table A.2   Ideals of Village Scouts*

1. Village scout is core of love, unity and friendship of all people in the nation in living together.
2. Village scout initiates, develops and builds up himself, the society, the group and the nation by group method or system.
3. Village scout believes in and acts in accordance with democretic way of administration with the King as the head and the way of life.
4. Village scout is good citizen who is loyal to the nation, religions, the King and will preserve Thai identity with his life.
5. Village scout believes in and acts strictly in accordance with the ideals, the Royal Policy, His mission, the regulations, pledges, traditions of village scout in deeds, words and mind.

*Reprinted without corrections from VS history (1983); (official publication of Village Scout Operations Center, Bangkok).

Table A.3   The Missions of Village Scouts of Thailand*

1. To recruit new members as many as possible, at least 3–5.
2. To abide by the regulations, pledges and traditions of boy scout strictly in deeds, words and heart.
3. To meet with one another all the time and to do deeds.
4. To cooperate with good government officials and do not cooperate with bad government officials.
5. Try to persuade the bad to become good. If not possible to do, cooperate with government officials to persuade them.
6. To spend free time usefully to develop one self, his community, the group and the country using group system.
7. Be loyal to the nation, the religions, and the King; to abide by the law, order, and good culture of the Thai nation.

*Reprinted without corrections fromVS history (1983); (official publication of Village Scout Operations Center, Bangkok).

Table A.4 Total Village Scout Initiation Sessions, Northern Provinces, Per Annum, 1971–1985

Year	Number of Sessions	Number of Initiates			Average No. Per Session	Percentage	
		Male	Female	Total		Male	Female
1971	8	1,265	735	2,000	250	63	37
1972	113	8,756	7,381	16,137	143	54	46
1973	412	9,733	12,661	22,394	54	43	57
1974	980	28,544	29,985	58,529	60	49	51
1975	1,493	89,763	88,486	178,249	119	50	50
1976	2,387	897,673	999,867	1,897,540	795	47	53
1977	1,796	387,846	376,435	764,281	426	51	49
1978	1,784	293,601	282,729	576,330	323	51	49
1979	1,277	199,796	275,435	475,221	372	42	58
1980	764	158,752	165,749	324,501	425	49	51
1981	265	19,975	18,875	38,850	147	51	49
1982	245	26,951	19,875	46,826	191	58	42
1983	191	20,310	15,794	36,109	189	56	44
1984	213	22,131	16,867	38,998	183	57	43
1985	200	20,778	17,042	37,820	189	55	45
Total	12,128	2,185,864	2,372,916	4,513,780	372	48	52

Source: Adapted from VS history (1987). Figures on number of initiations and number of initiates reprinted without change.

Table A.5 Initiation Statistics for South Central Provinces, 1971–1985 (*Phaak* 1, *Khet* 2)*

Province	Number of Initiations	Number of Initiates			Average No. Per Session	Percentage	
		Male	*Female*	*Total*		*Male*	*Female*
Prachinburi	170	29,116	28,816	57,932	341	50	50
Chachoengsao	99	17,349	11,481	28,830	291	60	40
Chonburi	177	28,649	22,993	51,642	292	55	45
Rayong	99	15,477	15,479	30,956	313	50	50
Trat	84	11,999	8,865	20,864	248	58	42
Samut Prakan	96	15,649	13,461	29,110	303	54	46
Saraburi	161	27,004	24,809	51,813	322	52	48
Prathum Thani	85	14,527	11,368	25,895	305	56	44
Ayutthaya	234	39,773	31,114	70,887	303	56	44
Lopburi	202	32,253	35,991	68,244	338	47	53
Nakhon Nayok	66	11,453	7,978	19,431	294	59	41
Chanthaburi	112	18,828	14,471	33,299	297	57	43
Total	1,585	262,077	226,826	488,903	308	54	46

Source: Adapted from VS history (1987). Figures on number of initiations and number of initiates reprinted without change.

Phaak means region; *khet* means division.

Table A.6 Initiation Statistics for Central Provinces, 1971–1985 (*Phaak* 1, *Khet* 7)*

Province	Number of Initiations	Number of Initiates			Average No. Per Session	Percentage	
		Male	Female	Total		Male	Female
Kanchanaburi	105	19,985	13,412	33,397	318	60	40
Suphanburi	211	36,007	29,004	65,011	308	55	45
Singburi	89	14,777	12,633	27,410	308	54	46
Chainat	102	16,239	12,698	28,937	284	56	44
Nonthaburi	68	10,226	9,380	19,606	288	52	48
Ratchaburi	216	47,612	42,999	90,611	419	53	47
Petchaburi	118	19,617	17,094	36,711	311	53	47
Prachuab Khiri Khan	147	25,137	24,062	49,199	335	51	49
Ang Thong	103	21,277	11,468	32,745	318	65	35
Samut Songkhram	108	13,590	13,155	26,745	248	51	49
Samut Sakhon	84	14,446	11,224	25,670	306	56	44
Nakhon Pathom	155	27,987	17,652	45,639	294	61	39
Total	1,506	266,900	214,781	481,681	320	55	45

Source: Adapted from VS history (1987). Figures on number of initiations and number of initiates reprinted without change.

Phaak means region; *khet* means division.

Table A.7 Initiation Statistics for Northeastern Provinces, 1971–1985 (*Phaak 2, Khet 3*)*

Province	Number of Initiations	Number of Initiates			Average No. Per Session	Percentage	
		Male	*Female*	*Total*		*Male*	*Female*
Ubon Ratchathani	258	43,165	22,085	65,250	253	66	34
Sisaket	258	43,999	19,614	63,613	247	69	31
Surin	219	39,190	20,891	60,081	274	65	35
Buriram	180	35,029	14,702	49,731	276	70	30
Nakhon Ratchasima	392	58,705	33,564	92,269	235	64	36
Chaiyaphum	217	33,397	18,224	51,621	238	65	35
Yasothon	119	17,696	8,845	26,541	223	67	33
Total	1,643	271,181	137,925	409,106	249	66	34

Source: Adapted from VS history (1987). Figures on number of initiations and number of initiates reprinted without change.

*Phaak means region; khet means division.

Table A.8 Initiation Statistics for Northeastern Provinces, 1971–1985 (*Phaak* 2, *Khet* 4)*

Province	Number of Initiations	Number of Initiates			Average No. Per Session	Percentage	
		Male	Female	Total		Male	Female
Loei	135	19,233	10,501	29,734	220	65	35
Nong Khai	221	34,923	18,684	53,607	243	65	35
Udon Thani	447	80,150	45,550	125,700	281	64	36
Roi Et	165	34,918	13,529	48,447	294	72	28
Nakhon Phanom	290	36,785	27,015	63,800	220	58	42
Kalasin	217	33,702	17,194	50,896	235	66	34
Maha Sarakham	131	24,141	9,166	33,307	254	72	28
Khon Kaen	220	27,617	23,204	**60,821****	**276**	**45**	**38**
Sakhon Nakhon	183	28,011	15,723	43,734	239	64	36
Mukdahan	59	8,225	4,347	12,599	214	65	35
Total	**2,037**	**337,705**	**184,940**	**522,645**	**257**	**65**	**35**

Source: Adapted from VS history (1987).

Phaak means region; *khet* means division.

**Boldface reflects an error in the figures. I have retained the uncorrected figures.

Table A.9 Initiation Statistics for Northern Provinces, 1971–1985 (*Phaak* 3, *Khet* 5)*

Province	Number of Initiations	Number of Initiates			Average No. Per Session	Percentage	
		Male	Female	Total		Male	Female
Chiang Mai	346	56,161	38,252	94,413	273	59	41
Lamphun	103	17,356	**10,995****	**32,351**	**314**	**54**	**46**
Lampang	162	26,980	16,084	43,064	266	63	37
Phrae	133	22,495	17,533	40,028	301	56	44
Nan	117	20,521	14,615	35,136	300	58	42
Chiang Rai	237	48,396	24,625	73,021	308	66	34
Phayao	46	7,065	4,962	11,757	256	60	40
Mae Hong Son	37	4,813	3,222	8,035	217	60	40
Total	**1,184**	203,787	**134,018**	337,805	285	60	40

Source: Adapted from VS history (1987).

Phaak means region; *khet* means division.

**Boldface reflects errors in official figures. I have retained the uncorrected figures.

Table A.10 Initiation Statistics for North Central Provinces, 1971–1985 *(Phaak 3, Khet 6)**

Province	Number of Initiations	Number of Initiates			Average No. Per Session	Percentage	
		Male	Female	Total		Male	Female
Uthai Thani	141	22,740	18,870	41,610	295	55	45
Nakhon Sawan	384	59,292	51,793	111,085	289	53	47
Kamphaeng Phet	151	26,610	15,658	42,268	280	63	37
Tak	87	13,892	8,236	22,128	254	63	37
Sukhothai	198	37,308	25,923	63,231	319	59	41
Phitsanulok	178	30,500	22,805	53,305	299	72	42
Uttaradit	168	26,116	20,761	46,877	279	56	44
Phetchabun	218	33,212	22,432	55,644	255	60	40
Phichit	166	29,619	20,151	49,770	300	60	40
Total	**1,691**	**279,292****	**206,638**	**485,930**	**287**	**57**	**43**

Source: Adapted from VS history (1987).

*Phaak means region; *khet* means division.

**Boldface reflects errors in official figures. I have retained the uncorrected figures.

Table A.11 Initiation Statistics for Southern Provinces, 1971–1985 (*Phaak 4, Khet 8*)*

Province	Number of Initiations	Number of Initiates			Average No. Per Session	Percentage	
		Male	*Female*	*Total*		*Male*	*Female*
Nakhon Si							
Thammarat	347	49,258	33,332	82,590	238	60	40
Surat Thani	224	26,993	23,476	50,469	225	53	47
Krabi	64	9,060	9,953	19,013	297	48	52
Phuket	26	2,855	5,824	8,679	333	33	67
Chumphon	104	19,492	21,737	41,229	396	47	53
Phangnga	78	7,380	4,963	12,343	158	60	40
Rayong	35	4,187	3,977	8,164	233	51	49
Total	**874****	119,225	103,262	222,487	255	54	46

Source: Adapted from VS history (1987).

Phaak means region; *khet* means division.

**Bold number indicates error in official figures. I have retained the uncorrected figures.

Table A.12 Initiation Statistics for Southern Provinces, 1971–1985 (*Phaak 4*, *Khet 9*)*

Province	Number of Initiations	Number of Initiates			Average No. Per Session	Percentage	
		Male	*Female*	*Total*		*Male*	*Female*
Phatthalung	90	12,548	4,361	16,909	188	74	26
Yala	97	10,785	4,554	15,339	158	70	30
Satun	50	6,116	1,792	7,908	158	77	23
Songkhla	284	35,766	17,087	52,853	186	68	32
Narathiwat	82	10,594	3,883	14,477	177	73	27
Trang	118	16,493	6,929	23,422	198	70	30
Pattani	85	8,844	4,074	12,918	152	68	32
Total	806	101,146	42,680	143,826	178	70	30

Source: Adapted from VS history (1987). Figures on number of initiations and number of initiates reprinted without changes

*Phaak means region; *khet* means division.

Table A.13 Summary: Initiation Statistics by Region and Division (*Phaak, Khet*), 1971–1985

Khet/ Phaak	Number of Initiations	Number of Initiates Male	Female	Total	Average No. Per Session	Percentage Male	Female
1/2	1,585	262,077	226,826	488,903	308	54	46
1/7	1,506	266,900	214,781	481,681	320	55	45
Bangkok*	403	64,759	57,687	122,446	304	53	47
Total	**3,494**	**593,736**	**499,294**	**1,093,030**	**313**	**54**	**46**
2/3	1,643	271,181	137,925	409,106	249	66	34
2/4	2,037	337,705	184,940	522,645	257	65	35
Total	**3,680**	**608,886**	**322,865**	**931,751**	**253**	**65**	**35**
3/5	1,184	203,787	134,018	337,805	285	60	40
3/6	1,691	279,292	206,638	485,930	287	57	43
Total	**2,875**	**483,079**	**340,656**	**823,735**	**287**	**59**	**41**
4/8	874	119,225	103,262	222,487	255	54	46
4/9	806	101,146	42,680	143,826	178	70	30
Total	**1,680**	**220,371**	**145,942**	**366,313**	**218**	**60**	**40**
Total for 4	11,729	1,906,072	1,308,757	3,214,829	274	59	41

*The totals by region and division do not tally with totals by year. I cannot explain the discrepancy. All figures on the number of initiations and number of initiates are reprinted without change from VS history (1987).

Table A.14 Incident Statistics and RTG/CPT Personnel Losses,* 1965–1985 (Jan.–March)

Year	CPT Personnel Losses Killed	Wounded	Arrested	Defected	RTG Personnel Losses Killed	Wounded	Clash	Attack
2509 (1966)	99	20	1,445	1,459	87	72	154	—
2510 (1967)	169	43	1,244	482	134	132	232	5
2511 (1968)	148	54	613	846	188	368	372	5
2512 (1969)	111	15	226	284	163	324	290	5
2513 (1970)	97	38	326	191	241	337	258	37
2514 (1971)	201	76	613	834	361	646	365	36
2515 (1972)	309	92	1,145	898	592	1,496	680	57
2516 (1973)	255	78	457	653	358	813	475	42
2517 (1974)	215	67	260	766	241	651	415	26
2518 (1975)	258	117	111	325	277	748	281	24
2519 (1976)	311	184	302	460	451	1,263	470	57
2520 (1977)	607	265	1,032	1,234	482	1,693	1,050	84
2521 (1978)	582	294	338	828	597	1,915	967	60
2522 (1979)	583	326	600	1,945	439	1,289	732	26
2523 (1980)	316	48	316	1,543	423	1,179	770	22
2524 (1981)	201	34	286	2,322	459	1,264	704	19
2525 (1982)	94	62	196	2,071	225	742	405	15
2526 (1983)	23	13	60	941	74	478	193	2
2527 (1984)	9	4	29	346	105	462	164	—
2528 (Jan.–Feb. 1985)	—	—	11	18	19	68	41	—
	4,588	1,830	9,610	18,446	5,916	15,941	9,018	522

Source: Adapted from Kerdphol (1986:186).

*RTG = Royal Thai Government; CPT = Communist Party of Thailand.

Notes

Introduction: Toward an Anthropology of the Right

1. See B. Anderson (1991), P. Anderson (1974), Bendix (1969), Foucault (1979), Fox (1990), Geertz (1963), Gellner (1983), Gramsci (1971), Hobsbawm (1990), Lifton (1969), Miliband (1969), B. Moore (1966), Poulantzas (1973), A. Smith (1973), Tilly (1975), and E. Weber (1976).
2. Although this phrase is often translated as King, Nation, and Religion (e.g., Vella 1978), I prefer to maintain the order in which Thais use the phrase.
3. The deliberate manipulation of mass psychology was quite clear in my interview with the movement's official founder, Police Major General Somkhuan Harikul. In explaining various elements of the initiation ritual he commented at one point, "We used techniques such as stimulating competition, giving praise and awards, to create a climate. We used processes of mass psychology to create a group sense of unity" (Harikul interview 1991).
4. Likhit Dhiravegin's survey of high-ranking officials from various ministries was an early attempt to study the political attitudes of bureaucrats. His survey revealed a spectrum of opinion ranging from conservative to liberal. Among other variables, he concluded that younger officials, and particularly those with higher levels of education, tended to be more liberal (1973). Other interesting discussions of divisions among the elite can be

found in Hewison (1981, 1989), Samudavanija, Snitwongse, and Bunbongkarn (1990), and Suehiro (1989).

5. See also discussions in Laclau (1977) and Poulantzas (1974).

6. This explicit association with the Boy Scouts helped provide an aura of political innocence to the Village Scouts. The Thai Boy Scout organization was formed in 1911 and involves village schoolchildren from elementary school on up. In fact, these two organizations were different, the Boy Scouts a long-standing organization intended for youth and the Village Scouts a newly created institution designed for adults in order to sway the political balance within the Thai nation-state.

1. Magic and Mayhem of Ritual and Class

1. *Phaa yan* are sacred cloths with magical designs and mantras believed to be imbued with protective powers. They are usually written by a monk or elder seen as having sacred knowledge, much of it based upon a knowledge of astrology. See Tambiah (1984) for discussion.

2. Scott McNabb notes that initiates were screened and that not all who wished to join could (1978:143). The exclusivity may have been more rhetorical than actual. Although some said only virtuous people with morality and compassion for others could join, others suggested it was good for selfish people and even leftists to join, because then they would see the errors of their earlier ways and reform.

3. Significantly, this story was published in an article by the national head of the Village Scouts, Major General Charoenrit Chamrasromrun (see Muecke 1980:n413).

4. A number of other sources also describe the movement as fascist (Bell 1978:69; Flood 1977:19; Girling 1981:209; Mallet 1978; Turton 1978:128; van Praagh 1977:298). Village Scouts were not supposed to have uniforms. Nonetheless the maroon kerchief was visible identification and had the same effect as a full uniform. According to criticism in newspaper editorials of the period, some troops actually wore uniforms in addition to the kerchief.

5. See appendix, tables A1.4–A1.13, for details. Thailand's total population was approximately forty million in the mid-1970s and 45 percent were younger than fifteen (Knodel, Chamratrithirong, and Nibhon 1987:28; Mudannayake et al. 1975:E4).

6. I do not wish to do more than broach the vast subject of gender relations in Thailand. The role of women in the initiation appears to reflect more the attitudes of the urban elite toward the ideal role of women than the actual role of women in village life. Rural Thailand is matrilocal, unlike Chinese-influenced urban society, which is patrilineal, and women play an important role in the domestic economy. In the Village Scout organization the president was usually a man, but one of the two vice presidents was usually

a woman. Furthermore, although the male president and vice president were generally chosen for their wealth and political prominence, the female vice president frequently was chosen for her youth and beauty and often even her singing and dancing abilities. In addition to serving as vice presidents, women performed gender-specific functions during the camp-fire phase of the initiation rite, such as dancing and distributing flowers to honored guests (usually male). They also did much of the morning marketing and cooking in color groups.

Interestingly, over time more and more women took over serious leadership roles in the movement. Thus the current district head of Village Scouts in San Patong District is a woman, the wealthy widow of a well-known rice merchant. Similarly, a woman served as head of the Village Scouts in Bangkok (see the appendix to Sivaraksa 1985). See chapters 5 and 6 for further discussions of the role of women in the movement.

7. The official figures on the relative percentages of male versus female initiates do not fully tally. The overall summary of membership year by year suggests that of 4,513,780 members, 2,327,916, or 52 percent, were women. The overall summary of initiates in all provinces suggests that of 3,214,829 initiates, 1,308,757, or 41 percent were women. I cannot explain the discrepancy in figures, other than to assume errors in math or copying (see appendix, tables A1.4 and A1.13, for both breakdowns). I believe the lower percentage based upon the provincial figures is the more accurate. A perusal of the seventy provinces for which data are available (from a total of seventy-two) shows that in the vast majority the percentage of women was less than 50 percent. Eight provinces had percentages of 30 percent and less, particularly provinces in the Northeast and the Muslim provinces of the South. My own data from northern Thailand also support the lower percentage (see chapter 5).

8. This adoption of communist organizing strategies was stated explicitly in many newspaper articles of the period. The recruitment policy changed after 1976, with the institution of village-based recruitment (see chapter 5).

9. *Nawaphon* means 'ninth force', an allusion to the king, who is the ninth king in the Chakri dynasty, or King Rama IX. For more on Nawaphon see also Girling (1981:156) and Keyes (1973).

10. In my interviews with him Somkhuan Harikul was vague about Village Scout involvement in the events of October 6. He volunteered that he got little sleep for several nights during that time, adding that he was summoned to meet with the prime minister, Seni Pramoj. Seni was concerned that the Village Scouts might attack Government House. Somkhuan Harikul told Seni that he could not stop the Village Scouts from exercising their right to rally but that he would make every effort to ensure that no violence occurred. Somkhuan Harikul went on to say that a box of maroon

scout kerchiefs had been reported missing from Petchaburi Province. He suggested that whoever was planning the coup could have arranged to have the scout kerchiefs stolen in order to put the Village Scouts in a bad light.

Photographs show men with Village Scout kerchiefs participating in the violence at Thammasat University. Dr. Puey makes specific mention of the Village Scouts at various points of his chronicle, beginning at 5:50 A.M., when "some members of the Red Gaurs and the village scouts tried to break through the campus gate by using a bus that they had hijacked several hours earlier" (Ungphakorn 1977:6). It is not clear who would have masterminded the theft of kerchiefs and to what end. Somkhuan Harikul did not deny Village Scout participation in other gatherings elsewhere in Bangkok on that day.

11. This figure was provided by Somkhuan Harikul (1992 interview). The scouts disbanded only after the crown prince and Somkhuan Harikul personally addressed the crowds. The crown prince spoke to the gatherings at the statue of Rama V and at the racegrounds, informing them that the "National Administrative Reform Council" had taken over the government and martial law was being introduced. He assured them he was unharmed, thanked them for their concern, and asked them to return home peacefully. Somkhuan Harikul addressed the crowds of Village Scouts gathered at the zoo (1992 interview). Most scouts complied.

12. Although it is clear that the overall number of new initiations has declined, there is some debate about how to interpret this decline. See discussion in chapter 8.

13. As I note in the introduction, because I accept the argument regarding the "relative autonomy" of the state, I include state factions as well as class fractions.

14. Much of the earlier anthropological literature on ritual focuses on its use in small-scale, more "egalitarian" societies.

15. The literature on the political applications of ritual has been expanding rapidly in recent years (e.g., Apter 1992; C. Bell 1992; Bloch 1986; J. Comaroff 1985; Comaroff and Comaroff 1993; Corrigan and Sayer 1985; Geertz 1977; Gluckman 1965; Handelman 1990; Hobsbawm and Ranger, eds. 1983; Kertzer 1988; Lane 1981; Lukes 1975; Moore and Myerhoff 1977; Mosse 1975; Turner 1988; Valeri 1985; Wilentz 1985). James Peacock's *Rites of Modernization: Symbolic and Social Aspects of Indonesian Proletarian Drama* (1968) is one of the few works by an anthropologist to consider a working-class performance, although the emphasis in this work is primarily to understand *ludruk* drama as a rite of transition into modern society rather than as an expression of class tensions. Some interesting work is being done on the use of ritual by corporations (see Kondo 1990; Nash 1989).

16. Although class is a major subject within the discipline of sociology,

Blumberg writes that the ideology of classlessness has affected American sociology, "the practitioners of which were often led to play down the importance of class in this country." He continues, "In fact, the tradition of classlessness narcotized thinking about social class for decades" (1980:10).

17. Because many public rituals originated in the mist of historical time, it is often difficult to determine definitively who created the ritual and in whose interest. Consequently, some theorists have suggested that rituals be viewed as "culturally produced texts" (e.g., Marcus and Fischer 1986:61). The impossibility of determining authorship has only compounded the problem.

18. These ideas can be traced to earlier scholars such as Fustel de Coulanges (*The Ancient City* 1956 [1864]) and Robertson Smith, albeit in a more inchoate form (see Munn 1973 for an interesting discussion of the early history of symbolism and ritual).

19. In the case of certain rituals in the Soviet Union Christel Lane suggests that the "first impetus came from lower political cadres rather than from the top of the political apparatus" (1981:33).

20. For similar observations see Goody (1961:152), Lukes (1975:291), Shils (1968:744), and M. Wilson (1971:66).

21. Because many of these scholars were working in what they considered "egalitarian" societies, issues of social stratification appeared to be irrelevant. Thus, for example, although the Ndembu had slavery, V. Turner notes that "in an egalitarian society like that of the Ndembu, slaves were not markedly exploited, and in fact were regarded more as relatives than chattels" (1957:189).

22. Although Foucault presents ritual as an element of premodern society, I believe that rituals of intimidation are also an element of modern society. The military parades of totalitarian societies are one obvious example.

23. As Christel Lane notes, many newly created state rituals in the Soviet Union faced significant problems of efficacy (see discussion 1981:193).

24. Most state rituals draw heavily from preexisting popular rituals (e.g., Bloch 1986, 1987; Hobsbawm and Ranger, eds. 1983). Even the Nazi state, whose leaders "boasted that they had invented something new" in their grandiose state mass rites, have been shown to have drawn from earlier working-class rituals (Mosse 1975:73). Similarly, Christel Lane writes that "Soviet ritual specialists have shown a keen awareness of the existence of class sub-cultures and have endeavoured, where possible, to select only the ritual of the exploited classes, of the ordinary people" (1981:231).

25. Definitions of *ritual* vary. As Leach writes, "[There is] the widest possible disagreement as to how the word ritual should be understood" (1968:526). Similarly, Crocker observes, "There are as many definitions of ritual as there are anthropologists" (1973:49). For various definitions see Leach

(1968), Lukes (1975), Munn (1973:580), Peacock (1968:6), Shaughnessy, ed. (1973:47), V. Turner (1967:19; 1988), Zuesse (1987:405).

26. Moore and Myerhoff go on to elucidate six formal properties of ritual by which even new rituals appear to celebrate tradition; these are repetition, acting, stylization, order, evocative presentational style, and its collective dimension (1977:7–8).

27. Scholars debate whether King Mongkut was building upon the Brahmanical rites of divine kingship or was downplaying them (see Tambiah 1976: 226–7; Riggs 1966:99). Whatever the assessment of the position of the Brahmanical elements, scholars agree that Mongkut certainly increased the Buddhist components (Griswold 1961:18). In addition to Buddhacizing existing court rituals King Mongkut intimated his modernizing role by adapting Western models. Borrowing Western birthday celebrations, Mongkut instituted festivals to commemorate the birth, enlightenment, and death of the Buddha. Because such festivals were apparently celebrated in ancient India, the innovation was presented as a revival of a lost tradition (Riggs 1966:105). Mongkut also initiated the annual practice of observing the king's birthday and the anniversary of his coronation (Tambiah 1976: 227; see Riggs 1966:105 for more detailed description of birthday celebrations). The pattern set by King Mongkut was continued by his successor and son, King Chulalongkorn, with an increasing incorporation of European protocol. As Tambiah explains, King Chulalongkorn felt "the need to present an image of monarchy more suited to European notions as well as to his program of modernization" (1976:228). Nonetheless none of the rites of kingship was trimmed, and King Chulalongkorn held an elaborate haircutting, or tonsure, ceremony for his heir apparent (see Gerini 1895; Wales 1931).

28. See Riggs 1966:100–105 for an interesting analysis of the linkage of monarch and people through the kathin.

29. Although modern Thai scouting is generally traced to both Lord Baden-Powell and King Rama VI, Rama VI evidently traced the lineage of Thai scouting to Ayuthayan days. He said that he had conceived of the idea to establish a corps to experiment with war games at Saranrom Palace in 1905, based upon an earlier group called the Wild Tigers and Peeping Cats, founded during King Naresuan's reign in the seventeenth century (for further discussion see Chakrabongse 1960:275; Graham 1924:241; Vella 1978:29; see also Bowie 1993).

30. He paid particular attention to Pra Ruang, the king who defeated the Khmer and established the first Thai kingdom of Sukhothai in the thirteenth century, and Uthong, the founder of the kingdom of Ayuthaya of the fourteenth century.

31. For a discussion of Buddhist national rites see Wells (1939). For a discus-

sion of kathin ceremonies in the modern context see Gray (1986). For discussions of rituals in the context of nation building see Bowring ([1857]
1969), Vandergeest (1990), Irvine (1982), B. Smith (1978), and Wales
(1931). For descriptions of various rituals in Thailand at the village level
see Tambiah (1970), deYoung (1955), R. Davis (1984), and Kingshill
(1991). In none of these national rites is there anything but the weakest of
parallels with the Village Scout initiation ceremonies.

32. In some sense parallels can be drawn between the Village Scout structure
and "rites of royal entry." As Kertzer explains, "By staging large-scale rites
in localities scattered throughout the realm, people were better able to
identify with the power of the ruler, and, at the same time, the sub-
servience of local authorities to the central ruler was made clear"
(1988:22). The fourteenth-century Javanese procession, the fifteenth-cen-
tury progresses of Queen Elizabeth I, or the travels made by the Moroccan
kings from the seventeenth to the nineteenth centuries, which Geertz
describes (1977), exemplify the practice. Another parallel can be found in
new nations where the center of state power is weak. Kertzer cites the
example of Tanzania where the government organized regular local meetings of the national party. Despite the linguistic and religious diversity of
Tanzania, Kertzer suggests, "In the past, many of these people had been
considered foreigners; but now, as they are all busy performing the same
rites, they have been redefined as fellow countrymen" (1988:23).

33. As a de novo rite the movement might have been expected to fizzle rapidly.
In his fascinating account of German state rituals Mosse gives examples of
state-created rites that fail. One such example was the Sedanstag begun by
Emperor William II in 1871; it failed in the end "because it had been organized from above in a conservative manner, had stressed discipline, and
gradually excluded popular participation" (1975:91).

2. Genesis in Conflict

1. The hill tribe villages in the area of the BPP school were Phuukhiithao,
Phuupayaab, Khaopuu, Khaoyaa, and Baan Thapbyyk (VS history 1984:19).
This area is sometimes referred to as the triprovince area. Administratively,
the area was the dividing line between the Second Army in the Northeast
and the Third Army in the North and was also the dividing line between
the fourth and sixth police regions, as well as the junction of three
provinces (Tanham 1974:58).

2. My sources for this overview are my interviews with Somkhuan Harikul,
supplemented by Village Scout histories (see VS history 1984, 1987).

3. According to official figures, the total number of government personnel
killed in 1968 was 188, and 368 were wounded in a total of 372 clashes
(Kerdphol 1986:186). Somkhuan Harikul could not recall the official fig-

ures of how many people were killed or wounded in this particular attack (1992 interview).

4. Boy Scouting was one program BPP officers often promoted in villages where they worked. The Wood Badge training is an eight-day course in leadership skills for adults involved in the Boy Scout organization. The course originated in England when Lord Robert Baden-Powell determined that the organization's leaders would benefit from additional training. In England the Wood Badge sessions train people who train troop leaders, whereas in the United States the Wood Badge sessions train both trainers of the troop leaders and the troop leaders.

According to Guy Eichsteadt, assistant scout executive of the Four Lakes Council (Madison, Wisconsin) of the Boy Scouts of America, participants are taught eleven basic leadership skills during the eight days. They are divided into eight-person patrols and given various tasks. Part of the training involves keeping the participants so uncertain of what they are supposed to be doing at a given time that they become intensely frustrated. On the third day the organizers explain that this exercise is deliberate and intended to teach the participants to keep their troops informed. The frustration also has the positive consequence of fostering camaraderie among participants.

Similarly, participants receive no praise for tasks performed during the first few days, regardless of how well they are executed. Again this serves to generate frustration. Finally, on about the fourth day the participants are urged to learn a useful lesson from this exercise, namely, to praise followers for good work.

Throughout the week participants are kept to a rigid time schedule from 7 A.M. to 9 or 9:30 P.M. each day. By the end of the session participants are exhausted but feel exhilarated. As Eichsteadt explains, "By the end, eight strangers have become eight good friends." At the conclusion the participants receive a Wood Badge Award, which consists of two pieces of wood on a leather thong reminiscent of an African wooden bead necklace. The king of Thailand wears the Wood Badge Award on his scout uniform (1993 Eichsteadt interview).

5. It is not clear whether the Thai version differed from the American Wood Badge training camp of eight days or if this is a typographical error or mistaken recollection (see VS history 1984:21).

6. Thailand shares more than three thousand miles of border with its neighbors, Burma, Cambodia, Laos, and Malaysia.

7. The four villages were Baan Lao Koh Hok, Baan Saeng Phaa, Baan Naa Saak, and Baan Muang Phrae. The session was held at Baan Lao Koh Hok village in Tambon Saeng Phaa, Khingamphur Phyyn Haew, Amphur Daan Saaj, in Loei Province (VS history 1977:26). For pilot session details see chapter 3.

8. Tanham writes of "economic plenty," adding that "there has always been

plenty of land for all" and that "socioeconomic mobility is considerable" (1974:38–39). Similarly, Thompson and Adloff attribute communism's earlier failure to attract an indigenous following in Thailand to such factors as "the widespread peasant proprietorship of the land" and "the absence of intense economic misery" (1950:52; see also D. Wilson 1959, 1962).

9. Major uprisings in the North included the Phrayar Phaab rebellion in 1889 (McGilvary 1912:305; Bristowe 1976:149; Tanabe 1984:75–110; T. Bunnag 1977:66; H. Taylor n.d.); the Mae Ngat revolt in Chiang Mai province of 1902 (Ramsay 1979); the Shan uprising in Lampang and Phrae in 1902 (H. Taylor n.d.; Bristowe 1976:108–20; T. Bunnag 1977:152–53, 1967; and Ondam 1971). There was also unrest in the Northeast in 1895, 1901 to 1902, 1924, and 1936 (Nartsupha 1984, Murdoch 1974, Keyes 1977, Ishii 1975, and Tej Bunnag 1968). As late as the mid-1930s the northern monk Khruubaa Siwichai became the catalyst for popular resistance to central Thai encroachments (see Tambiah 1976:245–49).

10. A complete inventory of these local protests has never been made. Nonetheless some sense of the protests is provided by W. A. Briggs, who wrote of the period at the turn of the century, "In Chieng Mai no less than seven court houses were destroyed by fire and looted" (Briggs 1902).

11. The reasons for this early concern with communism are not clear. Although Tanham says that communists played no role in the coup, he suggests that perhaps the Thai government was uneasy "over the excessive claims of the communists" and so enacted the anticommunist law (1974:30). Government concerns may also have been a response to the fact that from 1927 on, after the split in China between the Kuomintang and communists, Chinese immigrants came "almost exclusively" from the communist regions of China (Thompson and Adloff 1950:52–53). For more on this early period see Brimmell (1959), Buntrigswat (n.d.), Caldwell (1976), Flood (1975), McLane (1966), Randolph and Thompson (1981), Thompson and Adloff (1950), van der Kroef (1974), and D. Wilson (1959).

12. Thailand lifted its anticommunist law in 1946 in order to gain the Soviet Union's vote for Thailand's membership in the United Nations. However, the law was reinstated the following year, with the coup of Field Marshal Phibun Songkhram in 1947 (Tanham 1974:31; see also Thompson and Adloff 1950:59).

13. Sarit's initial coup took place on September 16, 1957.

14. There was dissension within the CPT over the adoption of armed struggle. Prasert Sapsunthorn, a member of Parliament from Surat Thani Province and a CPT Central Committee member, was a leading opponent; he argued that struggle within the democratic process would attract more mass support. Following the Third National Congress in 1961, Prasert was expelled from the party as a traitor (Wongtrangan 1984:178). Even in 1965 many in

the CPT did not feel ready to begin active armed struggle and, accordingly to Tanham, did so largely in response to pressure from the Chinese Communist Party (1974:44). See discussions in Tanham (1974:43), Turton, Fast, and Caldwell, eds. (1978:164), and Wongtrangan (1984:178).

15. McGehee, a former CIA agent, provides a telling critique of official figures on guerrilla strength. He notes that Thai intelligence services were unable to recruit agents from the CPT directly and relied on numerous second- or third-hand reports (1983:89–90).

16. Tanham also laments the lack of adequate information on the attacks, leaving unclear their size, intensity, nature, and objectives.

17. Gurtov (1970:17) and Lovelace (1971:78) suggest that Chinese assistance to the CPT began after the Tonkin Gulf incident in mid-1964. Van der Kroef disagrees, suggesting that as early as 1962 the Chinese had denounced the Thai government and that Thais were being trained in China (1974:113).

18. Randolph and Thompson give a second reason, namely, the intent of Communist China to topple the Thai government. However, as they point out, "Despite a good deal of propaganda support, Chinese material and organizational support was never large" (1981:15). Also see Tanham (1974: 43–44) for a discussion of why mid-1965 was chosen as the time to launch overt insurgency.

19. Girling (1981:236) summarizes the financial significance of U.S. assistance to Thailand:

> The total U.S. regular military assistance to the Thai armed forces from 1951–1971 amounted to $935.9 million. This was the equivalent to 59 percent of the total Thai military budget for the same period ($1,366.7 million). In addition, the United States provided a further $760 million in "operating costs," for acquisition of military equipment, and in payment for the Thai division in Vietnam ($200 million over four years). U.S. base construction—notably the B-52 base at Utapao, half a dozen other airfields, and the Sattahip navy facilities—amounted to a further $205 million. Finally, expenditure by U.S. military personnel in Thailand (around 50,000 at their peak in 1968–69) for rest and recreation, and other items, added a further $850 million or so.
>
> In addition to the 50,000 U.S. troops stationed in Thailand, 6,500 U.S. troops arrived each week on "rest and recreation" tours from Vietnam (Phillips 1987:6). Not including the Thai military and police forces trained by the United States, Girling writes, "At the peak of base construction, the United States employed, either directly or through Thai contractors, 44,000 Thais—while the

livelihood of another 50,000 or more (shopowners, taxi drivers, bar girls, and hired wives) depended on the U.S. presence.

20. Various scholars also believe "certain national Thai characteristics and aspects of Thai history and culture" inhibited communist organizing (Tanham 1974:36). Among these factors Buddhism and the character of Thai political parties are often mentioned.

21. In the triprovince area alone Race estimated that five hundred tribal people lived in refugee centers and the remainder of the approximately eight thousand tribal residents had fled into the forest where, according to police reports, "many of the young men were now cooperating with the hundred or so communist-led tribal activists" (1974:107; see also van der Kroef 1974:122).

22. General Saiyud Kerdphol describes an increase in guerrilla strength in the North from about 300 fighters in 1967 to nearly 2,000 by the end of the second period in 1970 and a growth from 400 communist guerrillas in the South in 1968 to about 1,100 by 1970 (Kerdphol 1986:117).

23. Ironically, some Thai military officers criticized the U.S. military in Vietnam for its excessive use of force; however, the Thai military repeated many of those errors (see Tanham 1974:92 for discussion).

24. Several scholars suggest that "in the village it is not deprivation that matters, but relative deprivation" (Tanham 1974:72–73). Many counterinsurgency experts believed that the government need not be "concerning itself with agricultural or commercial development" (Tanham 1974:73). Even Snitwongse suggests that villagers did not expect development projects from the government and that they already saw "the Bangkok government's role as legitimate" (1985:253). Instead, I would suggest that absolute deprivation was no less important than relative deprivation in forming villagers' political sympathies. See Bowie (1988) for an account of nineteenth-century peasant attitudes toward the state.

25. About 90 percent of ARD's initial funds were used in constructing roads (Chaloemtiarana 1979:264).

26. This social awareness appears to have shaped various aspects of the Village Scout movement. It likely contributed to Somkhuan Harikul's insistence that the Village Scout leadership be kept independent of government officials. In the early stages of the movement government officials were barred from leadership positions in any individual Village Scout "troop." Village Scout training also encouraged villagers to report cases of government corruption or abuses of power; this policy can also be seen as resulting from Somkhuan Harikul's view that the corruption of government officials was an important factor in the spread of communism.

27. The name of the National Information Psychological Operations Organization was changed to Office of National Psychological Operations in 1971.

28. In 1966 Graham Martin, the U.S. ambassador to Thailand, appointed Peer
de Silva as special assistant for counterinsurgency to coordinate and regulate
"all U.S. activities, military and civil, which are directly related to the problem of insurgency in Thailand" (Tanham 1974:131). Tanham was his successor, serving in that position from April 1968 to May 1970. Although overlapping jurisdictions continued to cause confusion, Martin sought to unify
the approach to counterinsurgency and "prevent the over-militarization
which had occurred in Vietnam" by ensuring that the American Military
Assistance Command in Thailand (MACTHAI) was not the primary counterinsurgency body (Tanham 1974:131–35). De Silva became the liaison
with General Saiyud Kerdphol, director of operations at CSOC, and an officer from the U.S. Information Service (USIS) was assigned to de Silva's staff
and made liaison with CSOC on psychological operations (Tanham 1974:
134). De Silva believed that civil actions and psychological operations that
would win the villagers to the government's side were important; General
Saiyud Kerdphol proved sympathetic, and the two met weekly until CSOC
was taken over by the Second Army in October 1967 (1974:135).

Tanham continued De Silva's work. Although Tanham believed that
Americans should not participate directly in the counterinsurgency effort,
he acknowledged "some participation had nevertheless crept in; for example, U.S. Air Force and Army personnel were at that time directly engaged
in civic action in the Northeast" (1974:145; see also McGehee 1983).
Tanham also describes having "developed close working relationships with
officers in CSOC, the Army, National Security Command, Police, Department of Local Administration (DOLA), ARD, and Community Development
(CD), as well as with many provincial officials" (Tanham 1974:249).

29. As Lobe writes, "This assistance was the first (and, as it turned out, most
dramatic) effort of the U.S. to systematically distort the Thai political system. By 1956, the police were strong enough to challenge the military for
ascendancy over the country" (1977:19).

30. Lobe notes that none of the Sea Supply advisers had any experience or
expertise in police methods but rather were military men with experience
in paramilitary operations. Their skills included small-unit warfare, intelligence, radio and vehicle maintenance, and parachuting. None of the equipment Sea Supply provided was intended for ordinary police officers. Rather,
Lobe writes, "it consisted primarily of carbines, mortars, bazookas, hand
grenades, medical supplies, parachutes, equipment for base camps, communications equipment, and later, artillery, tanks and helicopters" (1977:23).

31. In addition to rural counterinsurgency training the Bangkok Metropolitan
Police were given advanced riot control training (Lobe 1977:41).

32. By 1964 three thousand bpp members had completed unit retraining in counterinsurgency tactics and five hundred elite bpp personnel had undergone a twelve-month course in counterinsurgency given by U.S. Special Forces (Lobe 1977:42).

33. Although I agree that the emphasis placed on counterinsurgency in Thailand and the very development of the Border Patrol Police cannot be fully understood without an understanding of U.S. involvement, I do not believe that the Village Scout movement was the simple brainchild of U.S. counterinsurgency. From the overall history of the development of the Thai Border Patrol Police it would be easy to conclude that U.S. counterinsurgency forces were directly involved with the Thais in creating the scout movement. Indeed Girling has written that the Village Scout movement "bears the hallmarks of American counterinsurgency work in Vietnam and elsewhere" (1981:213; see also Flood 1977b).

Certainly, "winning hearts and minds" was frequently touted as being part of the U.S. counterinsurgency agenda. As an official Agency for International Development (aid) memorandum stated, "Civic action is a way to win the people over to one's sides; and it is cheaper and more effective than wars" (Lobe 1977:79). However, a closer examination of U.S. counterinsurgency strategies in Vietnam reveals a greater use of force, even in psychological warfare, than is connoted by the phrase "winning hearts and minds." As Lobe explains,

> Until 1964, the cia had been in charge of the war efforts, and limited its activities to political counter-insurgency—propaganda, civic action, indoctrination, and "winning hearts and minds." As the situation in Vietnam seemed to grow more urgent and the massive influx of U.S. armed forces began, cia programs were militarized. Politicization gave way to combat. *Winning hearts and minds through selective assassination gave way to annihilation and relocation.*
>
> (Lobe 1977:46; emphasis added)

The Village Scout movement did not involve selective assassination or relocation of population into strategic hamlets.

Nor did the Village Scout movement seek to implement development programs. Typical American initiatives in Thailand included giving selected villagers paramilitary training, building subdistrict (*tambon*) police stations, and establishing civic action programs. The Village Scout movement provided no direct benefits to villagers in the form of better health care or agricultural gains, as are provided ideally through civic action programs; this was purely a psychological appeal to villagers to convince them the government cared about them.

I have not been able to find any direct parallels with U.S. or other contemporary counterinsurgency efforts elsewhere. Although psychological warfare has long been used, and American counterinsurgency experts such as Colonel Edward Lansdale were well known for their efforts to use cultural beliefs and superstitions for psychological warfare purposes, I can find no other example of a nationalistic ritual lasting five days, with patriotic training and sleep deprivation as major components (However, Rutten [1992] describes a current program in the Philippines that bears remarkable similarities). Nonetheless many scholars wonder whether the Thais were likely to independently develop a format with age reduction (regression; see chapter 6 for details), dancing, mixed sleeping quarters, skits with cars and airplanes, and the like. Somkhuan Harikul denies direct American involvement (1994 interview).

34. See also D. Wilson (1962:274).

35. Lobe and Morell go so far as to suggest the only authority to which the BPP was answerable was the palace (1978:169).

36. By 1954 Somkhuan Harikul had already undergone training in guerrilla warfare. In 1955 he had his first course in military intelligence. In 1959 he received additional training specifically in the field of psychological warfare.

37. The use of nationalistic right-wing mass organizations to support besieged governments is nothing new. Nor are political applications of scouting. In fact Michael Rosenthal (1986) has suggested that the Boy Scouts were political from their inception. Many people with whom I have spoken have seen parallels between the Village Scout movement and right-wing movements in a variety of countries, including Vietnam, Indonesia, Philippines, Japan, and China (discussions with professors Ruth Dunnell of Kenyon College and Al McCoy of the University of Wisconsin, and Robert E. Jones, a former State Department official). Nonetheless the development of a five-day initiation rite able to produce hysteria among its participants is quite extraordinary.

3. The Expansion: The Monarchy and the Middle Classes

1. The session was held at Baan Saimuun, Tambon Ummao, Amphur That Phanom in Nakhon Phanom Province (VS history 1984:29).

2. The initiation was held at the BPP Region 4 headquarters at Camp Seni Ronnayuth in Udon Thani Province. It is likely that various individuals contributed to the royal decision to attend. The invitation to the king and queen was arranged through Somkhuan Harikul's superior officer, Major General Charoenrit Chamrasromrun, who had attended an earlier initiation session as master of ceremonies and later became head of the Village Scout Operations Center of Thailand, and Lieutenant General Suraphon Chulabrahm, then the deputy commanding general of the BPP and later director of the BPP (1991 interview; Morell and Samudavanija 1981:242).

Suraphon in particular commanded considerable trust and respect from numerous quarters, including the king, the CIA, and most top army leaders (Lobe and Morell 1978:170). No doubt the positive impression on the princess mother was another contributing influence.

3. Somkhuan Harikul described this timeframe when I interviewed him in 1991, but a semiofficial biography published by his friends and colleagues on the occasion of his sixtieth birthday and retirement, says the audience occurred ten weeks later (VS history 1984:31). Somkhuan Harikul insisted to me that the audience was immediately after the initiation.

4. This is the minimum staff needed for a ritual to initiate 250 to 300 people. During 1976 the average number of initiates per ritual was 795 (see appendix, table A1.4).

5. Important personal alliances often date to school days. General Suraphon Chulabrahm, the head of the BPP, graduated from Chulachomklao Military Academy in the class of 1940. Among his classmates were several individuals important in the Village Scouts. One was General Saiyud Kerdphol, the head of Communist Suppression Operations Command (CSOC) and later the supreme commander of the Royal Thai Armed Forces. General Saiyud Kerdphol served as master of ceremonies for the pilot initiation session of the Village Scouts held in 1970. As head of CSOC (renamed the Internal Security Operations Command, or ISOC, in 1974), General Saiyud Kerdphol was important to the Village Scout movement both because of his political philosophy and his personal connections. The civil-police-military concept, which became the basis for the Thai counterinsurgency effort of CSOC, is attributed to General Saiyud Kerdphol. According to this approach, countering insurgency is not just a military problem. Assuring good government and improving the social and economic conditions of the villagers were more important (see Tanham in Kerdphol 1986:2). As General Saiyud Kerdphol writes, "The loyalties of the villagers, rather than the destruction of the insurgents, should be the main objective" of counterinsurgency efforts (1986:77).

Other important classmates included Major General Sanga Kittikachorn of the BPP, Chartchai Choonhawan, and Serm na Nakorn. Sanga was the younger brother of Thanom Kittikachorn, the prime minister of Thailand when the Village Scout movement was beginning. Chartchai was the head of the Thai Nation political party, the party actively involved in the Village Scouts and responsible in large measure for their mobilization on October 6. Chartchai later became prime minister. Serm was a leader of the October 6 coup and army commander in chief and later supreme commander of the armed forces (Girling 1981:n129, n225).

6. *Daily Times*, June 2, 1976. The working relationship of the royal secretary and the Ministry of Interior was no doubt facilitated by another set of per-

sonal links. The royal secretary to the king was Campen Charusathien, whose brother, Field Marshal Praphat Charusathien, was then minister of interior.

7. However, as will become clear in chapter 4, even royal sponsorship was not enough to prevent the public outbreak of the rivalries that inevitably developed between the BPP and the Ministry of Interior for overall administrative control of the Village Scout movement. The rivalries were not resolved until 1978 (and then in part), only because the movement was loosing its momentum.

8. The session I observed had a budget of 15,000 baht. This was seen as a bare-bones figure and proved insufficient. In Bangkok the average session was apparently costing 30,000 to 40,000 baht (U.S. $1,500 to $2,000) in 1976 for an initiation of four hundred to five hundred people (see Kriangsak Lohachaala 1976:67). The more expensive initiations had lavish props such as huge papier-mâché tiger heads as portals through which initiates passed to enter the camp. Staff members—not the initiates—were provided with meals and a small per diem for their participation. In addition Natee Pisalchai, a Thai writer, explains that trainees "were required to: buy expensive badges and colored group photographs; contribute 40–50 baht daily for food; make religious donations, and pay for the elaborate costumes used for the beauty and dance competitions" (quoted in Anderson 1977:28).

9. See Kerdphol (1986:82). Such village-oriented projects included the Village Defense Corps, the Village Security Officers, the Peoples' Assistance Teams, the Census Aspiration Teams, the Village Security Force, the Border Security Volunteer Teams, and even the Hunter-Killer Teams.

10. This strategy was not new. McGehee describes its use in his book (1983: 104).

11. Charges of lèse majesté have invariably been brought by the government and not directly by a representative of the monarchy. The charge of lèse majesté has proved useful at various times to governments seeking to hide their activities from public comment by associating with the monarchy. See Anderson (1977:23–24) and Streckfuss (1995) for further discussion.

12. A commonly cited manifestation of sacred power is invulnerability—a gun aimed at an invulnerable person will not fire its bullets; if fired, the bullets will not enter that person's body. This belief is widespread throughout mainland Southeast Asia. In addition to bullets, the body of someone who is invulnerable cannot be penetrated by knives and even needles. See Tambiah (1984) for discussion of amulets.

13. Kingshill does not provide the wording of the question. He notes that those who defined monarchy gave the following descriptions: "1) when the king is above the law, 2) the old (Thai) government, 3) the government, and 4) a Buddhist country" (1991:245).

14. All Thai men are encouraged to ordain as monks at least briefly during their lives. Even today government officials are allowed to take a leave of absence to spend up to three months in the monkhood. King Mongkut had been the abbot of Wat Bovornives until he ascended the throne. King Chulalongkorn, King Vajiravudh, and King Prajadhipok were all monks at this temple, as was King Bhumiphol's father, Prince Mahidol.

15. A military coup in November 1951 suspended the constitution and dissolved Parliament. The new government justified its action with the assertion that the "present world situation has fallen into a generally critical condition due to the danger of the Communist aggressive threat" (in Wilson 1962:28). Upon his return from the United States in 1955 Field Marshal Phibun Songkhram allowed political parties to register in anticipation of elections, set for February 1957. Under his prime ministership the government also undertook measures to decentralize power to local governments in 1955 (see discussion in Wilson 1962:29–32).

16. That Sarit was conscious of this issue was made clear in an interview in 1958, when he said, "Anyone can launch a revolution, but the snag about it is that, once a revolution is staged, how to win public approval" (Darling 1962:171).

17. The countries were Vietnam, Indonesia, Burma, Malaysia, Pakistan, Australia, New Zealand, Japan, the Philippines, England, West Germany, Portugal, Spain, Switzerland, Denmark, Norway, Sweden, Italy, Belgium, France, Luxembourg, the Netherlands, and the United States.

18. The king has an experimental farm, a rice mill, and a dairy factory on the palace grounds (Morell and Samudavanija 1981:68). He frequently distributes rice seeds to farmers when he visits rural areas. He has also set up an experimental farm at Hubkraphong in Petchaburi, in addition to several projects in the North to help the hill tribes.

19. In the royal kathin ceremony the king presents gifts to the monks. Under the new constitutional governments the barge procession had been discontinued (Chaloemtiarana 1979:321–24).

20. Reading the king's comments from March 13, 1969, is instructive:

> Law and reality may be in conflict. In fact, there are quite a few loopholes in the law because we have structured our legal precepts and our government by relying on foreign principles without really considering the condition of the people. Worse than that, we did not take into account that government administration sometimes does not reach the people, thus forcing them to establish their own law. . . .

> We do not wish to have communist terrorists in Thailand. But we are creating them when we point at self-governing villagers who are orderly and democratic, charging them with having trespassed on

reserved forest land and driving them out. How should they know
that those areas are in a conservation category, since there have been
no government officials in the area to tell them so? Yet we repress
those ordinary villagers under the assumption that they ought to
know the law.

(Morell and Samudavanija 1981:68)

21. NSCT was founded on December 20, 1969. It was composed of the
elected presidents of all student bodies. During its early years it was primarily engaged in humanitarian causes, such as projects to aid the poor and
provide relief to flood victims (Punyodyana 1975:192; see also R.
Zimmerman 1978 for discussion of student organizations).

22. Although most accounts of October 14 focus on the role of the university
students, Boonsanong Punyodyana notes that people from many walks of
life took part. Among those who were killed or wounded, "more were
non-students than students." Hence he suggests, "The less privileged elements in Thai society had fought more aggressively against the status quo
under the military regime than the more privileged ones" (1975:193).

23. As is customary in the deaths of important figures, their funeral was
delayed until the following year. It was a state occasion with the king and
queen lighting the funerary pyre. Hundreds of thousands attended, including me.

24. Between the convention and the assembly phase significant shifts in the relative percentages occurred. Although the low number of military and
police officers at the convention (14 percent) was replicated in the
National Assembly, the number of rural leaders declined from 27 percent
to 6 percent, and the number of civil servants increased from 13 to 37 percent (Keyes 1987:87).

25. When the Village Scout movement was founded, the king established
twelve guidelines for the administration of the scout movement (see
appendix, table A1.1). These guidelines suggest the king was interested in
the development of a popular organization that was independent of government control as a way to check corruption and double-check village
grievances. As the staff training manuals explain, the movement was to
"avoid abuse of status and power by stressing democratic methods" and
"avoid involvement with money, as it easily leads to bribery" (Muecke
1980:423). In addition the king was supporting a nonmilitarized movement that would not use weapons. The goal was to encourage unity, and
uniforms and other means of identifying scouts according to status or class
were forbidden.

26. Furthermore not all royal projects succeed. A notable example of a royal
program that failed to garner support was land reform; the king donated
tens of thousands of rai for land reform, urging others to follow suit.

Virtually no one did. Another royal project involved an effort to encourage
the growth of red kidney beans; although many villagers grew kidney
beans, the project failed because of marketing difficulties.

27. U.S. troops began their withdrawal on March 20, 1976. The withdrawal
    was completed in July 1976, except for 270 advisers who remained (P. Bell
    1978:69).

28. In 1960 the average per capita income in northeastern Thailand, the poor-
    est and most underdeveloped region of the country, was 19.2 percent of
    the average per capita income in Bangkok. By 1970 this figure had declined
    to 16.2 percent. Even in the central region, the most prosperous region in
    the country, the average per capita income was 45.5 percent of the average
    per capita income of Bangkok; by 1970 this figure had declined to 41.5
    percent (Keyes 1987:92).

29. Only 10 to 15 percent of all credit was provided through official govern-
    ment or bank sources at the legal interest rate of 10 to 14 percent per year
    (Turton 1978:116). Once villagers were forced to borrow money at pri-
    vate rates, they had little hope of repaying it. The average farm family's
    debt was about U.S.$200, as compared to an average family income of not
    more than $300 a year; some families earned as little as $25 a year (Morell
    and Samudavanija 1981:209; see also Turton 1978:113 and Phelan
    1975:14).

30. The World Bank set tenancy at 40 percent in the central plains region at
    this time, but only 12 percent for the nation as a whole. Other sources put
    the national figure at 50 percent and suggest tenancy rates average 75 per-
    cent in the seven central provinces around Bangkok (Ping 1978:42).

31. Kamol Janlekha's 1955 study of a village in the central plains revealed 37
    percent of the villagers were tenants and 22 percent were laborers; in
    other words 59 percent were landless (Potter 1976:179). Kaufman's study
    of another central Thai village revealed 23.7 percent landless laborers
    (1960:55, 60). Piker writes that in his central plains village 60 percent of
    the families "are either landless or own so little land (5 rai or less) that they
    must subsist largely on the basis of wage labor" (1964:21, 35). Even in the
    Northeast, where land is somewhat more evenly distributed within villages
    than in other regions of the country, problems of landlessness and land
    insufficiency were considerable. Tambiah notes 10.8 percent were landless
    (1970:24). Keyes notes considerable out-migration from the northeastern
    village he studied, commenting that 18 percent lacked sufficient land on
    which to grow rice (Potter 1976:185; see Potter 1976, Bruneau 1984,
    Chiengkul 1983, and Turton 1978 for further details).

32. Farmers' demands included passage of the Land Rent Act, allocation of
    land for planting in 1975, issues of title deeds to farmers squatting on
    denuded forest reserve land, land reform legislation, suspension of all

court cases involving farmers charged with unwitting use of the land of absentee owners, release of farmers arrested for trespass, and the lifting of martial law in many outlying provinces, which prevented villagers from demonstrating (Turton 1978:122–23).

33. The Land Rent Control Act was primarily aimed at easing the plight of tenants; it required a contract for all tenancies for six-year periods and limited the maximum rent to one-third of the crop. The Land Reform Act set a maximum ceiling on landholdings at fifty rai. Although it appeared to be a step forward, the act had numerous loopholes that vitiated its effectiveness. Enough time was provided in the act for large landowners to either sell their lands or redistribute them in such a way that they appeared to be in compliance. Little land was actually distributed to landless villagers (see Turton 1978:120).

34. The high rate of tenancy in the northern provinces was one reason for this rapid growth.

35. A labor protection law was passed in 1956, but it was annulled eighteen months later, in October 1958, by Sarit's coup. For more on early labor history see Chandravithun (1982), Morell and Samudavanija (1981:181–86), Mudannayake et al. (1975), Schut (1975), and Mabry (1977).

36. Morell and Samudavanija note that a survey conducted by the Labor Department in late 1974 found that 44 percent of employers had not adjusted to the 20-baht minimum-wage rate set by the government in June 1974; 48 percent were not observing regulations regarding labor protection; 36 percent did not provide their workers with paid holidays; and 36 percent did not observe the labor law concerning use of women and child labor. Furthermore they add that in some factories, if a worker were sick, "his or her wages were reduced at a rate of 20 baht per day of time off, although he or she was receiving only 12 baht a day" (1981: 194–95). Nonetheless a survey by a group of Thammasat University lecturers in 1975 found the average rate of profit in the industrial sector to be 117 percent per year, the highest profit rate anywhere in Southeast Asia (Morell and Samudavanija 1981:195).

37. As Clark Neher explains, in 1971 the economic growth rate dropped precipitously, from 11.8 percent per year during the latter half of the 1960s to 2.8 percent in 1971 (1975:1098). Furthermore Thailand had a significant trade imbalance with Japan. In early 1973 the U.S. dollar was devalued by 10 percent, but the Thai Ministry of Finance retained a 20-to-1 parity between the baht and the dollar. As a result prices for commodities within Thailand began to rise rapidly. The oil increase by the Organization of Petroleum Exporting Countries (OPEC) further exacerbated this inflationary trend (see Morell and Samudavanija 1981:194).

38. Associations were restricted to a single industrial site; workers employed

in different industries or in different provinces were prohibited from joining the same association. All workers applying for membership in an association had to be at least eighteen years of age and to have been employed for
at least six months by the company in which the association was being
formed (Morell and Samudavanija 1981:188–89).

39. This federation has also been translated into English as the Federation of
Labor Unions of Thailand. The Labor Council of Thailand led campaigns
to subsidize the price of rice for urban workers, to extend the labor laws,
and to upgrade the Labor Department to ministerial status. It also provided advice to workers involved in labor disputes and assisted them in
forming unions. Long-range plans called for the establishment of a full-
time staff to provide organizational, negotiation, and legal services (Mabry
1977:939).

40. Puey Ungphakorn writes that Wattana was asked by General Saiyud
Kerdphol, the head of ISOC, to return from the United States to teach psychological warfare techniques at ISOC (1977:11).

41. Not all in the military supported Nawaphon. General Krit Sivara publicly
denounced the demagoguery of its leadership (Flood 1977a:39). Reports
suggest that ISOC later discontinued its official support of Nawaphon,
although some of its officials continued their support in their capacity as
private citizens. Morell and Samudavanija suggest that some ISOC officials
were concerned that they were lending support to Wattana's personal
ambitions (1981:240).

42. Thanin Kraivichien, the man who became prime minister after the
October 6 coup, was a member of Nawaphon. Another prominent member was an activist right-wing monk named Kittiwutho Bhikkhu, who generated tremendous controversy in a Buddhist society when he suggested
that killing communists was not demeritorious. Kittiwutho Bhikkhu had
close ties to right-wing elements in the military, many of whom were
involved in ISOC, even allowing his monastery to become a military training camp for Nawaphon members (see Keyes 1977 for details; see also
Jackson 1989:147–54; Suksamran 1982:92–99, 132–57).

43. Others involved with the Red Gaur groups were General Vitoon Yasawat,
former leader of the CIA-hired Thai mercenary forces in Laos, and General
Chartchai Choonhawan, a leading figure in the Thai Nation Party (Anderson
1977:n28). Both men were involved with the events of October 6, 1976.

44. In August 1976 the private home of Prime Minister Kukrit was stormed by
drunken policemen (for an analysis of violence in Thai society see
Anderson 1990).

45. These domestic policies included the minimal land reform efforts, minimal
efforts to improve the situation for workers, a modest corruption suppression program, and under Kukrit the Tambon Development Program,

which channeled additional government resources into rural areas. Conservatives also objected to the foreign policy initiatives to allow more open dialogue with Vietnam, Cambodia, and Laos.

46. Anderson portrays the entire Thai bourgeoisie as moving to the right. I believe the Thai bourgeoisie split, with some moving right and others moving left. After all, the university students leading many of the demonstrations were members of bourgeois families. Furthermore support for the return of the military was by no means unanimous. This opposition was manifested in August 1976 when Praphat attempted to return to Bangkok but was driven away by massive demonstrations led by university students. As Morell and Morell point out, these protests "achieved a good deal of public support" (1977:337). Further evidence of this split can be seen in the membership of the CPT, which drew many of its members from the Thai middle classes.

47. The elected government's foreign policy initiatives also concerned the king, with their "concessions to communism" and consequent dangers to Thai security (Morell and Morell 1977:338–39). Morell and Morell note that the king's main advisers came from institutions ranging from the Internal Security Operations Command to the Siam Commercial Bank, adding that "he neither requested nor received opinions from reform leaders" (1977:338–39).

48. Morell and Samudavanija claim that "90 percent of the Scouts are poor rural people" (1981:245). By contrast Natee Pisalchai suggests that "most of the people who joined the program were reasonably well off" (B. Anderson 1977:28). I believe the differences between these authors can be resolved by understanding the different phases of the movement.

49. See chapter 4 for more detailed discussion.

50. Many scholars have speculated about what provoked the turn to the right of villagers on October 6. I believe that few ordinary villagers were in fact involved in the events of October 6. Instead the Village Scouts who participated in these events were more likely to have come from the district towns near Bangkok, as well as Bangkok itself. When I interviewed Somkhuan Harikul he said that the BPP trucks picked up Village Scouts on fairly short notice from the provincial centers, further supporting my view that few villagers would have been involved.

4. The Moratorium: Fissures on the Right

1. See *Thai Rath* and *Daily News*, November 16, 1976; see also Kriangsak Lohachaala 1976:69.

2. The official figure for arrests at Thammasat University is 3,059 people (see R. Zimmerman 1978:58). However, many more were arrested in Bangkok in the days that followed and up-country as well. According to Marut Bunnag, official figures given in December 1978 indicated 5,788 detainees

had been released and another 255 would be released soon, thus suggesting the number of those arrested was close to 6,000. The Co-ordinating Groups for Religion estimated that the actual number of detainees was closer to 8,000 (Bunnag 1979:62).

3. Thanin had given lectures on anticommunist tactics to the Thai National Defense College and to ISOC (Shawcross 1976:61). One of Thanin's first actions in government was to establish an anticorruption committee. Interestingly, Kershaw sees the king's choice of the civilian Thanin as part of the monarch's continuing alliance against military power (1979:262).

4. In addition to Thanin the right-wing Democrat Samak Sunthorawej was appointed minister of interior, and three military leaders involved in the coup were appointed as deputy prime minister and minister and deputy minister of defense (Girling 1981:215). Just how conservative the government was can be read in Thanin's statement at a news conference: "When you deal with politics, you've got to be wary of the middle ground because that is where the communists creep in, disguised as liberals." (Girling 1981:215).

5. The new constitution mentioned the king in more than half of the twenty-nine articles (Marks 1977:62).

6. In a later interview the deputy minister of interior commented on the need felt by the BPP for tighter control of the movement. He also commented on budgetary considerations and the need to keep expenses down as much as possible so that financing new sessions would not be a burden to anyone (Siam Rath, December 8, 1976).

7. Not surprisingly, considerable tension was rumored to exist between Somkhuan Harikul and Charoenrit Chamrasromrun (see Muecke 1980: 409).

8. The government required village children to attend only to the fourth grade at this time. Consequently, the greatest number of teachers worked in rural elementary schools and came under the Ministry of Interior. Secondary schools were more likely to be located in the larger towns and cities. Teachers in secondary schools were also involved in providing staffing for the Village Scout movement, although their numbers were fewer. To the extent they were involved, these teachers came under a different ministry, the Ministry for Education.

9. After the fifth session they received their Village Scout kerchiefs and were allowed to return to their duties.

10. In one district in which I lived two local instructors in particular had developed a reputation for taking advantage of young initiates. Their peccadilloes became publicly known when they were arrested for drunken brawling in another province. At the time they were with two girls from the district they had met during the course of their last initiation session.

11. The royal injunction notwithstanding, the Village Scouts were always a political movement in the sense that they were a government-organized effort to counter communist insurgency. Muecke comments that in the Thai context, "'Extra-political' carries the de facto definition of 'not involved in the election process'" (1980:422).

12. One columnist protested, "I became a Village Scout in order to become close to villagers and to help develop and improve local communities. . . . There is nothing in the scout ideology that says we should serve politicians or political groups such as Nawaphon" (*Daily Times*, April 6, 1976).

13. The Bangkok governor, Thammanun Thienngen, who was involved in the rapid growth of the scout movement in Bangkok, was a member of the conservative wing of the Democrats.

14. *Prachachaat*, August 6, 1976. The incident occurred in February 1976 at a Village Scout initiation in Phyathai district in Bangkok. At the time Pramarn Adireksan was deputy prime minister and minister of defense.

15. *Prachachaat*, August 6, 1976. There was also talk of using the Village Scouts as official poll watchers and observers during the election campaigns (*Siam Rath*, March 8, 1976).

16. Rather than insinuate an oblique critique of communism and encourage a greater focus on national unity, as was often done, Charoenrit Camrasromran made direct and explicit attacks on communism. At many initiation sessions he would have Laotians, who had fled the new socialist government, speak on the evils of communism (*Prachachaat*, August 6, 1976).

17. *Siam Rath* was owned and edited by M. R. Kukrit Pramoj, who served as prime minister for much of the civilian period, so it is not surprising that this newspaper was among the boldest in its willingness to criticize Charoenrit Camrasromran and the Village Scouts.

18. It is easy to see this mobilization of up-country Village Scouts as a dress rehearsal for the much larger rallying of scouts on October 6.

19. Lobe writes, "In fact, many observers believe that the generals outmaneuvered the ideological Right by conducting the coup d'etat when they did. The generals, who are now in tenuous control, would like business to go on as usual (including the heroin trade, graft, rake-offs, and all the other important activities of the Thai military-business elite), but are opposed by the Prime Minister, the King, and their many well-organized legal and extra-legal fanatic followers" (1977:122).

20. Girling emphasizes as primary factors necessary for successful military coups the following: "Thai-Chinese and foreign business enterprises, agencies of the U.S. government, and most conspicuously in recent years, the monarchy" (1981:129).

21. Praphat was allowed to return to Thailand again after the coup, in January 1977 (Van Praagh 1977:302).

22. Anderson (1977:28). As Morell and Samudavanija write:

> Information about who actually ordered armed BPP and other
> police units into this area on the night of October 5 remains unavail-
> able. Did the military issue this order? If so, which faction? Did the
> police hierarchy itself order it? Did the palace, acting unilaterally
> (there is a special relationship between the palace and the BPP)? Did
> the Seni government? This vital fact remains unclear, though it is
> certain that some official order had to have been issued that evening,
> particularly since BPP units had to be brought into Bangkok from
> their upcountry garrisons.
>
> (1981:282)

23. There have been rumors that Krit's death occurred under mysterious circumstances after eating mangoes and sticky rice. With the exile of Field
Marshals Thanom Kittikachorn and Praphat Charusathien in October
1973, General Krit Sivara became the major military figure for much of
the civilian era. Closely associated with General Krit were his two successors as army commander: General Bunchai Bamrungphong, who became
army commander in October 1975 and later deputy prime minister in the
Thanin government and the first Kriangsak government, and General Serm
na Nakorn, army commander in chief from 1976 to 1978 (Girling 1981:
228–29; Morell and Samudavanija 1981:267). Although Krit died in April
1976, his supporters were members of NARC who later took power on
October 6.

24. The roots of the Thai Nation Party can be traced to what is called the Soi
Rajakhruu clique dating from the 1950s. The clique was formed by
Chartchai's father, General Phin Choonhavan, and Police General Phao
Siyanon. This faction receives its name from the fact that the leading fami-
lies in this clique, Choonhavan, Adireksan, and Siriyothin, all live on Soi
Rajakhruu. Pramarn Adireksan is married to Chartchai Choonhavan's
sister.

25. General Vitoon, also a former leader of the CIA-hired Thai mercenary
forces in Laos, was an opponent of Praphat's (Girling 1977:391). Vitoon
was among the military generals who had approached Kris Sivara in mid-
1973 to seize power from Thanom and Praphat. After October 14 Major
General Vitoon was given the post of assistant director general of the
police department (Morell and Samudavanija 1981:148–49).

26. As Morell and Samudavanija explain, "About six of the Democrats' central
committee members . . . had close links with leaders of the Thai Nation
party" (1981:268). Both the conservative wing of the Democrat Party and
the Thai Nation Party had close ties to the Village Scout movement.

27. General Pramarn is also known as an important businessman. He was pres-

ident of the Thai Industries Association and the Thai Textile Manufacturers
Association; for years he worked closely with Japanese enterprises, particularly with Japanese joint ventures in the textile industry (Girling 1981:
103, 181, 198; Morell and Samudavanija 1981:319). Given Pramarn's
interests in the textile industry, it is hardly surprising that he was opposed
to the organizing activities among workers and students characteristic of
the civilian period. Pramarn moved his adherents into positions of power at
the expense of Krit and the exiled Praphat factions (Girling 1981:205).

28. Thammanun was Samak's political mentor, bringing Samak into the
Democrat Party in the 1960s and assisting in Samak's first successful election to the municipal assembly in 1968. As governor of Bangkok
Thammanun openly supported Samak in the 1975 general election.
However, it seems this close relationship came to an end after the 1976
coup, because three months later the Thanin government—with Samak as
minister of interior—dissolved Thammanun's Bangkok municipal government (see Somvichian 1978:836).

29. Although a two-party coalition—Democrat (114 seats) and Social Action
(45 seats)—was formed, the king reportedly expressed his disapproval of
this coalition, and it collapsed (Morell and Samudavanija 1981:272–73; see
also Keyes 1987:98).

30. They were deputy interior ministers Samak Sunthornawej and Sombun
Sirithorn (Morell and Samudavanija 1981:272–73).

31. The three ministers were Damrong Latthaphiphat, Surin Masadit, and
Chuan Leekphai (for profiles of these and other cabinet members see
Business in Thailand, May 1976).

32. Instead, as a result of the intense factional competition following October
6, Vitoon was sent to Japan as the government liaison to oversee Thai students studying there (Morell and Samudavanija 1981:321).

33. Dr. Somchai Rakvijit was the chief of the research department of ISOC and
a former employee of the Pentagon's (Mallet 1978:95).

34. The victim was Major General Arun Devathasin (for details see Darling
1978). Both the shooting and the execution were unprecedented in the history of Thai coup making. Usually, coups are nonviolent, at least internally,
and the losing parties generally leave the country for a time.

35. Chalard was executed without trial on April 20, 1977. Eighteen other co-
conspirators were sentenced in early May to prison terms ranging from
five to twenty years. Two others, including the manager of the Dusit Thani
Hotel, were sentenced to life in absentia. Eleven of those sentenced were
police or army officers. Others were politicians, government officials,
and journalists. Among those arrested were Chalard's son and Pichai
Wassanasong, a prominent television commentator, and Raksat
Wattanapanich, director general of the Department of Public Relations.

All were pardoned by Kriangsak in December 1977 (Darling 1978:156; R. Zimmerman 1978:107).

36. At first the prime minister personally ordered the radio station closed and Colonel Uthan arrested. Later a compromise was worked out at a secret meeting of senior military figures that resulted in a temporary suspension of the radio station's operations and the transfer of Colonel Uthan (Peagam 1977:9).

37. The successful coup of October 1977 is further evidence of the political instability of the various military factions. However, in this coup the relevant factions were not oriented toward drawing the Village Scouts into their machinations.

38. This is particularly ironic given the close association of the king with the Village Scout movement. However, it seems that the king was known to be deeply distrusting of the Thai Nation leaders, and Thai Nation leaders were heavily involved in Village Scout activities (see Mallet 1978:91). Consequently, it is not clear which military faction had the king's sympathies on October 6.

39. After the unsuccessful coup attempt in March 1977 there was a purge of journalists, radio and TV personalities, and members of the Thai Nation Party (Girling 1977:400). However, the Praphat wing of the military, headed by General Yot Thephasdin, continued to maneuver against Admiral Sangad Chaloryu and General Kriangsak (Girling 1977:404). General Saiyud Kerdphol, head of ISOC, also was increasingly vocal in his criticism of the Thanin government (Somvichian 1978:835).

40. This assessment of the attitude of the Thanin government toward the Village Scout movement was seconded by Somkhuan Harikul. I asked him which of the three post-1976 prime ministers—Thanin, Kriangsak, and Prem—he considered most supportive of the Village Scout movement. He named Kriangsak, because the Village Scout Operation Center was given official status under Kriangsak (1992 interview).

41. As a signal of royal approval Thanin was appointed by the king to membership in the privy council two months after he had been ousted by the October 1977 coup (Girling 1981:n217).

42. A journalist, Kukrit had a regular newspaper column in *Siam Rath* and "reading between the lines of Kukrit's journalism is something of a national past-time of the middle class" (Kershaw 1979:261). Kukrit wrote of "the baleful influence of Dowager Empresses in Chinese history." He also wrote "at some length in praise of Queen Elizabeth II of Great Britain in her Jubilee Year, pointing out that despite Britain's loss of empire, and economic decline, the glory of the English throne had grown, thanks to the dignity of its incumbent and her ability to retain the love of the vast majority of

her people." As Kershaw observes, "Some readers were quick to assume an adverse comparison with developments in Thailand" (1979:261).

43. As Marks notes, the crown prince Vajiralongkorn, "never noted for his brilliance, had been sent to the Australian Military Academy rather than West Point for fear he might fail the engineering-saturated curriculum" at West Point (1977:56).

44. Samak was deputy minister of interior in the Seni government; he became minister of interior in the Thanin government.

45. The crown princess is actually his second-eldest daughter. His eldest daughter married a commoner and hence is officially no longer considered a member of the royal family.

46. The VOPT broadcast continued,

> The government report stated that while on the helicopter, the princess was informed of injuries to two BPP's, so she ordered the helicopter to pick them up. What about people in the area who are now facing difficulties and hardships, those whose relatives were killed or wounded by the police and volunteers, whose houses and farmland were destroyed, and whose children, wives, and sisters were raped or killed? Princess Wiphawadi never paid any attention to these people or asked about them. On whose side was Princess Wiphawadi? Why was she out there and for what purpose? Whose interest did she serve?
>
> (Marks 1977:64–65).

47. Patrice de Beer's chronology suggests that there were earlier critiques as well, although Thirayut's received considerable attention (1978).

5. Setting the Agrarian Stage

1. The district education officer told me in February that the initiations would resume the following month, although he said no specific locations or dates had been determined. Charoenrit Chamrasromrun also announced in an interview in mid-February that he anticipated that initiation sessions would resume in March (*Baan Muang*, February 14, 1977).

2. Initially, in the 1920s the Chinese Communist Party (CCP) saw itself as the party of the proletariat in accord with the current Marxist-Leninist interpretations and, accordingly, attempted to organize the urban-based proletariat into a network of industrial unions. The Kuomintang purge of 1927–28, in which thousands of cadre were killed, forced the CCP to find a new strategy based not in urban unions but the peasantry. Consequently, in the Chinese revolution "peasants ended up providing *both* the revolutionary insurrectionary force and the organized popular basis for the consolidation of revolutionary state powers" (Skocpol 1979:236).

3. Samsen Village and Samsen Subdistrict are fictitious names. With this

exception, I have not changed the names of the district or the other subdistricts within it.

4. I was specifically warned not to return to any of the villages I had visited in the course of researching an article on the FFT. I also was told that Village Scouts had been alerted to watch for my presence. In retrospect, what happened was somewhat humorous. The American consulate had also received this threat but misfiled it under the last name of Barry. Months later an alert consular official made the connection and passed on the warning.

5. See discussion of landlessness in chapter 3.

6. They came from the Socialist Party and the New Force Party. Of the 269 seats in the National Assembly, 37 seats were held by members of the three left-wing parties, the Socialist Party of Thailand, the United Socialist Front, and the New Force Party. For further analysis, see Morell and Samudavanija (1981:113).

7. At the time newspapers said that the car belonged to Dr. Boonsanong Punyodyana, secretary general of the Socialist Party of Thailand. In fact the car belonged to Boonyen Wothong, a member of the steering committee of the Socialist Party of Thailand who had come to help Insorn campaign. For more on Boonyen, see Morell and Samudavanija (1981:302–303).

8. Dr. Boonsanong was not driving the car when the guns were found, and it is widely assumed that these guns were planted.

9. The election campaign of 1976 was the bloodiest and most violent in Thai history. Dr. Boonsanong was assassinated on February 29, 1976. For interview with him see Peagam (1975), reprinted in *Bulletin of Concerned Asian Scholars* 9 (3) (July–September) 1977: 50–51.

10. Personal conversation with a factory manager.

11. Because membership in these organizations often overlapped, it was at times difficult to know the primary affiliation of those present at various confrontations in the area.

12. The tension between university and vocational students has historical roots. In general university students are more likely to be urban and of Chinese-Thai heritage. Vocational students are more likely to be Thai and from less prominent families. On October 14, 1973, vocational students were on the front lines and hence the receiving end of the military brutality. After the coup the vocational students resented that they were not included as equal partners in the National Student Center of Thailand (NSCT). The right was able to effectively manipulate this rift, both in Bangkok and elsewhere, with the vocational students forming the core of the Red Gaurs and other violent gangs. (See Morell and Samudavanija 1981:241, R. Zimmerman 1978).

13. Chayan Vaddhanaphuti also notes this pattern of elite involvement in the northern district of Mae Taeng where he conducted his fieldwork. The

chairman of the Village Scout troop in his area was the kamnan and the other troop leadership positions were chosen from other village headmen in the tambon as well as other rich villagers (Vaddhanaphuti 1984:330).

14. As I explained in chapter 2, the Wood Badge is awarded to those who have received special leadership training. Forty or fifty Wood Badge Scouts were living in all of San Patong District, most of them merchants in the district town. Because this store owner was a merchant, he was in frequent contact with the other merchants, and he was invited to become a Wood Badge Scout.

15. Questions continued about the happiness of the new couple. Villagers were concerned about the lack of education of the royal consort and questioned whether first cousins should marry. Her miscarriage in April served to confirm their doubts.

16. The American ambassador to Thailand was also in the procession.

17. The questions were simple. One teacher asked the queen if she was hot in the afternoon sun. The queen replied that she had just been distributing scout insignia and had been in the hot sun for five hours straight. A girl from the village in which I lived asked whether the royal children were then studying for their exams. The queen replied that that was indeed the case.

18. The Martyrs of October 14 were those killed in the prodemocracy uprising of October 14, 1973, that led to the expulsion of the military dictatorship and issued in the three-year civilian period. Their cremation rites were held on October 14, 1974.

19. I do not know whether any of the scout chapters arranged for a second anniversary celebration, but many chapters held a celebration to mark the first anniversary of their scout initiation.

20. Celebrating the king's birthday was a long-standing custom in which both Village Scouts and ordinary citizens were active. The crown prince's up-country wedding receptions appeared to have been overwhelmingly organized and attended by Village Scouts.

21. The head of the Bangkok Bank, Chin Sophanpanich, was chosen to be president of the committee. Other members were Baanjyyt Chonwicharn, president of the Thai Industrial Board; Thaworn Phonpraphaa, director of Sayam Kolkaan Co.; and Uthaen Dejaphaibul, president of the board of directors of Sri Nakorn Bank; all were named vice presidents (*Siam Rath*, December 21, 1976).

22. The meeting was held February 7 to 9 at Khon Kaen in the Northeast; the southern meeting was held at Songkhla from February 14 to 16; the central regional meeting at Chonburi from February 21 to 23; and the northern regional meeting at Chiang Mai from February 28 to March 2 (*Tawansayam*, February 9, 1977). Such national representatives as the deputy minister of

interior, Damrong Sunthornsarathun, and the head of the scouts, Charoenrit Chamrasromrun, were in regular attendance.

23. The regional meetings appear to have been inconclusive. Participants at the northeastern regional meeting recommended ending all unnecessary extravagances, including holding beauty pageants, hosting lavish dinners, and sponsoring other expensive events in the name of the Village Scouts. They reiterated that Village Scouts should focus on activities for the common good, such as fostering health care, providing charitable assistance for those in need, and supporting government officials by being exemplary citizens (*Tawansayam*, February 11, 1977). They also reaffirmed that Village Scouts should make every effort to be thrifty and to buy goods made in Thailand rather than imported items (*Baan Muang*, February 14, 1977). However, the broader problems of staffing, funding, and the movement's susceptibility to partisan politics remained unresolved.

At the end of the fourth regional meeting Major General Charoenrit Chamrasromrun of the BPP, the national head of the Village Scouts, announced a few additional conclusions. To avoid infiltration villagers were to scrutinize the prospective candidates; this would now be easier because each initiation would draw solely from people of that area. He also announced that the initiation session program would be changed to include more vocational or occupational training or help in setting up agricultural cooperatives. To minimize the possibility of nonscouts' wearing stolen kerchiefs, Charoenrit Chamrasromrun announced that a different company would make the scout insignia and that security would be beefed up at the factory that would be producing scout insignia. Furthermore any scouts who, after investigation, were found guilty of conduct unbecoming to a scout would have their scout insignia confiscated (*Chaw Thai*, April 8, 1977).

24. No one has written in detail of the early training sessions because, as Muecke notes, "Written publications of the organization, such as training manuals, are not distributed to the public, and it is difficult for persons who are not members of the organization to attain access to information on the Village Scouts" (1980:n408). Thai writer Natee Pisalchai's account is one of the few descriptions extant. If his account of the session in which he participated is representative of other sessions of the day, their content was much more highly politicized than the session I observed after the moratorium. Natee Pisalchai describes one skit as including a mock garroting of "bad students" (cited in B. Anderson 1977:30). Interestingly this session was held at Nakhon Pathom, not far from Camp Naresuan (where the BPP officers involved in October 6 were based); the initiates were taken on a trip to Camp Naresuan. This session took place shortly before the actual garroting of the student activists just before October 6 (in B. Anderson 1977:30). By contrast the session I observed seemed to emphasize unity,

even to the point of trying to teach errant communist guerrillas the errors of their ways and bring them back into the family. These variations in initiations may not be reflected in the training manuals, because they may have been the ad-libs of individual instructors.

25. See also *Tawansayam*, April 10, 1977, and *Thai Rath*, April 14, 1977.

26. Three main categories differentiated the levels of communist insurgency in a given area, namely, white, pink, and red. White areas were those under unchallenged government control; pink were those with potential or incipient communist activity; and red were those areas with existing insurgent activity no longer subject to government control.

27. This problem was clear in the efforts of scout chapters in San Patong District to organize postinitiation events.

28. As Somkhuan Harikul explained, national officials felt that 500 was far too many and that any session reached maximum effectiveness at about 200 to 250 people (1991 interview). According to the overall figures, the average number of members for a single session in 1976 was 795, but after the moratorium ended the overall average declined (see appendix, table A1.4). Chayan Vaddhanaphuti also notes that "the number of trainees decreased substantially in the late 1970s" (1984:532). The session that Chayan observed in 1978 had "not more than two hundred people attending the session. . . . By contrast, I was told that in the mid-1970s, a training session usually attracted 400–500 trainees" (1984:558–59). Chayan attributes these smaller sessions to lack of interest. Although I agree that by 1978 lack of interest was definitely a factor, I also believe that the session size was deliberately restricted as a result of the reformatting.

29. Some have suggested that funds came from secret budget allocations; these funds were earmarked for counterinsurgency work and did not have to be accounted for in the same manner as regular government funds.

30. He didn't specify what kind of medications were being distributed, other than "*yaa kae myaj*," or anti-illness medicine.

31. None of these complications stopped this session from being a propaganda event. The day the scarves were being distributed, the governor flew in by helicopter. There were also rumors that the king might fly in and hand out the scarves in person, but this didn't happen. Nonetheless the governor's visit was recorded by TV cameras and broadcast on the news.

32. Expenses included matching shirts for the staff and costumes and sets, particularly for the evening performances. Not included was the more optional expense of building a huge tiger face as a doorway. Some tiger entrances even had lights that flashed at night.

33. To give some idea of how challenging obtaining reliable interviews from villagers can be, I tried to get a sense of how long village fairs had encoun-

tered problems of violence. The first person I asked said, "since time immemorial," and the second person said it was only a recent problem.

34. Saensak Muangsurin was a Thai boxer who became a national celebrity in Thailand when he won a world championship in boxing.

35. I asked why there was so little discussion at the meeting. One villager explained that because this was a Village Scout affair, villagers did not feel it was their decision to make.

36. Attitudes toward dancing vary somewhat in various regions of the country. In the 1970s northern Thai married women rarely danced in public. Unmarried village girls would have few occasions to dance, except as part of a temple festival. The dancing in the Village Scout initiation was seen as particularly degrading because it involved Western-style dancing such as the bump, and the ludicrous duck-waddle dance. There is no physical contact in traditional Thai *ramwong*. The physical contact common in Western-style dancing violates the matrilineal spirit line (*phii buu yaa*) of northern Thai society.

37. Housing assignments were intended to encourage people from different villages to get to know each other better.

6. From Humor to Hysteria: Turning Villagers into Subjects

1. The instructors were quite deliberate in their use of these techniques as devices to keep initiates awake. In commenting on the clothing the staff wore one lead instructor added that they intentionally wore brightly colored jackets ranging from lime green to pink to keep people awake.

2. In the session I observed some people, especially some young female initiates, quietly swapped groups. As I noted in chapter 5, some parents allowed their daughters to join only if they were in the same color group as another village girl they knew or with a trusted host family.

3. At the sessions observed by Muecke the gauntlet began with a run through a huge tiger's mouth made of papier-mâché (1980:414). The full session I attended had insufficient budget, so no one constructed a tiger face. At yet another session I attended, the tiger mask was decorated with electric lights; entering it to attend the evening campfire created a dramatic impression.

4. As I noted in chapter 5, I had the impression that the number who wanted to join was about equal to the number of places for initiates. There were certainly not another three hundred who wanted to join, and no one to my knowledge cried upon being informed that all the places were filled.

5. The bogeyman of communist infiltration was picked up by villagers. When they attended initiation sessions elsewhere, everyone made sure to check whether everyone had their scout scarves. They did not want to be refused entrance to the evening campfire ceremonies under suspicion of being

communist agents infiltrating to cause trouble. Because I did not have a
scout scarf, they even discussed whether I could accompany them. They
eventually decided that I could go along because I had been a Girl Scout in
my country.

This invocation of communist infiltration appealed to a strong insider-
outsider mentality current among villagers. Although the family is their primary sphere of reference in daily life, the village is the dominant sphere of
reference vis-à-vis the outside world. Villagers from other villages, let alone
total strangers, are viewed with suspicion. Villagers take pride in their village. Clearly, the scout movement was attempting to broaden that identification to include the entire Thai nation.

6. The Three Refuges is one of the most frequently repeated Buddhist chants:
"I take refuge in the Buddha. / I take refuge in the Dharma [the teachings
of the Buddha]. / I take refuge in the Sangha [the monastic order]."

7. Although the Village Scout movement did not have uniforms, instructors
wore matching outfits to make them easily identifiable. During formal
parts of the initiation they also wore their Boy Scout or Girl Scout uniforms, substituting their Village Scout kerchiefs for those of the familiar
scouting organizations.

8. This explanation overlooks the fact that, although scouts in other countries
of the world have scout oaths, the oaths are not identical; elsewhere scouts
are not pledging loyalty to the Thai Nation, Religion, and King.

9. The number 108 is frequently used in Thai to refer to a large number and
also has astrological significance. There are presently 131 member associations in the World Scout Conference.

10. Many villagers believed when they joined that becoming a scout would
entitle them to free medicine and medical care at the local government
hospital.

11. The injunction to be kind to animals suggests Buddhist tenets against
harming living creatures.

12. Muecke describes the map she saw as follows: "A cartoon figure on the
map shows an army-helmeted, bullet-belted soldier sketched with stereotyped Vietnamese features, his huge gaping mouth biting the northeastern
portion of Thailand that bulges eastward to Laos and Kampuchea, while his
greedy eyes stare at the northeast region of Thailand" (1980:417; see also
Winichakul 1994:80).

13. In Muecke's account these skits occur on the last two nights. In her account
she also notes that "so heated is the emotion in portraying this scene that,
during at least three separate performances in one province, the man portraying the traitor was actually wounded" (1980:419).

14. A form of doing battle in this period. Hot sand was poured over enemy
soldiers as they stormed city walls.

15. At the quarters where I was staying, the household head asked the initiates to be more helpful. He complained that his wife was being left to do their dishes and other miscellaneous tasks. Because the color group had only three women, the men were going to have to help with the cooking and cleanup.

16. Cleanliness was heavily emphasized. Each morning the sleeping quarters of the trainees were inspected and points given. At the beginning of each morning session the scouts were reminded not to forget to clean the kitchens or toilets in their residences and to remember to pick up litter lying around outside their homes. During a break on the morning of the second day people were told to pick up any litter they saw lying about the meeting hall. The scouts did so but were not told what to do with the litter. They ended up dropping it on the ground next to their seats.

On the morning of the third day the instructors took time to impress upon trainees the importance of having clean quarters and personages. Certain color groups received cleanliness awards. As the color group was recognized, the group head was to come forward and receive a green flag in recognition. The potentially serious tone of this exercise was undercut by the scout instructors who were stealing flags. Everyone laughed, but the group heads looked quite chagrined. Once the heads had retrieved their color-group flags, they assembled in a neat row in the center. With the color-group flags and cleanliness flags before them, all sang a song, part of the lyrics to which were "Don't hate working, or the country will never progress."

To offset disappointed hopes and encourage continued efforts the instructors reminded everyone not to worry, that the next day was another opportunity to win the award for their group. The next day everyone won the cleanliness awards, although not before two trainees were made to do the duck-waddle dance because their shirts were not neatly tucked in. I could see no relationship between the actual cleanliness of the sleeping quarters and the awards. On the fourth day in particular the residence in which I was sleeping was quite disorganized. The scouts had so little time to sleep that no one wanted to get up to make breakfast. Consequently, breakfast was finally made in a mad rush and no one had time to finish the dishes. The wife of the house owner ended up doing them. Nonetheless the intention was to encourage a sense of the importance of tidiness and order among the trainees, with the implication that if everyone were tidy (*riaprooj*), everything in the nation would also fall in order (*riaprooj*).

17. The official explanation notwithstanding, I was struck by one villager who commented that fire is used because it has the power to burn everything, including evil and desire (*kiilet* in Thai; *kilesa* in Sanskrit), so that only the good remains.

18. He played the roles of Phrayar Chakkri, the bellicose instructor, and the royal messenger in various skits.

19. Given the close ties of the designers of the Village Scout movement to U.S. advisers, the reference to the United States may reflect both their own views and those of villagers about the "land of plenty."

20. Despite the admonition given to all scouts not to let nonscouts borrow their kerchiefs, I noticed among the "senior" scout visitors several local village youths who were not scouts. The skits performed by the villagers included a market woman who was trying to sell her wares, a girl being sold by a pimp to a brothel in Bangkok, and the like.

21. Many of the visiting scout troops included a group of younger women in their delegation; their primary function was to perform Thai-style dances to head up their procession.

22. There is no kingdom of Samsen. The name is based on the fictitious name for the host village, Samsen.

23. Interestingly, the people singled out for testing at each stop were the male president and female vice president elected that morning.

24. This scenario was somewhat risqué. As the travelers took their seats, a male instructor performed a supposedly comical strip-tease routine, taking off a red dress, a bra, and then running out in his undershorts. Two royal attendants then entered carrying a picture of a coconut tree in the shape of a woman. Using mime, the attendants picked or stroked the coconuts, or breasts, and threw them to the initiates.

25. While interviewing an instructor I suggested that this incident appeared to undermine the whole point of the scout initiation. Although the session attempted to generate villagers' loyalty and trust in public leaders, in this case the scout instructors they admired had made a mistake and rendered them targets of public humiliation. This instructor laughed at my comment, saying that I misunderstood the intent of this incident. The point of the exercise was to build up the meaning of the scout kerchief in the minds of the trainees. They were to feel that they had not received their kerchiefs lightly but had earned them. I observed no tears, only bewilderment, on the faces of the disgraced scouts. However, this instructor said he had noticed tears welling up because they were sad that after all this they might not receive the scout kerchief.

26. The points presented different somewhat from the official royal policies (see appendix, table A1.1). See also Muecke (1980:423).

27. Many scarves were blessed at Wat Phra Kaew, the famous temple in Bangkok. Others were blessed by Luang Buu Waen, the most famous monk in northern Thailand at the time.

28. The troop number and initiation dates are fictitious.

29. The initiation session clearly took its toll on older initiates. The oldest woman at the session had been the good-natured brunt of many jokes. However, she seemed to have reached a breaking point by the fourth night

when she was dressed up in a cape and told to parade around the campfire circle as a beauty queen. She was too tired to walk straight. By the following morning she was ill and in the infirmary. She had to be escorted onto the stage in the afternoon to receive her royal kerchief. Another initiate, who suffered from epilepsy, had a seizure on the fourth night and was given special dispensation to rest at home rather than in the first aid center.

30. It should be noted that the color groups had never been alone long enough or been assigned difficult enough tasks to give rise to any internal conflict.

31. A mere shout or an incongruous sound of laughter that succeeded in capturing the initiates' attention would have been enough to break the spell. Significantly, throughout the closing ceremony both the perimeter and the immediate area were cordoned off and curious villagers were kept at a remote distance. The catcall of this villager went unnoticed by the exhausted, zombielike initiates.

7. Mixed Metaphors: The Class Struggle Unmasked

1. The state further reinforced the ideology of the king and queen as parents of the nation in its subsequent decision to celebrate Mother's Day on the queen's birthday and Father's Day on the king's birthday.

2. Villagers who considered themselves people of means and influence commented after the session that it was fortunate that they had not been singled out to do the duck waddle because they would have refused.

3. In fact the hand is frequently used in right-wing discourse to symbolize both unity and hierarchy. According to this analogy, the hand makes a strong fist when all the fingers work together, yet each finger has a different size and role in society. All fingers are not equal.

4. Muecke notes that some scout troops did in fact set up cooperative insurance programs for troop members.

5. Someone also told me about a case from a neighboring village. The villager awoke in the middle of the night to feel his penis shrinking. As he was rushed to the hospital by his mother, he held on for dear life to what remained.

   The criticism of the Vietnamese fell for the most part on sympathetic ears. Although there is also animosity toward the Chinese, the Vietnamese have intermarried less with the ethnic Thai. Because of the fighting in Vietnam many Vietnamese fled to Thailand, particularly during the 1940s. Because many had come from North Vietnam, they were suspected of having communist affiliations. During their past few decades in Thailand many had been able to establish shops and become more prosperous than the surrounding villagers. In Chiang Mai many of the knitting factories were owned by Vietnamese. Many local village girls (including girls from Samsen) had gone to work in these knitting factories under conditions reminiscent of Charles Dickens's England. (For more on the Vietnamese in Thailand see Poole 1970.)

6. These skits were performed by the initiates, but the plots were usually suggested by the instructors assigned to each color group.

7. By evoking the specter of Thailand's neighbors the scout movement aroused historical memories of innumerable wars between Thailand and neighboring Burma, Laos, Cambodia, and Vietnam. These were not wars of democracy against communism but wars for land and labor. These wars evoked among villagers fears of being uprooted from their homes and turned into slaves. Intruders included officialdom. Historically villagers fled whenever they got word that a feudal lord or official was en route and hid their daughters and oxen (see Bowie 1988).

8. In view of the Village Scouts' discouragement of strikes and demonstrations one wonders what the movement means by *democracy*. Although the subject of October 6, 1976, was broached only once by a scout instructor during the initiation, I was surprised that it was mentioned at all. The instructor noted that the events of October 6 demonstrated clearly the importance of maintaining the democratic system. To those familiar with the accounts of Western journalists and others, suggesting that October 6 was connected to the preservation of democracy was strange; this was the day that the popularly elected government of M. R. Seni Pramoj was replaced by military rule. Indeed, as Muecke comments, "Popular definitions of political terms often differ from standard international definitions of these terms. For example, in Thai society the terms democracy and communism are considered antithetical, often simply signifying 'right' versus 'wrong.' Thus, autocratic or militarist regimes of Thailand have called themselves 'democratic' because they are anti-communist" (1980:407).

9. Although villagers were provided with no channels to report their grievances, the Village Scout movement encouraged its members to report activities "dangerous to society" to the authorities.

10. Samsen had about fifteen heroin addicts at the time.

11. See Samruam Singh, "A Curse on Your Paddyfields," and other short stories for examples of villagers' perspectives (Bowie, ed. 1991).

12. Not a traditional village custom, this in fact was the first birthday party ever celebrated in the village. Its novelty was reflected in the birthday fare, noodles fried in sauce (*phat sii-iaw*).

13. The headman also said that because he had wanted to be elected to the scout leadership, he had actively encouraged villagers to join. However, although villagers wanted to support him, they were too busy to join.

14. James Scott defines *patron-clientship* as a "largely instrumental friendship in which an individual of a higher socio-economic status (patron) uses his own influence and resources to provide protection or benefits, or both, for a person of lower status (client) who, for his part, reciprocates by offering general support and assistance, including personal services, to the patron"

(1977:125). See Schmidt et al., eds. (1977) for a collection of the seminal essays on this subject.

15. Even this action was criticized as token charity. A villager cited this aphorism: "Give a man a fish and he eats one day; show a man how to fish and he eats for the rest of his life."

16. Muecke provides a similar summary, suggesting the reasons villagers join the scouts:"1) political advantage; 1) trade and business advantage; 3) opportunity to get close to one's superiors; and 4) opportunity to demonstrate one's loyalty to and affection for the country, religion and the King" (1980:412).

17. Interestingly, although scout events had also been planned for Bangkok, they were felt to be too politically sensitive and were canceled. However, the Chiang Mai provincial gathering was not called off. It was a massive gathering. Samsen scouts estimated that twenty to thirty thousand scouts were present. I have no way to verify this figure, but it is reasonable to conclude that it was a large event.

No doubt also related to the continuing sensitivity of past political events, the military TV and radio stations held a marathon fund-raiser to raise money for disaster relief on October 14, the anniversary of the popular uprising of 1973 that ousted the military government of the time.

18. As Lobe explains the recruitment strategy behind the development of village defense units,

According to these U.S. experts, counter-insurgency was the "denial to the insurgents of village supporters without whom jungle soldiers (insurgents) could not continue to operate." A defense force, recruited from the village in which it would serve, and given political indoctrination and motivation, would provide the best possible armed protection and buttress village allegiance to the government. Army veterans, unemployed youths, and unmarried men, who had been the major source of insurgent support, were to be the recruitment targets for these village defense units. This, the thinking went, would deny the communists support and give many marginal villagers prestigious opportunities.

(1977:67)

19. This overall data may be biased because my informants, a school principal and kamnan, both long-term residents in the subdistrict, may have been more likely to hear of wealthier villagers from neighboring villages than poorer ones; however, wealthier villagers were more likely to be able to afford initiation expenses and the extra transportation costs involved in attending an initiation session away from their village.

20. Even the former prime minister of Thailand, Field Marshal Thanom,

whose return to Thailand sparked the violence of October 6, was called a communist by some villagers.

21. Government officials and military troops have frequently been criticized for demanding chickens and liquor from villagers.

22. The urban and Chinese populations prefer nonglutinous rice. Northern and northeastern villagers prefer glutinous rice.

23. Indicative of the growing tension was the storming of a truck on July 4, 1978, by desperate villagers who thought the truck was carrying rice. It turned out to have been carrying soybeans.

24. Another villager expressed his view of the scout movement by asking, "What do you get from it? Not so much as a dried piece of fish."

25. Conversations I had with participants and instructors indicated that each session was similar to the one I described in Samsen. The only exception was the initiation at Mae Win District. Of course the villagers of Samsen insisted that the scout instructors told them that the initiation in their sub-district had been the most fun. A couple of instructors verified this, but they were in a "drinking circle" (*wong lau*) with Samsen villagers when they said this. They could provide no specific details of what it was that was more fun.

26. This plant had been imported from Java (hence its name; *cawaa* means java) by King Rama V for its beauty but had adapted so well that it had taken over many canals and riverways.

8. Declawing the Tigers

1. In 1978 the initiations continued apace, in part because plans made during the Thanin government were simply completed under Kriangsak.

2. This observation was made by Marjorie Muecke, in conversation with the author, July 22, 1978.

3. Kriangsak's base of power within the military was relatively narrow. A staff officer, he had risen to power through positions in the Ministry of Defense and the Supreme Command headquarters rather than through army troop commands, "the first army prime minister in forty-six years to have done so" (Morell and Samudavanija 1981:278).

4. As soon as Thanin was ousted, the king appointed him to the privy council (Keyes 1987:102).

5. As Admiral Sangad, spokesman for the military coup, explained, Thanin's twelve- to sixteen-year timetable for the democracy development plan "was too long and was not according to the wishes of the people" (Girling 1981:218).

6. Kriangsak's more liberal policies included his promise to hold elections within a year; his ending of Bangkok's curfew; his selection of a broader spectrum of advisers, including the progressive New Force Party leader, Dr. Krasae Chanawong; his willingness to consider labor union and rural grievances; and his reopening communication with North Vietnam and

China (Morell and Samudavanija 1981:278). In September 1978 he granted amnesty to the "Bangkok 18," arrested in October 1976. He eased press censorship. He worked with moderate union leaders to increase the minimum wage in Bangkok from 28 to 35 baht per day (20 baht equaled U.S.$1) in 1978 and to 45 baht in October 1979. Cards issued to poor people gave them access to free medical care. Land reform continued to languish, but 1979 was declared the Year of the Farmer. A new constitution, approved in December 1978, transformed the appointed national assembly into an appointed upper house of 225 members and an elected lower house of 301. Nonetheless many repressive programs of the post-1976 period continued. The military buildup continued, with defense still the largest single item in the 1979 budget (Girling 1981:219). Similarly, the anticommunist laws remained in place, with a dramatic expansion of the search and seizure authorities of government officials (see Girling 1981:219–23 for more detailed discussion).

7. I was not able to pinpoint the date of this meeting, other than that it was held circa October and definitely before November 14 when I interviewed a senior scout who had been at the meeting. Chapter heads and Wood Badge scouts appear to have been the primary participants.

8. The explanation for the center's creation was given in officialese; it included such reasons as ensuring that scout activities would be in accord with the declared intentions of the scouts and the king's guidelines; safeguarding the scouts would not be used for political purposes; facilitating the coordination of all government agencies involved; ensuring that scout activities were "by the people, for the people, and of the people"; and ensuring the security of Nation, Religion, and King (*Saanprachachon*, May 1, 1978:7, 16).

9. Although the Thanin government had closed down many newspapers and magazines, the Kriangsak government was only minimally more liberal. Newspapers and magazines were gradually allowed to reopen, but stringent controls remained and were reinforced. In November 1978 amendments to the existing anticommunist act empowered authorities to close newspapers whenever the government considered doing so to be appropriate (Girling 1981:n220).

10. To what extent there were in fact conflicts between these two men and to what extent those in the Kriangsak government were trying to foment division between these two men in unclear. When I interviewed Somkhuan Harikul, he praised Charoenrit Chomrasromrun as one of the those unusual bosses who was able to accept innovation by his subordinates (see VS history 1984). Even today these two now-retired BPP commanders have offices directly across the hall from each other.

11. See also *Thai Rath*, April 25 and 27, 1978, and *Siam Rath Weekly*, April 30, 1978, p. 4.

12. The decision to suspend VOPT broadcasts has also been interpreted as a
voluntary decision by the CPT. Some observers suggest that the VOPT
broadcasts were suspended because of Chinese pressure on the " 'outlawed
communist guerrilla movement in Thailand to join the army-backed government in Bangkok in a de facto united front against Vietnam,' while
another [group of observers] believes that the CPT leadership decided to go
off the air until the party could resolve its internal differences" (cited in
Girling 1981:284).

13. With the illnesses of both Mao Zedong and Zhou Enlai intense infighting
erupted within the Chinese party leadership. As power increasingly shifted
to Deng Xiaoping, four other high-ranking party figures, Zhang Chunqiao,
Wang Hongwen, Yao Wenyuan, and Mao's wife, Jiang Qing, became
branded as the Gang of Four. Mao is said to have instigated this phrase,
warning them not to become a "faction of four" (Li 1994:584). Immediately after Mao's death on September 9, 1976, party factionalism intensified. Amid rumors of coups and countercoups the Gang of Four was
arrested on October 6. Jiang Qing and Zhang Chunqiao were sentenced to
death, but their sentences were reduced to life imprisonment in 1983.
Jiang Qing committed suicide in prison in 1991. Wang Hongwen received
life imprisonment and Yao Wenyuan was sentenced to twenty years. For a
fascinating account of this period see Li (1994).

14. Deng Xiaoping visited Thailand in November 1978 and at his request
attended the ordination of the crown prince as a Buddhist monk (Girling
1981:283).

15. Kramol Tongdhamachart's article on the April 1979 election does not
mention them once (1979b).

16. The top four parties were Social Action, with 82 seats, followed by Thai
Nation (Chart Thai), with 38 seats; Thai Citizen (Prachakorn Thai), with
32 seats; and Democrat (Prachatipat), also with 32 seats (Tongdhamachart
1979b:215). Before drawing conclusions about the right-wing drift of Thai
public opinion it is important to note that only 24 percent of eligible voters cast ballots, compared with 47 percent in April 1976. In Bangkok only
19.5 percent of those eligible voted (Keyes 1987:101). The strength of the
Thai Nation Party had actually fallen since the 1976 election when its candidates had won 56 seats (Keyes 1987:102).

17. The Thai Nation Party continued to gain seats in the assembly. In the April
1983 elections the party won 73 of 324 seats. This base, together with support from other members, was sufficient for Pramarn to make a bid for the
position of prime minister. The effort was premature and failed. However,
Chartchai Choonhavan succeeded, becoming prime minister in 1988. His
government was deposed in the coup of February 23, 1991. Because of factionalism Chartchai broke away from the Thai Nation Party and formed a

new party, Chart Patthana. Chart Patthana was part of the Chuan Leekphai cabinet. As a result of the elections of July 2, 1995, the Chuan government collapsed and the Chart Patthana Party became part of the opposition. However, as a result of this same election, Banharn Silpa-archa, the leader of the Thai Nation Party, became prime minister.

18. Scouts submitted a letter signed on behalf of twenty-four Village Scout districts representing 100,000 members in Bangkok urging that legal action be taken (Sivaraksa 1985:337–38). Sulak was arrested on August 5, as were two other people involved in the publication of a book considered subversive (see the appendix in Sivaraksa 1985). At the time rumors of a coup against the Prem government were rampant. As one politician explained, "Some group is intentionally lighting the fire by stirring them [Village Scouts] for use as an instrument as has happened before in Thai political history" (Foreign Broadcast 1984).

19. One of the last incidents involving Village Scouts occurred when a small group of Village Scouts rallied in support of the crown prince after an incident with the Japanese government; this rally, which occurred in August 1986 was short lived and uneventful.

20. Somkhuan Harikul confirmed that he had intervened (1994 interview). Although the Village Scouts remained dormant, the Red Gaurs participated on behalf of the military government.

21. Kriangsak declared 1979 the Year of the Farmer and reinstituted a variation of Kukrit's tambon development program.

22. The largest grassroots paramilitary organization was called Oh Soh (*asaasamak pongkaan chaat*), or National Defense Volunteers. Each village selected about ten "volunteers" who received paramilitary training and weapons. Unlike the Village Scouts, only men were involved. These volunteers came under the army and hence more directly under Kriangsak's control. The first training session of this paramilitary local defense force was held in early March 1978 in the area in which I was living. A second session followed two weeks later. About 570 villagers were trained in the first session and another 603 in the second session. Other organizations followed, including the Toh. Soh. Poh. Choh. (*Thai asaa pongkaan chaat*), or Thai National Defense Volunteers, organized by ISOC and working closely with the BPP and the Tahaan Phraan, a paramilitary group under the army.

23. I thank Bob Jones, Al McCoy, John Smail, and Ruth Dunnell for sharing their comparative insights about Vietnam, the Philippines, Indonesia, and China, respectively.

Bibliography

Interviews

Guy Eichsteadt, assistant scout executive, Four Lakes Council, Boy Scouts of
 America. Interview by author. March 23, 1993. Madison, Wisconsin.
Somkhuan Harikul. Interviews by author. February 4, 1991, and January 1992.
 Bangkok.
———. Interview by author. September 1994. Telephone.

Village Scout Histories

I relied on three histories of the Village Scouts, two official and one semiofficial,
in writing this book. None is signed. For simplicity's sake I refer to each generi-
cally in the text as VS history, followed by its respective date.

VS history. 1983. *The Village Scouts of Thailand*. Official publication available from
 the Village Scout Operations Center, Bangkok. August 9.
VS history. 1984. *Phontamruat trii Somkhuan Harikul* (Major General Somkhuan
 Harikul). Sixtieth birthday retirement commemoration. Semiofficial Village
 Scout history available from the Village Scout Operations Center, Bangkok.
 December 13.

VS history. 1987. *Prawsatisaat luuksyachaawbaan naj phrabohrommarachaanukhroh* (History of the Village Scouts Under Royal Patronage). Official publication available from the Village Scout Operations Center, Bangkok. December 5.

Sources in Thai

Anonymous. "Luuksyachaawbaan" (Village Scouts). 1975. *Anusaan Oh. Soh. Thoh* (Bulletin of the Tourist Organization of Thailand) 16 (5) (December): 20–23, 62–67.

Atsaceri. 1977. "Luuksyachaawbaan 'palang mai' khuan chaj haj thuuk withii" (Village Scouts, a New Force: Should Be Used Properly). *Siam Rath Sabdaawicharn* (Siam Rath Weekly) 23 (36): 10, 17.

Chan Liankhrya. 1976. "Paj duu khaw oprom luuksyachaawbaan" (Going to Watch a Village Scout Initiation), *Saanprachaachon* (People's News) 13 (540) (April 16): 11, 15.

Chom Phumiphaak. 1981. "Kitcakaam luuksyachaawbaan kap kaan pluukfang cariyatham" (Village Scout Activities and the Instilling of Morality). *Waarasaan Kaansyksaa* (Journal of Education) 16 (6) (November–December): 22–25.

Kawiirat Khunnaphat. 1986. "Luuksyachaawbaan: bang sing bang yaang caak 6 tulaakhom 2519" (Village Scouts: A Few Things from October 6, 1976). *Waarasaan Thammasatsaan* (Thammasat University Journal) 15 (3): 151–65.

Klum Phadungtham. 1981. *Raw khyy phuu bohrisut: ekasaan aanging thaang prawati-saat banthyyk hetkaan 6 tulaa 2519* (We Are the Innocent: Documents Refer-ring to the History of October 5, 1976). Bangkok: Bohrisat Saamakkhiisaan Camkat.

Kriangsak Lohachaala. 1976. "Luuksyachaawbaan krungthepmahaanaakhohn" (Village Scouts in Bangkok), *Nithetsarn* (Journal of Communication Arts) 5 (3) (December): 65–70.

Pramuan Rutcanasewii. 1976. "Luuksyachaawbaan" (Village Scouts). *Mahaathaj* (Ministry of Interior) 1 (14) (July): 46–48; (August 1976): 61–63; (August): 48–50.

Prasong Miisiri. 1976. "Luuksyachaawbaan" (Village Scouts). *Saanprachaachon* (People's News) 13 (540) (April 16): 10, 12–14.

Ruciraa Thongwet. 1978. "Kaanoprom luuksyachaawbaan" (Village Scout Initiations). *Saphayaakohn Manut* (Human Resources: Training and Develop-ment Journal) 2 (7) (3d quarter): 22–25.

Sirinthorn Kiratibutr. 1985. "Phlaeng plukcaj thaj 1932–1982" (Thai Nationalistic Songs, 1932–1982). Master's thesis, Chulalongkorn University, Bangkok.

Tej Bunnag 1967. "Kabot phuumiibun phaak isaan" (The Holy Man Uprisings in the Northeast). *Sangkhomsaat Parithat* (Social Science Review) 5:78–86.

———. 1968. "Kabot ngiew muang phrae (The Shan Uprising in Muang Phrae). *Sangkhomsaat Parithat* (Social Science Review) 6:67–80.

Magazines and Newspapers in Thai

Baan Muang
Chaw Thai
Chawnaa Thai
Daily Times
Jaturat
Prachachaat
Prachathipatai
Saanprachaachon
Sayamsaan
Siam Rath
Tawansayam
Thai News
Thai Rath

English-Language References

Abercrombie, Nicholas and Bryan S. Turner. 1978. "The Dominant Ideology Thesis." *British Journal of Sociology* 29 (2): 149–70.

Ahmad, Eqbal. 1971. "Revolutionary War and Counter-Insurgency." *Journal of International Affairs* 25 (1): 1–47.

Alapuro, Risto. 1976. "Regional Variations in Political Mobilisation." *Scandinavian Journal of History* 1:215–42.

Alexander, Bobby C. 1987. "Ceremony." In Mircea Eliade, ed., *Encyclopedia of Religion*, pp. 179–83. New York: Macmillan.

Allen, Douglas. 1976. "Universities and the Vietnam War: A Case Study of a Successful Struggle." *Bulletin of Concerned Asian Scholars* 8 (4): 2–16.

Allen, William Sheridan. 1984. *The Nazi Seizure of Power: The Experience of a Single German Town, 1922–1945*. New York: Franklin Watts.

Alpern, Stephen I. 1975. "Insurgency in Northeast Thailand: A New Cause for Alarm." *Asian Survey* 15 (8): 684–92.

Anderson, Benedict. 1977. "Withdrawal Symptoms: Social and Cultural Aspects of the October 6 Coup." *Bulletin of Concerned Asian Scholars* 9 (3) (Special issue): 13–30.

———. 1990. "Murder and Progress in Modern Siam." *New Left Review* 181:33–48.

———. 1991. *Imagined Communities: Reflections on the Origins and Spread of Nationalism*, revised 2d ed. New York: Verso.

Anderson, Benedict and Ruchira Mendiones, eds. 1985. *In the Mirror: Literature and Politics in Siam in the American Era*. Bangkok: Editions Duang Kamol.

Anderson, Perry. 1974. *Lineages of the Absolutist State*. London: Verso.

Andrews, James M. 1935. *Siam: Second Rural Economic Survey, 1934–1935*. Bangkok: Bangkok Times Press.

Anonymous. 1976. "Military Coup in Thailand." *Journal of Contemporary Asia* 6 (4): 424–31.

Appadurai, Arjun. 1981. "Royal Rituals and Cultural Change." *Reviews in Anthropology* 8 (spring): 121–38.

———. 1990. "Disjuncture and Difference in the Global Cultural Economy." *Public Culture* 2 (2) (spring): 1–23.

———. 1991. "Global Ethnoscapes: Notes and Queries for a Transnational Anthropology." In Richard G. Fox, ed., *Recapturing Anthropology*, pp. 191–210. Sante Fe: School of American Research Press.

Apter, Andrew. 1983. "In Dispraise of the King: Rituals 'Against' Rebellion in Southeast Africa." *Man* 18:521–34.

———. 1992. *Black Critics and Kings: Hermeneutics of Power in Yoruba Society.* Chicago: University of Chicago Press.

Arendt, Hannah. 1951. *The Origins of Totalitarianism.* New York: Harcourt, Brace and World.

Asiaweek. 1977. "A Most Gentle Coup." *Asiaweek*, November 4, 1977, pp. 16–20.

Aya, Rod. 1975. "The Present as 'Jumbo History': A Review Article." *Race and Class* 17 (2): 179–88.

Barraclough, Geoffrey. 1979. *The Origins of Modern Germany.* New York: Paragon.

Bayly, C. A. 1988. "Rallying Around the Subaltern: Review of *Subaltern Studies*, by Guha, Ranajit (ed.)." *Journal of Peasant Studies* 16 (1): 110–20.

Beattie, John. 1966. "Ritual and Social Change." *Man* 1 (1): 60–74.

Bechhofer, Frank and Brian Elliot. 1975. "Persistence and Change: The Petit Bourgeoisie in Industrial Society." *Archives Européennes de Sociologie* 16: 74–99.

Bell, Catherine. 1992. *Ritual Theory, Ritual Practice.* New York: Oxford University Press.

Bell, Peter. 1969. "Thailand's Northeast: Regional Underdevelopment, 'Insurgency,' and Official Response." *Pacific Affairs* 42 (1): 47–54.

———. 1978. " 'Cycles' of Class Struggle in Thailand." In Andrew Turton, Jonathan Fast, and Malcolm Caldwell, eds., *Thailand: Roots of Conflict*, pp. 51–79. Nottingham, England: Russell Press.

———. 1982. "Western Conceptions of Thai Society: The Politics of American Scholarship." *Journal of Contemporary Asia* 12 (1): 61–74.

Bellah, Robert N. 1967. "Civil Religion in America." *Daedalus* 96:1–21.

Ben-David, Clark and Terry Nichols, eds. 1977. *Culture and Its Creators: Essays in Honor of Edward Shils.* Chicago: University of Chicago Press.

Bendix, Reinhard. 1969. *Nation Building and Citizenship.* Garden City, New York: Doubleday Anchor.

Bennett, W. Lance. 1979. "Imitation, Ambiguity, and Drama in Political Life: Civil Religion and the Dilemmas of Public Morality." *Journal of Politics* 41: 106–33.

Bessel, Richard. 1978. "Eastern Germany as a Structural Problem in the Weimar Republic." *Social History* 3 (2): 199–218.

Binns, Christopher A. P. 1979. "The Changing Face of Power: Revolution and Accommodation in the Development of the Soviet Ceremonial System: Part I." *Man* 14:585–606.

Bix, Herbert. 1987. "Class Conflict in Rural Japan: On Historical Methodology." *Bulletin of Concerned Asian Scholars* 19 (3): 29–52.

Blackbourn, David. 1984. "Peasants and Politics in Germany, 1871–1914." *European History Quarterly* 14 (1): 47–75.

Blaufarb, Douglas S. 1977. *The Counterinsurgency Era: U.S. Doctrine and Performance 1950 to the Present.* London: Free Press.

Blessing, Werner K. 1978. "The Cult of Monarchy, Political Loyalty, and the Workers' Movement in Imperial Germany." *Journal of Contemporary History* 13:357–75.

Bloch, Marc. 1961. *The Royal Touch: Monarchy and Miracles in France and England*, trans. J. E. Anderson. New York: Dorset.

Bloch, Maurice. 1977. "The Past and the Present in the Present." *Man* (new series) 12:278–92.

———. 1986. *From Blessing to Violence: History and Ideology in the Circumcision Ritual of the Merina of Madagascar.* Cambridge, England: Cambridge University Press.

———. 1987. "The Ritual of the Royal Bath in Madagascar: The Dissolution of Death, Birth, and Fertility into Authority." In David Cannadine and Simon Price, eds., *Rituals of Royalty: Power and Ceremonial in Traditional Societies*, pp. 271–97. Cambridge, England: Cambridge University Press.

Block, Fred. 1977. "The Ruling Class Does Not Rule: Notes on the Marxist Theory of the State." *Socialist Revolution* 7 (33) (May–June): 6–28.

Blumberg, Paul. 1980. *Inequality in an Age of Decline.* New York: Oxford University Press.

Bourdieu, Pierre. 1977a. "Symbolic Power." In Denis Gleeson, ed., *Identity and Structure: Issues in the Sociology of Education.* Natterton, Driffield, England: Studies in Education.

———. 1977b. *Outline of a Theory of Practice.* Cambridge, England: Cambridge University Press.

Bowie, Katherine. 1975a. "Testing the North's Political Mood." *Bangkok Post Sunday Magazine*, June 29, p. 6.

———. 1975b. "When Free Enterprise Alienated a Village." *Bangkok Post Sunday Magazine*, August 3, p. 7.

———. 1988. Peasant Perspectives on the Political Economy of the Northern Thai Kingdom of Chiang Mai in the Nineteenth Century: Implications for the Understanding of Peasant Political Expression. Ph.D. diss., University of Chicago.

——. 1992. "Unraveling the Myth of the Subsistence Economy: Textile Production in Nineteenth-Century Northern Thailand." *Journal of Asian Studies* 51 (4): 797–824.

——. 1993. "Transnational Bricolage: Nationalism, Class, and the Village Scout Movement of Thailand." Paper read at Culturalism, Nationalism, Trans-nationalism Conference, November 1–2, 1993, University of Chicago, Chicago.

——. Forthcoming. "The Alchemy of Charity and Class: Buddhist Merit-Making in Northern Thailand." *American Anthropologist.*

Bowie, Katherine, ed. and trans. 1991. *Voices from the Thai Countryside: The Short Stories of Samruam Singh.* Monograph #6. Madison, Wisconsin: Center for Southeast Asian Studies, University of Wisconsin.

Bowie, Katherine and Brian A. Phelan. 1975. "Who's Killing the Farmers?" *Bangkok Post Sunday Magazine*, August 17, pp. 5–7.

Bowring, Sir John. [1857] 1969. *The Kingdom and People of Siam,* Vol. 1. Singapore: Oxford University Press.

Bradley, William, David Morell, David Szanton, and Stephen Young. 1978. *Thailand, Domino by Default? The 1976 Coup and Implications for U.S Policy.* Papers in International Studies, Southeast Asian Series No. 46. Athens, Ohio: Ohio University, Center for International Studies.

Braudel, Fernand. 1980. *On History*, trans. Sarah Matthews. Chicago: University of Chicago Press.

Bremner, Robert H. 1984. "Review of *Building Character in the American Boy: The Boy Scouts, YMCA, and Their Forerunners, 1870–1920*, by David I. Macleod." *American Historical Review* 89:1169–70.

Briggs, W. A. 1902. Letter to Board of Foreign Missions. Presbyterian Church USA. Siam Letters and Correspondence, 1840–1910. Microfilm vol. 271, letter 7. Philadelphia.

Brimmel, J. H. 1959. *Communism in Southeast Asia: A Political Analysis.* London: Oxford University Press.

Bristowe, W. S. 1976. *Louis and the King of Siam.* London: Chatto and Windus.

Brow, James. 1988. "In Pursuit of Hegemony: Representations of Authority and Justice in a Sri Lankan Village." *American Ethnologist* 15 (2): 311–27.

Brown, Ian. 1988. *The Elite and the Economy in Siam, c. 1890–1920.* Singapore: Oxford University Press.

Bruneau, Michel. 1984. "Class Formation in the Northern Thai Peasantry, 1966–1976." *Journal of Contemporary Asia* 14 (3): 343–59.

Bunbongkarn, Suchit. 1987. *The Military in Thai Politics, 1981–1986.* Singapore: Institute of Southeast Asian Studies.

Bunnag, Marut. 1979. "Legal Aspects of Human Rights: The Thai Case." *Contemporary Southeast Asia* 1 (1): 51–65.

Bunnag, Tej. 1977. *The Provincial Administration of Siam, 1892–1915.* Kuala Lumpur: Oxford University Press.

Buntrigswat, Maj. Sanchai. n.d. *Thailand: The Dual Threats to Stability in a Study of Communist Insurgency and Problems of Political Development.* Bangkok: Borpit Co.

Calavan, Kay Mitchell. 1974. Aristocrats and Commoners in Rural Northern Thailand. Ph.D. dissertation, University of Illinois at Urbana-Champaign.

Caldwell, Malcolm. 1976. "Thailand: Towards the Revolution." *Race and Class* 28 (2): 129–53.

Cannadine, David and Simon Price, eds. 1987. *Rituals of Royalty: Power and Ceremonial in Traditional Societies.* Cambridge, England: Cambridge University Press.

Cardoza, Anthony L. 1982. *Agrarian Elites and Italian Fascism.* Princeton, N.J.: Princeton University Press.

Carnoy, Martin. 1984. *The State and Political Theory.* Princeton, N.J.: Princeton University Press.

Cassels, Alan. 1975. *Fascism.* Arlington Heights, Ill.: Harlan Davidson.

Chakrabongse, Prince Chula. 1960. *Lords of Life: A History of the Kings of Thailand.* Bangkok: DD Books.

Chaloemtiarana, Thak. 1979. *Thailand: The Politics of Despotic Paternalism.* Bangkok: Social Science Association of Thailand and Thai Khadi Institute, Thammasat University.

Chandravithun, Nikom. 1982. *Thai Labour: A Long Journey.* Bangkok: Thai Watana Panich Co.

Chayan Vaddhanaphuti. See Vaddhanaphuti, Chayan.

Cheal, David J. 1979. "Hegemony, Ideology, and Contradictory Consciousness." *Sociological Quarterly* 20:109–17.

Chiengkul, Witayakorn. 1983. "The Transformation of the Agrarian Structure of Central Thailand, 1960–1980." *Journal of Contemporary Asia* 13 (3): 340–60.

Chitakasem, Manas and Andrew Turton. 1991. *Thai Constructions of Knowledge.* London: School of Oriental and African Studies, University of London.

Chomsky, Noam. 1984. "The Vietnam War in the Age of Orwell." *Race and Class* 25 (4): 41–60.

Choonhavan, Kraisak. 1982. "Interview." *Journal of Contemporary Asia* 12 (4): 510–16.

———. 1984. "The Growth of Domestic Capital and Thai Industrialization." *Journal of Contemporary Asia* 14 (2): 135–46.

Christensen, Scott. 1991. "Thailand After the Coup." *Journal of Democracy* 2 (3): 94–106.

Cleary, M. C. 1987. "Priest, Squire, and Peasant: The Development of Agricultural Syndicates in South-West France, 1900–1914." *European History Quarterly* 17 (2): 145–64.

Clutterbuck, Richard L. 1966. *The Long Long War: Counterinsurgency in Malaya and Vietnam.* New York: Praeger.

Cohen, Abner. 1979. "Political Symbolism." *Annual Review of Anthropology* 8:87–113.

Cohen, Paul. 1981. The Politics of Economic Development in Northern Thailand, 1967–1979. Ph.D. diss., University of London.

Cohen, Ronald. 1973. "Political Anthropology." In John J. Honigmann, ed., *Handbook of Social and Cultural Anthropology*, pp. 861–81. Chicago: Rand McNally.

Cohn, Bernard S., and Nicholas B. Dirks. 1988. "Beyond the Fringe: The Nation State, Colonialism, and the Technologies of Power." *Journal of Historical Sociology* 1 (2): 224–29.

Colley, Linda. 1986. "Whose Nation? Class and National Consciousness in Britain, 1750–1830." *Past and Present* 113:97–117.

Comaroff, Jean. 1985. *Body of Power, Spirit of Resistance.* Chicago: University of Chicago Press.

Comaroff, Jean and John Comaroff. 1991. *Of Revelation and Revolution: Christianity, Colonialism, and Consciousness in South Africa,* Vol. 1. Chicago: University of Chicago Press.

———,eds. 1993. *Modernity and Its Malcontents: Ritual and Power in Postcolonial Africa.* Chicago: University of Chicago Press.

Comaroff, John. 1989. "Images of Empire, Contests of Conscience: Models of Colonial Domination in South Africa." *American Ethnologist* 16 (4): 661–85.

Combs-Schilling, M. E. 1989. *Sacred Performances: Islam, Sexuality, and Sacrifice.* New York: Columbia University Press.

Conroy, Hilary. 1981. Letter to the Editor. "Concerning Japanese Fascism." *Journal of Asian Studies* 40 (2): 327–28.

Contursi, Janet A. 1989. "Militant Hindus and Buddhist Dalits: Hegemony and Resistance in an Indian Slum." *American Ethnologist* 16 (3): 441–57.

Cooper, Frederick and Ann L. Stoler. 1989. "Tensions of Empire: Colonial Control and Visions of Rule." *American Ethnologist* 16 (4): 609–21.

Cooper, Robert G. 1979. "The Tribal Minorities of Northern Thailand: Problems and Prospects." *Southeast Asian Affairs 1979*, pp. 323–32. Singapore: Institute of Southeast Asian Studies.

Copeland, Matthew P. 1993. "Contested Nationalism and the 1932 Overthrow of the Absolute Monarchy in Siam." Ph.D. diss., Australian National University.

Corner, Paul. 1979. "Fascist Agrarian Policy and the Italian Economy in the Inter-War Years." In John A. Davis, ed., *Gramsci and Italy's Passive Revolution*, pp. 239–74. New York: Barnes and Noble.

Corrigan, Philip and Derek Sayer. 1985. *The Great Arch: English State Formation as Cultural Revolution.* New York: Basil Blackwell.

Coyle, R. G. 1985. "A System Description of Counterinsurgency Warfare." *Policy Sciences* 18:55–78.

Crocker, Christopher. 1973. "Ritual and the Development of Social Structure: Liminality and Inversion." In James D. Shaughnessy, ed., *The Roots of Ritual*, pp. 47–86. Grand Rapids, Mich.: William B. Eerdmans.

Cullen, Stephen. 1987. "The Development of Ideas and Policy of the British Union of Fascists, 1932–1940." *Journal of Contemporary History* 22:115–36.

Currey, Cecil B. 1988. *Edward Lansdale: The Unquiet American*. Boston: Houghton Mifflin.

Dale, Richard. 1977. "The Eroding of the White Redoubt: The Study of Insurgency and Counterinsurgency in the Context of Southern Africa" (book review). *Armed Forces and Society* 3 (4): 655–70.

Darling, Frank C. 1960. "Marshal Sarit and Absolutist Rule in Thailand." *Pacific Affairs* 33 (4) (December): 347–60.

———. 1962. "Modern Politics in Thailand." *Review of Politics* 24:163–82.

———. 1974. "Student Protest and Political Change in Thailand." *Pacific Affairs* 47 (1) (spring): 5–19.

———. 1978. "Thailand in 1977: The Search for Stability and Progress." *Asian Survey* 18 (2) (February): 153–63.

Davidson, Alastair. 1984. "Gramsci, the Peasantry, and Popular Culture." *Journal of Peasant Studies* 11 (4): 139–54.

Davies, Derek and Paisal Sricharatchaya. 1986. "Thai Monarchy." *Far Eastern Economic Review* (January 23): 22–28.

Davis, Richard B. 1984. *Muang Metaphysics: A Study of Northern Thai Myth and Ritual*. Bangkok: Pandora.

Deal, Douglas. 1975. "Peasant Revolts and Resistance in the Modern World: A Comparative View." *Journal of Contemporary Asia* 5 (4): 414–45.

de Bary, William Theodore, ed. 1960. *Sources in Chinese Tradition*, Vol. 2. New York: Columbia University Press.

de Beer, Patrice. 1978. "History and Policy of the Communist Party of Thailand." In Turton, Fast, and Caldwell, eds., *Thailand: Roots of Conflict*, pp. 143—58.

Desai, Santosh N. 1980. *Hinduism in Thai Life*. Bombay: Popular Prakashan Private.

deYoung, John E. 1955. *Village Life in Modern Thailand*. Berkeley: University of California Press.

Dhiratayakinant, Kraiyudht, ed. 1975. *Thailand: Profile 1975*. Bangkok: Voice of the Nation.

Dhiravegin, Likhit. 1973. *Political Attitudes of the Bureaucratic Elite and Modernization in Thailand*. Bangkok: Thai Watana.

Dirlick, Arif. 1975. "The Ideological Foundations of the New Life Movement: A Study in Counterrevolution." *Journal of Asian Studies* 34:945–80.

Dodd, William Clifton. 1923. *The Tai Race: Elder Brother of the Chinese*. Cedar Rapids, Iowa: Torch Press.

Dolgin, Janet L., David S. Kemnitzer, and David M. Schneider, eds. 1977. *Symbolic Anthropology: A Reader in the Study of Symbols and Meanings*. New York: Columbia University Press.

Durkheim, Emile. 1915. *The Elementary Forms of the Religious Life*, trans. Joseph Ward Swain. New York: Free Press.

Duss, Peter and Daniel I. Okimoto. 1979. "Fascism and the History of Pre-War Japan: The Failure of a Concept." *Journal of Asian Studies* 39 (1): 65–76.

Dutt, Palme R. 1974. *Fascism and Social Revolution: A Study of the Economics and Politics of the Extreme Stages of Capitalism in Decay*. San Francisco: Proletarian Publishers.

Elliot, David. 1978. *Thailand: Origins of Military Rule*. London: Zed Press.

Emerson, Rupert. 1960. *From Empire to Nation*. Boston: Beacon Press.

——. 1966. "Paradoxes of Asian Nationalism." In Robert O. Tilman, ed., *Man, State, and Society*, pp. 247–58. New York: Praeger.

Esposito, Bruce J. 1970. "Can a Single Spark Ignite a Paddyfield?: The Case of Thai Insurgency." *Asian Studies* 8 (3): 318–25.

Evans, Peter B., Dietrich Rueschemeyer, and Theda Skocpol, eds. 1985. *Bringing the State Back In*. Cambridge, England: Cambridge University Press.

Evans, Richard J. and W. R. Lee, eds. 1986. *The German Peasantry*. New York: St. Martin's Press.

Firth, Raymond. 1967. *Tikopia Ritual and Belief*. Boston: Beacon Press.

——. 1973. *Symbols, Public and Private*. Ithaca, N.Y.: Cornell University Press.

Fischer, Joseph, ed. 1973. *Foreign Values and Southeast Asian Scholarship*. Research Monograph No. 11. Berkeley: Center for South and Southeast Asian Studies.

Fletcher, Miles. 1979. "Intellectuals and Fascism in Early Showa Japan." *Journal of Asian Studies* 39 (1): 39–63.

Flood, Thadeus. 1975. "The Thai Left Wing in Historical Context." *Bulletin of Concerned Asian Scholars* (April–June): 55–67.

——. 1977a. "The Vietnamese Refugees in Thailand: Minority Manipulation in Counterinsurgency." *Bulletin of Concerned Asian Scholars* 9 (3) (July–September): 31–47.

——. 1977b. "Village Scouts: The King's Finest." *Indochina Chronicle* (January–February): 19.

Foreign Broadcast Information Service. 1984. "Mobilization of Village Scouts Condemned by MP." Microfiche News Summary for July 27. Joint Publications Research Series, Asia: SE Asia Reports.

Forgacs, David, ed. 1988. *An Antonio Gramsci Reader*. New York: Schocken.

Foucault, Michel. 1979. *Discipline and Punish: The Birth of the Prison*. New York: Vintage.

Fox, Richard G., ed. 1990. *Nationalist Ideologies and the Production of National Cultures*. American Ethnological Society Monograph Series #2. Washington, D.C.: American Anthropological Association.

——. 1991. *Recapturing Anthropology: Working in the Present.* Santa Fe: School of American Research Press.

Frank, Andre Gunder. 1975. "Anthropology = Ideology; Applied Anthropology = Politics." *Race and Class* 17 (1): 57–68.

Friedrich, Paul. 1977. *Agrarian Revolt in a Mexican Village.* Chicago: University of Chicago Press.

Fussell, Paul. 1983. *Class: A Guide Through the American Status System.* New York: Summit Books.

Fustel de Coulanges, Numa Denis. [1864] 1956. *The Ancient City: A Study on the Religion, Laws, and Institutions of Greece and Rome.* Garden City, N.Y.: Doubleday.

Galey, Jean-Claude, ed. 1990. *Kingship and the Kings.* New York: Harwood Academic.

Gallagher, Tom. 1984. "Salazar's Portugal: The 'Black Book' on Fascism." *European History Quarterly* 14 (4): 479–88.

Ganjanapan, Anan. 1984. The Partial Commercialization of Rice Production in Northern Thailand, 1900–1981. Ph.D. diss., Cornell University.

Gardner, Brian. 1968. *Mafeking: A Victorian Legend.* London: Sphere Books.

Gates, Hill and Robert P. Weller. 1987. "Hegemony and Chinese Folk Ideologies." *Modern China* 13 (1): 3–16.

Geertz, Clifford. 1977. "Centers, Kings, and Charisma: Reflections on the Symbolics of Power." In Joseph Ben-David and Terry N. Clark, eds., *Culture and Its Creators.* pp. 150–71. Chicago: University of Chicago Press.

——. 1980. *Negara: The Theater State in Nineteenth Century Bali.* Princeton, N.J.: Princeton University Press.

——, ed. 1963. *Old Societies and New States.* London: Free Press of Glencoe.

Gellner, Ernest. 1983. *Nations and Nationalism.* Ithaca, N.Y.: Cornell University Press.

Geneletti, Carlo. 1975. "The Political Orientation of Agrarian Class: A Theory." *Archives Européennes de Sociologie* 16:55–73.

Gentile, Emilio. 1986. "Fascism in Italian Historiography: In Search of an Individual Historical Identity." *Journal of Contemporary History* 21:179–208.

Gerini, Gerolamo Emilio. [1895] 1976. *Chulakantamangala: Or, the Tonsure Ceremony as Performed in Siam.* Bangkok: Siam Society.

Gesick, Lorraine. 1983. *Centers, Symbols, and Hierarchies: Essays on the Classical States of Southeast Asia.* Monograph Series No. 26. New Haven, Conn.: Yale University Southeast Asian Studies.

Gidiri, A. 1974. "Imperialism and Archaeology." *Race and Class* 15 (4): 431–59.

Girling, John L. S. 1977. "Thailand: The Coup and Its Implications." *Pacific Affairs* 50 (3): 387–405.

——. 1981. *Thailand: Society and Politics.* Ithaca, N.Y.: Cornell University Press.

——. 1984. "Thailand in Gramscian Perspective." *Pacific Affairs* 57 (3): 385–403.

Gluckman, Max. 1965. *Politics, Law and Ritual in Tribal Society.* Oxford, England: Basil Blackwell.

Goldschläger, Alain. 1982. "Toward a Semiotics of Authoritarian Discourse." *Poetics Today* 3:12–20.

Goody, Jack. 1961. "Religion and Ritual: The Definitional Problem." *British Journal of Sociology* 12:142–64.

——. 1977. "Against 'Ritual': Loosely Structured Thoughts on a Loosely Defined Topic." In Sally F. Moore and Barbara G. Myerhoff, eds., *Secular Ritual.* The Netherlands: Van Gorcum.

Gottdiener, M. 1985. "Hegemony and Mass Culture: A Semiotic Approach." *American Journal of Sociology* 90 (5): 979–1002.

Graf, Christoph. 1987. "The Genesis of the Gestapo." *Journal of Contemporary History* 22:419–35.

Graham, W.A. 1924. *Siam.* London: Alexander Moring/De La More Press.

Gramsci, Antonio. 1971. *Selections from the Prison Notebooks,* trans. Quinton Hoare and Geoffrey Nowell Smith. New York: International Publishers.

Gray, Christine E. 1986. Thailand: The Soteriological State in the 1970s. Ph.D. diss., University of Chicago.

——. 1991. "Hegemonic Images: Language and Silence in the Royal Thai Polity." *Man* 26:43–65.

Greene, Nathanael, ed. 1968. *Fascism: An Anthology.* New York: Thomas Y. Crowell.

Greene, Stephen. 1971. Thai Government and Administration: The Reign of Rama VI, 1910–1925. Ph.D. diss., University of London.

Gregor, A. James and Maria Hsia Chang. 1979. "National Fascismo and the Revolutionary Nationalism of Sun Yat-sen." *Journal of Asian Studies* 39 (1): 21–37.

Griffiths, B. 1993. "The Role of Vocational Students During the Democracy Period in Thailand from 1973 to 1976." Northern Illinois University, DeKalb. Class paper.

Grill, Johnpeter Horst. 1982. "The Nazi Party's Rural Propaganda Before 1928." *Central European History* 15 (2): 149–85.

Griswold, A. B. 1961. *King Mongkut of Siam.* New York: Asia Society.

Gua, Bo. 1975. "Opium, Bombs, and Trees: The Future of the H'mong Tribesman in Northern Thailand." *Journal of Contemporary Asia* 5 (1): 70–81.

Guerin, Daniel. 1973. *Fascism and Big Business.* New York: Monad Press/Pathfinder Press.

Gunn, Geoffrey C. 1987. "Minority Manipulation in Colonial Indochina: Lessons and Legacies." *Bulletin of Concerned Asian Scholars* 19 (3): 20–28.

Gurevich, Robert. 1975. "Teachers, Rural Development, and the Civil Service in Thailand." *Asian Survey* 15 (10) (October): 870–81.

Gurr, Ted Robert. 1970. *Why Men Rebel.* Princeton, N.J.: Princeton University Press.

Gurtov, Melvin. 1970. "China's Policies in Southeast Asia: Three Studies." *Studies in Comparative Communism* (July–October): 13–68.

Hall, Stuart. 1988. "The Toad in the Garden: Thatcherism Among the Theorists." In Cary Nelson and Lawrence Grossberg, eds., *Marxism and the Interpretation of Culture*, pp. 35–57. Chicago: University of Illinois Press.

Halliday, Fred. 1977. "British Mercenaries and Counterinsurgency." *Race and Class* 14 (2): 163–71.

Hamilton, Nora. 1982. *The Limits of State Autonomy: Post Revolutionary Mexico.* Princeton, N.J.: Princeton University Press.

Handelman, Don. 1990. *Models and Mirrors: Toward an Anthropology of Public Events.* Cambridge, England: Cambridge University Press.

Hanks, Lucien M. 1968. "American Aid Is Damaging Thai Society." *Transaction* (October): 29–34.

Hanley, Mary Lynn. 1989. "Girl Guides Inspire Health in Thailand's Poor Northeast." *Source* 1 (3): 15–17.

Hanna, Willard A. 1964. *Eight Nation Makers: Southeast Asia's Charismatic Statesmen.* New York: St. Martin's Press.

Hannerz, Ulf. 1987. "The World in Creolization." *Africa* 57 (4): 546–59.

Hantover, Jeffrey P. 1978. "The Boy Scouts and the Validation of Masculinity." *Journal of Social Issues* 34 (1): 184–95.

Haseman, John B. n.d. *The Thai Resistance Movement During the Second World War.* Bangkok: Chalermnit Press.

Heinze, Ruth-Inge. 1974. "Ten Days in October—Students Versus the Military: An Account of the Student Uprising in Thailand." *Asian Survey* 14 (6): 491–508.

Henriksen, Thomas H. 1977. "Portugal in Africa: Comparative Notes on Counterinsurgency." *Orbis* 21 (2): 395–412.

Herring, Ronald J. 1978. "Share Tenancy and Economic Efficiency: The South Asian Case." *Peasant Studies* 7 (4): 225–49.

Hewison, Kevin J. 1981. "The Financial Bourgeoisie in Thailand." *Journal of Contemporary Asia* 11 (4): 395–412.

———. 1989. *Power and Politics in Thailand.* Manila: Journal of Contemporary Asia Publishers.

Hindess, Barry, and Paul Q. Hirst. 1975. *Precapitalist Modes of Production.* London: Routledge and Kegan Paul.

Hindley, Donald. 1968. "Thailand: The Politics of Passivity." *Pacific Affairs* 41 (3): 355–71.

Hinton, William. 1966. *Fanshen: A Documentary of Revolution in a Chinese Village.* New York: Random House/Vintage Books.

Hoagland, John H. 1971. "Changing Patterns of Insurgency and American Response." *Journal of International Affairs* 25 (1): 120–41.

Hobsbawm, Eric. 1983. "Introduction: Inventing Traditions." In Eric Hobsbawm and Terence Ranger, eds., *The Invention of Tradition*, pp. 1–14. Cambridge, England: Cambridge University Press.

———. 1990. *Nations and Nationalism Since 1780: Programme, Myth, Reality.* Cambridge, England: Cambridge University Press.

Hobsbawm, Eric and Terence Ranger, eds. 1983. *The Invention of Tradition.* Cambridge, England: Cambridge University Press.

Holmes, Kim R. 1982. "The Forsaken Past: Agrarian Conservatism and National Socialism in Germany." *Journal of Contemporary History* 17:671–88.

Hong, Lysa, 1982. "Thailand in 1981: Reformulating the Polity from Within?" *Southeast Asian Affairs* Singapore: Institute of Southeast Asian Studies.

Huntington, Samuel P. 1975. *Political Order in Changing Societies.* New Haven, Conn.: Yale University Press.

Ibrahim, Zawawi. 1983. "Perspectives Toward Investigating Malay Peasant Ideology and the Bases of Its Production in Contemporary Malaysia." *Journal of Contemporary Asia* 13 (2): 198–209.

Ingersoll, Daniel W. Jr. and Gordon Bronitsky, eds. 1987. *Mirror and Metaphor: Material and Social Constructions of Reality.* Lanham, Maryland: University Press of America.

Ingram, James C. 1971. *Economic Change in Thailand, 1850–1970.* Palo Alto, Calif.: Stanford University Press.

Irvine, Walter. 1982. The Thai-Uan "Madman" and the Modernizing, Developing Thai Nation, as Bounded Entities Under Threat: A Study in the Replication of a Single Image. Ph.D. diss., University of London.

Ishii, Yoneo. 1975. "A Note on Buddhistic Millenarian Revolts in Northeastern Siam." *Journal of Southeast Asian Studies* 6 (2): 121–26.

Jackson, Peter A. 1989. *Buddhism, Legitimation, and Conflict: The Political Functions of Urban Thai Buddhism.* Singapore: Institute of Southeast Asian Studies.

Jacobitti, Edmund E. 1980. "Hegemony Before Gramsci: The Case of Benedetto Croce." *Journal of Modern History* 52:66–84.

Janlekha, Kamol Odd. 1955. A Study of the Economy of a Rice-Growing Village in Central Thailand. Ph.D. diss., Cornell University.

Jeshuran, Chandran, ed. 1985. *Governments and Rebellion in Southeast Asia.* Singapore: Institute of Southeast Asian Studies.

Jumbala, Prudhisan. 1974. "Toward a Theory of Group Formation in Thai Society and Pressure Groups in Thailand After the October 1973 Uprising." *Asian Survey* 14 (6): 530–45.

Kalela, Jorma. 1976. "Right-Wing Radicalism in Finland During the Interwar Period." *Scandinavian Journal of History* 1:105–24.

Kamenka, Eugene, ed. 1973. *Political Nationalism—The Evolution of the Idea.* Canberra: Australian National University Press.

Kapferer, Bruce. 1988. *Legends of People—Myths of State: Violence, Intolerance, and*

Political Culture in Sri Lanka and Australia. Washington, D.C.: Smithsonian Institution Press.

Karnow, Stanley. 1983. *Vietnam: A History.* New York: Viking.

Karunan, Victor P. 1984. *A History of Peasant Movements in Thailand and the Philippines.* Hong Kong: Plough Publications.

Kasza, Gregory J. 1984. "Fascism from Below?: A Comparative Perspective on the Japanese Right, 1931–1936." *Journal of Contemporary History* 19:607–29.

Kaufman, Howard. 1960. *Bangkhuad: A Community Study in Thailand.* Locust Valley, N.Y.: J. J. Augustin.

Kelly, John D. and Martha Kaplan. 1990. "History, Structure, and Ritual." *Annual Review of Anthropology* 19:119–50.

Kent, Peter C. 1987. "Review of *The Vatican and Italian Fascism*, by Pollard, John F." *European History Quarterly* 17 (3): 386–88.

Kerdphol, General Saiyud. 1986. *The Struggle for Thailand: Counterinsurgency, 1965–1985.* Bangkok: S. Research Center Co.

Kershaw, Roger. 1979. "Three Kings of Orient: The Changing Face of Monarchy in Southeast Asia (Part 1, 2, and 3)." *Contemporary Review* 234:200–6, 256–65, 299–304.

Kertzer, David I. 1979. "Gramsci's Concept of Hegemony: The Italian Church-Communist Struggle." *Dialectical Anthropology* 4 (4): 321–28.

———. 1988. *Ritual, Politics, and Power.* New Haven, Conn.: Yale University Press.

Keyes, Charles. 1973. "Ethnic Identity and Loyalty of Villagers in Northeastern Thailand." In John T. McAlister Jr., ed., *Southeast Asia: The Politics of National Integration*, pp. 355–65. New York: Random House.

———. 1977. "Millennialism, Theravada Buddhism, and Thai Society." *Journal of Asian Studies* 36 (2): 283–302.

———. 1978. "Political Crisis and Militant Buddhism in Contemporary Thailand." In Bardwell L. Smith, ed., *Religion and Legitimation of Power in Thailand, Laos, and Burma*, pp. 147–64. Chambersburg, Pa.: Anima Books.

———. 1987. *Thailand: Buddhist Kingdom as Modern Nation-State.* Boulder, Colo.: Westview Press.

Keyes, Charles, ed. 1991. *Reshaping Local Worlds: Formal Education and Cultural Change in Rural Southeast Asia.* Monograph No. 36. New Haven, Conn.: Yale University Southeast Asian Studies.

Kheng, Cheah Boon. 1988. "The Erosion of Ideological Hegemony and Royal Power and the Rise of Postwar Malay Nationalism, 1945–1946." *Journal of Southeast Asian Studies* 19 (1): 1–26.

Kidd, Ross. 1983. "Popular Theater and Popular Struggle in Kenya: The Story of Kamiriithu." *Race and Class* 24 (3): 287–304.

Kiernan, Ben. 1979. "The 1970 Peasant Uprising in Kampuchea." *Journal of Contemporary Asia* 9 (3): 310–24.

Kingshill, Konrad. 1991. *Ku Daeng—Thirty Years Later: A Village Study in Northern Thailand, 1954–1984.* Special Report No.26, 1991. De Kalb: Northern Illinois University.

Knodel, John, Apichat Chamratrithirong, and Debavalya Nibhon. 1987. *Thailand's Reproductive Revolution: Rapid Fertility Decline in a Third-World Setting.* Madison: University of Wisconsin Press.

Knox, MacGregor. 1982. *Mussolini Unleashed, 1939–1941: Politics and Strategy in Fascist Italy's Last War.* Cambridge, England: Cambridge University Press.

Koch, H. W. 1975. *The Hitler Youth.* New York: Dorset Press.

Kogan, Norman. 1969. "The Origins of Italian Fascism." *Polity* 2 (1): 100–105.

Kohn, Hans. 1965. *Nationalism: Its Meaning and History.* Princeton, N.J.: D. Van Nostrand.

Kolko, Gabriel. 1973. "The United States and the Philippines: The Beginning of Another Vietnam?" *Journal of Contemporary Asia* 3 (1): 70–84.

Komer, Robert W. 1971. "Impact of Pacification on Insurgency in South Vietnam." *Journal of International Affairs* 25 (1): 48–69.

Kondo, Dorinne K. 1990. *Crafting Selves: Power, Gender, and Discourses of Identity in a Japanese Workplace.* Chicago: University of Chicago Press.

Kraivixien, Tanin. 1982. *His Majesty King Bhumibol Adulyadej: Compassionate Monarch of Thailand.* Bangkok: Katavethin Foundation.

"Labour 3: The Keys to Industrial Accord." 1975. *Investor: Thailand*, August 1975, pp. 23–32.

Laclau, Ernesto. 1977. *Politics and Ideology in Marxist Theory.* London: NLB.

Lane, Christel. 1981. *The Rites of Rulers: Ritual in Industrial Society—The Soviet Case.* Cambridge, England: Cambridge University Press.

Lane, Robert E. 1962. *Political Ideology.* New York: Free Press.

Laqueur, Walter, ed. 1976. *Fascism: A Reader's Guide.* Berkeley: University of California Press.

Leach, Edmund R. 1968. "Ritual." In David L. Sills, ed., *International Encyclopedia of the Social Sciences,* Vol. 13, pp. 520–26. New York: Macmillan/Free Press.

———. 1984. "Glimpses of the Unmentionable in the History of British Social Anthropology." *Annual Review of Anthropology* 13:1–23.

Lears, T. J. Jackson. 1985. "The Concept of Cultural Hegemony: Problems and Possibilities." *American Historical Review* 90 (3): 567–93.

Lehman, F. K. 1981. "On the Vocabulary and Semantics of 'Field' in Theravada Buddhist Society." *Contributions to Asian Studies* 16:101–11.

Levi-Strauss, Claude. 1967. *Structural Anthropology.* Garden City, N.Y.: Basic Books.

Lewis, Gavin. 1978. "The Peasantry, Rural Change, and Conservative Agrarianism: Lower Austria at the Turn of the Century." *Past and Present* 18:119–43.

Lewis, Ioan. 1977. *Symbols and Sentiments: Cross-cultural Studies in Symbolism.* London: Academic Press.

Li, Zhisui. 1994. *The Private Life of Chairman Mao: Memoirs of Mao's Personal Physician.* Trans. Professor Tai Hung-chao. New York: Random House.

Lifton, Robert J., M.D. 1969. *Thought Reform and the Psychology of Totalism: A Study of "Brainwashing" in China.* New York: W. W. Norton.

Lissak, Moshe. 1976. *Military Roles in Modernization: Civil-Military Relations in Thailand and Burma.* Beverly Hills, Calif.: Sage.

Lobe, Thomas. 1977. *United States National Security Police and Aid to the Thailand Police.* Monograph Series in World Affairs, vol. 14, no. 2.

Lobe, Thomas and David Morell. 1978. "Thailand's Border Patrol Police: Paramilitary Political Power." Part 4; In Louis Zurcher and Gwyn Harries-Jenkins, eds., *Supplementary Military Forces: Reserves, Militias, Auxiliaries*, pp. 153–78. Beverly Hills, Calif.: Sage.

Lomax, Louis E. 1967. *Thailand: The War That Is, The War That Will Be.* New York: Random House/Vintage Books.

Long, Ngo Vinh. 1973. *Before the Revolution: The Vietnamese Peasants Under the French.* Cambridge, Mass.: MIT Press.

Loomis, Charles P. and J. Allan Beegle. 1946. "The Spread of German Nazism in Rural Areas." *American Sociological Review* 11 (6): 724–34.

Lovelace, Daniel D. 1971. *China and "People's War" in Thailand, 1964–1969.* Berkeley: University of California Center for Chinese Studies.

Lukes, Steven. 1975. "Political Ritual and Social Integration." *Sociology: Journal of British Sociological Association* 9 (2): 289–308.

Lyttelton, Adrian. 1979. "Landlords, Peasants and the Limits of Liberalism." In Davis, John A., ed., *Gramsci and Italy's Passive Revolution*, pp. 104–35. New York: Barnes and Noble.

Mabry, Bevars D. 1977. "The Thai Labor Movement." *Asian Survey* 17 (10): 931–51.

MacDonald, Ian. 1975. "Some Thoughts on Fascism Today." *Race and Class* 16 (3): 295–304.

MacDonald, Robert H. 1981. "The Wolf That Never Slept: The Heroic Lives of Baden-Powell." *Dalhousie Review* (Canada) 61 (1): 5–26.

Machiavelli, Niccolo. [1517] 1961. *The Prince*, trans. George Bull. Baltimore: Penguin Classics.

Macleod, David I. 1985. Letter to the Editor. *American Historical Review* 90 (4): 1060–61.

———. 1993. *Building Character in the American Boy: The Boy Scouts, YMCA, and Their Forerunners, 1870–1920.* Madison: University of Wisconsin Press.

Mallet, Marian. 1978. "Causes and Consequences of the October '76 Coup." In Turton, Fast, and Caldwell, eds., *Thailand: Roots of Conflict*, pp. 80–103. Nottingham, England: Russell Press.

Marcus, George E. and Michael M.J. Fischer. 1986. *Anthropology as Cultural Critique: An Experimental Moment in the Human Sciences.* Chicago: University of Chicago Press.

Markovits, Andrei S. and Frank E. Sysyn, eds. 1982. *Nationbuilding and the Politics of Nationalism: Essays on Austrian Galicia.* Cambridge, Mass.: Harvard University Press.

Marks, Thomas A. 1977. "The Status of the Monarchy in Thailand." *Issues and Studies* 13 (11): 51–70.

——. 1980. "Thailand—The Threatened Kingdom." *Conflict Studies* (January–February 1980): 1–20.

Marriott, McKim. 1963. "Cultural Policy in the New States." In Geertz, ed., *Old Societies and New States*, pp. 27–56.

Marx, Karl and Friedrich Engels. [1925] 1970. *The German Ideology*, ed. C. J. Arthur. New York: International Publishers.

——. 1968. *Karl Marx and Frederick Engels: Selected Works.* New York: International Publishers.

Maza, Sarah. 1989. "Domestic Melodramas as Political Ideology: The Case of the Comte de Sanois." *American Historical Review* 94 (5): 1249–64.

McClintock, Michael. 1985a. *The American Connection.* London: Zed Books.

——. 1985b. "U.S. Military Assistance to El Salvador: From Indirect to Direct Intervention." *Race and Class* 26 (3): 63–82.

McCormack, Gavan. 1982. "Nineteen-Thirties Japan: Fascism?" *Bulletin of Concerned Asian Scholars* 14 (2): 20–32.

McCoy, Alfred W. 1991. *The Politics of Heroin: CIA Complicity in the Global Drug Trade.* New York: Lawrence Hill Books

McCracken, Grant. 1984. "The Precoronation Passage of Elizabeth I: Political Theater or the Rehearsal of Politics?" *Canadian Review of Sociology and Anthropology* 21 (1): 47–61.

McGehee, Ralph W. 1983. *Deadly Deceits: My Twenty-Five Years in the CIA.* New York: Sheridan Square Publications.

McGilvary, Daniel. 1912. *A Half Century Among the Siamese and the Lao.* New York: Fleming H. Revel.

McKinley, Gareth. 1985. "Knights, Pawns . . . and Kings." In Sulak Sivaraksa, ed., *Siamese Resurgence*, pp. 394–406. Bangkok: Asian Cultural Forum on Development.

McLane, Charles B. 1966. *Soviet Strategies in Southeast Asia: An Exploration of Eastern Policy Under Lenin and Stalin.* Princeton, N.J.: Princeton University Press.

McNabb, Scott F. 1978. Study-Service in Thailand: The Case of the Maeklong Integrated Rural Development Project. Ph.D. diss., University of Virginia.

Mead, Margaret. 1973. "Ritual and Social Crisis." In Shaughnessy, ed., *The Roots of Ritual*, pp. 87–101.

Mechling, Jay. 1980. "The Magic of the Boy Scout Campfire." *Journal of American Folklore* 93 (367): 35–56.

Mendick, Hans. 1987. " 'Missionaries in the Row Boat'? Ethnological Ways of

Knowing as a Challenge to Social History." *Society for Comparative Study of Society and History* 29:76–98.

Merelman, Richard M. 1969. "The Dramaturgy of Politics." *Sociological Quarterly* 10 (2): 216–41.

Mezey, Michael L. 1973. "The 1971 Coup in Thailand: Understanding Why the Legislature Fails." *Asian Survey* 13:306–17.

Mezey, Susan Gluck. 1975. "Political Socialization and Participation Among University Students in Thailand." *Asian Survey* 15 (6): 499–509.

Miliband, Ralph. 1969. *The State in Capitalist Society: An Analysis of the Western System of Power.* New York: Basic Books.

Mintz, Sidney. 1977. "The So-Called World System: Local Initiative and Local Response." *Dialectical Anthropology* 2:253–70.

Mitchell, Timothy. 1990. "The Invention and Reinvention of the Egyptian Peasant." *International Journal of Middle East Studies* 22:129–50.

Moeller, Robert G. 1981. "Dimensions of Social Conflict in the Great War: The Views From the German Countryside." *Central European History* 14 (2): 142–68.

Mokarapong, Thawatt. 1972. *History of the Thai Revolution: A Study in Political Behavior.* Bangkok: Chalermnit.

Moore, Barrington Jr. 1966. *Social Origins of Dictatorship and Democracy.* Harmondsworth, England: Penguin University Books.

Moore, Sally Falk and Barbara G. Myerhoff. 1977. *Secular Ritual.* Assen, The Netherlands: Van Gorcum.

———, eds. 1975. *Symbol and Politics in Communal Ideology: Cases and Questions.* Ithaca, N.Y.: Cornell University Press.

More, Sir Thomas. [1516] 1964. *Utopia*, ed. Edward Surtz. New Haven, Conn.: Yale University Press.

Morell, David. 1972. "Thailand: Military Checkmate." *Asian Survey* 12 (2) (February): 156–67.

———. 1975. "Alternatives to Military Rule in Thailand." *Armed Forces and Society* 1 (3): 287–301.

Morell, David and Chai-anan Samudavanija. 1981. *Political Conflict in Thailand.* Cambridge, Mass.: Oelgeschlager, Gunn & Hain.

Morell, David and Susan Morell. 1977. "Thailand: The Costs of Political Conflict." *Pacific Community* 8 (2) (January): 327–40.

Morrow, Michael. 1972. "Thailand: Bombers and Bases-America's New Frontier." *Journal of Contemporary Asia* 2 (4): 382–402.

Mosel, James N. 1963. "Communication Patterns and Political Socialization in Transitional Thailand." In Lucien W. Pye, ed., *Communication and Political Development*, pp. 184–228. Princeton, N.J.: Princeton University Press.

Mosse, George L. 1975. *The Nationalization of the Masses.* Ithaca, N.Y.: Cornell University Press.

Mudannayake, Ivan, John Weller, Katherine Bowie, Marcia Brewster, and Brian Phelan. 1975. *Thailand YearBook, 1975–1976*. Bangkok: Temple Publicity Services.

Muecke, Marjorie A. 1980. "The Village Scouts of Thailand." *Asian Survey* 20:407–27.

Mugabane, Bernard Makhosezwe. 1979. *The Political Economy of Race and Class in South Africa*. New York: Monthly Review Press.

Mukherjee, Mridula. 1988. "Peasant Resistance and Peasant Consciousness in Colonial India: 'Subalterns and Beyond.'" *Economic and Political Weekly* 23: 2174–85.

Muller, Klaus-Jurgen. 1976. "French Fascism and Modernization." *Journal of Contemporary History* 11:75–107.

Munck, Thomas. 1986. "Review of *Power in the Blood: Popular Culture and Village Discourse in Early Modern Germany*, by David Warren Sabean." *European History Quarterly* 16 (2): 222–23.

Munn, Nancy D. 1973. "Symbolism in a Ritual Context: Aspects of Symbolic Action." In John J. Honigmann, ed., *Handbook of Social and Cultural Anthropology*, pp. 579–612. Chicago: Rand McNally.

Murashima, Eiji. 1988. "The Origin of Modern Official State Ideology in Thailand." *Journal of Southeast Asian Studies* 19 (1): 80–96.

Murdoch, John B. 1974. "The 1901–1902 'Holy Man's' Rebellion." *Journal of the Siam Society* 62 (1): 47–67.

Nakano, Ako. 1990. "Death and History: An Emperor's Funeral." *Public Culture* 2 (2) (spring): 33–40.

na Pombhejara, Vichitvong. 1979. "The Kriangsak Government and the Thai Economy." *Southeast Asian Affairs 1979*, pp. 312–22. Singapore: Institute of Southeast Asian Studies.

na Ranong, Lydia S. 1975. "Thai Foreign Policy Since October 1973." *Southeast Asian Affairs 1975*, pp. 196–200. Singapore: Institute of Southeast Asian Studies.

Nartsupha, Chatthip. 1984. "The Ideology of Holy Men Revolts in North East Thailand." In A. Turton and S. Tanabe, eds., *History and Peasant Consciousness in Southeast Asia*, pp. 111–34. Osaka, Japan: National Museum of Ethnology.

Nash, June C. 1981. "Ethnographic Aspects of the World Capitalist System." *Annual Review of Anthropology* 10:393–423.

———. 1989. *From Tank Town to High Tech: The Clash of Community and Industrial Cycles*. New York: State University of New York Press.

Nations, Richard. 1977. "Kriangsak Hints at Change." *Far Eastern Economic Review* 98 (47) (November 25): 10–12.

Neher, Clark D. 1975. "Stability and Instability in Contemporary Thailand." *Asian Survey* 15 (12): 1097–1113.

———. 1979. *Modern Thai Politics: From Village to Nation*. Cambridge, Mass.: Schenkman.

——. 1991. *Southeast Asia in the New International Era*. Boulder, Colo.: Westview Press.

Nelson, Cary and Lawrence Grossberg, eds. 1988. *Marxism and the Interpretation of Culture*. Chicago: University of Illinois Press.

Ng, Ronald C.Y. 1970. "Some Land-Use Problems of Northeast Thailand." *Modern Asian Studies* 4 (1): 23–42.

Nicholas, Ralph. 1965. "Factions: A Comparative Analysis." In Michael Banton, ed., *Political Systems and the Distribution of Power*, pp. 21–61. Association of Social Anthropologists Monograph #2. London: Tavistock.

Nordstrom, Carolyn and JoAnn Martin, eds. 1992. *The Paths to Domination, Resistance, and Terror*. Berkeley: University of California Press.

Ohnuki-Tierney, Emiko. 1987. *The Monkey as Mirror: Symbolic Transformations in Japanese History and Ritual*. Princeton, N.J.: Princeton University Press.

——. 1990. "Introduction." In Emiko Ohnuki-Tierney, ed., *Culture Through Time: Anthropological Approaches*, pp. 1–25. Palo Alto, Calif.: Stanford University Press.

O'Neil, Wayne. 1971. "Thailand: America's Troubled Ally." *Journal of Contemporary Asia* 1 (4): 55–59.

Onchan, Tongroj, ed. 1990. *A Land Policy Study*. Monograph #3. Bangkok: Thailand Development Research Institute Foundation.

Ondam, Bantorn. 1971. "The Phrae Rebellion: A Structural Analysis." *Cornell Journal of Social Relations* 6 (spring): 84–97.

Ongsuragz, Chantima. 1965. *The Stages of Political Development*. New York: Alfred A. Knopf.

——. 1982. "The Communist Party of Thailand: Consolidation of Decline." *Southeast Asian Affairs*, pp. 362–74. Singapore: Heinemann Educational Books.

Orgel, Stephen. 1975. *The Illusion of Power: Political Theater in the English Renaissance*. Berkeley: University of California Press.

Ortner, Sherry B. 1978. *Sherpas Through Their Rituals*. Cambridge, England: Cambridge University Press.

——. 1984. "Theory in Anthropology Since the Sixties." *Comparative Studies in Society and History* 26:126–66.

——. 1991. "Reading America: Preliminary Notes on Class and Culture." In Fox, ed., *Recapturing Anthropology*, pp. 163–89.

Ozouf, Mona. 1988. *Festivals and the French Revolution*, trans. Alan Sheridan, Alan. Cambridge, Mass.: Harvard University Press.

Patnaik, Arun K. 1988. "Gramsci's Concept of Common Sense: Toward a Theory of Subaltern Consciousness in Hegemony Processes." *Review of Political Economy, Special Issue. Economic and Political Weekly* 23 (5): 2–10.

Payne, Stanley G. 1980. *Fascism: Comparison and Definition*. Madison: University of Wisconsin Press.

——. 1986. "Fascism and Right Authoritarianism in the Iberian World-The Last Twenty Years." *Journal of Contemporary History* 21:163–77.

Peacock, James L. 1968. *Rites of Modernization: Symbolic and Social Aspects of Indonesian Proletarian Drama.* Chicago: University of Chicago Press.

Peagam, Norman. 1975. "Rumblings from the Right." *Far Eastern Economic Review* 89 (July 25): 13–14.

———. 1977. "Political Stability at Stake." *Far Eastern Economic Review* 95 (February 11): 8–10.

Phelan, Brian. 1975. "The Land Squeeze." *The Investor* (Thailand) 7 (8): 7–17.

Phillips, Herbert P. 1965. *Thai Peasant Personality: The Patterning of Interpersonal Behavior in the Village of Bang Chan.* Berkeley: University of California Press.

———. 1987. *Modern Thai Literature with an Ethnographic Interpretation.* Honolulu: University of Hawaii Press.

Pike, Douglas. 1966. *Viet Cong: The Organization and Techniques of the National Liberation Front of South Vietnam.* Cambridge, Mass.: MIT Press.

Piker, Steven. 1964. An Examination of Character and Socialization in a Thai Peasant Community. Ph.D. diss., University of Washington.

Ping, Ho Kwan. 1978. "Thailand's Broken Ricebowl." *Far Eastern Economic Review* (December 1): 40–46.

Pinto, Antonio Costa. 1986. "Fascist Ideology Revisited: Zeev Sternhell and His Critics." *European History Quarterly* 16 (4): 465–83.

Plekhanov, George. 1940. *The Role of the Individual in History.* New York: International Publishers.

Pollard, Vincent K. 1971. "Southeast Asian Regionalism." *Journal of Contemporary Asia* 1 (4): 45–54.

Pollini, Maria Grazia. 1983. "Recent Interpretations of Mussolini and Italian Fascism." *Politico* 48 (4): 751–64.

Poole, Peter A. 1970. *The Vietnamese in Thailand: A Historical Perspective.* Ithaca, N.Y.: Cornell University Press.

Popkin, Samuel, L. 1979. *The Rational Peasant.* Berkeley: The University of California Press.

Potter, Jack M. 1976. *Thai Peasant Social Structure.* Chicago: University of Chicago Press.

Poulantzas, Nicos. 1973. *Political Power and Social Classes*, trans. Timothy O'Hanen. London: New Left Books.

———. 1974. *Fascism and Dictatorship: The Third International and the Problem of Fascism.* London: NCB.

"Probe Ordered in Mock Hanging." 1976. *Bangkok Post*, October 6, p. 1.

Punyodyana, Boonsanong. 1975. "The Revolutionary Situation in Thailand." *Southeast Asian Affairs 1975*, pp. 187–95. Singapore: Institute of Southeast Asian Studies.

Pye, Lucian W. and Mary W. Pye. 1985. *Asian Power and Politics: The Cultural Dimensions of Authority.* Cambridge, Mass. Harvard University Press.

Rabinbach, Anson. 1978. "Politics and Pedagogy: The Austrian Social Democratic Youth Movement, 1931–1932." *Journal of Contemporary History* 13: 337–56.

Rabinow, Paul. 1975. *Symbolic Domination: Cultural Form and Historical Change in Morocco.* Chicago: University of Chicago Press.

Race, Jeffrey. 1972. *War Comes to Long An: Revolutionary Conflict in a Vietnamese Province.* Berkeley: University of California Press.

———. 1974. "The War in Northern Thailand." *Modern Asian Studies* 8 (1): 85–112.

———. 1977. "The Future of Thailand." *Pacific Community* 8 (2) (January): 303–26.

Rafael, Vicente L. 1990. "Patronage and Pornography: Ideology and Spectatorship in the Early Marcos Years." *Comparative Studies in Society and History* 32 (April): 282–304.

Rajaretnam, M. 1975. "Courts, Camps, and Constitutions: The Game of Politics in Thailand." *Southeast Asian Affairs 1975*, pp. 171–86. Singapore: Institute of Southeast Asian Studies.

Ramsay, James Ansil. 1979. "Modernization and Reactionary Rebellions in Northern Siam." *Journal of Asian Studies* 38 (2): 283–97.

Randolph, R. Sean, and W. Scott Thompson. 1981. *Thai Insurgency: Contemporary Development: The Washington Papers,* Vol. 9, no. 81. Beverly Hills, Calif.: Sage.

Rappaport, Roy A. 1979. *Ecology, Meaning, and Religion.* Richmond, Calif.: North Atlantic Books.

Ratanapat, Nuttanee. 1990. King Vajravudh's Nationalism and Its Impact on Political Development in Thailand. Ph.D. diss., University of Northern Illinois.

Rearick, Charles. 1977. "Festivals in Modern France: The Experience of the Third Republic." *Journal of Contemporary History* 12:435–60.

Rebel, Hermann. 1989. "Cultural Hegemony and Class Experience: A Critical Reading of Recent Ethnological-Historical Approaches (Part One)." *American Ethnologist* 16 (1): 117–36.

Rejali, Darius M. 1993. *Torture and Modernity: Self, Society, and State in Modern Iran.* Boulder, Colo.: Westview Press.

Renard, Ronald D. 1980. Kariang: History of Karen-T'ai Relations from the Beginnings to 1923. Ph.D. diss., University of Hawaii.

Reynolds, Craig J., ed. 1991. *National Identity and Its Defenders: Thailand, 1939–1989.* Monash Papers on Southeast Asia, No. 25. Victoria, Australia.

Reynolds, Craig J. and Lysa Hong. 1983. "Marxism in Thai Historical Studies." *Journal of Asian Studies* 43 (1): 77–104.

Reynolds, Frank E. 1977. "Civic Religion and National Community in Thailand." *Journal of Asian Studies* 36 (2): 267–82.

———. 1978. "Sacral Kingship and National Development: The Case of Thailand." In Bardwell L. Smith, ed., *Religion and Legitimation of Power in Thailand, Laos, and Burma,* pp. 100–10.

Richardson, Michael. 1976. "Thailand: How the Right Won." *National Times* (November 29–December 4): 48–51.

Ricoeur, Paul. 1965. *History and Truth*, trans. Charles A. Kelbley. Evanston, Ill.: Northwestern University Press.

Riggs, Fred W. 1966. *Thailand: The Modernization of a Bureaucratic Polity*. Honolulu: East-West Center Press.

Rosenthal, Michael. 1980. "Knights and Retainers: The Earliest Version of Baden-Powell's Boy Scout Scheme." *Journal of Contemporary History* 15: 603–17.

———. 1986. *The Character Factory: Baden-Powell and the Origins of the Boy Scout Movement*. London: Collins.

Roth, David F. 1976. "Dimensions of Policy Change: Toward an Explanation of Rural Change Policies in Thailand." *Asian Survey* 16:1043–63.

Rude, George. 1968. *Captain Swing*. New York: W. W. Norton.

Rutten, Rosanne. 1992. " 'Mass Surrenders' in Negros Occidental: Ideology, Force, and Accommodation in a Counterinsurgency Program." Paper presented at 4th International Philippine Studies Conference, Australian National University, Canberra, July 1–3.

Sabean, David. 1978. "Small Peasant Agriculture in Germany at the Beginning of the Nineteenth Century: Changing Work Patterns." *Peasant Studies* 7 (4): 218–24.

Sahlins, Marshall. 1985. *Islands of History*. Chicago: University of Chicago Press.

Saiyud Kerdphol. See Kerdphol, Saiyud.

Salvemini, Gaetano. 1971. *Under the Axe of Fascism*. New York: Citadel Press.

Samudavanija, Chai-anan and Sukhumbhand Paribatra. 1987. "In Search of Balance: Prospects for Stability in Thailand During the Post-CPT Era." In Kusuma Snitwongse and Sukhumbhand Paribatra, eds., *Durable Stability in Southeast Asia*, pp. 187–233. Singapore: Institute for Southeast Asian Studies.

Samudavanija, Chai-anan, Kusuma Snitwongse, and Suchit Bunbongkarn. 1990. *From Armed Suppression to Political Offensive: Attitudinal Transformation of Thai Military Officers Since 1976*. Bangkok: Institute of Security and International Studies, Chulalongkorn University.

Sangchai, Somporn. 1976. "The Rising of the Rightist Phoenix." *Southeast Asian Affairs 1976*, pp. 357–93. Singapore: Institute of Southeast Asian Affairs.

San Juan, E. Jr. 1973. "Reactionary Ideology in Philippine Culture." *Journal of Contemporary Asia* 3 (4): 414–26.

Sarti, Roland. 1970. "Fascist Modernization in Italy: Traditional or Revolutionary" *American Historical Review* 75 (4): 1029–45.

Schmidt, Steffen W., James C. Scott, Carl Lande, and Laura Guasti, eds. 1977. *Friends, Followers, and Factions: A Reader in Political Clientelism*. Berkeley: University of California Press.

Schneider, Jane. 1977. "Was There a Precapitalist World System?" *Journal of Peasant Studies* 6:20–28.

Schneider, Peter. 1986. "Rural Artisans and Peasant Mobilisation in the Socialist International: The Fasci Siciliani." *Journal of Peasant Studies* 13 (3): 63–81.

Schut, Jan. 1975. "Focus on Labor: Are the Laws at Fault?" *The Investor (Thailand)*, June, pp. 7–16.

Scott, James C. 1976. *The Moral Economy of the Peasant.* New Haven, Conn.: Yale University Press.

——. 1977. "Patron-Client Politics and Political Change in Southeast Asia." In Steffen W. Schmidt, James C. Scott, Carl Lande, and Laura Guasti, eds. *Friends, Followers, and Factions: A Reader in Political Clientelism*, pp. 123–46. Berkeley: University of California Press.

——. 1985. *Weapons of the Weak: Everyday Forms of Peasant Resistance.* New Haven: Yale University Press.

——. 1987. "Resistance Without Protest and Without Organization: Peasant Opposition to the Islamic 'Zakat' and the Christian Tithe." *Society for Comparative Study of Society and History* 2:417–52.

——. 1990. *Domination and the Arts of Resistance: Hidden Transcripts.* New Haven, Conn.: Yale University Press.

Sean, Randolph R. and W. Scott Thompson. 1981. *Thai Insurgency: Contemporary Developments*, Washington Paper 9. Beverly Hills, Calif.: Sage.

Searle, Chris. 1984. "Maurice Bishop on Destabilisation: An Interview." *Race and Class* 25 (3): 1–13.

Sereseres, Caesar D. 1978. "Guatemalan Paramilitary Forces, International Security, and Politics." In Zurchert and Harries-Jenkins, eds., *Supplementary Military Forces: Reserves, Militias, Auxiliaries*, pp. 179–99.

Shanin, Teodor. 1978. "The Peasants Are Coming: Migrants Who Labor, Peasants Who Travel, and Marxists Who Write." *Race and Class* 19 (3): 277–88.

Shaughnessy, James D., ed. 1973. *The Roots of Ritual.* Grand Rapids, Mich.: William B. Eerdmans.

Shawcross, William. 1976. "How Tyranny Returned to Thailand." *New York Review of Books,* December 9, pp. 59–62.

Shih-fu, Lo. 1972. "The Thai Communists' Two-Front Warfare." *Issues and Studies* 8 (6): 57–67.

Shils, Edward. 1968. "Ritual and Crisis." In Donald R. Cutler, ed., *The Religious Situation*, pp. 733–48. Boston: Beacon Press.

Shils, Edward and Michael Young. 1953. "The Meaning of Coronation." *Sociological Review* 1:63–81.

Sivanandan, A. 1979. "Malcolm Caldwell" (editorial). *Race and Class* 20 (4): 329–30.

Sivaraksa, Sulak. 1985. *Siamese Resurgence.* Bangkok: Asian Cultural Forum on Development.

———. 1988. *A Socially Engaged Buddhism*. Bangkok: Inter-Religious Commission for Development.

Skocpol, Theda. 1979. *States and Social Revolutions*. Cambridge, England: Cambridge University Press.

Smethurst, Richard J. 1974. *A Social Basis for Prewar Japanese Militarism: The Army and the Rural Community*. Berkeley: University of California Press.

Smith, Anthony D. 1973. "Nationalism." *Current Sociology* 21 (3): 5–176.

Smith, Bardwell L., ed. 1978. *Religion and Legitimation of Power in Thailand, Laos, and Burma*. Chambersburg, Pa.: Anima Books.

Smith, Raymond. 1984. "Anthropology and the Concept of Social Class." *Annual Review of Anthropology* 13:467–94.

Snitwongse, Kusuma. 1985. "Thai Government Responses to Armed Communist and Separatist Movements." In Chandrun Jeshuran, ed., *Governments and Rebellions in Southeast Asia*, pp. 247–75. Singapore: Institute of Southeast Asian Studies.

Snitwongse, Kusuma and Suchit Bunbongkarn. 1990. *From Armed Suppression to Political Offensive*. Bangkok: Institute of Security and International Studies.

Snowden, Frank M. 1972. "On the Social Origins of Agrarian Fascism in Italy." *Archives Européennes de Sociologie* 13 (2): 268–95.

Somvichian, Kamol. 1978. " 'The Oyster and the Shell': Thai Bureaucrats in Politics." *Asian Survey* 18 (8): 829–37.

Spjut, R. J. 1978. "A Review of Counter-Insurgency Theorists." *Political Quarterly* 49:54–64.

Springhall, John. 1987. "Baden-Powell and the Scout Movement Before 1920: Citizen Training or Soldiers of the Future?" *English Historical Review* (October):934–42.

"Srisuk Admits Police Behind Garrottings." 1976. *Bangkok Post*, October 5, p. 1.

Stachura, P. D. 1973. "The Ideology of the Hitler Youth in the Kampfzeit." *Journal of Contemporary History* 8 (3): 155–67.

Stauder, Jack. 1974. "The 'Relevance' of Anthropology to Colonialism and Imperialism." *Race and Class* 16 (1): 29–51.

Stifel, Laurence. 1976. "Technocrats and Modernization in Thailand." *Asian Survey* 16 (12): 1184–96.

Streckfuss, David. 1995. "Kings in the Age of Nations: The Paradox of Lèse Majesté as a Crime in Thailand." *Comparative Studies in Society and History* 7 (3): 445–75.

Strong, Roy. 1984. *Art and Power: Renaissance Festivals, 1450–1650*. Suffolk, England: Boydell Press.

Stubbs, Richard. 1989. *Hearts and Minds in Guerrilla Warfare*. Singapore: Oxford University Press.

Sudhamani, S. R. 1978. "Major Components in Thai Politics, 1958–1963." *International Studies* 17 (2) (April–June): 227–97.

Suehiro, Akira. 1989. *Capital Accumulation in Thailand, 1855–1985.* Tokyo: Center for East Asian Cultural Studies.

Suhrke, Astri. 1970. "The Thai Muslims: Some Aspects of Minority Integration." *Pacific Affairs* 43 (4) (winter 1970–1971): 531–45.

Sukontarangsi, Swat. 1968. *Development of Thai Educational Bureaucracy.* Bangkok: National Institute of Development Administration.

Suksamran, Somboon. 1982. *Buddhism and Politics in Thailand: A Study of Socio-political Change and Political Activism of the Thai Sangha.* Singapore: Institute of Southeast Asian Studies.

Summers, Anne. 1987. "Scouts, Guides, and VADS: A Note in Reply to Allen Warren." *English Historical Review* (October): 943–47.

Suriyamongkol, Pisan. 1988. *Institutionalization of Democratic Political Processes in Thailand: A Three-Pronged Democratic Polity.* Bangkok: Thammasat University Press.

Tambiah, Stanley Jeyaraja. 1969. "Animals Are Good to Think and Good to Prohibit." *Ethnology* 8:424–59.

——. 1970. *Buddhism and the Spirit Cults in Northeast Thailand.* Cambridge, Mass.: Cambridge University Press.

——. 1976. *World Conqueror and World Renouncer.* Cambridge, Mass.: Cambridge University Press.

——. 1979. "A Performative Approach to Ritual." *Proceedings of the British Academy* 65:113–69.

——. 1984. *The Buddhist Saints of the Forest and the Cult of Amulets.* Cambridge, Mass.: Cambridge University Press.

Tanabe, Shigeharu. 1984. "Ideological Practice and Peasant Rebellions: Siam at the Turn of the Twentieth Century." In Andrew Turton and Shigeharu Tanabe, ed., *History and Peasant Consciousness in Southeast Asia*, pp. 75–110. Osaka, Japan: National Museum of Ethnology.

Tanham, George K. 1974. *Trial in Thailand.* New York: Crane, Russak.

Tannenbaum, Edward R. 1972. *The Fascist Experience: Italian Society and Culture, 1922–1945.* New York: Basic Books.

Tapp, Nicholas. 1989. *Sovereignty and Rebellion: The White Hmong of Northern Thailand.* New York: Oxford University Press.

Taussig, Michael T. 1987. *Shamanism, Colonialism, and the Wild Man: A Study in Terror and Healing.* Chicago: University of Chicago Press.

Tawney, R. H. 1931. *Equality.* London: G. Allen and Unwin.

Taylor, Hugh. n.d. "Autobiography of Hugh Taylor." Phayab College Library, Chiang Mai, Thailand.

Taylor, J. L. 1990. "New Buddhist Movements in Thailand: An 'Individualistic Revolution,' Reform and Political Dissonance." *Journal of Southeast Asian Studies* 21 (1): 135–54.

Taylor, Simon. 1981. "Symbol and Ritual Under National Socialism." *British Journal of Sociology* 32 (4) (December): 504–20.

Terwiel, B. J. 1983. *A History of Modern Thailand, 1767–1942*. New York: University of Queensland Press.

Theeravit, Khien. 1979. "Thailand: An Overview of Politics and Foreign Relations." *Southeast Asian Affairs 1979*, pp. 299–311. Singapore: Institute of Southeast Asian Studies.

Thompson, E. P. 1974. "Patrician Society, Plebian Culture." *Journal of Social History* 7:277–304.

Thompson, John B. 1990. *Ideology and Modern Culture*. Palo Alto, Calif.: Stanford University Press.

Thompson, Robert. 1966. *Defeating Communist Insurgency. Studies in International Security 10*. London: Chatto and Windus.

Thompson, Virginia and Richard Adloff. 1942. "Nationalism and Nationalist Movements in Southeast Asia." In Rupert Emerson, ed. *Government and Nationalism in Southeast Asia*, pp. 125–222. New York: Institute of Pacific Relations.

———. 1950. *The Left Wing in Southeast Asia*. New York: William Sloane Association.

———. [1941] 1967. *Thailand: The New Siam*. New York: Paragon Book Reprint Corp.

Tilly, Charles, ed. 1975. *The Formation of National States in Western Europe. Studies in Political Development 8*. Princeton, N.J.: Princeton University Press.

Tilton, Timothy Alan. 1975. *Nazism, Neo-Nazism, and the Peasantry*. Bloomington: Indiana University Press.

Tomosugi, Takashi. 1969. "The Land System in Central Thailand." *Developing Economies* 7 (3): 284–308.

Tongdhamachart, Kramol. 1979a. "Thailand's 1978 Constitution and Its Implications." *Contemporary Southeast Asia* 1 (2): 125–40.

———. 1979b. "The April 1979 Elections and Postelection Politics in Thailand." *Contemporary Southeast Asia* 1 (3): 211–31.

Trager, Frank N. and William L. Scully. 1975. "Domestic Instability in Southeast Asia." *Orbis* 19 (3): 971–89.

Trocki, Carl A. 1981. "Power and Paradigms. Review Essay: Thailand." *Bulletin of Concerned Asian Scholars* 13 (2): 64–73.

Trotsky, Leon. 1971. *The Struggle Against Fascism in Germany*. New York: Pathfinder Press.

Turner, Henry Ashby Jr. 1972. "Fascism and Modernization." *World Politics* 24 (4): 547–64.

Turner, Victor. 1957. *Schism and Continuity in an African Society: A Study of Ndembu Village Life*. Manchester, England: Manchester University Press.

——. 1967. *The Forest of Symbols: Aspects of Ndembu Ritual*. Ithaca, N.Y.: Cornell University Press.

——. 1969. *The Ritual Process: Structure and Anti-Structure*. Chicago: Aldine.

——. 1988. *The Anthropology of Performance*. New York: PAJ Publications.

Turton, Andrew. 1977. "Laos: A Peasant People's Struggle for National Liberation." *Race and Class* 18 (3): 279–92.

——. 1978. "The Current Situation in the Thai Countryside." In Turton, Fast, and Caldwell, eds., *Thailand: Roots of Conflict*, pp. 104–42.

Turton, Andrew and Tanabe Shigeharu, eds. 1984. *History of Peasant Consciousness in Southeast Asia*. Senri Ethnological Studies #13. Osaka, Japan: National Museum of Ethnology.

Turton, Andrew, Jonathan Fast, and Malcolm Caldwell, eds. 1978. *Thailand: Roots of Conflict*. Nottingham, England: Russell Press.

Ungphakorn, Puey. 1977. "Violence and the Military Coup in Thailand." *Bulletin of Concerned Asian Scholars* 9 (3) (Special issue): 4–12.

Utrecht, Ernst. 1972. "The Indonesian Army as an Instrument of Repression." *Journal of Contemporary Asia* 2 (1): 56–67.

Vaddhanaphuti, Chayan. 1984. "Cultural and Ideological Reproduction in Rural Northern Thai Society." Ph.D. diss., Stanford University, Palo Alto, Calif.

——. 1991. "Social and Ideological Reproduction in a Rural Northern Thai School." In Charles F. Keyes, ed., *Reshaping Local Worlds: Formal Education and Cultural Change in Rural Southeast Asia*. Yale Southeast Asia Studies Monograph #36. New Haven, Conn.: Yale University Southeast Asian Studies.

Valeri, Valerio. 1985. *Kingship and Sacrifice: Ritual and Society in Ancient Hawaii*, trans. Paula Wissing. Chicago: University of Chicago Press.

Van Beek, Steve and Vilas Manivat, eds. 1983. *Kukrit Pramoj: His Wit and Wisdom*. Bangkok: Duang Kamol Editions.

Vandergeest, Peter. 1990. Siam into Thailand. Ph.D. diss., Cornell University.

——. 1993. "Constructing Thailand: Regulation, Everyday Resistance, and Citizenship." *Comparative Studies in Society and History* 35 (1): 133–58.

van der Kroef, Justus M. 1974. "Guerrilla Communism and Counterinsurgency in Thailand." *Orbis* 18 (1): 106–39.

——. 1977. "Thailand: A New Phase in the Insurgency." *Pacific Community* 8 (4) (July): 606–24.

van der Meer, C. L. J. 1981. *Rural Development in Northern Thailand: An Interpretation and Analysis*. Groningen, The Netherlands: Krips Repro Meppel.

Van Gennep, Arnold. [1909] 1960. *The Rites of Passage*. Chicago: University of Chicago Press.

Van Praagh, David. 1977. "The Outlook for Thailand." *Asian Affairs* 4 (5): 290–305.

——. 1989. *Alone on the Sharp Edge: The Story of M. R. Seni Pramoj and Thailand's Struggle for Democracy.* Bangkok: Duang Kamol Editions.

Vella, Walter F. 1978. *Chaiyo!: King Vajiravudh and the Development of Thai Nationalism.* Honolulu: University Press of Hawaii.

Viksnins, George J. 1973. "United States Military Spending and the Economy of Thailand, 1967–1972." *Asian Survey* 13 (January–June): 441–57.

Vincent, Joan. 1978. "Political Anthropology: Manipulative Strategies." *Annual Review of Anthropology* 7:175–94.

Wales, Horace Geoffrey Quaritch. 1931. *Siamese State Ceremonies: Their History and Function.* London: B. Quaritch.

Wallerstein, Immanuel. 1974. *The Modern World System I: Capitalist Agriculture and the Origins of the European World-Economy in the Sixteenth Century.* New York: Academic Press.

Walter, Eugene Victor. 1969. *Terror and Resistance: A Study of Political Violence with Case Studies of Some African Communities.* New York: Oxford University Press.

Walzer, Michael. 1967. "On the Role of Symbolism in Political Thought." *Political Science Quarterly* 82:191–205.

Wanrooij, Bruno. 1987. "The Rise and Fall of Italian Fascism as a Generational Revolt." *Journal of Contemporary History* 22:401–18.

Warner, W. Lloyd. 1961. *The Family of God: A Symbolic Study of Christian Life in America.* New Haven: Yale University Press.

——. 1962. *American Life: Dream and Reality,* rev. ed, Chicago: University of Chicago Press.

Warren, Allen. 1986. "Sir Robert Baden-Powell: The Scout Movement and Citizen Training in Great Britain, 1900–1920." *English Historical Review* (April): 377–98.

Wasserman, Gary. 1973. "Continuity and Counterinsurgency: The Role of Land Reform in Decolonizing Kenya, 1962–1970." *Canadian Journal of African Studies* 7 (1): 133–48.

Webb, R. A. F. Paul. 1986. "The Sickle and the Cross: Christians and Communists in Bali, Flores, Sumba, and Timor, 1965–1967." *Journal of Southeast Asian Studies* 17 (1): 94–112.

Weber, Eugen. 1976. *Peasants into Frenchmen: The Modernization of Rural France, 1870–1914.* Palo Alto, Calif.: Stanford University Press.

Wechsler, Howard J. 1985. *Offerings of Jade and Silk: Ritual and Symbol in the Legitimation of the T'ang Dynasty.* New Haven, Conn.: Yale University Press.

Wedel, Yuangrat. 1982. "Current Thai Radical Ideology: The Returnees from the Jungle." *Contemporary Southeast Asia* 4 (1): 1–18.

Wehner, Wolfgang. 1973. "American Involvement in Thailand." *Journal of Contemporary Asia* 3 (3): 292–305.

Welch, David. 1987. "Propaganda and Indoctrination in the Third Reich: Success or Failure?" *European Historical Quarterly* 17 (4): 403–22.

Weller, Robert P. 1987. "The Politics of Ritual Disguise: Repression and Response in Taiwanese Popular Religion." *Modern China* 13 (1) (January): 17–39.

Wells, Kenneth Elmer. 1939. *Thai Buddhism: Its Rites and Activities.* Bangkok: Bangkok Times Press.

West, F. J. Jr. 1985. *The Village.* Madison: University of Wisconsin Press.

Wilentz, Sean, ed. 1985. *Rites of Power: Symbolism, Ritual, and Politics Since the Middle Ages.* Philadelphia: University of Pennsylvania Press.

Williams, Raymond. 1976. *Keywords.* London: Fontana.

———. 1977. *Marxism and Literature.* New York: Oxford University Press.

———. 1981. *Culture.* Glasgow: William Collins.

Willis, Paul. 1977. *Learning to Labour: How Working-Class Kids Get Working-Class Jobs.* New York: Columbia University Press.

Wilson, David A. 1959. "Thailand and Marxism." In Frank Trager, ed., *Marxism and Southeast Asia.* Palo Alto, Calif.: Stanford University Press.

———. 1962. *Politics in Thailand.* Ithaca, N.Y.: Cornell University Press.

Wilson, Monica. 1954. "Nyakyusa Ritual and Symbolism." *American Anthropologist* 56 (2): 228–41.

———. 1971. *Religion and the Transformation of Society.* Cambridge, England: Cambridge University Press.

Wilson, Stephen. 1980. "For a Sociohistorical Approach to the Study of Western Military Culture." *Armed Forces and Society* 6 (4): 527–52.

Winichakul, Thongchai. 1994. *Siam Mapped: A History of the Geo-Body of a Nation.* Honolulu: University of Hawaii Press.

———. 1993. "Tuning the Nation: Political Songs at War in Thailand." Paper read at the Annual Meeting of the Association for Asian Studies, Los Angeles, March 25.

Wiskermann, Elizabeth. 1969. *Fascism in Italy: Its Development and Influence,* 2d ed. London: Macmillan.

Wistrich, Robert S. 1976. "Leon Trotsky's Theory of Fascism." *Journal of Contemporary History* 11:157–84.

Wit, Daniel. 1968. *Thailand: Another Vietnam?* New York: Charles Scribner's Sons.

Wolf, Eric R. 1969. *Peasant Wars of the Twentieth Century.* New York: Harper and Row.

Wongtrangan, Kanok. 1983. *Change and Persistence in Thai Counter-Insurgency Policy.* Paper #1. Bangkok: Chulalongkorn University Press.

———. 1984. "The Revolutionary Strategy of the Communist Party of Thailand: Change and Persistence." In Lim Joo-Jock and S. Vani, eds., *Armed Communist Movements in Southeast Asia,* pp. 133–82. Aldershot, England: Gover Publishing.

Woodside, Alexander B. 1976. *Community and Revolution in Modern Vietnam.* Boston: Houghton Mifflin.

Wright, Erik Olin. 1985. *Classes*. London: Verso.

Wright, Erik Olin et al. 1989. *The Debate on Classes*. London: Verso.

Wright, Joseph J. Jr. 1991. *The Balancing Act: A History of Modern Thailand*. Bangkok: Asia Books.

Wyatt, David K. 1982. "The 'Subtle Revolution' of King Rama I of Siam." In David K. Wyatt and Alexander Woodside, eds., *Moral Order and the Question of Change: Essays on Southeast Asian Thought*, pp. 9–52. Monograph Series No. 24. New Haven, Conn.: Yale University Press.

Xuto, Somsakdi. 1987. *Government and Politics of Thailand*. Singapore: Oxford University Press.

Yano, Toru. 1968. "Land Tenure in Thailand." *Asian Survey* 8 (10): 853–63.

Young, Michael. 1953. "The Meaning of the Coronation." *Sociological Review* (new series) 1:63–81.

Zehner, Edwin. 1990. "Reform Symbolism of a Thai Middle-Class Sect: The Growth and Appeal of the Thammakai Movement." *Journal of Southeast Asian Studies* 21:402–26.

Zimmerman, Carle C. 1931. *Siam Rural Economic Survey, 1930–1931*. Bangkok: Bangkok Times Press.

Zimmerman, Robert F. 1976. "Insurgency in Thailand." *Problems of Communism* 25 (3): 18–39.

———. 1978. *Reflections on the Collapse of Democracy in Thailand*. Occasional Papers Series No. 50. Singapore: Institute of Southeast Asian Studies.

Zuesse, Evan M. 1987. "Ritual." In Mircea Eliade, ed., *Encyclopedia of Religion*, Vol. 12, pp. 405–22.

Index

❧

With the exception of Thai authors whose works are cited in the text using the English-
language convention of last name first, all Thai names are listed first name first.